GETTING MORE FOR YOUR MONEY

GROSSET & DUNLAP
Publishers • New York

Copyright © 1980, 1982 Council of Better Business Bureaus, Inc.
and The Benjamin Company, Inc.

All rights reserved
Library of Congress catalog card number: 81-71070
   ISBN: 0-448-16617-8

Portions of this book formerly published as *Guide to Wise Buying* by The Benjamin Company, Inc.

First Grosset & Dunlap edition 1982
Printed in the United States of America

Contents

You and the Better Business Bureau   6

Advertising   12
Air Conditioners   22
Animals   29
Antiques   31
Apartments   33
Appliances   36
Audio Equipment   39
Automobiles   47
Banks and Savings Institutions   68
Basement Waterproofing   72
Bicycles   74
Calculators   77
Camps   79
Carpet and Floor Covering   81
Charitable Giving   86
Clothing   89
Condominiums and Cooperatives   100
Contracts   103
Cosmetics   105
Credit and Installment Buying   108
Day-Care Centers   115
Dishwashers   117
Door-to-Door Selling (Direct Selling)   118
Drugs, Nonprescription   123
Drugs, Prescription   128
Dry Cleaning   131
Employment   135
Encyclopedias   140

Energy   142
Fire Protection Systems   147
Food Shopping   150
Franchises   161
Fraud and Deception   164
Funerals   170
Furnaces   173
Furniture   176
Furs   182
Gardening and Lawn Care   185
Gasoline and Gasoline-Saving Devices   188
Hair Dryers   190
Health and Medicine   192
Hearing Aids   198
Home Maintenance and Improvement   202
Housing, Home Buying   212
Insulation   223
Insurance, Health   226
Insurance, Home   232
Insurance, Life   235
Jewelry   240
Land Purchases   248
Legal Services   252
Magazine Subscriptions   255
Mail-Order Shopping   258
Mattresses and Foundations (Box Springs)   262
Mobile Homes   264
Motorcycles   268
Moving   271
Musical Instruments   276
Nursing Homes   279
Nutrition   282

Painting and Paints	285	Tires	342
Photographic Equipment	288	Toys	346
Power Tools	296	Travel, Travel Agents	348
Prices and Sales	298	Typewriters	351
Radios	305	Vacuum Cleaners	353
Ranges	307	Warranties	355
Refrigerators and Freezers	310	Watches	361
Refunds and Exchanges	314	Water-Conditioning Equipment	363
Roofs and Roofing	316	Work-at-Home Schemes	365
Safety	320	If You Are Dissatisfied	368
Schools, Home Study	326		
Schools, Vocational	329	*Directory of Better Business Bureaus*	375
Sewing Machines	332		
Storm Windows and Doors	334		
Televisions	336	*Index*	380

Foreword

TODAY'S CONSUMER WANTS and needs complete, factual knowledge about products and services available in the marketplace. *Getting More For Your Money* provides information and advice on business practices as well as on the goods and services being offered. The contents are based on extensive resources used by the Council, and supplemented by sixty-eight years of Better Business Bureau experience.

Whether you are shopping for a refrigerator, getting your car repaired or signing a contract for installing home insulation, this book is designed to help you get better value for your money. We urge you to refer to the book frequently, especially before making any major purchase. Consumers who "investigate before they invest" are more likely to be satisfied customers — which benefits both the consumer and business.

— William H. Tankersley
President
Council of Better Business Bureaus, Inc.

You and the Better Business Bureau

MAKING A PURCHASE, even a minor one, is always an important investment. You spend most of your waking hours working to earn money. And if you spend more money than necessary on buying the things you need or want, you waste both time and energy. That is why you should take advantage of the advice offered by the Better Business Bureau.

The facilities of the nation's 152 Better Business Bureaus — offering files, contacts and staffs of experts — are available to the public at large. When you need factual information before making an important purchase, when you have a specific question or a complaint about a business or service, all you have to do is get in touch with your nearest Better Business Bureau.

BBB services are free. There are no charges, no strings attached. The business community supports the Better Business Bureau, which in turn provides consumers with the free service.

HOW THE BBB BEGAN
Approximately one hundred years ago, the seeds of industrial growth in the United States began to flourish. Homesteaders poured west to take up land claims; the great railroads spanned the continent; open-hearth fires glowed in the steel mills that pounded out the sinews of a burgeoning nation. It was the age of the industrial titans. And the chief concern of many Americans was to apply their energies to exploiting the continent, and each other.

These were days of unrestrained commerce, with a philosophy of *caveat emptor* (let the buyer beware) prevailing. It was up to the buyer to keep from being swindled.

Goods were advertised in a freewheeling, P.T. Barnum style, without code or standards. The con men of the day advertised "Complete Sewing Machines for 25 Cents," and mailed out twelve needles in cambric packages to the innocents who rose to the bait. A "bona fide" offer of a genuine, steel-engraved portrait of General Grant for 25 cents turned out, on receipt, to be a one-cent stamp. But these frauds were minor compared to the concoctions of alcohol compounds or opium derivatives sold to a trusting public as cure-alls "for man or beast." And then there were the guileless investors in land or stock promotions who seldom received even so much as a needle or a one-penny stamp for their money.

Honest businessmen therefore advertised cautiously, if at all —

fearful lest the public lump them with promoters of patent medicines, oil stocks, gold mines and land speculation.

In 1872 Congress voted "Fraud Order" powers to the U.S. Postmaster General, enabling postal inspectors to go after the mail swindlers. This move, however, had little impact on advertising. Mail-order commerce was in danger of foundering on the shoals of dishonesty and mistrust.

Then, in 1909, one Samuel C. Dobbs, sales manager of a nationally known corporation and later president of the Associated Advertising Clubs of the World, launched a crusade for honesty in advertising. By 1911 the crusade was making strides. John Irving Romer, publisher of *Printers Ink*, persuaded a lawyer friend of his to draw up a model statute to deal with sharp practices, fraud and deception in advertising. Known as the "Printers Ink Statute," the law in one form or another has since been adopted by most states. It makes dishonest advertising illegal.

In that same year the Advertising Men's League of New York formed a "vigilance committee" to fight dishonesty in advertising. In 1912 the organization branched out into a National Vigilance Committee. Within a year most big cities had established such committees.

Many people wonder how the Better Business Bureau got its name. As vigilance committees formed and reformed, local groups tested various names. The name "Better Business Bureau" was among them, and it caught on rapidly. Within a decade it came into universal use and some tentative moves were made toward a federation of the vigilance committees and the Better Business Bureaus. That federation is known today as the Council of Better Business Bureaus.

The BBB movement became international in 1928 with the founding of the first Canadian Bureau; they number sixteen today. Later, Israel and Venezuela established Better Business Bureaus.

Over the years the Better Business Bureaus have forged for themselves a well-earned reputation, not only throughout the United States but around the world, for the protection of the consumer in initiating and maintaining ethical standards in advertising and selling practices and for the encouragement of self-regulation in the business community.

THE BBB IN ACTION

This historical thumbnail sketch of the growth of ethical standards in advertising and selling is in itself reassuring. It is an indication that the picturesque but uncomfortable period when swindlers felt free to fleece their victims without fear of reprisal belongs to the past. *Getting More For Your Money* should help you to protect yourself against any of the special brands of trickery that still exist. At the same time it will teach you something else — that most businessmen today are honest.

Still, even now, there are swindlers out to take the public, and the unwitting player in a confidence game could be *you*.

GETTING MORE FOR YOUR MONEY

Let us take a typical day at a typical Better Business Bureau as an illustration of the kind of problems that the BBBs throughout the country are asked to handle.

As the office opens in the morning, the telephone switchboard is buzzing, and the various experts and specialists find themselves hard pressed to keep up with the continuing avalanche of questions and complaints.

A woman is on the phone, almost in tears. "I had a man come over to put a new thermostat on my refrigerator. That was three days ago. He charged me $31.50 and it still doesn't work! Now he tells me he won't come back until next Thursday."

Another woman reports that her air conditioner was fixed four weeks ago at a cost of $78.75. "Water dripped all over the floor just the same. I called the man yesterday, and he said he'll get here when he can. I called him again this morning and he yelled, 'I'll get there! I'll get there!' But I haven't seen any sign of him yet."

A man calls up to describe his daughter's experience with an employment agency. The agency sent her to apply for a job, which she accepted. Shortly, however, the company informed her that she was not, after all, suitable for the job. The agency had just called her to say that she owed them a fee.

Another man tells the sad story of his new car. He has driven it in to his dealer for repairs ten times by appointment. It hasn't been repaired yet. "They always tell me they're too busy that day," the man reports.

But not everyone who phones is in trouble. There are also many calls from people who have learned to get in touch with the BBB *first* and thereby stay out of trouble. They have learned one of the basic rules for getting one's money's worth:

Check on your suppliers and service organizations before you commit yourself so that you will deal only with reliable businessmen.

Here's how this works:

A woman who owns some valuable oriental rugs asks for information on a rug-cleaning firm that has been recommended to her. She gets it almost instantly. "This firm was established in 1926 and our files show a satisfactory customer-experience record."

A consumer wants advice on buying a swimming pool. The BBB pamphlet that covers the subject extensively will be sent and will probably provide all the answers to his questions.

A man who has bought a suite of furniture complains that three months later he is still waiting for delivery, despite repeated telephone calls to the dealer. He is advised to submit his complaint in writing, setting forth dates, money paid and so on, so that the BBB can decide how to proceed.

A woman reports that she has received merchandise she never

8

ordered. She is advised that by law she is under no obligation either to pay for such goods or to return them.

Another woman has had a dishwasher installed, but it doesn't work. The first thing she should do, she is told, is to get in touch with the dealer from whom she bought the equipment. If she is unable to get a satisfactory adjustment, then she should feel free to contact the BBB for a review and consideration of her problem.

A man inquires about a firm selling uniforms by mail. The BBB reply is: "Our files on this company show complaints about long delays in deliveries which the company has not adjusted."

One call concerns misrepresentation on the part of a door-to-door salesman. A woman's husband has signed a contract to take a course in electronics. The salesman had assured the couple that if for any reason the husband was unable to attend, his enrollment fee would be refunded. This point was not stipulated in the contract, however, and when the husband found he could not attend, the school refused to refund his fee. The couple were told that, while the Better Business Bureau would try to help them, it had to be pointed out that signed contracts are binding and that oral promises not contained in those contracts are difficult to prove.

HOW THE BETTER BUSINESS BUREAU CAN HELP YOU

Millions of inquiries and complaints are received annually by all the Better Business Bureaus combined. The more calls, the better, because it means so many more informed consumers who can expect and get their money's worth. The aims of the Better Business Bureaus today are threefold:

- ☐ to protect the buying power of the consumer;
- ☐ to encourage honesty in business;
- ☐ to inform the public on how to do business so the consumer can buy intelligently and gain maximum satisfaction from his purchases.

If you, in your capacity as a consumer, have questions regarding the reliability of any firm you plan to deal with, check with your BBB. A call may save you from buying unwisely.

Here, specifically, are some of the things a Bureau can do for the consumer:

Give pertinent information. The Better Business Bureaus keep files on large numbers of individual business firms and organizations in their particular areas and can provide you with information on them. They can give you basic facts such as how long the firm has been in business, whether or not customers have had problems, the nature of their problems and the manner in which the firm resolved them. The BBB can also provide factual information on charitable solicitations. The BBB gives you the facts; you must draw your own conclusions.

GETTING MORE FOR YOUR MONEY

Handle complaints. You've bought a washing machine, it doesn't work, and the store won't give you satisfaction. Or the TV set you just purchased produces a jumpy picture and the store manager says he is too busy to talk to you. What now? The BBB will determine if this is the sort of complaint that it can handle. If so, it will then take the matter up with the firm. If there appears to be a reason for checking into the pattern of the firm's practices, a shopper from the Bureau may be sent to size up the situation as well. If you have a legitimate complaint against an ethical firm, the BBB will almost always be able to help you settle it quickly.

Check on advertising claims. Experts read ads regularly, looking for unrealistically low prices, tricky phrases, phony illustrations, deceptive offers of free merchandise with purchases and fictitious claims of "Below Our Cost."

For example, a BBB executive noticed that a given dealer was offering a new model sedan at an implausibly low price. He suspected that none of these automobiles would be sold at this price and that they were advertised merely as a come-on to trick prospective purchasers into buying a higher-priced car. He dispatched a Bureau shopper to try to buy this particular car. Within a matter of days, five shoppers visited the agency. All were informed that the cars had been sold — but the ad continued to run. Armed with these facts, the Bureau contacted the dealer, and the misleading ad was discontinued.

An ad offering a one-carat "perfect" diamond solitaire ring for $500 sounded suspicious, so a BBB shopper purchased the ring. It was submitted to a diamond-testing organization for analysis. Result: the imperfections were so obvious that the use of the word "perfect" in the advertising copy obviously could not be supported. The advertiser was consulted, whereupon assurance was given that the claim "perfect" would not be made again.

There are other situations in which one businessman will complain about the practices of another. For example, a home improvement contractor saw a competitor's advertisement offering to install 1,200 square feet of aluminum siding for $349. He was outraged, knowing this could not be done. He called the Better Business Bureau to protest that his competitor was running a phony ad. BBB shoppings were conducted and, on the basis of findings, advertising was discontinued.

Such trade complaints are helpful because they come from men and women who know what they are talking about and are able to provide the BBB with specific facts. In the long run, such complaints benefit the consumer as well.

Develop standards for advertising and selling. The BBB has helped to evolve ground rules by which businesses are guided in the creation of their advertising and the sales promotion of their products and services. This is a major and continuing activity of the Better Business Bureaus that provides an additional benefit to the public.

One of the major functions of the Better Business Bureaus is to help you, the consumer, go out into the marketplace well prepared. But the area of buyer-seller relationship and of product quality is a broad one. The BBBs restrict their activities to questions of honesty and ethical practices in business.

It may be helpful to list some of the things Bureaus do *not* do for the general public:

- ☐ They do not handle complaints about the pricing of goods and services. This is a matter between merchant and customer. Only if there is misrepresentation will the Better Business Bureau act.
- ☐ They do not appraise products. For instance, whether one appliance is better than another is not within a BBB's province.
- ☐ They do not give legal advice or recommendations. They give you facts. While they advise you of the complaints they have received about a firm you have inquired about, they do not go beyond these facts. They expect you to form your own conclusions and to act accordingly.

The BBB's contribution is affirmative. It is intended to guide you toward intelligent buying by providing you with the know-how for making sensible choices and then leaving you free to exercise your own judgment.

The Better Business Bureau System is proud to present *Getting More For Your Money* and it is hoped you will find in it some answers to your buying problems.

Advertising

(See also PRICES AND SALES)

ACCORDING TO SOME CRITICS of the advertising field, the "Great American Merchandising Method" is so effective that it sells large quantities of unnecessary goods and services to millions of easily led people. Other observers, as well as practitioners of the profession, are convinced that many consumers block out most ads. One study shows, for instance, that a mere 12 percent of the viewers of prime-time television shows remember the next morning the commercials they must have seen the night before.

The truth about the effectiveness of the industry is likely to be found, as truths often are, somewhere between the two extremes.

Wise consumers use advertising.

They are not manipulated by it.

Much of this chapter deals with various types of deceptive advertising, and how to avoid them. However, it is very important for consumers to recognize how advertising can assist them in making wise buying decisions.

In today's complex economy, advertising is essential. Through the use of advertising, we are provided with information on the wide variety of products and services available from a large number of sellers. Whether the ads are found in newspapers or magazines, on television or radio, or even in the classified pages of the phone book, here are some of the ways advertisements can help:

1. They provide information on new or unknown items, creating a demand for newer and, in many cases, better products and services.
2. They give details on performance or special characteristics of existing products, especially those that change from time to time.

> Advertising is communication from a vendor (manufacturer, retailer, etc.) directed to potential buyers of goods and services. Any medium can carry the message — TV, radio, magazines, newspapers, billboards, transportation posters, direct mail, skywriting, bus benches, store circulars, hang tags on appliances, furniture and clothing, packaging and labeling materials, coupons and catalogs.

3. They supply daily price information of vital interest to the inflation-conscious consumer, including timely information on legitimate and money-saving "specials" and sales.
4. They also tell consumers the location of specific sellers, thereby saving them time and money in finding certain products and services.

In the best of all possible worlds, the principles enunciated by the Better Business Bureau code would be adhered to by vendors at all levels, from mass merchandisers to the neighbor down the block who is selling a used car. Manufacturers and retailers who wish to keep the customers they have and to increase their share of the market find that they must be careful with their claims.

Wise buyers analyze advertising. A quick survey of the following techniques will help:

- ☐ Separate information from puffery.
- ☐ Recognize meaningless coined words and no-promise promises.
- ☐ Identify misplaced emphasis.
- ☐ Recognize "guilt-producing" ads.
- ☐ Bring up useful questions in regard to price advertising.

The BBB Code of Advertising

Better Business Bureaus throughout the country have devised a "Code of Advertising" for the guidance of advertisers, advertising agencies and the media. The code's basic principles, listed below, deserve consideration by the public as well as by the advertising profession.

- ☐ The primary responsibility for truthful and nondeceptive advertising rests with the advertiser. Advertisers must be prepared to substantiate any claims or offers made *before publication or broadcast* and, upon request, present such substantiation promptly to the advertising medium or the Better Business Bureau.
- ☐ Advertisements which are untrue, misleading, deceptive, fraudulent or falsely disparaging of competitors shall not be used.
- ☐ An advertisement as a whole may be misleading although every sentence separately considered is literally true. Misrepresentation may result not only from direct statements but by omitting or obscuring a material fact. This kind of advertising must not be used.

PUFFERY, SUPERLATIVE CLAIMS
Is Product X the best . . . the most effective . . . the greatest ever?

Superlative statements, like other advertising claims, generally fall into one of two categories: objective (factual) or subjective (puffery).

Objective claims are statements of fact, and as such, they can either be proved or disproved. They are concerned with the tangible qualities and performance values of a product or service that can be measured against accepted standards or tests.

Subjective claims, on the other hand, are expressions of opinion or personal evaluation; in advertising they tend to concern themselves with the intangible qualities of a product or service — such as taste, beauty, aroma or style. In general, they cannot be proved or disproved.

The Better Business Bureau Code of Advertising points out that:

> Concern for the public's confidence in advertising generally has led many users and readers of advertising to condemn the use of any superlative. While superlative factual claims substantiated by the advertiser may be used, it is recommended that self-discipline be observed in their use. Similarly, subjective claims which may tend to mislead should be avoided.

In recent years superlative claims have become less fashionable in the language used by advertisers, probably due to the public's growing demand that claims be substantiated.

Puffery, however, is a constant — even in staid retail catalogs. For example:

THIS 2-PIECE SET FEATURES:

★ **Fashionable shirt-jacket**
★ **Stylish flare-leg pants with comfortable elasticized waist**
★ **Machine-washable fabric that needs little or no ironing**

SHIRT-STYLE PANTS SET. In easy-care polyester double-knit. Button-front shirt jacket, sport-pointed collar, mock cuffs and front patch pockets. Matching flare-leg pants with smooth-fitting elasticized waistband. Machine wash warm, tumble dry . . .

There are no outright lies in this copy, but the style makes cheap construction sound exciting. The words "fashionable" and "stylish" are empty expressions of opinion — puffery. The described merchandise turns out to be so innocuous that the word "fashionable" could only be used in relation to this style in the sense that many women are wearing pants. And since when has an elasticized waistband ever been "smooth-fitting"? To fit well and smoothly, waistbands must be cut to size.

One can, however, ignore the nonsense and the excitement in the copy and find valid reasons for buying one of these suits:

1. The suit is simple and practical — just the sort of thing you might like to jump into when you drive the children to school and then go shopping. You might even wear it to the office occasionally.
2. It is an inexpensive wardrobe-filler.
3. It requires little maintenance.
4. The catalog retailer has a reputation for providing serviceable merchandise at generally fair prices.
5. The retailer states and carries out a policy that unsatisfactory merchandise can be returned.

Having considered these factors, a wise buyer might decide to buy the merchandise — *in spite of*, not because of, the catalog copy.

In general, the less there is to say about a given piece of merchandise, the more puffery is likely to be used in ad copy.

Some products, such as washing machines, are easily described in realistic terms. Varied speeds for wash and spin cycles either are or are not available. There is or there is not a water-level selector. The manufacturer does or does not provide a warranty.

Of products whose attributes are less tangible, there is little or nothing to say. Perfumes and shaving lotions immediately come to mind. Is a fragrance sensual? Mysterious? Entrancing? Crisp? Masculine? The essence of femininity? Objective proof of any of these qualities would be hard to come by. Advertising copy is inevitably subjective. Buying decisions will be equally subjective. Fragrances are variable: they are not only different things to different people; they are different things *on* different people.

Consider cosmetics and the ads that sell them. Some face creams "lubricate" or "moisturize." Sometimes they turn into "cremes" and are described with meaningless coined words, such as "aqualucent" or "ultra something-or-other." When you respond to the advertising, you supply your own definition or coined words, depending upon what function you wish your face cream or "creme" to perform.

Other make-ups and facial treatments hide themselves — they are so "natural" no one knows they're there.

Products such as soft drinks, alcoholic beverages, tobacco products and a variety of luxury items are often sold via mood or image advertising. Scotch is consumed by opinion leaders in rooms filled with mellow wood, sporting prints and oriental rugs. Or perhaps it is displayed upon sensuous satin. Soft drinks represent a life style — young, gregarious and free. The person from cigarette country is lean, tanned and blue-jeaned. Clothing and fabrics are made for "your" kind of life, which is, no doubt, fashionable and exciting.

This is not to say that products advertised by way of coined words, moods and images are bad. They can be very good indeed. But the fact remains that it is necessary to cut through quantities of underbrush in

GETTING MORE FOR YOUR MONEY

the ad copy, *if* you choose to pay attention to the ads at all.

Wise buyers choose products on the basis of their own assessment of quality and value.

No-promise promises involve such meaningless phrases as "may help" or the slightly more authoritative but equally meaningless "may *actually* help." If the product *doesn't* clear your skin, make your hair lustrous, or make the itch go away, the implication is that you are one of those recalcitrant people who are beyond help. Tough.

Misplaced emphasis in advertising is apparent when some irrelevant aspect of a product or service is stressed instead of the factors on which a rational buying decision should be based. Anytime you shop for a personal loan, for example, you need hard information from several lending institutions which will enable you to compare the amounts of money you will pay for the loan. Because the advertising of credit terms is governed by detailed regulations — and because rates charged by lending institutions for personal loans are variable — it is impossible to gather the information you really need from advertising. Therefore, the friendliness of the loan officers and the ease with which you may file an application are emphasized.

Neither the mood set by an effective ad nor the ease with which you may file an application should limit the time and energy you spend shopping for the most favorable interest rate you can get.

The guilt-producers of advertising would have you believe that you shouldn't "skimp," for example, when it comes to buying expensive snack foods for your children. Other guilt-producers sell some arbitrary standard of home maintenance which is often irrelevant to the busy household whose members are involved in work, child care and community activities. In such homes, choices among empty-calorie snack foods, soaps, cleaning preparations and the like rank low on the priority list. Intellectually, many consumers are aware that such guilt-producing ads are irrelevant to the lives they lead. But how do consumers react emotionally? If the ads were not effective, they would certainly be discontinued. Think about it.

Price advertising (see also PRICES AND SALES) can provide important where-to-buy information. It can also be misleading.

For years Better Business Bureaus have frequently found deception in such claims as

"We sell for less . . ."

"Less than cost . . ."

"We will NOT be undersold . . ."

"Below wholesale . . ."

"Below original wholesale cost . . ."

A basic rule to remember in regard to price advertising is that normally only wholesalers, who sell to retailers, sell at wholesale prices. No retailer who hopes to stay

ADVERTISING

in business can regularly sell below cost, although they may from time to time feature an item at a wholesale price.

Other potentially misleading price claims are found in relation to such phrases as these:

"List price $45.95. Our price . . ."

"25% below manufacturer's suggested list price . . ."

"Suggested retail price, $43.00. Our price . . ."

Wise consumers are not taken in by such statements. Prices are variable. "List" or "Manufacturer's suggested retail prices" are likely to be higher than the prices for which merchandise of many kinds sell in various market areas. In any case, prices are too variable *within* market areas for any "list price" to be consistently applicable.

Price advertising can be misleading in another sense as well: it may fail to disclose extra charges for such services as installation and delivery. *If advertised prices do not include all the applicable costs to consumers, Better Business Bureaus recommend that the ad disclose that there are other costs.* When *all* charges are identified and priced, it is easier for customers to determine the total cost of the product.

Perhaps a study of some actual advertisements will help you guard against misleading ads:

1. "No Limit! 3 Rooms": This offer sounds like a great buy until you read the small print and think about the amount of carpet actually being offered. Then you discover that the low price quoted is "based on 36 sq. yds." That amount of carpet is an 18' by 18' square — considerably less than the actual size of three rooms.

GETTING MORE FOR YOUR MONEY

2. This ad offers a "free" bed frame when you buy a mattress and matching box springs. As it turns out, the shopper who doesn't want the "free" frame can buy the mattress and box springs for $15 less than the advertised price. In other words, the frame is by no means "free."

3. "Own this Huge Pool": This is an example of bait advertising. The pool in the picture is only an "artist's rendering" (*see the small print*). Once you get to the dealer you find that there is no pool available for $696 which resembles the picture in the ad. The pool you had in mind to buy, based on the ad, is available for nearly three times that amount.

18

ADVERTISING AND CHILDREN

Children may be excessively vulnerable to advertising. Or they may become critics and skeptics at a very early age.

Wise parents will help their children become wise buyers at the earliest possible age. Youngsters enter into their lifelong roles as consumers from the time they are first attracted by advertised toys, games and foods. An important contribution to the young consumer's learning experiences will be the parents' ongoing effort to help the child develop independent judgment.

A balanced middle course is in order in helping youngsters learn to be wise buyers. Try these ideas:

☐ Examine your own attitudes toward advertising. Help the children learn to ask constructive questions: "That space station looks *enormous*. How do you suppose they get it all into the little box we saw at the toy shop?" "Do you think a toy motorcycle can really work like that on the carpet in the playroom . . .?" "Plastic is very light. Could the bulldozer move all that sand if it's made of plastic?"

☐ Teach about nonnutritious foods and drinks by setting a good example: "Sure, that tastes good for a little while, but you really need a balanced diet."

☐ Trips to the supermarket can be learning experiences for young children if you let them see you make out a shopping list and — more important — see that you stick to it. This will help youngsters distinguish between nutritional needs and nonessentials. *Caveat:* Try this only when you have plenty of time and patience for constructive communication.

☐ Help children develop "money sense" by starting an allowance system early. If you help the children plan a budget — so much for lunch at school, so much for school supplies; this to save, that for the movies — they will be off to a good start in making essential consumer choices.

☐ Help them learn from experience. "Battery-operated toys can be expensive to run because you really have to have fresh batteries all the time. Do you want to spend your allowance on that sort of thing?"

☐ Toys should not be guilt-producers. This kind of experience is best avoided: If that Slam-Bang Flying Widget doesn't fly, if the battery-operated doll gurgles instead of talks and can't make it across the room when she "walks," it would be best to help the child understand that fantasy elements are used in advertising. The fragile mechanism inside the doll was never constructed to withstand long hours of use. This kind of understanding will be much healthier than having to assume guilt for a "broken" toy. Perhaps the next toy on your child's shopping list will be something strong and child-powered or a tasteful item from a craft shop.

GETTING MORE FOR YOUR MONEY

Remember that children will inevitably reflect their parents' attitudes toward spending goals and consumer choices. If parents are consistent tryers-out of new products, the children may see no reason why the same attitude should not extend to the "New Improved Superspecial Flying Widget," even though they know very well that the first one didn't work. If your children believe everything they hear in advertising, it's time to take a long, close look at your own attitudes.

HOW TO COMPLAIN

If you have purchased a product on the basis of advertised performance claims only to find that actual performance falls far below your expectations, *it is your responsibility to complain.*

If you believe a firm makes untrue or inaccurate claims in its national advertising, you can register your complaint with the National Advertising Division (NAD) of the Council of Better Business Bureaus (845 Third Avenue, New York, N.Y. 10022). Complaints concerning advertising directed to children should be directed to the Children's Advertising Review Unit, NAD, at the same address.

NAD reviews and investigates all the complaints it receives. Complaints that are disputed — those that NAD is unable to resolve — are referred to the National Advertising Review Board (NARB).

NARB is a self-regulatory appellate body established in 1971 by four associations: the American Advertising Federation, the American Association of Advertising Agencies, the Association of National Advertisers and the Council of Better Business Bureaus. Its objective is to sustain high standards of truth and accuracy in national advertising.

Local Better Business Bureaus receive and act on complaints concerning local advertising.

When you register a complaint, be sure to identify the offending ad. If you question or complain about a national television advertisement, for example, identify:

☐ the brand name of the product;
☐ the name of the advertiser;
☐ when (date and time) and where (channel and city) the ad appeared.

You may wish to complain about an advertisement in a newspaper or magazine or about a display in a retail store or service showroom. You may question a billboard, a direct-mail advertisement or a message on a package you buy. Be specific as to where the message appeared. If possible, supply a copy of the advertisement.

From time to time NARB reviews broad areas of responsibility in advertising (e.g., product advertising and consumer safety; advertising and women). Trends in advertising and public concerns in such areas are watched closely, and panels of experts serve as consultants in the preparation of position papers and/or statements on advertising practices.

> **National advertising** originates with businesses selling goods or services on a national or broad regional basis.
>
> **Local advertising** originates with local businesses and appears only in the communities served by these businesses.

Always:
- ☐ Put your complaint in writing.
- ☐ Be specific about where and when the advertisement appeared.
- ☐ If your complaint concerns a printed ad, send a copy with your letter.

WHAT HAPPENS WHEN YOU FILE A COMPLAINT?

NAD will review and evaluate the complaint and the advertising claims. After evaluation, complaints are brought to the attention of the advertiser, who is asked to provide proof that the claims or statements are true and accurate. If necessary, NAD will seek the advice of outside experts in the evaluation of the advertiser's proof (substantiation).

After a complete review of all the evidence presented by complainants, advertiser and consultants, NAD will arrive at a decision. It may decide that the advertising claims have not been substantiated and ask the advertiser to take appropriate action — to discontinue or change the ad. If the advertiser agrees to do so, the matter is considered closed.

Or NAD may decide, after investigation, that the advertiser's claims have been substantiated and no further action is necessary.

Whatever the decision of the NAD, the complainant is always notified.

There is also a third possibility:

If NAD asks the advertiser to change or discontinue the advertising and doesn't get cooperation, the National Advertising Review Board is asked to act on the matter.

NARB will then appoint a five-member panel to review the problem. Complainants are notified of the panel meeting in advance so that they have the opportunity to appear as witnesses or to submit additional testimony in writing. The panel evaluates the NAD investigation, the original complaint and the substantiation of claims presented by the advertiser. If the complaint is considered valid, the advertiser is again asked to make appropriate changes in his claims. If he refuses to cooperate, NARB's chairman will publicly refer the matter to an appropriate government enforcement agency. Whatever the result — whether the final decision is favorable or unfavorable to the advertiser — NARB's panel report will be published.

Air Conditioners

AIR CONDITIONERS DO MORE than cool the air. They also regulate humidity and clean and circulate the air.

Air-conditioning equipment ranges from small window-size units produced for use in one room or in an efficiency apartment, to central systems that cool private homes, to major units for use in apartment and office buildings. Window models are household appliances. They can be moved from home to home and, in some cases, from room to room within a home. Central systems, once installed, are an integral part of the dwelling. These should be purchased with the same care afforded the home heating system — after careful consideration of cost, efficiency and maintenance factors.

Anyone in the market for air-conditioning equipment should take these important factors into consideration before making a final decision:

- ☐ the cooling capacity of the unit and the size of the area it will serve;
- ☐ the Energy Efficiency Rating (EER);
- ☐ the cost and complexity of installation.

The cooling capacity of any air-conditioning system must be tailored to the area it will serve. An oversized unit will not only be more expensive than necessary, but it will cause uncomfortable variations in temperature and is likely to cool the area so quickly that moisture will remain in the air, resulting in a "clammy," instead of comfortable, environment. An undersized unit cannot be expected to perform. It would be false economy to buy one.

Cooling capacity is measured by the number of British thermal units (Btu) of heat the equipment can remove from the air in one hour. This is the consumer's only meaningful standard of measurement. "Horsepower" and "amperage" have no relation to cooling capacity, though both terms are sometimes used in advertising. The Btu/h (British thermal units per hour) capacity is clearly marked on the nameplate of each unit.

For purposes of comparison, the quarterly Directory of Certified Room Air Conditioners published by the Association of Home Appliance Manufacturers (AHAM) lists the capacity in Btu/h for the products of manufacturers who participate in its certification program. This directory may be available for inspection at your dealer or you may purchase a copy of the current edition from AHAM, 20 North Wacker Drive, Chicago, Illinois 60606.

AIR CONDITIONERS

To determine the cooling capacity required for a limited area, use the following formula:

(W × L × H × I × E)/60 = Btu/h capacity needed,

where W = width of room in feet
L = length of room in feet
H = height of room in feet
I = insulation factor (if there is a floor or a well-ventilated ceiling or attic above the area to be cooled, multiply by 10; if there is no such insulation or protection, or if the room has an especially large window area, multiply by 18)
E = exposure factor (when the longest room dimension faces north, multiply by 16; east, 17; south, 18; and west, 20)

More complex computation is required to arrive at the cooling capacity needed for large areas or for several rooms. You may want to write for a copy of the **Cooling Load Estimate Form** (see pp. 24—25) published and distributed free of charge by AHAM (see p. 22 for address). If the form seems overly complicated to you, enlist the services of a reliable contractor or dealer. Better still, get Cooling Load Estimates from several dealers.

The **Energy Efficiency Rating (EER)** of air conditioners is not related to cooling capacity. Unit A and Unit B may be comparable in their ability to maintain constant, comfortable temperature and humidity levels but Unit A, with an EER of 9.5, will use less energy and cost less to operate than Unit B, with an EER of 5.9.

Check the label for EER information.

EERs range up to 11.6. *The higher the number, the more efficient the unit.* The most efficient room air conditioners may be larger and heavier than their mid-range counterparts and they may also have a higher initial cost, but remember that they cost less to operate — a factor that will compensate for the higher initial cost over a period of a few years.

Many units now in use were produced before the EER was added to label information. Owners of these units may use information available on the nameplate to determine the EER:

Divide the Btu/h by the wattage (power) required for operation.

$$\frac{Btu/h}{w} = EER$$

GETTING MORE FOR YOUR MONEY

COOLING LOAD ESTIMATE FORM

Customer _____ Estimate by _____ Date _____

HEAT GAIN FROM	QUANTITY	FACTORS					Btu/Hr (Quantity x Factor)
		NIGHT	DAY				
			No Shades*	Inside Shades*	Outside Awnings*	(Area x Factor)	
1. WINDOWS: Heat gain from sun.							
Northeast	___ sq ft	0	60	25	20		___
East	___ sq ft	0	80	40	25	Use	___
Southeast	___ sq ft	0	75	30	20	only	___
South	___ sq ft	0	75	35	20	the	___
Southwest	___ sq ft	0	110	45	30	largest	___
West	___ sq ft	0	150	65	45	load	___
Northwest	___ sq ft	0	120	50	35		___
North	___ sq ft	0	0	0	0		___

*These factors are for single glass only. For glass block, multiply the above factors by 0.5; for double-glass or storm windows, multiply the above factors by 0.8.

2. WINDOWS: Heat gain by conduction. (Total of all windows.)					
Single glass	___ sq ft	14	.... 14		___
Double glass or glass block ..	___ sq ft	7	.... 7		___
3. WALLS: (Based on linear feet of wall.)			Light Construction	Heavy Construction	
a. Outside walls					
North exposure	___ ft	30	...... 30 .... 20		___
Other than North exposure. ..	___ ft	30	...... 60 .... 30		___
b. Inside Walls (between conditioned and unconditioned spaces only)	___ ft	30	.... 30		___
4. ROOF OR CEILING: (Use one only.)					
a. Roof, uninsulated	___ sq ft	5	.... 19		___
b. Roof, 1 inch or more insulation.	___ sq ft	3	.... 8		___
c. Ceiling, occupied space above.	___ sq ft	3	.... 3		___
d. Ceiling, insulated with attic space above	___ sq ft	4	.... 5		___
e. Ceiling, uninsulated, with attic space above	___ sq ft	7	.... 12		___
5. FLOOR: (Disregard if floor is directly on ground or over basement.)	___ sq ft	3	.... 3		___
6. NUMBER OF PEOPLE:	___	600	.... 600		___
7. LIGHTS AND ELECTRICAL EQUIPMENT IN USE	___ watts	3	.... 3		___
8. DOORS AND ARCHES CONTINUOUSLY OPEN TO UNCONDITIONED SPACE: (Linear feet of width.)	___ ft	200	.... 300		___
9. SUB-TOTAL	x x x x x	x x x x x	x x x x x		___
10. TOTAL COOLING LOAD: (Btu per hour to be used for selection of room air-conditioner(s).)	___	(Item 9) X ___	(Factor from Map) = ___		

NOTE: See Reverse side for instructions on use of this form.

Published and distributed by the
Association of Home Appliance Manufacturers
20 North Wacker Drive   Chicago, Illinois 60606
Phone A. C. 312 / 984-5800

AIR CONDITIONERS

INSTRUCTIONS FOR USING COOLING LOAD ESTIMATE FORM FOR ROOM AIR CONDITIONERS
(FROM AHAM STANDARD RAC-1)

A. This cooling load estimate form is suitable for estimating the cooling load for comfort air-conditioning installations which do not require specific conditions of inside temperature and humidity.

B. The form is based on an outside design temperature of 95 F dry bulb and 75 F wet bulb. It can be used for areas in the continental United States having other outside design temperatures by applying a correction factor for the particular locality as determined from the map.

C. The form includes "day" factors for calculating cooling loads in rooms where daytime comfort is desired (such as living rooms, offices, etc.), as well as "night" factors for calculating cooling loads in rooms where only nighttime comfort is desired (such as bedrooms). "Night" factors should be used only for those applications where comfort air-conditioning is desired during the period from sunset to sunrise.

D. The numbers of the following paragraphs refer to the correspondingly numbered item on the form:

1. Multiply the square feet of window area for each exposure by the applicable factor. The window area is the area of the wall opening in which the window is installed. For windows shaded by inside shades or venetian blinds, use the factor for "Inside Shades." For windows shaded by outside awnings or by both outside awnings and inside shades (or venetian blinds), use the factor for "Outside Awnings." "Single Glass" includes all types of single-thickness windows, and "Double Glass" includes sealed air-space types, storm windows, and glass block. Only one number should be entered in the right-hand column for item 1, and this number should represent *only the exposure with the largest load*.

2. Multiply the total square feet of *all* windows in the room by the applicable factor.

3a. Multiply the total length (linear feet) of all walls exposed to the outside by the applicable factor. Doors should be considered as being part of the wall. Outside walls facing due north should be calculated separately from outside walls facing other directions. Walls which are permanently shaded by adjacent structures should be considered as being "North Exposure." Do not consider trees and shrubbery as providing permanent shading. An uninsulated frame wall or a masonry wall 8 inches or less in thickness is considered "Light Construction." An insulated frame wall or a masonry wall over 8 inches in thickness is considered "Heavy Construction."

3b. Multiply the total length (linear feet) of all inside walls between the space to be conditioned and any unconditioned spaces by the given factor. Do not include inside walls which separate other air-conditioned rooms.

4. Multiply the total square feet of roof or ceiling area by the factor given for the type of construction most nearly describing the particular application. (Use one line only.)

5. Multiply the total square feet of floor area by the factor given. Disregard this item if the floor is directly on the ground or over a basement.

6. Multiply the number of people who normally occupy the space to be air-conditioned by the factor given. Use a minimum of 2 people.

7. Determine the total number of watts for lights and electrical equipment, except the air conditioner itself, that will be *in* use when the room air-conditioning is operating. Multiply the total wattage by the factor given.

8. Multiply the total width (linear feet) of any doors or arches which are continually open to an unconditioned space by the applicable factor.

   NOTE—Where the width of the doors or arches is more than 5 feet, the actual load may exceed the calculated value. In such cases, both adjoining rooms should be considered as a single large room, and the room air-conditioner unit or units should be selected according to a calculation made on this new basis.

9. Total the loads estimated for the foregoing 8 items.

10. Multiply the sub-total obtained in Item 9 by the proper correction factor, selected from the map, for the particular locality. The result is the total estimated design cooling load in Btu per hour.

E. For best results a room air-conditioner unit or units having a cooling capacity rating (determined in accordance with the AHAM Standards Publication for Room Air Conditioners, RAC-1) as close as possible to the estimated load should be selected. In general, a greatly oversized unit which would operate intermittently will be much less satisfactory than one which is slightly undersized and which would operate more nearly continuously.

F. Intermittent loads such as kitchen and laundry equipment are not included in this form.

RAC-1   Printed in USA

WINDOW-MODEL AIR CONDITIONERS

Installation. Window-model units — the ones generally available to the public at the retail level — usually require a minimum of time and effort for installation, but *be sure to follow manufacturer's instructions carefully.*

Some units designed primarily for through-the-wall installation may also be used for window installation. Again, manufacturer's instructions must be carefully followed. Through-the-wall units should be installed by a heating and air-conditioning contractor.

Before any air conditioner is installed, make sure that the electrical wiring is adequate for its operation. Inadequate wiring will waste power, reduce efficiency and may damage the unit. It can also be dangerous.

Have the wiring checked to make sure the circuit you plan to use has the right amperage (strength of electric current) and voltage (pressure in the power line) *before* the unit is installed. Follow these instructions:

1. Use a clear line — not one already loaded with appliances.
2. Make sure the outlet is properly grounded. Never remove the grounding prong from a three-prong plug.
3. Never attempt to connect a 208-V unit to a 115-V (normal household) line, nor a 115-V unit to a higher-voltage line intended for appliances such as an electric range or clothes dryer.
4. If possible, install your air conditioner in a shaded window, but avoid areas where outside dust, odors or pollen will be drawn into the unit.
5. Keep warm air out of cooled areas by weather-stripping doors and windows and keeping them tightly closed. Leave storm windows on, but make sure some can be opened so the room can be aired.
6. Close the fireplace damper.
7. Seal openings to the attic and other cooled areas.
8. Reduce solar heat by keeping shades and window blinds closed during the day. Reflecting glass, double-pane windows, awnings, overhangs, louvered sun screens, plantings, fences or adjoining buildings all help to diminish solar heat.
9. Never block the back of the unit.
10. Insulation helps. A minimum "R" value of 30 is recommended for ceilings, an "R" value of 13 for walls (see INSULATION).

Maintenance. Keep air-conditioning equipment clean. Use the dusting brush attachment of your vacuum cleaner to keep the vents free of dust. Clean or change the filters every month or so, and make sure the air flow is not blocked by dust, leaves, bugs, outside obstructions or frost on the condenser coils. Never remove the filter to get more air.

If unusual odors or smoke are detected, if the fan or cooling action stops or if the unit doesn't sound "right," turn it off and call for service.

Have air conditioners cleaned and checked at the beginning of each cooling season, and make sure each unit is cleaned before it is stored or covered for the winter.

CENTRAL AIR-CONDITIONING SYSTEMS

Central air-conditioning systems are composed of one or more basic air-conditioning units powered by gas or electricity, plus a mechanism for distributing conditioned air throughout the living space and the ducts through which the air moves. There are two principal types: **split system** and **single-package units**.

Most single family homes have a split system which places the evaporator coil and a fan inside the house and the condensing unit outside. This saves interior space and minimizes operating noise inside the house.

Single-package units have all elements of the system in one package, with an air-exhaust connection to the outdoors.

Most central systems are installed in basements, but they may also be installed in a crawl space, an attic or even a closet. If a split system is used in a home with central warm-air heating, the evaporator coils are usually installed on top of the furnace; the furnace fan is then used as the distribution mechanism for both warm and cool air. The accompanying unit is placed on a concrete slab near the wall of the house. A single-package unit is placed near the furnace and tied in with existing ductwork.

A total comfort system is more elaborate than the basic central system. Its additional components are an air cleaner, a power humidifier and, sometimes, an odor-control device.

Installation. Most homes can be centrally air-conditioned. Cost and complexity of installation will depend upon the size and construction of the individual home. Like room air-conditioning equipment, central systems must be tailored to the house and the family they will serve. No contractor can provide a reliable estimate until he has seen the home.

If a central system is to be added to an existing house, registers may have to be changed, ducts must be altered or added, and it may be necessary to add roof and wall insulation. Additional electrical work will be a necessity in houses that lack adequate wiring.

The best time of year to have air conditioning installed is when you don't need it. Contractors are more readily available (and are likely to charge less) during the fall and winter when they are less in demand.

Contractors and bids. Choosing a reliable, competent contractor may be the most important aspect of your buying decision. Start by asking friends and neighbors for their recommendations. It is important to know the contractor's reputation for economical and efficient installation of the equipment and for reliable service later. Follow these guidelines:

☐ Check the reputations of several contractors with friends and

neighbors, and your Better Business Bureau.
- Have each contractor submit a written estimate. The estimate should include a full description of the system to be installed and the additional work required for installation of ducts, registers and electrical wiring. (To prepare the estimate, the contractors should use an "Air Conditioning and Refrigeration Institute Cooling Load Calculation Form" or some comparable standard procedure.)
- Compare more than costs. Check the size of the equipment each contractor plans to use. If the size varies significantly, something is wrong. You should ask each contractor to explain how he arrived at his estimate of the required cooling capacity.
- Compare warranties. Most reputable contractors warrant their installation work for one year. Most manufacturers warrant equipment for the same period of time, with a four-year extension on the compressor.
- The contractor you choose should provide at least one "call back" free of charge after installation to check the system.

Operation. A routine yearly checkup performed by the air-conditioning specialist who installed the system should be enough to keep your air-conditioning equipment operating efficiently and economically.

To maintain maximum operating economy and efficiency, follow these suggestions:
- Keep heat out of the house. Use drapes, blinds and curtains to keep the sun out. Trees and shrubs will also help reduce solar heat.
- Find a comfortable thermostat setting and avoid changing it. A change of one or two degrees in the thermostat setting can have a considerable effect on operating costs. In the interest of energy conservation, a setting of 78° F or higher is urged by federal agencies.
- Keep the outside unit clear of shrubbery and grass.
- Cut down on heat-producing activities during the hot hours of the day. For example, schedule cooking for early morning and late afternoon hours. The same is true for humidity-producing activities such as bathing and mopping.

About "brown-outs." Operation of a central cooling system when voltage is reduced by 5 or even 10 percent will not damage the equipment. Central air-conditioning units are manufactured to tolerate this.

To help save electricity during a brown-out, raise the thermostat a few degrees. Central systems should not be turned off during a brown-out.

If electric power is temporarily cut off, the thermostat switch should be turned to the OFF position to avoid contributing to a sudden surge of demand for electricity when power is restored.

Animals

FROM HAMSTERS TO HORSES, pets provide companionship and amusement for adults and valuable learning experiences for children. They can also demand — and should receive — a great deal of time and attention.

Selection of the source of a pet, its accompanying guarantee and the animal's health at the time of purchase are the major factors that should influence all buying decisions in this area.

Look for these characteristics in a pet shop or kennel:

- ☐ Animals should be well groomed and clean.
- ☐ Cages should be large enough to allow the animals to move about.
- ☐ Cages and feeding trays should be clean.
- ☐ Animals should be alert, energetic and responsive. Listless animals may be a signal of problems in the shop.
- ☐ Pets should be sold with a guarantee allowing replacement or refund for diseased animals for a specified period of time. A full guarantee for an unlimited time should be allowed to cover congenital defects. Twenty-four or forty-eight hour guarantees are meaningless. This is not enough time to allow for examination by a veterinarian and/or for infection to develop. (Distemper, the most common killer of animals, has an incubation period of seven days.)

According to a pet dealer association, an excellent way to make sure the dealer is ethical is to determine whether he is willing to offer a cash refund. This is a definite indication that he is confident of the health of his animals. Ideally, all contracts should give the customer the option of accepting a cash refund or a new animal.

If the animal you purchase has received its initial immunizations at the pet shop, get a certificate of vaccination signed by the veterinarian showing when the animal was inoculated, for what, and when it will need booster or follow-up shots.

Healthy cats and dogs have smooth, glossy coats, clear eyes, white teeth, firm, pink gums, and clear skin with no dryness or scaliness. Check for these characteristics, but make sure to arrange for a thorough checkup by a veterinarian to confirm the animal's good physical condition *before* the sale is final.

The general health of fish and birds is hard for most shoppers to evaluate, but a few basic rules apply:

- ☐ Fish should have flexible, free-flowing fins and even-textured scales (sick fish often have worn-looking patches on their bodies). Make sure the fish you choose are neither listless nor tend to hover at the top of the aquarium.

☐ Birds should be alert and responsive. If a bird sits quietly with feathers fluffed up, it is ill. This is an indication that it is rapidly losing body heat and is trying to keep itself warm. Other symptoms of illness in birds include loss of appetite, excessive thirst, discharge from eyes and nostrils, watery discolored droppings, and convulsions or shock. Again, birds should be bought with a guarantee allowing for refund or replacement if illness should develop.

Pet record

It's a good idea to keep a permanent record of your pet, which contains such information as its date of birth, license number, the dates of its inoculations and other pertinent facts on its medical care. This information can prove quite helpful for your own use as well as for your veterinarian's.

PURCHASE RECORD

From: Name _____
Address _____
Date: _____
Contact: _____
Telephone Number: _____
Price: _____
Breed: _____

VITAL STATISTICS

Name: _____

Pedigreed description
Born: _____
Sex: _____
Sire: _____
Dam: _____
Litter Number: _____
AKC (Pet): _____
AKC (Dealer): _____
Papers Sent: _____
Papers Received: _____

HEALTH RECORD

Veterinarian: _____
Address: _____
Telephone: _____
Immunization record (dog):
(Temporary)   Due   Given
    Distemper   ____   ____
    Hepatitis   ____   ____
    Leptospirosis   ____   ____
(Adult)
    Distemper   ____   ____
    Hepatitis   ____   ____
    Leptospirosis   ____   ____
Rabies vaccination: _____
(Yearly booster)
    Rabies _____
    D-H-L _____
Immunization record (cat): _____
Feline pneumonitis _____
Booster
Feline Distemper _____
Booster _____
Rabies Vaccination: _____

GENERAL MEDICAL RECORD (Fish, Birds, Other Pets)

1. _____
2. _____
3. _____

Antiques

ANTIQUES IS A TERM that covers a wide area and is not easily defined. For those who enjoy "antiquing," an activity that has risen in popularity in recent years, there are several criteria to use in choosing an antique: age, quality of workmanship, excellence of design and condition. How rare an item is can also be important; copies of a piece of antique china are not as desirable as the original piece itself. To determine for sure whether or not an item is an antique, it's a good idea to get advice from a reputable antique dealer or from someone knowledgeable in the field.

Reasons for collecting antiques are as various as the collectors themselves. Some people buy antiques as investments, some out of simple nostalgia, some for esthetic reasons. Any or all of these reasons can motivate a collector who, for example, likes the patina and texture of old wood and who believes that old furniture will appreciate instead of depreciate in value.

Whatever the motivation, the best place to launch a search is in a good library, where illustrated reference materials provide a range of information on period styles and designs. Next, visits to museums, the local historical society and a range of "historic houses" are in order.

The safest place to buy is an established antique shop run by a dealer who knows what he's selling.

Estate and country auctions are fun and they can, occasionally, be profitable — but mostly for dealers and experienced buyers.

Buying should go slowly. A heavy investment in Victoriana can be a problem if your taste changes after a few years (as taste usually does) and you find the simple lines of Windsor chairs and the muted colors of oriental rugs now suit you better.

Read a variety of advertisements for antiques. Classifications such as "fine," "excellent" and "good" should be self-explanatory. A "fine" example of an eighteenth-century New England Windsor bow-back side chair should mean that it is not only a fine example of its kind, but that it has not been restored or refinished.

"Restored" to a serious collector or dealer is tantamount to "damaged." Once restored, the "fine" Windsor chair is only an attractive piece of furniture. If more than 10 percent of it has been replaced, it is no longer an antique.

"Refinished" is another problem category. The patina of that same Windsor chair is irreplaceable and unmistakable to the serious collector. The best-preserved wood should only be cleaned with mild soap and water, wiped dry with a soft cloth and then — *perhaps* — oiled or waxed. A greater change to the original finish may drastically lower the value of the piece.

"As is," applied to anything from antiques to used cars, means the item is offered for sale and the customer takes it as he or she finds it. It could mean the piece is a battered reproduction, or that it has been badly restored or poorly refinished. There is no guarantee of its value or of its period.

"In the rough" may be a better gamble. It usually means that, whatever the item, it is in its original condition. Like "as is" pieces, these are purchased without pedigree or guarantee. Inspect them carefully to make sure they are not reproductions or damaged pieces.

Consider major purchases as major investments — they should always be accompanied by a written guarantee consisting of a detailed description of the object and the seller's statement of when and where it was made.

Apartments

(See also CONDOMINIUMS AND COOPERATIVES; HOUSING, HOME BUYING; MOVING)

APARTMENT LIVING IS "right" for many people — for confirmed city dwellers and for others who prefer the relative absence of responsibility to the care and maintenance of a one-family home.

Established apartment houses develop a character of their own, just as established neighborhoods do. For this reason it is important to choose an apartment with an atmosphere that is right for your individual taste and needs. Finding a suitable apartment is well worth a long, careful search, complete with visits long enough to assess the neighborhood and the building and to get a sense of whether or not you'd be compatible with the neighbors.

THE SEARCH

If you are moving into a city new to you, the services of a reputable apartment rental agency may be worth having. Consulting someone who is familiar with neighborhoods, buildings and apartments can save a great deal of time and effort. *But remember:* apartment rental agencies are only referral services. The agencies get most of their listings from newspaper ads. Charges are made on a fee basis, and can be substantial.

With or without the services of a broker, you might enjoy thorough explorations of the neighborhoods you like. You can search for "Vacancy" and "Apartment Available" signs on your own, getting acquainted with doormen and building superintendents in the process and chatting with tradesmen and shopkeepers to assess the atmosphere of the place. You will want to explore in the evening as well as in the daytime to check such important factors as the general sense of security (or lack of it) in the neighborhood and the cleanliness of the streets.

Make a list of the qualities that are important to you in choosing the area and the kind of apartment house you want to live in, and keep them in mind while you search. Use these guidelines:

The neighborhood
☐ Are the streets well-lighted at night? Acceptably neat in the daytime?
☐ Where would you call the police or fire department (outside your own apartment) in an emergency?

- ☐ Is there a good selection of medical and dental services close by? Where is the nearest hospital?
- ☐ How close are you to parks and other recreational facilities? Are neighborhood public recreation areas clean, well kept and well lit?
- ☐ Are there supermarkets, neighborhood groceries and other shops and restaurants close by?
- ☐ Where would the children go to school? Visit the school to see that its atmosphere meets your standards.

The building
- ☐ Is the entrance hall acceptably clean and neat?
- ☐ Is there a doorman on duty at night? Around the clock? Are guests *always* announced? If there is no doorman, is there a speaker system that allows you to confirm the identity of visitors? Is the outside door kept locked?
- ☐ Are hallways, stairways and elevators well lighted and secure?
- ☐ Is there a resident superintendent? If not, whom do you contact in case some sort of emergency occurs when he is not available? (The availability of the building superintendent is important to apartment dwellers — he can be as important as the landlord to the comfort, cleanliness and security of the building you live in.)

The apartment
- ☐ How much room do you need? Could you be comfortable in a studio apartment (one big room, small kitchen and bathroom)? Must you be able to provide space for out-of-town visitors? How about separate rooms and play space for the children? Keep looking until you find the space you need for your life style.
- ☐ Check for cross-ventilation and/or air conditioning.
- ☐ Do the kitchen appliances work?
- ☐ Are there enough electric outlets with adequate voltage for your needs?
- ☐ Will the noise from other apartments disturb you? (Visit at night when everyone is at home to check the kinds and degree of noise.)

THE LEASE

The lease — the contract under which you rent your apartment — should protect you as well as it protects the landlord. Like all other contracts, it must be taken seriously and read carefully.

Expect the standard lease to provide for a security payment, equal to at least one or two months' rent, which protects the landlord against damage to his property through the tenant's carelessness and/or against the tenant's falling behind in rent or absconding. This payment should be returned to you when you leave the apartment, minus, of course, any bona fide charges for damage, clean-up, etc. *Check the provisions concerning the security deposit in your lease.* Some states have passed legislation restricting the amount of the security deposit and limiting the amount of time the landlord can retain your deposit after you move out. In many areas, the security deposit must be placed in an escrow account where it will gain interest. Be sure you are familiar with your state's law.

If your lease is to protect your rights as a tenant, it should contain in writing all promises made by the landlord or rental agent. Find out:

- [ ] Who is responsible for repair or replacement of such items as broken windows, damaged screens, plumbing, etc.?
- [ ] Who is responsible for the repair of the appliances that come with the apartment?
- [ ] Does the lease list all the equipment that comes with the apartment? Usually this includes the refrigerator, stove, lighting fixtures, air-conditioning units and window blinds. (If other appliances or equipment are in the apartment, the lease should guarantee that they will remain if you want them or will be removed by the landlord if you don't want them. Otherwise, you will have to pay for having them disconnected and stored.)
- [ ] Does the lease provide for a decorating timetable, stating whether the landlord does the painting and how often?
- [ ] Does it specify building services, such as a round-the-clock attendant?
- [ ] Are pets allowed?
- [ ] Must you carpet the place? Some leases say that a tenant must carpet at least 90 percent of his apartment if the downstairs tenants complain of noise.
- [ ] Does the lease give you permission to sublet if you want to move before the lease is up or if you plan on being away for a lengthy period?
- [ ] Does it state how many persons may occupy the apartment? If so, does the figure allow for children or for friends and relatives who may join your household? Some landlords have demanded and received rent increases when tenants' families grow.
- [ ] Are utility charges included in the rent? The lease should say so.

When you inspect your lease, check to make sure all the blanks have been filled in correctly. Make sure that the rent stated is the amount agreed upon. Mistakes can occur even in the best of offices, and you don't want your rental agreement changed by way of a typing error.

Once you are satisfied with the terms of your lease, you may want to have it examined by your lawyer and/or by someone familiar with real estate law. Get explanations of any provision you don't understand. Better Business Bureaus report that their records of tenants' complaints indicate that many tenants are not fully aware of certain important clauses in their leases, such as the terms of renewal and conditions under which they can be dispossessed.

Appliances

(See also DOOR-TO-DOOR SALES; ENERGY; SALES CONTRACTS; WARRANTIES)

SMALL APPLIANCES — from blenders and broilers to coffeemakers and waffle irons — seem to multiply like so many rabbits in many homes. Opinions differ on the usefulness and practicality of powered gadgetry: some homemakers swear by electric can openers and complex slicer—chopper—grater machines; others feel that such items present more problems than they solve, and would rather stick to their twenty-year-old metal can opener and a good set of carbon steel knives.

Here are some general considerations that apply to the purchase of any new appliance.

- ☐ **Storage space.** Do you really have room for it? Will it be easily accessible when you need it?
- ☐ **Use.** How often will you use it? Often enough to make it a reasonable, practical purchase?
- ☐ **Maintenance.** Look it over carefully. Will it be difficult to clean?
- ☐ **Safety.** All electrical appliances should carry the Underwriters Laboratory seal. Gas appliances should bear the seal of the American Gas Association.
- ☐ **Operating cost.** This is generally a consideration only for major appliances such as water heaters, frost-free refrigerators, ranges and the like.

When these factors have been considered and you have decided that appliance A will be a valuable addition to the efficiency or comfort of your home, check product-rating publications that test and evaluate products. These publications are available on newsstands or in your local public library.

Choosing a dealer should be done as carefully as choosing which of several models of a particular appliance best suits your needs. If the equipment you want to buy requires professional installation, make sure to find out whether the dealer has included delivery and installation in the price. *Be on guard against dealers who advertise exceptionally low purchase prices and then levy additional charges for delivery, installation, service, etc.* Extra charges, when added to so-called "bargain prices," may add up to a greater price than you would have paid to a dealer who is more forthright about his terms and services.

> House brand or store brand appliances are made by national-brand manufacturers and sold under the private labels of national retailers. They are often good buys, manufactured to the retailer's specifications and warranted by the retailer. Compare prices. Compare warranties. Get information about the retailer's local service facilities.

Insist on seeing the warranty *before* you buy. This should always be a major factor in your buying decision (see WARRANTIES). Find out whether the warranty is "full" or "limited" — and what the limitations are. Find out where in-warranty service is provided and by whom. **Remember:** No appliance is a really good buy unless it works; if you are obliged to send a piece of household equipment to a service center six hundred miles away for repairs, the purchase might turn out to be more trouble than it's worth.

Follow the manufacturer's use and care instructions. Familiarize yourself with the operation of an appliance *before* you begin to use it. Whenever possible, have the equipment demonstrated in the store before you buy. Keep the operating instructions available for reference (file them with the warranty). Proper operation and care will make any appliance work more efficiently and last longer. Always consult the operating manual when something seems to be wrong with an appliance; you may be able to save the cost of a service call.

ENERGY COSTS AND SMALL APPLIANCES

There's no need to feel guilty about using that electric toothbrush, blender, mixer, coffeemaker, waste disposal or other small appliance. Utility rates vary and are continually going up, but an electric toothbrush costs only pennies a year to operate. The coffeemaker, operated about 120 hours per year, would use about 100 kilowatt hours and cost $10.00 or so annually. (A kilowatt hour is a thousand watts running for an hour or any other combination producing the same total, such as a 100-watt light bulb burning for 10 hours.) Color television costs under 5 cents per hour and an electric blanket will keep you warm for a few cents a night.

Although electric appliances abound in most American homes, it is not these appliances that send your utility bill sky-high. Instead, it is the major appliances — the necessities — which are the major energy eaters. These include the water heater, the range/oven, the refrigerator (especially the frost-free model), the clothes dryer and the air conditioner. Look for EER (Energy Efficiency Rating) labels on new major appliances and choose the most efficient models to gain lower operating costs. These models are likely to be more expensive to buy, but less expensive to operate. Consider compensating for a higher initial cost by long-term saving on utility bills (see ENERGY).

Used, second-hand? Reconditioned, rebuilt?
There are important differences among these categories.

True, you can save money by buying a used, second-hand appliance, but you must choose your dealer carefully. If your second-hand appliance is labeled "as is," you may be buying an unpleasant surprise. Unless your "bargain" is backed by a warranty or guarantee *in writing* from a reputable dealer, its purchase is a gamble — and you have little basis for complaint should something go wrong.

The term "reconditioned" implies that those repairs and adjustments have been made which are necessary to put the appliance in satisfactory operating condition *without reconstruction or rebuilding.*

"Reconstructed" or "rebuilt" implies that the appliance has been disassembled, reconstructed, repaired and refinished, including replacement of parts. This should mean that the machine is more than merely repaired or reconditioned — in other words, the reconstruction should provide nearly-new performance and a better warranty.

Compare prices, warranties and dealer service facilities. Base your buying decision on a careful evaluation of your needs and the dealer's reputation. If you are in doubt about the latter, check with friends, neighbors and your local Better Business Bureau.

Audio Equipment

(See also WARRANTIES)

YOUR BEST CHOICE WILL BE based on an inventory of your own needs, tastes and listening habits. To help you determine your needs, use the following checklist:

1. **What's your budget?**
   Audio equipment can cost hundreds or thousands of dollars. Within any price range, there is a wide variety of equipment to choose from.

2. **What do you want to hear?**
   The needs of a person who wants to build a music library by taping from FM will be very different from those of the person who has — or wants to build — an extensive record or tape collection.

3. **What is your current investment in records? Tapes? Eight-track cartridges? Prerecorded cassettes?**
   With more than 45,000 titles available, most people invest a considerable amount of money in recordings. Because of this investment, it's wise to put your money into equipment that will complement your past investments in recordings. For example, if you already have a lot of records or eight-track tapes, you may not be in the market for a system featuring a cassette tape deck.

4. **What are the conditions in your listening room?**
   A room with carpeting, open doorways and quantities of upholstered furniture may be acoustically "dead" and therefore require a more powerful amplifier. A "live" room requires less. Most rooms fall between these two extremes. Your listening room may be due for attention if you are in search of concert hall fidelity.

5. **What range of options do you need?**
   You may want to choose a sound system which allows a range of inputs including AM-FM radio, turntable, tape recorder, cartridge or cassette recorder and/or player.

6. **What sound quality are you looking for?**
   The best way to listen for the sound you like is to test a variety of equipment in several audio specialty stores. Experiment with the

volume, balance, bass and treble controls of each set. Test out both mono and stereo recordings (preferably *your own* records, which you've brought to the store with you) to help you judge the quality and accuracy of the sound system.

7. **What are your musical tastes?**
Background music played at moderate levels makes few demands on the range of your sound system. If there is a wide range of taste in your family — from baroque to Wagner to hard rock — and an equally wide range of preferred volume, you need an amplifier and speakers that can cope with broad dynamic contrast.

8. **Is space important?**
Modern solid-state equipment can pack a great deal of power, playing options and controls into a very small space. You no longer need to sacrifice quality or performance because your listening room is limited.

9. **Which are you interested in — stereophonic or quadriphonic sound?**
Stereophonic sound reproduction was a major step forward for audiophiles in the 1950s. The most recent development is the quadriphonic (four-channel) system. Two speakers are needed for stereophonic systems. For a quadriphonic system, you need four, two of which must be located in the back of the listening room. The objective of the quadriphonic system is to provide a 360° sound perspective, with more sound radiated indirectly rather than directly, adding depth and breadth to the sound quality.

10. **Are you knowledgeable about standards and rating specifications?**
If not, you should learn about them. Several different standards and rating specifications are used for the evaluation of audio amplifiers and/or the amplifiers built into packaged receivers. There are three major types of amplifier power specifications:

- ☐ continuous power (RMS);
- ☐ IHF power (Institute of High Fidelity);
- ☐ EIA music power (Electronics Industry Association).

Federal Trade Commission guidelines require manufacturers who advertise "power output" to disclose the rated minimum continuous output in watts, in addition to the following three related (and crucial) criteria:

- ☐ The speaker or load impedances set by the manufacturer. Impedance, simply defined, is the flow of alternating current. Components that must function together must have matched or comparable impedance values.
- ☐ The manufacturer's rated power band or power frequency response in Hertz (Hz).

AUDIO EQUIPMENT

☐ The manufacturer's rated percentage of maximum total harmonic distortion at the rated power.

11. **How about a compact system?**
    If you are relatively new to audio and want a system that has already been balanced and matched, a stereo compact system (including speakers, turntable and electronics) may be just the thing for you. Many manufacturers and dealers preselect components for a wide range of budget requirements and a wide range of listening needs. Listen to these systems and compare. If you find a system you like, your buying decision has been made for you and you can stop your research and comparison shopping immediately. You will have a wide range of choices among portables, all-in-one systems, etc. These are likely to be convenient to use and attractively designed. *And remember:* size is no longer related to quality.

12. **Are you interested in a console?**
    Many people choose to combine their sound systems with a quality piece of furniture by buying consoles. Usually, a console includes an automatic turntable, a stereo receiver and matched speakers, and sometimes a tape deck. Price depends on the type of cabinet and the sound system you choose.

13. **Do you need a component system?**
    If your interest in sound has turned into an audio hobby . . . if your listening taste and sound preference is better defined than it used to be . . . it may be time to upgrade your equipment.
    A component system generally includes a turntable, a receiver (tuner, preamplifier and amplifier), perhaps a tape recorder and/or cassette player, and speakers.
    Components can be upgraded by degrees without changing the whole system. You may wish to invest more in whatever part of the system is most important to you.
    Experts agree that a good rule of thumb for budgeting is to allocate 25 percent of the equipment budget for the turntable and phonograph cartridge, 45 percent for your receiver and 30 percent for your speakers. This should result in a basically balanced system.

Here are some details on the equipment used for a component system:
Tuner. A tuner is an electronic circuit designed to receive AM, FM stereo or other radio services. It's possible to buy one tuner to receive AM, another for FM, the two combined, or any other combination together with an amplifier and preamplifier.
Antenna. If you want to receive FM stations, you'll need a good FM antenna. Some manufacturers include indoor antennas with the FM units they sell; these are good enough for use in an apartment. For

optimum performance quality, it's a good idea to get an outdoor antenna.

Turntable. You'll need a turntable to play records; there are several different varieties available. You can buy a unit that changes records automatically in addition to playing them. Or you can choose a single-play automatic turntable that automatically plays records one at a time, but doesn't change them. You can also buy a turntable separate from the tone arm and phono cartridge which are usually included with it.

TAPE EQUIPMENT

The question occurs and recurs: I am about to buy my first tape recorder — should I buy a reel-to-reel, a cassette deck or a cartridge player? The answer is yes.

There is an almost endless list of uses for tape equipment, with a wide range of models and types of equipment available to fill the needs of hobbyists and/or listeners. Your satisfaction with the equipment you choose will depend, of course, on quality and reliability. But equally important to your continued satisfaction will be its suitability for the job you intend it to do. Here is a rundown of the main types.

Reel-to-reel (open reel). This is the original type of tape recorder, the kind still used by recording studios, radio stations and serious sound hobbyists. It is likely to be the most expensive to buy and to use: the initial cost is likely to be higher; tapes and tape consumption will be higher; and you will need more storage space, both for equipment and tapes. The best reel-to-reels maintain professional performance standards, have excellent recording capabilities, and are versatile and functional.

Tape reels, generally seven inches in diameter, must be placed on the machine and the tape threaded by hand from the "feed reel" across the recording/playback heads and onto the "take-up reel." There is usually a choice of at least two speeds on quality open reel recorders — 7½ or 15 inches per second (ips), or 3¾ or 1⅞ ips. The higher speeds produce higher fidelity. 7½ ips is regarded as the standard speed for open reel recordings.

Cassette. This type of recorder/player uses a standard thin compact cassette containing two small reels. The cassette snaps into the recorder/player; the operator does not touch the tape.

Either blank or prerecorded cassettes are available in standard 30-, 60- and 90-minute playing lengths. There are also 15-minute and (more fragile) 120-minute tapes.

Cassette tapes and players have changed a great deal since they were introduced as dictating equipment. Cassette tape decks are available in many forms, and with a great variety of engineering devices, such as the Dolby noise reduction system, long-lasting head materials and improved fidelity.

Standard advice is in order for potential buyers of cassette recorders: Listen a lot. Experiment with the mechanism *before* you buy. Base your final decision on individual needs and taste.

Cartridge. The eight-track cartridge player is the type commonly used in automobile stereo systems as well as for home and portable use. The standard tape cartridge is somewhat larger than a cassette and its operation is even more automatic. Cartridge players can provide quantities of music — the four pairs of stereo tracks are automatically played in sequence. Switching from track to track is usually automatic. A cartridge can accommodate up to the equivalent of two full LPs.

Recorders, players and decks. Each of the three types of tape instruments described above is available either as a deck or a complete self-contained unit. A **deck** is simply a recorder or player without amplifier or speakers which is designed to be plugged into a home music system.

A **player** is an instrument designed only to play back recorded tapes — it cannot make recordings. A **recorder** can make recordings *and* play them back, as well as play commercially recorded tapes. Most cartridge instruments are players, designed to play the enormous range of recorded eight-track cartridges now available, although cartridge recorders are also on the market. Cassette units are primarily sold as recorders, but players without the recording capacity are also on the market.

Which type is for you? If you are a serious audio hobbyist interested in "producing" your own tapes, the open reel machine is likely to be your choice. The higher initial and equipment costs (and the relative inconvenience of tape threading and storage of bulky tape reels) will be more than compensated for by the flexibility in editing and tape splicing, as well as the excellent sound reproduction characteristic of the best instruments of this type.

For listening, recorded stereo albums are available for all three types, with a somewhat wider variety offered in the cartridge format. The eight-track cartridge player, as noted, is widely used as a high-fidelity player for cars, homes, boats and for use outdoors as well (and the fidelity grows better with constant technological improvements). It is at its best in the presentation of album-length selections or background music, since it plays the album from start to finish without requiring any handling.

If outdoor listening is your pleasure, either a cartridge or cassette player, in combination with a built-in radio, will serve the purpose.

For recording music from the radio or phonograph, a good-quality cassette recorder or deck combines simplicity with good sound. Best results are obtained with patch cords plugged directly into the tape jacks of a stereo or hi-fi system. Cartridge recorders are fine for recording long album-type selections, but *cartridges cannot be rewound for rapid location of a specific selection.* They may be wound forward only and,

GETTING MORE FOR YOUR MONEY

since the tape is an endless loop, you will eventually get back to the selection you want. Cassettes, on the other hand, have both fast forward and rewind capacities. Most combination cassette recorders with AM-FM radios provide for direct recording from the built-in radio without the use of patch cords.

> If you choose a cassette player/recorder with the tape selector, bias and/or equalization switches, you will be able to choose among several different tapes available for several purposes. You would use a less expensive tape for practicing a speech or for talking a letter to a friend than you would use for recording music from an FM station. To decide whether these features would be useful to you, consider the various kinds of recording you will do and make your decision accordingly.

For recording speech, making "sound snapshots," talking letters, learning languages and memorizing speeches or dramatic roles, a cassette recorder is ideal. A unit capable of both battery and AC operation is versatile, usable both outdoors and at home.

Monaural, stereo and quadriphonic equipment. All modern recorders and players designed for high-fidelity music reproduction are capable of stereophonic operation, while the most compact battery-operated recorders are designed for monophonic use only. You can record monophonically with either a stereo or mono recorder. Tape itself is capable of extreme high-fidelity recording; the amplifier and speaker systems are generally the limiting factors in sound quality. So any stereo unit you choose should have good speakers or should be designed to record and play through your own hi-fi.

Quadriphonic reproduction is available on both open reel and cartridge equipment, and specially recorded four-channel cartridge tapes are available for them. Again, the limiting feature will be the capacity of the speakers and the acoustics in your listening room.

Special features or necessities?

VU (volume unit) meters. At their best, these give you a visible picture of your recording level so that you can avoid wrecking your recording with distortion. An accurate VU meter is an absolute necessity for anyone interested in producing clear "sound snapshots" or in recording live music.

Dolby noise-reduction system. This is a device that increases the signal-to-noise ratio by raising the volume of quiet passages prior to recording and lowering them to their original levels during playback. Without the Dolby system you will hear "tape hiss" behind the signal you want to hear on your tape. Dolby will add to the cost of your cassette recorder, but the extra cost for increased fidelity is likely to be a good investment.

AUDIO EQUIPMENT

Among other special features you may want to consider are:

☐ **Automatic cartridge and cassette changers,** for hours of uninterrupted music.
☐ **Automatic shut-off,** which turns off the power when the tape is over.
☐ **Automatic reverse for cassette and open reel recorders,** which eliminates the need to reverse the tape manually.
☐ **AC converters,** to permit battery recorders to be operated from the AC wall plug.
☐ **Pause controls,** which allow instantaneous start-up from a complete stop with none of the audible results you inevitably get from the Play/Record switch. This allows smooth recording of live music as well as commercial and click-free recording from FM. If the pause control is slow, however, a "smeared" note will result.
☐ **Front-loading cassette decks,** which are convenient if you need to store the deck on a narrow shelf with the controls and the loading mechanism easily at hand. Remember, though, that the loading deck must be at eye level to be useful — otherwise you can't see the VU meters and you can't tell whether the tape is malfunctioning. Top-loading models are often easier to clean.

Microphones. Most self-contained recorders come equipped with microphones: one for a monophonic recorder, two for stereo. The microphone with a portable cassette recorder usually has a built-in remote-control switch to let you start or stop the tape from the microphone itself. Recording decks generally are sold without microphones; you may choose them on your own to match your own requirements. Again, the requirements will vary with the kind of use you plan. For live music, you would want to choose maximum accuracy and range; for voice-only recording, a simpler, less expensive microphone will be adequate.

Types of tape. There are quantities of tape for various functions available in a confusing array of price ranges. Because tapes have different magnetic characteristics, choose the type of tape for which your cassette deck is designed — iron oxide, chrome or ferrichrome.

Tape storage. Magnetic tapes should always be stored in their original boxes or containers to protect them from dust. *Because a magnetic field can erase or distort the recordings, they should be kept away from such magnetic equipment as loudspeakers, amplifiers and magnetic microphones while in storage.*

THE AMPLIFIER
Even if you choose the simplest system available, it will contain an amplifier section. An amplifier is a circuit that takes weak signals from the program source and amplifies them to a powerful enough level to

activate a loudspeaker. Of course, the more sophisticated the system, the more complex the amplifier. If you choose a high-fidelity component system, it will have a control unit that will shape the outgoing signal, route signals to two or more speaker systems, handle two or more turntables, tape decks and so on.

Because of the technical nature of the products available in addition to the considerable cost, it's wise to do business with a knowledgeable and reputable dealer. Be sure to understand how a specific piece of equipment works before you buy it.

THE SPEAKERS

You'll need a set of speakers to complete your stereo system. Some speaker systems require more power than others; others take up a lot of space. Check with the dealer for advice on choosing the right speakers for your needs.

THE WARRANTY

The warranty on audio equipment you buy may differ from one manufacturer to another, even from dealer to dealer. In most cases, the warranty runs for a minimum of ninety days while others may extend for a year or longer. Some warranties cover parts and labor; others include parts only. Most of them require you to bring the audio product to an authorized service center for repair. Keep in mind that since the provisions of the warranties differ, it's a good idea to understand exactly what the warranty covers before you buy the audio equipment.

HOW ARE YOU GOING TO PAY FOR IT?

Purchasing audio products can be an expensive undertaking. Before buying, be sure to think about how you're going to pay the price. Some stores will let you finance the purchase through them, or you may want to go to a financial institution to borrow the money. If you decide to finance the amount due, know what your options are. Compare different types of loans and financing. Remember that lenders are required by law to spell out the amount of interest and other charges. Since credit costs money, it's wise to borrow only as much as you need.

SUMMING UP

- ☐ Know how you plan to use your audio equipment — the kind of music you listen to and/or want to record, the special uses you may find for a portable tape recorder, etc. — and remember that your own ears, your own plans must define the kind of equipment you choose.
- ☐ When buying a tape recorder, remember that cartridge, cassette and open reel units have different characteristics and uses. Familiarize yourself with them.
- ☐ Buy from a reputable dealer. Listen to the equipment and learn to operate it before you buy.
- ☐ Know and understand the terms of the warranty.

Automobiles

(See also ADVERTISING; CREDIT AND INSTALLMENT BUYING; GASOLINE AND GASOLINE-SAVING DEVICES; WARRANTIES; IF YOU ARE DISSATISFIED)

MOST AMERICAN MOTORISTS have no idea how much it costs to own and operate their cars. According to the American Automobile Association, it cost 24 cents per mile to own and operate an intermediate-size car in 1980. For the anticipated life span of the car (approximately ten years, or 100,000 miles), this totals $24,000!

Expenses for gasoline, repairs, parking, insurance, taxes and finance charges are included in these estimates. Operating costs vary from region to region. For example, they would be higher in Boston, New York City or San Francisco, and lower in Jacksonville, Montgomery or Fort Worth.

The most economical way to own a car, suggests the AAA, is to get all the mileage you can out of it instead of following the practice of trading for a new model every year or two. *Depreciation is the greatest single cost of owning and operating a new car.*

Depreciation is the difference between what you paid for your car and what you sell it for. To determine your annual depreciation expense, subtract the trade-in value of your car from the purchase price and divide by the number of years you plan to keep the car. Although repair bills increase with the age of any automobile, they will not equal the cost of depreciation paid by the car owner who trades in a car each year.

Remember: No matter how carefully a new car is operated and maintained, it will have lost one-quarter of its value at the end of its first year on the road. Trade-in values are variable and dependent upon unpredictable market conditions, so optimistic statements by salesmen in regard to a future trade-in value should be discounted.

Prepurchase research and decision-making are important to the choice of the best buy in automobile purchasing. Key items to consider, equally applicable to the purchase of new and used cars, are:

- ☐ How much can you afford to spend?
- ☐ How many people must the car accommodate? For what kind of driving?
- ☐ Which options do you really need? How much do they add to the cost of the car? It is important to consider not only the initial cost of each option, but the weight it will add and the accompanying

increased fuel consumption. Air conditioners, for example, add about one hundred pounds and impose a permanent fuel penalty whether the unit is operating or not; operation of the unit imposes a second fuel penalty, estimated at 1 to 2 miles per gallon.
- ☐ Consider operating costs. How many miles per gallon can be expected from each model? According to the U.S. Department of Transportation, gasoline expense is the highest single cost of operating a compact and subcompact, as well as the standard-size car. Until gasoline shortages occurred, the price of fuel had changed very little for some twenty years. However, the price of fuel rose sharply in late 1973 and 1979.
- ☐ What are the terms and conditions of the warranty? Legislation, effective July 4, 1975, has made automobile warranties easier to compare.
- ☐ How about financing? Use as much care in finding the best, most advantageous source of credit as you use for selection of the vehicle. *Before you sign*, take the seller's proposed purchase and finance contract to several banks, a credit union and even to a finance company to determine the differences in the price of borrowing.

Compare all the figures on each proposal: the sale price; the down payment required; the amount of the loan; the finance charge (always stated as an annual percentage rate); the number of monthly payments; how, when and where payments must be made; and the total contract amount (the amount of the loan plus the total amount of the finance charge). For example, if you buy a car for $7,000 and make a down payment of $1,000, you'll pay interest on the balance of $6,000. The total finance charge, added to the original sale price, will be the amount actually paid for the car.

Answers to these questions should be individually determined *before the shopping process begins*. Customers who have made their basic decisions on what kind of car they need and the amount of money they intend to spend are much less likely to be "traded up" — that is, sold merchandise more elaborate and more expensive than they need — than those who shop without research.

ADVERTISING PRACTICES
Some of the promotional material issued by new and used car dealers simply adds to the confusion of car shopping. The Better Business Bureau system, with help from the automotive industry, has developed voluntary standards for such advertising. If new and used car dealers follow these guidelines — or if consumers choose to do business only with those who do — there should be less confusion in the automotive marketplace.

Claims such as "like new," "never undersold," "factory to you," and "at cost" should be disregarded. For example, the "never undersold" claim is meaningless because no dealer can ever really know that his prices are lower than anyone else's — especially when advertising is prepared several days in advance and other dealers' prices can change by the time the ad appears.

Other suspect claims are:

☐ **"Factory equipped" or "fully equipped."** These terms do not have a universal meaning and therefore can be misleading. Advertising should clearly state exactly what "standard" and what "optional" equipment is being offered.

☐ **"List price."** An advertised "manufacturer's list price" or a "suggested retail price" is meaningless unless the higher price is the actual selling price of other dealers in a given area. If most other dealers are selling at a lower price, there is no "saving" or "special discount."

☐ **"Wholesale" or "factory to you."** These terms are misleading because they imply the dealer is selling cars by way of a system that avoids the routine channel from manufacturer to dealer to you, the retail buyer. Merchandise is sold to consumers at retail, *not wholesale.* The dealer must make a profit, or else he will not be able to stay in business.

☐ **"At cost," "below cost" or "below invoice."** These terms should not be used because the dealer's cost is dependent upon many variables, such as rebates from manufacturers for car sales which are not necessarily known to the dealer at the time an ad is placed.

The advertising standards also list specific guidelines for descriptions of new and used vehicles. A "new" car is defined as one that has never been sold, titled or registered. Such terms as "factory fresh" may not be used in advertising unless the car is, in fact, new.

Legitimate dealers do not confuse the issue by using terms that raise more questions than they answer. They do not, for example, advertise used cars — no matter how and by whom they were used — as new. If the wording of an ad for a new or used car seems vague, the potential buyer would be well advised to ask the dealer or his salesperson to get down to specifics and define his terms. Make sure the word "new" has exactly the same meaning to everyone involved in the transaction.

"Demonstrators" have never had day-to-day use by a consumer, nor have they been sold, titled or registered. Nevertheless, they have been used by the dealer, salespeople and by prospective buyers to demonstrate performance of the car. They should be so identified in advertising.

"Executive" or "official" cars have also been used — by manufacturer's representatives or by an executive of an authorized dealership. Verbal assurances that such vehicles "have not been driven much" or

GETTING MORE FOR YOUR MONEY

"have had the best of care" notwithstanding, they *must* be sold as used cars.

Any car that has previously been used as a taxi-cab or as a fleet, rental, lease, driver training, police, demonstrator, executive or company official vehicle should be so identified in advertising and be sold as a used car. The same goes for any car that has been wrecked or flooded, regardless of whether it was new at the time of the accident.

Terms such as "nearly new" or "like new" may not be used in advertising of a used car. Nor may the word "commercial" — or other similar vague terms — be used to describe such a vehicle.

BUYING A NEW CAR

Before you shop, consult all available sources of information to compare the attributes of various makes and models of new cars. Data on fuel consumption, safety features, operating factors such as ease of pick-up, efficiency of the steering and braking systems, the array of optional equipment and comparative repair statistics are available from consumer research publications and automotive magazines. Compare printed material from manufacturers which detail the specifications of new cars.

Test driving several models gives you the "feel" of each vehicle. It tells you which of the cars, if any, fit your driving style, your size, your "reach."

Check these important items:

- ☐ Make your test drive long enough so that you get an accurate feel of the vehicle's steering and braking systems and its stability.
- ☐ The driver's seat should be easily adjustable.
- ☐ Controls should work smoothly and pedal positions should be comfortable. All controls should be within easy reach when safety belts are fastened and correctly adjusted.
- ☐ You should have a clear view of all instruments and should be able to see clearly out the windshield, through the rear window and through each side. Inside and outside rear-view mirrors should be both easily adjustable and stable when adjusted.
- ☐ Make sure that windshield wiper and headlight switches, heater and ventilation controls are operable and within easy reach.

Questioning friends on the good and bad aspects of their new cars and on the after-purchase service by local dealerships may be helpful. This is a way to learn about design and operations problems that surface only after the car has been used for a few weeks or months. For example, you may learn about design factors that make simple repairs more expensive than they should be. The design of one luxury-model automobile required that the bumper be removed to replace a turn-signal bulb; the labor cost involved amounted to many times the cost of the bulb.

Design/repair problems of a given model may also be known to or identifiable by mechanics. Discussing the cars you are considering with your own trusted mechanic would certainly be worthwhile.

Better Business Bureaus can supply reports on the consumer complaint records of local automobile dealers you're thinking of doing business with. Take the time to secure copies of these reports and be especially careful to request information on the dealers' performance of in-warranty service. Your new-car warranty will be only as good as the dealer responsible for backing it up.

When you shop, ask dealers to supply written price quotations. Get the price of each piece of optional equipment you think you want, as well as the price of the car *without options*.

Compare prices, but don't base your buying decision on price alone. The dealer who offers the lowest initial price may not offer the kind of after-purchase service you may need. Furthermore, the dealer and his salesmen are professionals who sell every day of their lives; they are well able to give consumers the impression that whatever "deal" they happen to offer is the buy of a lifetime.

The salesperson who quotes unrealistically low prices may be using a sales techniques called "low balling," well known in the trade and condemned by reputable dealers. The method consists of quoting a price so low that customers stop shopping. The salesperson may even fill out a purchase order at the low price — a meaningless exercise if the order is not then approved by the dealer or an authorized representative. If you are offered some extraordinarily low price, don't stop shopping until you are notified that the transaction has been approved. Contact the dealer and get written confirmation of approval. Otherwise the salesperson can claim that a "mistake" was made on the original quote, and the dealer can demand a much higher price when the car is delivered. The result: a waste of time and money.

A second common, and unfair, sales practice is "high balling" — offering an unrealistically high price for the trade-in. The trade-in offer must also be approved by the dealer, and it is subject to revision. The day you deliver your old car and pick up the new one is not the time to find out that the trade-in value has decreased. Again, you face a waste of time and money.

Even if unethical sales practices have been used, it may not be a simple matter to get out of the deal — especially if you have made a deposit on the new car. A deposit is generally considered to be binding upon both buyer and seller. In most states, it is not refundable without specific prior agreement or unless the dealer is willing to make the refund. The deposit is refundable, however, if the transaction is rejected by the dealer or by a dealer-obtained finance company.

If your new car is being ordered from the factory, the date of delivery supplied by the dealer is no more than an estimate, based upon information supplied by the manufacturer to the dealer. Promises are meaningless unless they are in writing and are made a part of the contract, and this includes promises in regard to delivery dates.

BUYING A USED CAR

Some people prefer to buy used cars because they wish to avoid the cost of depreciation. Others simply cannot afford to buy new cars. Whatever the reason for choosing a used vehicle, the way to find the best buy is to follow procedures that will minimize the risks involved.

- ☐ Shop for the seller.
- ☐ Shop for the car.
- ☐ Don't shop alone.
- ☐ Shop for the financing.

Sellers of used cars can and should be checked with your local Better Business Bureau or consumer protection agency. (Many consumer protection agencies do not provide written reports on complaint records because their major functions are restricted to implementation of local consumer protection legislation and the direct handling of complaints.) Sellers include new car dealers, used car dealers, and car rental and leasing companies.

An additional source is the classified advertising section of local newspapers, where private owners advertise individual sales. It is possible to find a good buy from this source, but remember that private sellers cannot perform repairs or issue guarantees or warranties. Make sure that service and maintenance records are readily available, especially if the seller is also the original owner of the car.

Check the car. Whatever the source of a used car, a sales talk is not a reliable basis for a buying decision. The sales talk, obviously, is part of the salesman's job. It might even be true. Nevertheless, it is important to gather first-hand knowledge of the car before the purchase is made. Follow this procedure for an "on lot" inspection:

- ☐ Inspect the outside of the car. Look carefully at the sides, over the hood and trunk lid. Check for ripples or uneven spots in the paint, for unmatched color, a "gritty" paint surface and for rust spots. Check the bumpers for looseness. Any of these may indicate collision or body damage.
- ☐ Examine the doors, windows and trunk lid for close fit and ease of operation. These are indications of a well-maintained car.
- ☐ Check the tires. Uneven wear on the front tires usually indicates bad alignment or front end wear. Bald spots on the tires are an indication that the wheels need balancing.
- ☐ Inspect the end of the tailpipe. Black, gummy soot indicates worn rings or bad valves (that is, an oil-burning engine) and the possibility of expensive repairs later on.
- ☐ Move the front seat back and forth to make sure it locks in place and can be adequately adjusted. Check the adjustment of seat belts and shoulder harness. Check the carpet for wear and look for signs of rust under the mats and carpet. Inspect the

AUTOMOBILES

upholstery for bumps, sags, loose springs and surface wear.
- ☐ Check the accelerator and brake pedal pads for signs of excessive wear. If excessively worn on a "low-mileage" car, suspect the odometer reading.
- ☐ Start the engine. If it is difficult to start, check further for the cause: this can indicate a bad battery and/or electrical system or poor engine compression.
- ☐ While the motor is running, have the person accompanying you look for smoke from the exhaust. (Checking out a used car is *not* a one person job!) Continuous blue smoke means bad valves or rings. Repair will be serious and expensive.
- ☐ Test the "feel" of the engine. If you detect clunking or rumbling noises when the accelerator is partially depressed or when you release pressure on the accelerator, the car may have bad rods or bad bearings — and will be real trouble for the new owner.
- ☐ If the car has an automatic transmission, listen for a whining sound. Get out of the car and look underneath for signs of fluid leaks — not only on the ground, but on the underside of the engine, transmission and rear axle.
- ☐ Steering should be tight. The wheel should not have more than two inches of play. Stiffness or a clunking sound when the wheel is turned may signal front end problems.
- ☐ Check the brakes. The pedal should be firm and not spongy. Insist on having a front and rear wheel removed for inspection of the brake linings. Inspect the master cylinder and the inside of the wheels for signs of fluid leakage.
- ☐ Test all electrical items — windshield wipers, *all* lights, turn signals, heater, radio, air conditioner, etc.

If the car passes this on-lot inspection, the road test comes next.
The road test is essential. A good dealer will not only raise no objection to your thorough test of his vehicles, he should insist on it. *Never* buy a car you have not tested on the road. Again, take a friend along. If the dealer or salesperson insists on accompanying you, make sure that you do the driving and relegate the dealer to the back seat.

Use this checklist for your road test:
- ☐ Start and stop the car several times, using different rates of acceleration and braking. The car should pick up speed without hesitation. The brakes should provide an even, straight stop without pulling to one side or grabbing.
- ☐ Have your passenger watch for smoke from the tailpipe when you slow down. Smoke can signal bad rings and the need for a costly repair.
- ☐ Check the front end by turning corners at various speeds. If there is too much sway or stiffness, there could be a problem.
- ☐ Drive over a rough road and listen for looseness, rattles and clunking sounds.

Once the on-lot and road tests are completed, if the car still seems to be a good buy, have it checked again — by a professional. Take it to a repair shop, to a mechanic you trust, or to a diagnostic center for an assessment of current or potential problems. There is no reason to expect free diagnostic service of this kind, so be prepared to pay for it. The investment is worthwhile; it may help to avoid a costly wrong decision.

MAINTENANCE AND REPAIR

Maintenance and repair are not the same thing at all. Maintenance is the *preventive* attention automobiles should receive; repair is *corrective* — fixing ailing vehicle systems and replacing broken or worn-out parts.

Theoretically, the greater the degree of effective maintenance a car receives, the less likely it is to need extensive, expensive repairs as it grows older. Drivers of older cars — especially those intent on following the U.S. Department of Transportation's advice on economical car ownership — should follow maintenance directions to the letter. Owners of new cars *must* follow maintenance directions listed in their owner's manuals if they wish to keep their warranties in effect.

The best source for information on preventive maintenance is the owner's manual supplied by the manufacturer. Read it carefully and keep it in the glove compartment for ready reference. (Replacement copies can usually be secured from local automobile dealers or by writing to the manufacturer.)

Maintenance procedures, to be performed at specified intervals, include: oil changes, air, oil and gas filter replacement, replacement of hoses and belts, tune-ups, checking and correction of brake system, power steering, transmission and battery fluid levels.

The importance of proper, regularly scheduled preventive maintenance cannot be overemphasized. Equally important, however, is finding a competent, reliable mechanic to turn to when something goes wrong.

To most automobile owners, the mass of metal under the hood of a standard-size, option-filled automobile looks like an accident. Increasingly complex interrelated vehicle systems have made many cars difficult to diagnose and repair, a factor which may contribute to the American consumers' interest in simpler compact and subcompact models.

Industry representatives point to the success of programs like the voluntary testing and certification scheme for mechanics launched by the National Institute for Automotive Service Excellence (NIASE). This organization uses tests developed and administered by the Educational Testing Service of Princeton, New Jersey, to certify the competence of professional mechanics. It also publishes a national directory of a large number of employers of certified mechanics (available for $1.95 from NIASE, 1825 K Street N.W., Washington, D.C. 20036).

The alert consumer can protect himself by using defensive buying practices. Follow these guidelines:

- If something seems to be wrong with your car, check your owner's manual for clues to the ailment. In addition to providing information on the regular maintenance schedule, the manual may also help you troubleshoot common problems.
- If the car is still under warranty, repair work must be performed by an authorized franchised dealership that sells your make of car. Exceptions to this rule usually require prior approval from a regional office of the manufacturer (locations are usually listed in the owner's manual).
- If your car is not under warranty, you are free to shop for service. The best time to do this is *before* you need it. Check the consumer complaint records of local repair shops with your local Better Business Bureau. Ask friends and neighbors to recommend reliable mechanics.
- It's best to talk to the mechanic who will work on your car when you drive in for service. Be specific. Take time to communicate. Report unusual sounds — pings, whistles, clunks, squeals, rattles and knocks. Do they occur when the engine is warm? When it is cold? Does the sound go away as the engine warms up? How long has it been going on? Have you noticed any unusual odors? Has the "feel" of the car changed? Is it slower to start? Hard to steer? Does it pull to the left or right when you brake? Does it stall? Under what conditions? Describe symptoms, but don't try to diagnose the cause for the shop. If you tell the shop to replace the starter, when all the car needs is a loose wire connected, you'll end up paying too much.
- If you can't talk directly to the mechanic, communicate as

completely as possible with the service person who writes the repair order. Then check the order carefully. Once you sign a repair order, it becomes an authorization by you to have the shop make the repairs or adjustments listed, regardless of cost, unless you specify otherwise. If you don't understand the notations on the repair order, insist on an explanation. Find out how much the repairs will cost. Any repair establishment should be willing to supply specific cost estimates when a mechanic has had a chance to inspect the car. To make doubly sure nothing is done without your permission, have the service manager write on the repair order: *Make no repairs or replacements without the owner's permission.* And be sure to leave your phone number.

☐ Don't be surprised if you are told you must pay for diagnosis of automotive problems. A good deal of time and labor is required to examine properly an engine or transmission to achieve an accurate diagnosis of internal problems. Just be sure to find out how much the procedure will cost beforehand. (The only time you will be aware of this cost after it is performed is when you decide not to have the repair made. Otherwise, it will normally be a part of the charge for labor and parts.)

☐ Be wary of advertised offers to repair transmissions or fix brakes for a flat fee. Complex repairs to these systems can vary widely in cost from car to car, depending on the time and parts necessary to correct the problem.

Some shops lure customers with low-priced offers in their ads, then dismantle whatever system is involved and advise the owner that, due to "unexpected" problems, the repair will cost much more than the advertised price. At best, the owner may have to pay the basic fee to have his car put back together; at worst, an unreasonably high bill is presented for a shoddy repair.

☐ Deal with repair establishments that warrant their repairs — *and get the warranty in writing.* Be careful to note who the warrantor is.

☐ Make sure your bill itemizes all work performed. If there is a problem later, you can establish the date of the original repair and its coverage under a guarantee.

Many good repair shops allow the owner to take a test drive before the repair bill is paid. Or perhaps they state on the bill that the car has been road-tested by a mechanic. The road-test procedure is particularly important after repair to the brakes, transmission or other mechanical systems. If you are not allowed to take a test drive, insist on getting a firm guarantee for the work. Again, if at all possible, get all of this ironed out *before* you leave your vehicle for repairs.

If the same problems that were supposedly remedied recur, take the car back to the garage immediately. Take your receipt. Insist on an explanation and correction. If the problem is not corrected, report the situation to the local Better Business Bureau.

EMERGENCIES AND OUT-OF-TOWN REPAIRS
First follow these simple safety precautions:

- ☐ Get your car off the road, out of the flow of traffic.
- ☐ Signal the problem: tie a handkerchief to the door handle or to the antenna and turn on the emergency flashers. If it's dark, set out flares, spaced several yards from the vehicle to warn oncoming vehicles.

Then:

- ☐ If the problem is engine failure or an apparent electrical failure, make a quick check of the obvious but most frequently overlooked causes — being out of gas, having a loose fan belt or loose wires, blowing a fuse. Check your owner's manual for probable causes.

Protect yourself
- ☐ Spend some time finding a good repair shop.
- ☐ Make sure your car is in good condition before you start a trip.
- ☐ Don't leave your car unattended in a repair establishment you don't know.
- ☐ If your car seems to be developing a problem — if you hear unusual sounds or sense a difference in performance — don't just hope the problem will go away. Have it checked out while the car is still running. Then, if you question the first diagnosis, you still have time to get a second opinion.
- ☐ If you feel you have been dealt with dishonestly, complain (see IF YOU ARE DISSATISFIED).

- ☐ Call a repair shop or garage. Try to find a full-service dealership that sells your brand of car. If you belong to an automobile club, ask the local office to recommend a repair establishment.
- ☐ If your car must be towed, don't necessarily accept help from the first truck that appears. A dealer or an automobile club may provide service that will cost you less and get your car where you want it.

Above all, don't be talked into having your car towed to a repair shop recommended by the tow truck operator *unless you know something about the shop*. Some unscrupulous truck operators monitor police radio calls, find disabled cars and make their money from kickbacks paid by repair shops.

- ☐ If the garage operator suggests that your car needs major repairs, try to postpone them until you get back home — to your own trusted mechanic. If repair on the road is unavoidable, at least try calling the nearest Better Business Bureau to check on the

garage's reputation before you authorize any work.
- [ ] Again, once the car is in the garage, find out *in advance* how long the repairs will take, and get an estimate of the cost. Get a written repair order and ask to be called when the problem has been analyzed so that you can get a firm estimate. Then ask to be notified when the repairs are complete.

Get a second opinion if you doubt a mechanic's diagnosis of "necessary" repairs or replacements. As long as the car is running, you can always take it down the street to another shop.

If you have been involved in an accident:
- [ ] Either call the police or make sure someone else does before you leave the scene.
- [ ] If possible, stay with your car — but not in it, and not close to passing traffic. Injuries often occur to drivers attempting to make repairs or sitting in disabled cars in traffic.

RENTAL AND LEASING — HAVING A CAR WITHOUT OWNING IT

The difference between renting a car and leasing one is a matter of time. Rental cars are generally available for a day, a week or perhaps a month. For periods of several months up to a year or more, the lease — a long-term contract — replaces the rental agreement.

Terms and conditions of both kinds of contracts vary. Comparison shopping is a necessary prerequisite to finding the best deal.

Automobile rental. When the rental business began, it was geared largely to the needs of increasingly mobile business travelers. Their acceptance of the fly-and-drive idea soon spread to other segments of the community. City dwellers, for example, often prefer to have a car only when they need one and thus avoid the expense of automobile ownership in urban areas, where parking and storage space are at a premium.

Rental firms also provide the convenience of choosing from a "wardrobe" of cars — a variety of sizes, makes and models. They also assume the responsibility for maintenance and repair.

Sources for rental cars include national firms with coast-to-coast networks and offices in all major cities and airports. Other firms may have a single location or may be a branch of another business, such as an automobile dealership or service station. Depending upon the size and facilities of the individual firm, customers may be able to rent a car in Maine and leave it in California (although usually at added expense). Most firms require the car to be returned to the original location or charge an additional fee for the privilege of leaving it in another city.

Each firm has its own range of services. Customers should shop for the services they need.

AUTOMOBILES

Rental rates can be a source of confusion. They are based on a series of variable factors, including:

type and size of car;	insurance coverage;
length of rental period;	city-to-city drop-off
whether gasoline is or	privileges;
is not included;	season of the year;
mileage charges;	time of week.

In general, lower rates are charged for smaller cars. Standard-size automobiles and special vehicles such as station wagons carry higher prices.

Rental companies either set their prices at x amount per day plus y amount per mile, *or* at a given price per day which includes z amount of "free" miles. Some companies offer both plans; others, only one or the other. It is important to compare not only the rates of different firms, but also to check out the rental plans offered by each company. To find out which type of rental is best for you, estimate the length of time the car will be needed and the number of miles it will travel; then add up the cost of both ways. To demonstrate the comparative options and costs:

Company X offers a rate of $20.00 a day and 15 cents a mile.
Company Y offers a rate of $27.00 per day, with the first 100 miles "free" and a charge of 7 cents per mile for each additional mile.

A comparison of the two plans for a 300-mile trip gives these results:

Company X	**Company Y**
$20.00	$27.00 (100 miles included)
+45.00 (300 miles @ 15 cents)	+14.00 (200 miles @ 7 cents)
$65.00	$41.00

Company Y would clearly be the more economical choice — despite the fact that, under most unlimited mileage plans, the customer pays for the gasoline.

Weekly rentals usually offer a reduction in per-day cost, which may be roughly equivalent to paying for five days and having the use of the car for seven days. Monthly rates may provide additional savings.

It is always worthwhile to compare the costs of short-term rental plans as well. Consider:

Under plan A, the rental company offers a car for three days at a cost of $136.00, which includes unlimited mileage. The customer pays for the gasoline.

Plan B calls for rental at $26.00 a day and 20 cents per mile.

For a trip of three days and 500 miles, the following costs would be incurred:

GETTING MORE FOR YOUR MONEY

Plan A	Plan B
$136.00 (plus gasoline)	$ 78.00 ($26.00 per day for 3 days)
	100.00 (500 miles @ 20 cents/mile)
$136.00	$178.00

Plan A would be the better buy, depending on the cost of gasoline, of course. The most economical car to rent would be the smallest model available.

An important consideration in any cost comparison is to make sure similar types of car, comparable insurance coverage, drop-off privileges, etc., are being compared. Be cautious. Check out any company whose advertised rental rates seem unrealistically low. Rates for a so-called "12-hour day" certainly cannot be compared with a full 24-hour day, nor is it reasonable to compare the rate for a small compact with the rate for a standard-size car.

The wide range of options and rental plans is confusing — as confusing as the wide range of models, options and payment plans available in automobile sales. The potential confusion in each field can be used by unscrupulous operators to cloud the issues so that the customer doesn't know how much he's paying for what services. The consumer's first line of defense is a clear understanding of the issues and a clear understanding of any contract he signs.

Don't "assume" anything. Ask questions and insist on answers. If any rental agency representative can't or won't provide straight answers to straight questions, use the consumer's second defense — leave. Find another rental firm whose representatives will help you find the car you want to rent at the price you are willing to pay.

Remember: Reputable companies encourage their employees to help customers understand the terms and conditions of the contracts they sign.

Ask the representative to work out estimated costs for your particular trip under alternative rental plans. Again, reputable companies instruct their employees to provide this assistance.

Insurance. Most car rental companies include insurance as part of their service without additional charge. Standard liability, comprehensive and collision coverage — which most motorists buy from their own insurance companies — is a standard part of the rental agreement.

Liability coverage for the renter and other authorized drivers should be $100,000 to $300,000 for bodily injury liability; $25,000 for property damage, full fire and theft protection; and $100 to $150 deductible on collision damage to the rental vehicle. Some insurance provides for a $200 deductible on collision damage — so be sure to check the policy for this as well as all coverage limits.

For a small added charge, the firm will waive the deductible if full collision protection is desired. If you decide against purchasing this "extra" insurance, inspect the vehicle carefully for dents and scratches and have them noted on the contract *before* you leave the rental agency.

Also, take the time to see that the spare tire and emergency tools are in the trunk of your rental car.

Unless you take these precautions, you may be accused by a less-than-scrupulous rental firm of damaging the vehicle or of losing equipment that was never in the car. If they happen to have your cash deposit, you may never get it back if they have a claim of alleged damages against you.

Insurance usually covers the renter who signs the contract as well as other licensed drivers, including business associates and/or family members, who share the trip. Read the agreement carefully, however, to see if there are exceptions to this.

It is important to make sure insurance coverage is clearly understood — especially when dealing with a firm whose advertised rental rates are considerably lower than others.

Check the following:

- What is the stated dollar amount of coverage?
- Is the coverage the same as that afforded by your standard policy?
- If the coverage is inadequate, how much must you pay to get the insurance you need?
- Does the insurance cover other licensed drivers in addition to the person who signs the rental agreement?
- What "escape clauses" have been included that may invalidate the insurance if, for example, the car is returned late, parked unlocked, etc?

Never rent from a firm whose representative can't or won't supply complete insurance information.

LEASING

Automobile leasing is analogous to renting a house or apartment, as opposed to investing time and money in home ownership.

Total expenses in each case — for transportation and housing — are likely to be about the same. However, and this depends upon the terms of the lease, the lessor (the leasing company, the owner of the property) retains the responsibility for routine maintenance and repair of his property and for the payment of taxes and insurance.

The lessee (you) has no capital investment in the property and, when the lease expires, has no further claim upon it unless the lease is extended or the lease provides an option to buy.

Unless the particular lease so specifies, the lessor has no further claim upon the lessee — and it is in this area that problems can arise for people who choose to enter into long-term rental agreements without reading their contracts carefully.

It is vital that consumers understand all the terms of the lease. There are two kinds of automobile leases — "closed-end" and "open-end" — and there is an important difference between them.

☐ The "closed-end" lease contains a clear statement of the number of months (usually 12, 24 or 36) that the contract is to run. When the lease expires and the lessee has made the required number of payments, the car is returned to the lessor and the contract is terminated. The lessee has no further obligation.

☐ The "open-end" (or "finance") lease will usually have lower monthly payments, but the lessee may be required to make a hefty final payment when his lease expires to compensate the lessor for any loss sustained when the car is sold on the used car market.

A depreciation charge is included in all leasing agreements. It is based on the lessor's best estimate or prediction of the car's value at the end of the lease. This, in turn, is based upon the estimated use, estimated mileage, the type of vehicle involved, and two other important variables: the lessor's experience in predicting depreciation; and the state of the used-car market at the time the lease expires. The "depreciation reserve" included in each monthly payment may or may not cover the total depreciation of the vehicle. If, at the end of the lease period, the vehicle sells for more than the difference between the "net capitalized cost" and the "accumulated depreciation reserve," the lessee receives the difference — or an agreed-upon portion of the difference. If the car sells for less, the lessee must pay the difference to the leasing company.

The monthly charges are lower because the customer has elected to assume the risk for the unpredictable market value of the vehicle when the lease expires.

One automobile leasing firm suggests that consumers considering the leasing alternative move slowly, that leasing "should never be considered as a cure-all for your automobile problems":

Keep one thing in mind. Automobile leasing companies are not non-profit organizations. Leasing automobiles is a growing and profitable area of business which, in some major metropolitan areas, accounts for as much as 25 percent of the new car sales. What you see or hear may lead you to think you are getting a bargain, but remember that the company from which you are leasing your car has to — and will — make a profit.*

The major motivations toward leasing, according to this firm, are convenience, freedom from paperwork, and a fixed, budgetable cost for transportation. The customer gets what he pays for — the greater the degree of services provided by the lessor, the more the monthly payments will be. Again, the terms and conditions of each lease should be clearly understood by each party to the agreement.

Better Business Bureaus suggest that any leasing, rental, or pur-

---

*"The Truth about Automobile Leasing: A Guide for the Consumer," CCEC/McCULLAGH, 300 St. Paul Place, Baltimore, Maryland 21202.

chase agreement involving a major expenditure for any merchandise or service should not be signed until all the bids are in. Several vendors or lessors should be consulted and their offers compared. And certainly, all questions should be answered. CCEC/McCULLAGH suggests that potential customers put the following questions to their leasing companies:

Payments
- ☐ When do payments begin? At the time the contract is signed, the day the car is delivered, or on the next monthly billing date?
- ☐ How often will I be billed, and how soon must payment be made?
- ☐ What happens if a payment is late?
- ☐ When do payments stop — on the day the car is turned in, thirty days later, or when the car is sold?

While the car is in use
- ☐ What maintenance provisions are made by the leasing company?
- ☐ What will the leasing company do if the car breaks down during the warranty period? If the car is wrecked? If the car is disabled for any period of time?
- ☐ Will a temporary replacement be provided? Under what circumstances? For what period of time?
- ☐ Are there limitations and restrictions on the use of the car, such as other drivers, minors, trailer hitches, driving in Canada or Mexico?
- ☐ What are the mileage restrictions? How much will it cost if the mileage limit is exceeded?
- ☐ How much insurance is carried on the car, and who has the responsibility for insuring it?
- ☐ How are licensing and insurance renewals handled?

When the car is turned in
- ☐ What are the penalties if the car is turned in before the lease expires?
- ☐ What charges can I expect after the car has been turned in? On what basis will extra charges be made?
- ☐ What happens if I want to buy the car at the end of the lease? How much will I pay?
- ☐ Can the lease be extended or renewed? How will the monthly charges for such extension or renewal be determined?

The lease analysis forms on pp. 66-67 can be used to compare costs between leasing firms. They can also serve as outlines of information that potential leasing customers should have before any agreement is signed.

INSURANCE
Two important developments have occurred in the insurance field in recent years:

☐ Many states now have no-fault insurance legislation, which simplifies the claims process.
☐ Some insurance companies have produced (and are advertising) policies translated from legalese which the average layman can understand.

Insurance coverage is required for all car owners and drivers in many states, and financial responsibility laws in all states and the District of Columbia directly affect all motorists.

There are five basic kinds of automobile insurance:

Liability, the most important coverage, covers personal injury and property damage to others for which you (or another person driving your car) are held responsible. Liability insurance is usually purchased in a three-part series. A policy referred to as 10/20/5 (the minimum amount required by financial-responsibility laws in many states) means the insurer's liability is limited to $10,000 for injury to one person; $20,000 maximum for two or more persons in one accident, and $5,000 for property damage. This minimum coverage could be inadequate if your car seriously injures another person. Judgments of several hundred thousand dollars are not uncommon in personal injury cases.

Collision insurance covers damage to your own car, and these policies routinely contain "deductibles" available at $50, $100 or $250 levels. The higher the deductible — the amount you pay for damages to your own car before the insurance company picks up the rest of the bill — the lower the premium you pay. You may want to drop collision insurance after your car is several years old, if you want to assume the risk and write off casualty losses over $100 on your income tax if your car is subsequently damaged in an accident.

Comprehensive coverage protects against fire, theft, vandalism, riots and "natural cause" accidents resulting from hail, floods, hurricanes, etc. As in collision coverage, the higher the deductible, the lower the premium.

Medical payment insurance covers medical and hospital costs incurred by you or your passengers as the result of an automobile accident. Your need for this depends upon the kind and amount of medical and hospitalization insurance carried by you and your family.

Uninsured motorists insurance covers injuries or damages to you caused by another driver whose insurance is inadequate or nonexistent, or by a hit-and-run driver.

Premiums and coverage vary widely from company to company. Comparison shopping is important. Consumers are well advised to decide in advance how much of what kinds of coverage is needed and to contact representatives of several companies in order to compare costs.

The amount of the premium you will pay is based on a number of factors, including:

AUTOMOBILES

☐ the make, model, special equipment and the age of your car;
☐ how you use the car — pleasure, business, etc.;
☐ where you live;
☐ your driving record (and that of all other drivers);
☐ estimated annual mileage;
☐ your age and marital status;
☐ how many cars you insure with the same company.

Not all companies apply the same values to each of these variables. This is another reason to get bids from several firms.

The best way to keep your insurance rate down is to maintain a good driving record. Some companies offer discounts to accident-free drivers; some will cancel your policy after two or three costly accidents. In states where insurance is mandatory, high-risk drivers are insured under separate insurance plans called "assigned-risk pools." Since the risks are greater for the insurance company, these insurance rates are correspondingly higher.

Look for discounts. Special arrangements and lower premiums are sometimes granted to drivers of compact cars, and families with two (or more) cars may find coverage purchased for all the cars in the family is cheaper than insuring each one separately. Some firms offer a discount for "limited teenage use." Insurance rates rise dramatically for a young male under 25, but you may cut this increase if you demonstrate that his use of the car is infrequent. Driver-training discounts are another way to cut the cost of teenage driver insurance. The discount is available to graduates of an approved driver training program.

GETTING MORE FOR YOUR MONEY

Automobile Lease Analysis—Closed-End Lease
For Use In Comparing Lease Proposals

	Lessor No. 1		Lessor No. 2	
Type Of Vehicle And Optional Equipment Note: Make, Model and Equipment must be identical for an accurate comparison.				
	Per Month	Per Annum	Per Month	Per Annum
Lease Payments including administrative and service charges and applicable taxes				
1 – 12 Months	$	$	$	$
13 – 24 Months	$	$	$	$
25 – 36 Months	$	$	$	$
Total Lease Payments for ___ Months of the Lease	$	$	$	$
Breakdown Of Administrative And Service Charges				
Freight and Delivery	$		$	
Applicable Taxes	$		$	
License and Registration	$		$	
Insurance	$		$	
Maintenance	$		$	
Excess Mileage	$		$	
Approximate Reconditioning Charges At Termination	$		$	
Total Cost Of The Lease				
Mileage Limitation	_____ miles		_____ miles	
Per Mile Cost For Excess Mileage	_____ ¢ per mile		_____ ¢ per mile	
Insurance Coverage				
Bodily Injury (B.I.)	$		$	
Property Damage (P.D.)	$		$	
Comprehensive Deductible	$		$	
Fire and Theft	$		$	
Collision Deductible	$		$	
Maintenance Coverage				
Number of Replacement Tires				
Number of Lubrication and Oil Changes				
Other Services Provided				

AUTOMOBILES

Automobile Lease Analysis—Open-End Lease For Use in Comparing Lease Proposals				
	Lessor No. 1		Lessor No. 2	
Type Of Vehicle And Optional Equipment Note: Make, Model and Equipment must be identical for an accurate comparison.				
Cost of vehicle including optional equipment	$		$	
Freight and delivery charges.	$		$	
Dealer and lessor markup including preparation charges	$		$	
Total Capitalized Cost	$		$	
Lease Payments including administrative and service charges and applicable taxes	Per Month	Per Annum	Per Month	Per Annum
1–12 Months	$	$	$	$
13–24 Months	$	-$	$	$
25–36 Months	$	$	$	$
Depreciation reserve @ ___ % per month	$	$	$	$
Total Lease Payment	$	$	$	$
Total Payments During Period Of Lease	$		$	
	Total Depreciation Reserve for a ___ month lease will be $ ___ Estimated undepreciated balance on vehicle at: 12 Months . . . . . $ ___ 24 Months . . . . . $ ___ 36 Months . . . . . $ ___		Total Depreciation Reserve for a ___ month lease will be $ ___ Estimated undepreciated balance on vehicle at: 12 Months . . . . . $ ___ 24 Months . . . . . $ ___ 36 Months . . . . . $ ___	
Lease Termination Charges For: _____	$		$	
Total Cost of an Open-End Lease Will Depend on Resale Value of the Vehicle at the Expiration of the Lease.				
A. If Resale Value Exceeds Undepreciated Balance on Vehicle . . . Total Lease Payments +$ _____ Difference Between Resale Value And Undepreciated Balance −$ _____ Termination Charges +$ _____ Total Cost Of Lease $ _____		B. If Undepreciated Balance on Vehicle Exceeds Resale Value . . . Total Lease Payments +$ _____ Difference Between Resale Value And Undepreciated Balance +$ _____ Termination Charges +$ _____ Total Cost of Lease $ _____		

SOURCE: "The Truth about Automobile Leasing: A Guide for the Consumer." Form 2270 CCEC/McCULLAGH, 300 St. Paul Place, Baltimore, Maryland, 21202.

67

Banks and Savings Institutions

JUST AS YOU SHOP AROUND to get the best buy, it's important to compare different banking and saving institution services in order to get the most for your banking dollar. Like other businesses, financial institutions must earn money for their stockholders, investors, owners and depositors. Their services are not always free, and their charges vary. Wise consumers can use comparative shopping methods in deciding how to choose among the various financial services available.

There are several kinds of financial institutions:

Commercial banks (or full-service banks) are private corporations owned by their stockholders. Those organized under federal law are "national" banks, and those organized under state law are "state" banks. Most commercial banks are insured by the Federal Deposit Insurance Corporation (FDIC). Services provided include: checking accounts, savings accounts, consumer loans (automobile, home improvement and education) and mortgages on residential property.

Savings and loan associations (building and loan associations), like commercial banks are organized under state laws while others, known as federal savings and loan associations, operate under federal law. In general, savings and loan associations pay higher interest rates on deposits than commercial banks although that gap is narrowing. Federally chartered and most state-chartered associations are insured by the Federal Savings and Loan Insurance Corporation (FSLIC). Among the services offered are savings accounts, time deposits, passbook loans and consumer loans.

Mutual savings banks are technically owned by their depositors who have no management rights or responsibilities. The board of trustees directs the bank's operations and must act in the interest and to the benefit of the depositors. Mutual savings banks are chartered in only 17 states where they are supervised by state banking authorities. Deposits are insured by FDIC or by state deposit insurance funds. During the past few years, mutual savings banks have won the right to offer many services previously reserved to full service banks. In addition to the traditional savings accounts, you can get individual or joint checking accounts and home loans. The checking accounts will involve little or no service charge.

Credit unions are cooperative associations for people who have a common place of employment, or who belong to a professional association, etc. Credit unions are governed by members, and basically make low-cost loans to members as well as accept savings from members. The member is a shareholder, not a depositor. Credit unions are insured by the National Credit Union Administration (NCUA), or by state or private insurance programs. Services offered include savings accounts, loans, financial counseling, check cashing and group discount buying.

A sampling of banking services

Automatic line of credit. Depending on your credit rating, you can get a specified maximum amount of credit through your regular checking account or through a special checking service. This means you can write a check for more than your balance if you want to take advantage of a special sale on a major purchase, for example. Keep in mind, however, that an automatic line of credit can be a temptation to overspend.

Automatic bill paying. If you authorize them to do so, many banks will pay your bills, automatically deduct your insurance premiums, monthly car payments and other types of regular payments from your checking account.

Automatic savings. Your bank can transfer money from your checking account to your savings account at your request at specified times. The bank can also invest this money every month or quarter in U.S. savings bonds or mutual funds if you want.

Electronic funds transfer. Already operating in some parts of the country, this new system will allow you to make most financial transactions using a coded plastic card. This means you can pay for groceries, for example, by presenting the card and having money transferred electronically from your account to the store's. There are both advantages and disadvantages to this system which are currently being worked out.

Before deciding on a particular bank or savings institution, check the following:

☐ Is there a minimum required balance on regular checking accounts?
☐ What about a service charge for checks?
☐ Are there extra charges on other bank services such as safe deposit boxes?
☐ What about the availability of installment loans? At what interest rate?
☐ What about the availability and terms of mortgages?

- [ ] What types of savings plans are offered?
- [ ] What is the rate of interest on savings and how often is it compounded and credited?
- [ ] Are there any restrictions on withdrawing your money?
- [ ] Are your deposits federally or state insured?

CHECKING ACCOUNTS

Regular checking accounts usually require that you keep a certain amount of cash in the account. As long as you keep the minimum, you can write checks and make as many deposits as you want without paying a monthly service charge. Other banks require a monthly service charge and no minimum balance. Find out in advance which service is the most convenient for you. If you write a large number of checks each month, the regular account may be the most economical.

Special checking accounts don't require you to keep a minimum balance. But you usually have to pay a flat monthly service fee plus another 10 to 15 cents for each check you write. This type of account may be the best bet if you write only a few checks each month.

Negotiable Order of Withdrawal (NOW) accounts are checking accounts that earn interest or, to look at it another way, savings accounts on which an individual can write checks. Before opening a NOW account, be sure to comparison shop among financial institutions. Wise consumers should ask:

- [ ] What, if any, is the minimum balance requirement to earn interest?
- [ ] Is there a service charge each month; does it vary with the number of checks written or the minimum balance maintained?
- [ ] How many checks may be written without a service charge?
- [ ] If the account falls below a prescribed minimum balance, does the account stop earning interest?

SAVINGS ACCOUNTS

There are several different types of savings accounts. These range from an **individual account** opened by only one person with a small deposit to an **organization account** opened by someone in charge of an organization's funds. A **joint account** can be opened by two people, usually husband and wife, either of whom may deposit or withdraw funds. Also available are **school savings accounts** for your children and **voluntary trust accounts** in which you open an account for your child or another person.

Forms of savings accounts vary from one financial institution to another. Be sure to figure your needs, using the following as a guide.

Passbook savings accounts: You can deposit or withdraw any amount of money at any time. However, the interest you earn is the lowest compared to other major types of accounts. Interest is usually compounded annually, semiannually or quarterly. These accounts are federally insured or state insured, and funds can be used as collateral for personal loans. The balance of your savings is kept in a passbook where transactions are noted each time you make a deposit or withdrawal or when interest is credited.

Beyond passbooks, the prudent saver may want to consider:

All-Savers certificates: These are one-year savings certificates authorized under a law passed in 1981 by Congress as part of President Reagan's tax package. They bear an interest rate of 70 percent of the one-year Treasury Bill rate which is determined monthly. The certificates are available in varying denominations until the end of December 1982. For those filing individual income tax returns, the first $1,000 of interest is exempt from federal taxes; the first $2,000 of interest is exempt for those who file joint returns. Penalties for early withdrawal include loss of interest and tax exempt status.

Certificates of deposit: Depositing a specified amount over a certain time period in a bank, S&L or credit union earns more interest than a passbook. If the money is withdrawn before the time period is up, however, a severe penalty is imposed by federal law.

U.S. savings bonds: These are conservative time deposits commonly known as Series EE (matures in 5 years) and Series HH (matures in 10 years). The interest is exempt from state and local income taxes and the federal taxes may be deferred until the bonds are cashed in.

U.S. savings bonds: These are conservative time deposits commonly known as Series EE (matures in 9 years) and Series HH (matures in 10 years). The interest is exempt from state and local income taxes and the federal taxes may be deferred until the bonds are cashed in.

Money-market certificates: The investor can get a return comparable to T-bills with these time deposits at banks, S&Ls and credit unions. There is a minimum investment of $10,000 for 6 months, and the earnings are fully taxable.

Common stocks: These are investments that make the stockholder a part owner in a corporation. They are not insured, though the risk of loss with "blue-chip" major corporations is low. The more speculative stocks may bring higher risk but often offer potential for greater gain.

Mutual funds: An investment company which pools investors' funds and invests in stocks and bonds. The buying and selling decisions are made by professional managers who generally diversify the portfolio to minimize loss. Different funds are tailored to different goals; some seek high yield, others are more speculative with the goal of sacrificing present earning for possible greater gains.

Basement Waterproofing

BASEMENT WATERPROOFING measures are most economically and effectively accomplished when homes are under construction. Post construction waterproofing can be time-consuming, messy, expensive — *and* absolutely necessary.

There is no single quick-and-easy method to dry damp basements. The problem, if it is caused by mild seepage or condensation, can be simple to correct; but more extensive procedures are required for leaking walls or floors and for severe seepage problems.

Seeping and condensation both result in damp floors and walls, and they can occur simultaneously. To distinguish one from the other, tape a twelve-inch square of aluminum foil to the wall, taping all four sides to make the seal as airtight as possible. Check it in a day or two. If the side that was against the wall is wet, the problem is seepage; if the outside is wet, it's condensation.

To reduce condensation, you will need to insulate the water pipes and maintain a constant temperature in the basement — heat it in winter and keep the windows closed in summer. If these measures don't work you may have to invest in a dehumidifier.

If there is a mild seepage problem, a good waterproofing paint can stop it. Application of the paint can be a difficult, time-consuming job, so be sure to check with your paint dealer for pointers. You may want to delegate the job to a contractor. Severe seepage requires extensive correction, similar to the measures used to stop leakage.

Leakage may be caused by poor drainage, a high water table — or both. Bad drainage can be remedied by regrading the lawn so that the land slopes away from the house and by adding long splash blocks below the downspouts or underground piping to carry rain water away from the foundation walls.

To divert water leaking through the floor, you may need to install a sump (a receiving tank or well to collect water below the floor), a drain system and an electric pump.

To combat leakage (or severe seepage) through the walls, the outside of the basement walls must be excavated and coated with a membrane coating or a plastic film. Inside barriers such as waterproofing paints will not be adequate where there is enough water pressure to result in measurable amounts of water entering the basement.

BASEMENT WATERPROOFING

If the leakage or seepage is localized, you may be able to solve the problem by coating only a portion of the wall.

Beware of ads promising quick and easy solutions to this complex problem. The "clay injection" method of waterproofing, widely advertised over the last few years, has resulted in a substantial number of complaints to local Better Business Bureaus. The method involves pressure-pumping a substance called sodium bentonite into the land surrounding basement walls. The material is said to spread and seal the walls. However, many factors, such as soil characteristics, undetected rocks, the height of the water table and poor workmanship can prevent this method from working.

Find a reputable contractor.
- Start with recommendations from friends who have dealt with the same problem.
- Get two or three diagnoses and estimates.
- Check each contractor's complaint records with your local Better Business Bureau.
- Ask for the names of previous customers whom you may contact as references.
- Always deal with an established firm in the community — one likely to still be in business should problems arise at a later date. Remember that the home improvement contract should contain a guarantee that the work done will solve the problem, but the guarantee is only as good as the firm behind it.

Bicycles

(See also WARRANTIES)

BICYCLES PROVIDE ECONOMICAL transportation and excellent exercise for people of all ages.

They are available in a wide range of stores — discount houses, department stores, sporting goods shops, bicycle specialty shops and select hardware stores — for a wide variety of prices, from well under a hundred to several hundred dollars.

Whether you are in the market for a child's first two-wheeler or a complex ten-speed model for yourself or your teenager, the same basic buying rules apply. Follow these guidelines:

☐ Buy a bike that "fits." The frame size (measured from the pedal crank axis to the top of the seat tube) should be nine or ten inches less than the rider's inseam.

For a man's frame style (preferred by many women as well, because of the extra strength of the construction), the rider should be able to straddle the crossbar, both feet flat on the floor, with an inch of clearance between crossbar and crotch.

☐ Make sure the saddle height is right. The rider should be able to sit comfortably in riding position, one knee slightly flexed, when the pedal is at its lowest point.

Never buy a bike too big for a child on the theory that the right size would soon be outgrown.

It is a better idea to choose an easy-to-handle, properly sized model which can be sold or traded in for a larger size when the time comes.

An oversized bike can be a real safety hazard. Children whose arms are not long enough to make a full turn with the handlebars and whose feet won't touch the ground unless the bike is tilted at a 45-degree angle cannot have proper control of steering and braking mechanisms which would keep them safe in traffic.

Consider — and try out — several products in the two basic bike models:

- ☐ **Touring bikes** have upright handlebars and wide saddles. They weigh 35 to 40 pounds; most have three speeds.
- ☐ **Lightweights or racers** have dropped handlebars, narrow saddles and no fenders. The rider leans forward, a position that lowers wind resistance and makes pedaling more efficient. Body weight does not rest on the saddle, but is distributed more evenly, with arms and back muscles sharing the exercise. The bike weighs less than 30 pounds, and has anywhere from 5 to 15 speeds.

Some stores also carry different types of children's bikes, "high risers" which resemble motorcycles, folding bikes, tandem bikes, and unicycles.

The style to choose is the one most comfortable for you. Try renting various kinds of bikes for a day's try-out before you make a final decision on buying your own. You should also experiment with braking systems and gears. Only you can decide whether you are more comfortable with coaster or caliper brakes, for example, or a combination of the two.

- ☐ **Caliper brakes** are operated by a hand lever located on each handlebar. They provide smooth, straight stops, but they tend to slip in wet weather.
- ☐ **Coaster brakes,** activated by pressing backward on the pedals, are equally efficient in wet and dry weather.

Most racing bikes and many touring bikes come equipped with caliper brakes, but all-weather riders — students, commuters and serious hobbyists — may want to consider combining both systems for greatest efficiency and safety.

A second important reason to try before you buy is to decide on *the gear system* you can use most efficiently.

Choose among the once-standard single-speed models and the three-, five- and ten-speed styles. The *derailleur* gear system, usually found on five- and ten-speed models, changes the pedal-to-rear-wheel speed ratio by moving the chain from sprocket to sprocket as the rider shifts gears. Smooth operation of the gear system requires some practice and experimentation, but it makes cross-country and commuter riding easier.

Construction is also important. The more rigid the frame, the more efficient and responsive the bike will be. For this reason, the men's frame style with additional bracing provided by the crossbars is often easier to ride than the traditional women's style.

Check for proper alignment by walking the bike in the store, holding it upright by the saddle. Reject any bike that has a tendency to pull to one side.

ACCESSORIES

Choosing what accessories you will need is an essential part of the bicycle-buying experience. Any well-stocked bicycle shop or sporting goods store will carry a large range of accessories to enhance the practicality, efficiency, safety and/or appearance of your new "machine." First-time buyers should be aware that the quoted price of most standard models may not include such essential extras as a basic tool kit, front and back headlights and reflectors for night riding (required by law in many places), padlock and chain, a bell or air horn, saddlebag or panniers, and other such items that are crucial to insure even a minimum of convenience, safety and security. Before you decide that a given model is in your price range, be sure to take into account these essential extras, as well as any other items you think necessary (special rain gear, clips to fasten your feet to the pedals, carrier rack, etc.).

> Some retailers sell bikes unassembled, in boxes, and the buyer must accept the challenge of assembling the equipment or pay extra to have it done. Unless there is an experienced do-it-yourselfer in the family, it is probably a good idea to leave this chore to a professional.

DEALERS

Choose your dealer as carefully as you choose your bike. Unless there is a resident mechanical genius in your family or among your close friends, repair and maintenance should be performed by a professional. You will want to find a dealer who is competent to provide service.

Always check the reputation of a dealer — *whatever you're buying* — with friends, neighbors and with the local Better Business Bureau. Find out how dealers handle complaints in regard to both products and service. Check performance under the terms of the product warranty. And, by all means, check the warranty itself (see WARRANTIES). Never accept an oral promise of future maintenance and repair. Get the warranty in writing and take time to read it carefully. Make its coverage part of your buying decision.

Most communities have regulations about registering bikes. Some have inspection requirements as well. In any case, be sure your bike has a loud bell and dusk/night road visibility. Have a properly certified headlight with a 500-foot beam, a rear reflector with a 600-foot reflection, plus either spoke or pedal side reflectors. Also check your homeowner's insurance policy to see if it covers a bicycle. If it doesn't, it's a good idea to get a special policy; the cost usually runs about $10 a year for a $125.00 bicycle.

Calculators

(See also WARRANTIES)

SMALL ("pocket") electronic calculators are available in a larger range of models, with prices ranging from about ten dollars to hundreds of dollars. The greater the degree of sophistication — that is, the greater the number of mathematical functions the instrument can perform — the higher the price will be.

A simple machine capable of performing the four basic arithmetical functions (addition, subtraction, multiplication and division) and providing answers of up to eight digits should suffice for day-to-day use in business and by consumers interested in a fast, accurate method of balancing their checkbooks, keeping track of the grocery bill while shopping and computing taxes. More elaborate calculators, complete with memory unit and the capacity to perform trigonometric and logarithmic functions, are useful to advanced math students or to the engineer in the family.

Features to look for include:

☐ A "clear" key (usually marked CE) — the eraser — which removes the last entry without eliminating previous entries.
☐ A "constant" key (marked K), which allows multiplication or division of a series of numbers by the same number (constant) without requiring reentry of the constant for each operation.
☐ A "floating decimal," which places the decimal point at the correct place in the answer. "Fixed" decimal calculators round off results in division and multiplication at two decimal places; "floating decimal" capacity provides the ability to carry out the number of decimal places a computation should have within the eight-digit capacity of the calculator. Some calculators provide both floating and fixed decimal, allowing the user to "round off" or "carry out" the result at two or more decimal places.
☐ A "memory" key, which enables the calculator to store a past calculation and then bring it out again when needed.
☐ A "percentage" key, which simplifies figuring percentages — a useful feature for computing taxes, discounts, interest, etc.
☐ "Chain calculation" capability, which is usually a standard operation for most calculators. This means it is possible to run through a continuous series of operations (20 ÷ 3 × 6 + 12 — 8, etc.) without having to reach a total and clear the calculator after every step.

77

GETTING MORE FOR YOUR MONEY

☐ **"Underflow,"** which, on most calculators, is the ability to drop the last and least significant digits to the right when the answer has more features than the capacity of the display window.
☐ **"Zero suppression,"** the capacity to display only the digits required for the answer without including unnecessary zeros.

Before you buy any calculator, insist on a demonstration from a well-informed salesperson who can advise you on the use and functions of these instruments. If no such person is available, make sure to read the manufacturer's instructions carefully and insist on using the instrument yourself before you buy it.

Things to check before buying a calculator:

☐ **Ease of handling:** The keyboard should be convenient for your use; the keys should not be too small or too close together. Given the range of calculators on the market, there is no reason to settle for an instrument that fails to meet the individual's needs.
☐ **Ease of reading:** Answers should be flashed on a display window that is large enough and bright enough to read easily.
☐ **Display window capacity:** For most household arithmetical computations, an eight-digit display window is adequate. (Some models do come equipped with ten- or twelve-digit display windows, should your work require it.)
☐ **The power supply:** Does the calculator use batteries that must be replaced, or does it use a longer-life (but more expensive) rechargeable battery? Or does it come with a DC adaptor (still more expensive), which allows you to plug it into the household current through a regular wall socket?
☐ **Warranty and repair:** Despite the fact that calculators have no moving parts except the keyboard (the "brain" is a single silicon chip containing all necessary circuitry), the instruments can and do break down. Insist on seeing the warranty before you buy (see WARRANTIES). Defective calculators must be returned to the factory for repair, so find out who pays the postage and who is responsible — customer or retailer — for the return.

Some manufacturers and retailers provide a full one-year warranty. Others warrant their products for 90 days. Find out the length of the warranty and whether replacement and/or refund is allowed.

☐ **Cost of operation:** Many "pocket" calculators operate on disposable batteries, which are short-lived and more expensive to use than the models that operate on standard household current and/or on a rechargeable battery.

Camps

CAMPS — day camps or residential (sleep-away) camps — should be relaxed, casual, fun . . . and, most of all, safe. If your child is to stay in a recreational facility of any kind for any period of time, you should inspect the facilities yourself to see that they meet *your* standards. For starters, posted inspection licenses should tell you that the facilities meet minimum health and safety standards.
Use these guidelines to aid your assessment:

- What is the proportion of campers to counselors?
- What provision is made for counselors' time off? Does one counselor have to assume double responsibility?
- Who supervises the counselors? Are the camp administrators professionals in education or recreation?
- What do the children do when it rains? Are there adequate facilities for indoor games and sports?
- Rooms should be well-lighted, buildings safe and in good repair. If there are stairways leading to second-story sleeping quarters, check for sturdy handrails and stairs.
- Play equipment should be plentiful, in good repair and suited to the ages of the children.
- Who supervises water sports? Check to make sure that lifeguards are competent and capable. They should have had special courses in water safety, such as those provided by the Red Cross. This should be a *minimum* standard of competence; you will also want to inquire into the lifeguards' and instructors' experience in working with youngsters.
- Inquire into first aid and medical facilities. Accidents and minor injuries are almost inevitable; the staff should be competent to deal with these.
  You should also find out who attends to the campers' more serious medical problems, how often a doctor is available and how close medical personnel can be found.
- Inspect the kitchen and dining areas for cleanliness.
- Ask to see a week's menus. Check that a well-balanced, nutritious diet will be provided.

A good camp should have a well-rounded program designed to provide a range of learning and living experiences that will help youngsters learn and grow physically, emotionally, socially and intellectually. Set your own standards for day or residential camps — and don't settle for second best. Camping should be an enriching experience.

Check costs carefully. Before you enroll your child in any recreation facility, find out:

☐ What does the camp fee cover? Are there extra charges for special trips, for special courses such as horseback riding, for laundry, for craft equipment, etc.?

☐ What happens if your child must leave camp before the season is over? Must you pay for the full season?

☐ Camp fees are usually paid in advance. Do you get a full refund if your child cannot attend? Is there a cancellation fee?

SPECIAL ADULT CAMPS

Every year many *adults* pack up and go away to camp, too. The camps they choose offer a variety of services, everything from tennis lessons to comprehensive programs of weight reduction.

Before choosing such a special camp and putting your money (as well as yourself) in the hands of strangers, it's wise to do some checking. For example, find out the credentials of the camp "counselors" or professional staff. Are the facilities adequate? If possible, try to visit the camp for a quick inspection. If you are required to sign a contract, be sure to read and understand all of its conditions. Find out, too, what you need to do if you decide to cancel.

Carpet and Floor Covering

(See also WARRANTIES)

CARPETING CAN BE A major investment — in terms of both initial cost and upkeep, and the cost of replacing a bad buy when your "bargain" turns out to be worth exactly what you paid for it when the color changes or traffic patterns begin to show. The following factors should be considered before you enter into carpet-buying decisions.

Where will the carpet be used? High traffic areas require construction and fiber that wear well; a beaten path up the front stairway never improved anyone's home. Carpets for the kitchen, family room or bathroom should be easy to clean and durable, because they are constantly exposed to spills and stains. Less durable floor coverings can be purchased for bedrooms where traffic is lighter.

Who will use it? If there are young children, active teenagers and equally active adults in the family, the more durable and cleanable your carpet, the better the investment.

How about the future? If you have settled into a home to stay, wall-to-wall carpet will be a good investment. Otherwise, area rugs or room-size rugs, which you can take with you when you move, will be a better buy.

How much carpet do you need? Multiply the width of the room by its length to find the total number of square feet; divide by 9 to get the total square yards. For example, a 12 foot × 15 foot room would require about 20 square yards of wall-to-wall carpet. Before you buy, have an in-home interview with sales representatives from several local home furnishings stores. Get written estimates. If you are going to buy on a monthly payment plan, make sure the finance charges are added to the estimate.

How much can you afford to spend? Don't be talked into anything you can't afford. Determine your budget *before* you begin to look.

Here are a few tips on how to judge the quality of a rug or carpet:

- ☐ Examine the depth, thickness and density of the pile.
- ☐ See how the pile fibers are locked into or attached to the backing.
- ☐ Examine the quality and sturdiness of the construction and backing. Take a corner of the carpet or rug in your hand and bend it back. This is the the only way to get a clear view of the length and density of the pile and the number of strands of fiber twisted together to make one strand of yarn.

GETTING MORE FOR YOUR MONEY

A good carpet, no matter how it is constructed, has a closely packed pile firmly secured to the backing. The height of the pile is important, but the density or closeness of the surface yarns is more important for long wear.

A skimpy pile may feel luxurious when it is new, but it will crush easily and should not be used in a high-traffic area. A medium-height dense pile is a wise choice for living rooms, hallways or stairways. A short, dense loop pile with high twist will best avoid crush marks.

All carpet consists of pile and backing constructed in one of the following ways:

- **Tufted:** The pile yarns are inserted into a preconstructed backing. The backing may be coated with latex, or — in better-quality carpets — laminated with a second backing fabric. This is the most common construction method used today because it is quick and economical to manufacture.
- **Woven:** The pile and backing are interwoven on a loom in a single operation.
- **Needle-punched or nonwoven:** A core of fiber sheet and layers of loose fibers on each side are interlocked by a machine punching thousands of needles through them.
- **Knitted:** Pile yarns and backing are interlocked in a process very similar to hand knitting.

Terminology can be confusing, especially when a word like "broadloom" is often used in advertising with the implication that the term reflects a certain standard or quality. It doesn't. Broadloom simply refers to seamless carpet made on a broad loom, tufted or woven, regardless of fiber and content, and made in widths wider than six feet.

Rugs that do not pass inspection because they have some imperfection are classified as "seconds" or "imperfects." If you have any doubt about the quality of the carpet that interests you — especially if the price is low — make sure to confirm the quality. Have the salesman mark your sales slip "first quality, not seconds" to preclude any problem with the warranty at some later time.

The term "mill run" should not be used to disguise seconds or irregulars.

CARPET FIBERS

Before you decide on a particular carpet fiber, it's important to weigh any advantages and disadvantages of the types available. Be sure to ask the salesperson for information and advice. Choosing the right fiber for your needs can be a difficult and sometimes confusing process. Here are some guidelines to consider:

- **Wool** is the most expensive carpet material, but offers many excellent qualities. It is easy to clean, resistant to fire and soiling, durable and resilient.

- **Nylon** is less resilient than wool, but is less apt to be damaged by abrasion. Water-soluble stains can be cleaned up very easily. In some situations, nylon can generate static electricity unless metal fiber is included.
- **Rayon** is relatively inexpensive, but may not hold up very well under normal wear and tear.
- **Acrylics** look like wool, wear like nylon, resist soil and sunfading, and clean very easily. They tend to be flammable, however, so make sure there is at least 20 percent modacrylic included.

CARPET PADDING

A cushion makes a rug or carpet more comfortable to walk on. More important, it prolongs its life by absorbing the crushing and grinding of footsteps, and acting as a buffer against wear. A cushion also helps a carpet retain its texture and increases its sound-absorbing qualities.

The give or softness of a carpet cushion is not necessarily the key to quality. A cushion with too much give does not provide a firm enough base for maximum carpet protection. On the other hand, a very hard cushion will not be an adequate buffer against wear.

- **"All hair" padding** is made of selected cattle hair and is the most resilient of the fiber pads.
- **"Combination hair and jute"** is less expensive but not as resilient as all-hair padding.
- **"All jute"** is the material used in the least expensive cushions. Although resilient at first, it tends to break down and bunch up.
- **"Rubberized hair" cushion** consists of rubber-coated top and bottom with a center of blended hair. The coating holds the fibers firmly in place and gives the pad a clean, nonslip surface.
- **"Sponge rubber, foam rubber and urethane foam" cushions** provide good resilience and give soft but uniform support underfoot.

Some carpets are made with an attached padding, eliminating the need for a separate cushion.

THE DEALER

Because carpeting is an important purchase, expected to last longer and survive more constant use than the family car, it is a promising and productive field for unscrupulous dealers to take advantage of poorly informed customers.

A reputable dealer has the same policy for all his customers; service is designed to preserve the firm's reputation and to attract repeat business from satisfied customers. Check with friends and relatives who have shopped for carpeting recently to find out whether they are completely satisfied with the dealer they chose. A dependable dealer will help you make a practical and dependable purchase.

GETTING MORE FOR YOUR MONEY

Be wary of dealers who use these tactics:
Referral schemes: If a dealer attempts to sell you carpet under the guise that you can earn all or part of the cost of the carpet by referring to him other customers who may also buy, be cautious. The cost of the carpet may have been inflated to cover the "bonuses." Once you have signed a contract, you must pay, whether or not your referrals also buy.

Bait and switch: When a dealer advertises carpet by the room — for example, "Your living room, dining room and hall completely installed — 288 square feet — only $159," watch out! You may expect to discover, after the salesperson has shown up at your home, that the advertised carpet is of poor quality or your living room, dining room and hall are not the same size as the area in the advertisement. Once there, the salesperson will have the opportunity to sell you something you never expected to buy.

Also be wary of ads that quote a price per square foot. Wall-to-wall carpet is ordinarily sold by the square yard. When you compare prices, make sure you are comparing the same quantities.

Use this checklist to help with your buying decision:

- ☐ Select your retailer with care. You should feel free to depend on his counsel and advice.
- ☐ Consider the area where your carpet or rug will be used. Make preliminary measurements carefully to estimate size.
- ☐ Beware of "fantastic" bargains.
- ☐ Never buy a carpet that is not labeled as to fiber content.
- ☐ Take a carpet sample home. You need to see the color in your room.
- ☐ Once you have found the color and texture you like, consider the performance quality in relation to the traffic pattern and your own needs for cleanability and wear.
- ☐ Fiber content is important, but it should not be the sole consideration in your buying decision. Construction is equally important.
- ☐ Don't skimp on quality for carpets and rugs that will see constant duty in high-traffic areas.
- ☐ Read your contract or sales receipt for all essential information before you sign it.
- ☐ When a guarantee is offered, find out exactly what is covered and by whom. Get it in writing.
- ☐ Plan to give your carpet or rug good care. Your investment will last longer.

FLOOR COVERINGS

Before deciding on a floor covering be sure to determine your needs by asking a few questions: What kind of traffic does the room get? How often are things spilled and dropped? Do you want a smooth or embossed surface? What about maintenance of the floor? What color combinations are important. How much are you willing to spend?

Once you've determined your needs, the next step is to find out what type of flooring is available. Sheet or tile flooring materials are the most commonly used resilient floor coverings. Available materials include simple asphalt, linoleum, and vinyl as well as the more expensive grades with cushioned backing and no-wax surfaces.

Tile flooring is installed by cementing each tile into place to form a permanent floor. Sheet materials are also cemented, but are installed in wide rolls leaving few seams on the finished floor. Tiles generally are sold in twelve-inch squares; sheet materials come in rolls up to twelve feet wide. Whatever type of flooring material you choose, keep in mind that the denser the surface, the better it will wear.

Installation of flooring can be a difficult task even for the most experienced do-it-yourselfer. Proper measuring, cutting, maneuvering and joining of materials are essential. Those determined to install the flooring should know that tile flooring is easier to install than sheet flooring. It may not be practical to install sheet flooring in a room that has many irregularities or that does not have a clean, dry, smooth subfloor.

If you decide to have the flooring professionally installed, be sure to consult a well-established, well-informed dealer. Find out all the details of the warranty, and be sure to get the specifics of the job in writing (see WARRANTIES).

Maintenance. No-wax floorings should be vacuumed and damp-mopped from time to time to make sure dirt does not scratch the surface or become ground in. Other flooring should be cleaned with a mild floor cleaner on a regular basis. By applying a vinyl coating on the flooring you can help to conceal scratches and prolong the life of the floor.

Charitable Giving

PRIVATE GIVING TO charitable causes is a strong tradition in America. Contributions totaled over $47 billion in 1980, and nearly 90 percent came from individual donors.

Clearly, informed givers can exert a powerful influence on the welfare of our society. So, when you consider contributions of time, money or the use of your name, make sure your donation will serve the purposes you intend. Wise giving is informed giving.

The Council of Better Business Bureaus believes organizations soliciting the public for charitable contributions should provide, upon request, all information a potential donor might reasonably wish to consider. Responsible groups are usually happy to provide such information, so don't be shy. You have a right — in fact, a responsibility — as a wise giver to obtain answers to your questions about a group's operations.

Think of it this way: in choosing which medical research-assistance program, social welfare organization or educational program will receive the benefit of your contribution of time or money or your name on the letterhead, you are facing yet another responsibility as a wise buyer. Your donation will buy service or assistance for people or an organization you wish to help. You have every right to know that the recipients will receive the most for your money.

In some organizations a large percentage of freely given funds will be used to meet administration and fund-raising costs, and only a small percentage of the total budget is actually used for the stated purpose of the organization. But most charities, more genuinely charitable, channel larger proportions of their donations to programs and services.

If you want to make sure that your donation goes where you want it to go, never give to an organization whose operations you cannot check.

Use these guidelines for giving:

☐ Get the name and permanent address of the organization.
☐ Have the organization supply a financial statement and read it carefully. How much money was collected last year? How much spent? On what? Compare administration and fund-raising costs with program costs.
☐ Who operates the program? Sponsors, board members, leaders and operations personnel should be clearly identified.
☐ What do you know of the organization's services? Are they needed? Adequately staffed? Efficiently administered?

☐ What is the tax status of the organization? Is your contribution tax deductible?

If answers to any of your questions are not readily available from the organization itself, a call to the Better Business Bureau may get the answers for you — especially in regard to an organization actively soliciting in your area. You may request reports on nationally operating organizations from the Philanthropic Advisory Service (PAS), a division of the Council of Better Business Bureaus. Its address is: 1515 Wilson Blvd., Arlington, VA 22209.

HELP FOR THE HANDICAPPED . . . OR THE PROMOTER?

Sales presentations from organizations selling lightbulbs, brooms, magazines or other merchandise may originate from a *bona fide* charity or from a for-profit company that employs handicapped persons as sales representatives. Telephone or door-to-door solicitations are frequently used by such firms. Door-to-door sale of merchandise such as greeting cards, candles and wreaths are especially common during the holidays.

Use some caution before you buy.The cause as well as the product should be judged on its merits — not on the degree of sympathy aroused by the salesperson. When you are contacted:

☐ Ask whether the organization is nonprofit or profit.
☐ Get the name and address of the organization.
☐ Ask what portion of your payment will go to the organization.
☐ Keep copies of receipts and sales slips for your records.

LENDING YOUR NAME TO THE CAUSE

Serving as a sponsor or nominal head of a fund-raising drive, giving your time as a volunteer or neighborhood solicitor and serving on the board of charitable organizations are all important ways of giving.

Remember: When you allow your name to be used by any organization, it is assumed that you are also lending your active support to its activities and fund-raising procedures. Your name and your reputation are on the line. Before you agree to provide such support, it is doubly important to secure detailed information on the program, its resources and its fund-raising methods.

You would be well advised to get a copy of "Council of Better Business Bureaus Standards for Charitable Solicitations," a pamphlet published by the Council of BBBs, which sets forth voluntary standards for charitable organizations to follow in soliciting funds from the general public. Single copies are free to nonprofit groups. Send a stamped, self-addressed number 10 envelope with your request to the Philanthropic Advisory Service (for address, see above). Every three months the service publishes a list of soliciting organizations, showing whether their practices follow the "Council of Better

Business Bureaus Standards." The list includes the national and international organizations about which PAS receives the most inquiries, and is available to the public at $1.00.

The voluntary standard emphasizes the importance of full disclosure to contributors (and potential contributors) of the charity's full program and audited financial information, and suggests guidelines for fund-raising, including:

- ☐ At the time of appeal, soliciting organizations should provide to the public a clear and concise description of the programs and special projects for which contributions are being solicited.
- ☐ Organizations mailing unordered merchandise should clearly disclose that recipients are under no obligation to pay for or return the items received.
- ☐ Any offer of merchandise for sale made in conjunction with a charitable solicitation should clearly disclose the amount or percentage of money from the sale that will actually go to the organization for whose benefit the appeal is made.
- ☐ Any telephone appeal should accurately disclose at the outset of the call: (1) the name of the soliciting organization, (2) the purpose of the call, and (3) how further information on the organization can be obtained.
- ☐ Identification cards or badges containing the soliciting organization's name and address and the individual solicitor's name should be provided to all individuals who approach the public requesting contributions.

Remember: As a volunteer fund-raiser, *you* would be expected to answer reasonable questions about the organization. As a sponsor, *you* must have a clear idea of the organization's programs, activities, purposes and fund-raising procedures. Investigate before you invest your time.

Unordered merchandise

Direct-mail solicitations from charitable organizations sometimes contain unordered merchandise such as key rings, seals, pens, name labels and ties. You are not obligated to pay for or return such merchandise, and accompanying advertising/solicitation materials should disclose this fact. (You don't, as a matter of fact, have to pay for or return unordered merchandise sent to you by *any* organization — charitable or otherwise.) You may consider the item a gift, to use or dispose of as you choose. Furthermore, it is illegal for any organization to send you a bill for any unordered item.

   You may choose to donate to the organization but, before you do, make sure that it is truly a charity by checking with your local BBB.

Clothing

(See also DRY CLEANING; PRICES AND SALES)

YOU CAN DRESS WELL— even on a limited budget — if you:
- ☐ Shop wisely.
- ☐ Take time to plan your wardrobe carefully.
- ☐ Do some comparison shopping at home, using catalogs and ads in newspapers and magazines for ideas.
- ☐ Take advantage of end-of-season sales for next year's sportswear, winter coats and classic styles in basics.
- ☐ Choose the best quality you can afford for the items you wear *most*. (It's nonsense to reserve a major portion of your clothing budget for a rare "special occasion" outfit.)
- ☐ Learn to check care labels when you shop. Make maintenance cost part of your buying decision.

WARDROBE PLANNING

The top-of-the-moment fashion, fun for a season, is often this year's bad investment and next year's throwaway. Remember miniskirts? Hotpants? Nehru jackets? Fun to buy and fun to wear (but only for a short time), they are representative of the kind of clothing one buys not out of necessity but for pleasure. The objective is to budget and choose wisely, so that funds are available for pleasure as well as necessities. Therefore, wise buyers spend the major portion of their clothing budget on good classic clothing, the mainstay of a well-planned wardrobe.

Both men and women can save clothing dollars and build a more useful wardrobe by planning in accordance with their lifestyles.

Teenaged members of the family who find it extremely important to look "right" will be vulnerable to whatever fashion seems to be the necessity of the moment. But they will learn to be wise buyers and planners more quickly if they are allowed to make their own choices within a set budget. Accept the fact that a few expensive mistakes are inevitable. Mistakes have their uses; one learns from them. And the experience that goes with learning how to plan and use a budget is invaluable.

The youngest members of the family — the preschoolers — certainly don't need quantities of expensive clothing that they will soon outgrow. What they *do* need is comfortable, washable clothing that allows plenty of freedom to move in. Patient parents can help preschoolers (from about the age of four) exercise freedom of choice by allowing them to choose one new outfit from two or three pre-selected alternatives.

MAINTENANCE COSTS

Consider wardrobe maintenance part of your clothing budget (see DRY CLEANING). A washable, permanent-press garment may cost more than a comparable outfit that must be dry cleaned or laundered by a professional, but it is likely to be a better bargain when you consider the money you save on maintenance. The greater the amount of home-care clothing you own, the better balanced your clothing budget is likely to be.

Be sure to check care labels *before* you buy. Then follow their instructions. Be especially careful to preserve the wrinkle-resistant finish of wash-and-wear clothing. If they are dried at high heat and/or allowed to remain in the dryer after the cycle is complete, they will develop permanently dried-in wrinkles.

Understanding label language is a must for wise buyers. The following list of terms and definitions will guide you in shopping and maintenance.

- **Colorfast:** Sometimes this term is used loosely — the more specific the label, the more generally resistant to color change the fabric is likely to be. No fabric is *absolutely* colorfast, and not all "colorfast" fabrics resist fading caused by sun, water and perspiration. If the term is used as an absolute, it means that no noticeable color change will take place during the normal life of the garment.
- **Drip-dry:** A fabric that may be washed, *hung up to dry while wet,* and worn with little or no ironing. Care instructions often warn against wringing drip-dry fabrics.
- **Permanent press:** This term is self-explanatory. Permanent press garments are made to retain their shape permanently. These fabrics, useful as they are, can make alterations difficult; hemlines can often be shortened but not lengthened. Features include sharp creases, flat seams, and smooth surface texture.
- **Preshrunk:** Fibers or fabrics that have received a preshrinking treatment — often necessary for cotton and wool — to reduce residual shrinkage. The percent of residual shrinkage to be expected must be indicated on the label of treated merchandise. Preshrunk fabrics may shrink as much as 3 to 5 percent. Knitted fabrics may shrink up to 10 percent. When they are labeled "Sanforized," residual shrinkage may be reduced to 2.5 percent or less.
- **Spot-repellent:** Fabrics that have been surface-treated to resist

stains, so that anything spilled on them will not penetrate the weave and can be wiped off easily.
- **Wash-and-wear:** A quality usually provided by a resin finish applied to the fabric. Whether to wash-and-wear or wash-and-iron is a matter of personal choice. Care instructions specified on the label should be followed to the letter to insure that the "easy care" convenience you pay for will be retained for as long as possible.
- **Wrinkle-resistant:** Garments or fabrics that are treated to retain a smooth appearance. Wrinkles that may occur should hang out overnight. The protective resin finish also prevents shrinkage and gives some protection against spotting.

CHECK FOR QUALITY

When clothing is carefully put together, it will fit better, look better and wear better. Expect to pay for quality of construction, but don't assume that all expensive clothing is carefully constructed. In moderate and more expensive clothing, look for:

- Careful construction: the pattern should be matched well at seams, armholes and at the collar.
- Reinforced buttonholes, and buttons that are neither too large nor too small.
- Smooth seams: if the seams show signs of puckering when a garment is bought, they will only get worse with wear and laundering.
- Seams at least a half-inch wide, pinked or finished to guard against raveling.
- Adequate hem for the type of clothing, finished with tape if the material is likely to ravel.
- A well-fitted lining, tailored to be long enough and wide enough. Check the quality of the fabric lining.
- Check care instructions for lined garments. Manufacturers have been known to use incompatible fabrics, which result in a rude shock for consumers who find that the outside of the garment is washable and the nondetachable lining must be dry cleaned.
- Stitching is important. Stitches should be small and the thread should not pull.
- Sturdy clothing, intended for heavy wear, should have double stitching and should be reinforced at points of wear.

CHECK FOR FIT

It doesn't matter how much you paid for a garment if there is something "a little wrong" with the way it fits. If the set of the shoulders is not quite right or the way that a jacket, skirt or pair of pants hangs, find out whether alterations are practical *before* you buy.

Make sure you are buying in the proper size group for you. If you order clothing from a catalog, don't trust last season's measurements. Use current measurements, and check your dimensions with the size chart contained in most clothing catalogs.

Some unwise buyers may shop in particular departments for no better reason than habit. A teen-age girl, for instance, may be too tall for junior sizes but, for some reason, she continues to buy them. Shopping around will surely result in finding a store that has a tall girls' department. On the other hand, many older women can wear junior sizes, and these are the sizes they should buy.

SAVE AT CLOTHING SALES

Regular clothing sales offer excellent bargains. They are normally scheduled at specific times (see PRICES AND SALES) and you can watch for them in specialty shops, department stores, catalog retailers, discount houses and bargain basements.

At any sale the earliest bird inevitably finds the best buys. The longer a sale goes on, whether for hours or days the narrower your choice will be. If you plan your purchases well ahead, you can build up a complete wardrobe — all at sale prices.

Remember: The greater the markdown, the more closely you should examine sale merchandise for tears or defects, poor workmanship or a defective fit that may make the garment useless to you. You will often find that sale merchandise cannot be returned.

Unless the garment fills a true need in your wardrobe, don't buy it. If you do (and it doesn't), you haven't saved money — you've indulged yourself. If it's not the sort of thing you would normally choose, don't buy it; that particular color or cut will only clutter up your closet.

Be a wary buyer at "50 percent off" sales. If the store holding such a sale is not well established and known to you, you may be better off avoiding it. If you know the store, you are probably familiar with the price ranges of its merchandise. If the store is new to you, you have no way of knowing whether the prices were doubled just before the sale was announced. The question in the wise shopper's mind will be: 50 percent of *what*? Watch for these kinds of sales:

- **Reduced for clearance sales** offer best buys in men's, women's and children's clothing. Regular merchandise will carry prices well below the in-season prices. However, a store may also bring in additional merchandise on which the manufacturer and the retailer have taken a lower-than-usual mark-up to make these sales more attractive. *Always check for quality.*
- **Preclearance sales** may have less dramatic bargains, but they are still bargains. The choice will be wider than at regular clearances.
- **Special purchase sales** can yield savings. These generally offer items on which both the manufacturer and retailer have cut their usual mark-up to make the sale possible, or to dispose of slow-moving merchandise.

☐ National-brand men's clothing sales, which occur frequently, represent savings of at least 10 percent. It may not sound like a lot, but 10 percent off a $200 suit will save enough for a shirt or two. And here there can be no question about the values. The times for these sales vary, so watch for them in the newspapers.
☐ Men's and women's coat sales, and sometimes suit and rainwear sales, are scheduled for Columbus Day and Election Day. The stores often plan these sales well in advance and feature real bargains.
☐ Shoe sales, held usually in January and July, can net savings up to 50 percent on national brands.
☐ Accessory sales (on handbags, gloves, etc.) are usually scheduled in January and July and offer from moderate to sensational savings.

FIBERS

Understanding fibers is another "must" for the wise clothing buyer. It is a rare garment that is made of 100 percent anything, and the wide variety of trade names for synthetics can tax the memory.

The natural fibers seem to be making a slight comeback in clothing in the last few years. More often than not, though, you'll see ads that combine, say, "country tweed" photographs with copy containing a simple, truthful declarative statements that the "country tweed" look comes from polyester.

Natural fibers have certain advantages over synthetics, but they have disadvantages as well — remember ironing? Fabrics made of natural fibers are now likely to be more expensive than synthetics.

Use the guide on pp. 94—99 to help you (some fiber trademarks are listed in parentheses for each of the generic fiber groups).

Flammability

Every year there are serious injuries and deaths caused by burns associated with flammable fabrics. The federal Flammable Fabrics Act and the regulations that implement it set flammability standards and inform the public of the hazards arising from the use of flammable fabrics.

The issue of the flammability of children's sleepwear resulted in a complicated set of labeling requirements. Government regulations specify that all items treated with flame resistant chemicals must be labeled with precautionary washing instructions to protect them from elements that cause the chemical to deteriorate.

In addition, controversy over the use of tris phosphate to make sleepwear flame-retardant prompted consumers to discontinue buying sleepwear treated with it. At this time flame-retardant chemicals now being used to treat children's sleepwear are not considered harmful.

MAN-MADE FIBERS

Acetate and triacetate (Ariloft, Arnel, Celanese, Chromespun, Estron, Lanese, Loftura)

CHARACTERISTICS:
Soft, silklike texture; excellent draping qualities. Moth and mildew resistant. Low in price. Good wrinkle resistance, good crease retention; some dyes subject to atmospheric fading. Triacetate is less sensitive to heat, launders well; has poor abrasion resistance.

USES:
Children's wear, women's and men's sportswear and leisure wear, knitted fabrics, lingerie, curtains, draperies, upholstery fabrics, bedspreads, blankets. Also in blends with other man-made fibers.

CARE:
Dry-cleaning is recommended unless the care label indicates the fabric is washable. Low-heat setting should be used both for drying and pressing. Iron on wrong side while damp or use press cloth. Remove oily stains before washing.
(**Warning:** Nail polish remover and other solvents will dissolve acetate.)

Acrylic (Acrilan, Creslan, Fina, Orlon, Zefran)

CHARACTERISTICS:
Provides warmth and bulk without weight; soft and resilient, similar to wool. Low absorption. Wrinkle-resistant; retains pressed pleats, takes well to dyeing in bright colors. Resistant to sunlight, bleaches, moths and atmospheric fading. Blends well with other fibers.

USES:
A variety of knitted and woven apparel fabrics, blankets, rugs, deep-pile fabrics. Blended with high-strength rayon, this fabric is used for durable press fabrics.

CARE:
May be laundered or dry-cleaned — check the care label and follow the manufacturer's instructions. Acrylic blankets should be washed very much like those made of wool. Ironing temperatures for acrylics should not exceed 325°F. *Do not use steam on fur-like fabrics.*

Modacrylic (Acrilan, Elura, SEF, Verel)

CHARACTERISTICS:
Some modacrylic-fiber fabrics can be made to resemble fur or human hair. These fibers are highly resistant to chemicals, are nonflammable, durable, warm and quick-drying. They have good abrasion resistance, wrinkle recovery and shape retention. They are often bulky, have a soft texture and good resilience, and can be permanently pleated.

USES:
Wigs and hairpieces, blankets, carpeting, drapery and upholstery fabrics, furlike pile and napped fabrics for apparel and home furnishings.

CARE:
Follow manufacturer's instructions for care of furlike coats. Some can be dry-cleaned. Some modacrylic fabrics can be machine-washed and dried, using low temperatures. If you wash your modacrylics, use a fabric softener in the final rinse to minimize static electricity. If the garment needs touch-up ironing, use the lowest setting on your iron, the shortest contact time and a press cloth. Do not steam.

Nylon (Antron, Cadon, Cantrece, Caprolan, Enkaloft, Qiana, Zeflon)

CHARACTERISTICS:
Colorfast, strong, lightweight and resistant to abrasion, chemicals, moths and mildew. It is quick-drying, does not shrink and has natural wrinkle resistance and crease recovery. Nylon can be permanently pleated and it blends well with other fibers. Stretchable nylon yarns give elasticity to fabrics.

USES:
Widely used in hosiery, lingerie and many types of woven and knitted fabrics, as well as for apparel, bedspreads, carpeting, drapery and upholstery fabrics. Nylon fiber can be processed into stretch yarns, and it is widely used in blends to add strength and wash-and-wear characteristics to fabrics.

CARE:
Nylon can pick up colors from other fabrics, so whites should be washed separately. Washes easily, dries quickly, *should not be wrung or twisted*. White nylons tend to gray; they should be rinsed thoroughly (and bleached frequently with oxygen-based bleach). Little or no ironing is required; if ironing is necessary, use the lowest heat.

Olefin (Herculon, Marvess, Vectra)

CHARACTERISTICS:
Exceptionally colorfast, strong and lightweight, with a characteristic waxy feel. It sheds water, is resistant to abrasion and easy to clean, but has a low melting point.

USES:
Olefin fibers are used in knitted garments, hosiery, high-pile boot liners, neckties, children's sleepers, blankets, robes, belts, handbags, seat covers, upholstery fabrics, and indoor and outdoor carpets.

CARE:
This fiber is highly heat-sensitive and should not be exposed to

temperatures over 200°F. Olefin upholstery may be cleaned with a cloth and solvent.

Polyester (Avlin, Dacron, Fortrel, Kodel, Terylene, Trevira, Vycron, Zefran)

CHARACTERISTICS:
Strong; resistant to wrinkling, abrasion, sunlight, mildew and moth damage. Blends well with other fibers, holds pleats and trouser creases when heat-set. Does not shrink. Polyesters are comfortable to wear in warm weather, since the weave allows perspiration to evaporate.

USES:
When combined with other fibers, sensitized and cured by heat, polyester fibers are used for durable-press fabrics and garments. Elasticity of polyester fibers makes them useful in stretch fabrics. Blends are widely used for men's, women's and children's apparel, and for household items.

CARE:
Machine washing and drying preserves durable-press characteristics. The wash cycle should be followed by a cool rinse. Garments should be removed from the dryer promptly at the end of the cycle. Oily stains should be pretreated before washing.

Durable press garments should be washed in small loads (white polyesters should be washed separately). If touch-up ironing is required, use low heat.

Rayon (Avisco, Avril, Coloray, Eukrome, Xena, Zantrel)

CHARACTERISTICS:
Rayon can withstand higher temperatures than the other man-made fibers. It is inexpensive, blends well with other fibers, is highly absorbent, and is stable during laundering if resin-treated.

USES:
Alone or blended with natural fibers or other synthetics, rayon is widely used in wearing apparel. It is also found in home-furnishings fabrics for carpets, draperies, upholstery, blankets and table linens.

CARE:
Follow manufacturer's instructions as to washing or dry-cleaning. Many rayon fabrics can be washed and ironed like cotton. In blends, use the laundering method recommended for the fiber present in the highest percentage. Do not use chlorine bleach on resin-finished rayon unless the label states it is safe to do so. Do not wring or twist rayon fabrics.

Spandex (Duraspun, Glospan, Lycra, Spandelle, Stretch-Ever, Varene)

CHARACTERISTICS:
Lightweight with long-lasting elasticity and excellent resistance to abrasion, perspiration, and body and cosmetic oils. The filament yarn is usually wrapped with another textile fabric or blend.

USES:
Spandex is used for foundation garments, bathing suits, ski pants and snowsuits. It is also in fabric blends that require varying degrees of elasticity.

CARE:
Avoid exposure to high heat and strong chlorine bleach. Spandex may be machine-washed and tumble-dried at low temperature setting. It should *not* be ironed.

NATURAL FIBERS

Cotton

CHARACTERISTICS:
Durable, absorbent, resists abrasion. It shrinks, but shrinkage-control treatments reduce residual shrinking. Cotton wrinkles easily, but with resin finishes it gives excellent wash-and-wear performance. Blends of cotton and synthetic fibers, given special treatment, can give durable or permanent-press performance. Cotton fiber is weakened by exposure to sunlight. Vat-dyed cottons are colorfast to sunlight and good home laundering procedures.

USES:
Cotton is a versatile fiber that can produce sheer, medium, and heavy sturdy fabrics. It is used for a wide range of clothing for all ages, as well as for home furnishings fabrics.

CARE:
Untreated white and colorfast cottons may be laundered without special care other than following instructions as to the use of laundry equipment, detergents, bleaches, etc. Many things made of 100 percent cotton will have to be ironed. Follow manufacturer's instructions as to the care of resin-finished wash-and-wear cottons. Chlorine bleach should not be used on wash-and-wear cotton items unless the label states that the garment is bleachable. Durable-press items can be machine-washed and tumble-dried.

Flax (Linen)

CHARACTERISTICS:
Absorbent, dries quickly, carries heat away from the body, and has poor wrinkle resistance unless it is chemically treated. Special finishes are necessary to make linen mildew-resistant. Linen is lint-free,

lustrous, crisp-looking and strong. It is moth resistant, does not soil readily and launders easily. Vat-dyed linens are colorfast.

USES:
Like cotton, linen has been used for a wide range of apparel and home furnishings fabrics.

CARE:
Hand wash or machine wash according to type and weight of fabric. Do not use chlorine bleach on wrinkle-resistant (resin-treated) linen unless label says the item is bleachable. Linens should be well-damped and pressed with a hot iron. To increase the luster of the fabric, iron the wrong side first. To bring out the interesting texture of 100 percent linen, iron on the wrong side *only*.

Silk

CHARACTERISTICS:
Silk is second only to nylon in fiber strength. It has excellent draping qualities, is luxurious in appearance and takes dyes exceptionally well. It is a poor conductor of heat and therefore is warmer than cotton. Silk is sensitive to both acids and alkali, and is weakened by sunlight and perspiration. White silk fabrics tend to yellow with age or with exposure to heat or chlorine bleach. Silks with smooth surfaces do not soil easily.

USES:
Lingerie, ribbons, shoes, trimmings, umbrellas, drapes, curtains, upholstery fabrics, dresses, suits, blouses, lace, knitted ties, sweaters, scarves, etc.

CARE:
Some silks are washable, but unless they are so labeled they should be dry cleaned. They should be protected from perspiration, acid, alkali, chlorine bleaches, and high ironing temperatures. To hand wash, use a mild neutral soap, lukewarm water, oxygen-type bleach. Do not rub. Use very low ironing temperature, especially on white silk.

Wool

CHARACTERISTICS:
Wool yarns are classified as woolen or worsted. **Worsted yarns** are made of long, evenly combed fibers and are smooth and firm. **Woolen yarns** are softer, made of short, uncombed fibers. Wool has a natural resilience that makes it resist wrinkling. It is strong, durable, absorbent and takes dyes well.

USES:
Wool is available in a wide range of fabrics from sheer crepes to bulky

knits and tweeds and heavy fleeced coating fabrics. It has been used for sweaters, skirts, dresses, suits, underwear, coats and upholstery fabrics.

CARE:
Check the care label. Wool should be dry cleaned unless the label tells you it must be hand washed. For hand-washables, use cold water and cold-water soap; dry on a flat surface. Woolens that have been treated for shrink resistance may be machine-washable and dryable. Again, follow instructions carefully — gentle agitation or the soak method with liquid detergents and fabric softeners are often recommended. Chlorine bleach should never be used on wool.

STRETCH FABRICS AND LAMINATED FABRICS
These two developments in the textile industry appear both in clothing and home furnishings fabrics.

Stretch fabrics may be knitted or woven; they often provide long wear, excellent fit and shape retention and resistance to wrinkling. They are easy to care for and comfortable to wear. There are three varieties: vertical stretch, horizontal stretch and two-way stretch (horizontal *and* vertical). The latter is mainly in foundation garments and clothing for active sports. Single-way stretch fabrics are used in many kinds of clothing as well as in such household items as stretch slipcovers.

Laminated fabrics have a packing of polyurethane foam laminated (permanently attached) to the underside of the fabric. There are two kinds: a single laminate has fabric only on one side of the foam; a double laminate is a "foam sandwich." Laminated fabrics are used for dresses, coats, and jackets. They hold their shape well, are wrinkle-resistant and odor-resistant. *Check the care label before you buy* — follow the manufacturer's instructions as to washing or dry cleaninig.

Summing up
- ☐ Beauty, appropriateness, style, quality and the required care are the standards you should use to judge clothing.
- ☐ *Plan* family wardrobes. Each family member should learn to plan for a coherent, well-put-together wardrobe *instead of buying piecemeal.*
- ☐ Learn all you can about fibers and the fabrics made from them — each has its own special advantages.
- ☐ Know *current* size ranges and buy the right size for each member of the family.
- ☐ Check care labels. *Remember:* maintenance is part of the clothing budget.
- ☐ Save labels and hang tags.
- ☐ Keep a sales calendar and shop sales for value buying.

Condominiums and Cooperatives

(See also APARTMENTS; CONTRACTS; HOUSING)

CONDOMINIUMS AND COOPERATIVE apartment housing can offer the convenience of apartment living with some of the advantages of owning property.

The basic difference is that a condominium provides for individual mortgages to cover each resident's dwelling. The deed to a condominium apartment is recorded in the same way as the deed to a house. This allows the condominium owner to have his own personal mortgage, for which he is responsible and which can be refinanced if he wishes. The closing process is similar to a house closing and, therefore, the closing costs are somewhat higher than those incurred by a person buying a co-op.

Cooperative apartments must be paid for *in cash* at the closing. If sufficient cash is not available, you must obtain a personal loan with collateral from a bank. The size of the loan and the amount of collateral will vary according to current financial conditions and under variable local law. If you use stock as collateral, remember that the bank will only lend you two-thirds of the current market value of the negotiable stock (as protection for the bank in case of stock fluctuations). You will have to secure the remaining third of the cost to get the loan. The bank will hold the stock certificates for the duration of the loan, although you continue to receive the dividends.

Real estate taxes are paid by the corporation owning the co-op, but the tenant is allowed an income-tax deduction proportional to the amount of stock he or she owns. (If the tenant has borrowed money to buy the stock, the interest on that loan is also deductible.)

Certain tax advantages accrue to the benefit of both cooperative and condominium apartment owners in the deductions received for local taxes and mortgage interest. In addition to this, capital gains taxes can be deferred if a home is sold and the money reinvested in a co-op or condominium, or other real estate of equal or higher value.

The additional advantage of building up an equity in the property may also be beneficial.

If your apartment house turns into a condominium, and you don't want to buy, there is probably nothing you can do except move. Find out whether state law protects you: some states have laws giving you as much as four months to find another apartment and arrange to move. If you have a long-term lease, you cannot be evicted until it expires, provided, of course, that you comply with the terms of the lease.

When you buy a co-op . . .
- ☐ You own shares in a nonprofit corporation which holds title to the building.
- ☐ You hold a long-term proprietary lease on your apartment.
- ☐ You share real estate taxes and operating costs with the other owners.
- ☐ You have no personal liability for corporate obligations, since your status is that of a tenant. What this means is you are not responsible if the corporation cannot make its mortgage payments (though you lose your investment) or if someone is injured on the property outside your own apartment. On the other hand, if twenty apartments are contained in the building and only eighteen are purchased, costs which would normally be shared by twenty tenants must be borne by eighteen.

When you buy a condominium . . .
- ☐ You get a deed to your apartment.
- ☐ You are the owner, along with the other owners, of common areas such as the lobby, elevators, etc. Condominium owners have a different legal status from co-op owners and, therefore, different responsibilities, such as greater personal liability and, possibly, liability for a share of any contracts entered into by the condominium association, and for personal injury damages sustained by anyone in any of the common areas, such as the lobby. The seriousness of such risks can be reduced by adequate insurance coverage. The prospective purchaser should make sure that sufficient liability coverage is maintained for the entire condominium development.

BEFORE YOU BUY A CONDOMINIUM . . .
Remember that you will become part owner of the plumbing, wiring and other common structural elements of the building. If any of these have not been well maintained or are outmoded, you and the other new owners will have to bear the substantial cost of restoration. *Sometimes apartment dwellers are victimized in a conversion by speculative operators taking advantage of the current condominium boom to rid themselves of aging or undesirable buildings.*

Find out:

- ☐ Whether an engineering survey was made of the property and if any necessary work has been completed. Are there any housing violations outstanding?
- ☐ Have there been any improvements to enhance the livability of the building, such as the addition of a swimming pool or other community facility? Have kitchens and bathrooms been remodeled?

THE ROLE OF THE DEVELOPER

Get answers to these questions before you buy:

- ☐ Is the developer retaining control over certain elements of the project, such as recreational facilities or parking spaces? This can become a real problem because the developer could charge exorbitant fees for the use of these facilities. A potential problem related to the developer's role is that *if he buys a single condominium unit for his own use,* he could, as an owner, prevent any change in the declaration (or bylaws of the project) not to his liking. (Usually, 100 percent of the owners must agree to amendments of the declaration.)
- ☐ Find out whether the developer has reserved the right to control the condominium management or to add new facilities.
- ☐ Consider, also, whether you want a group, the condominium association, determining your future costs and expenses (in the way of monthly maintenance fees).

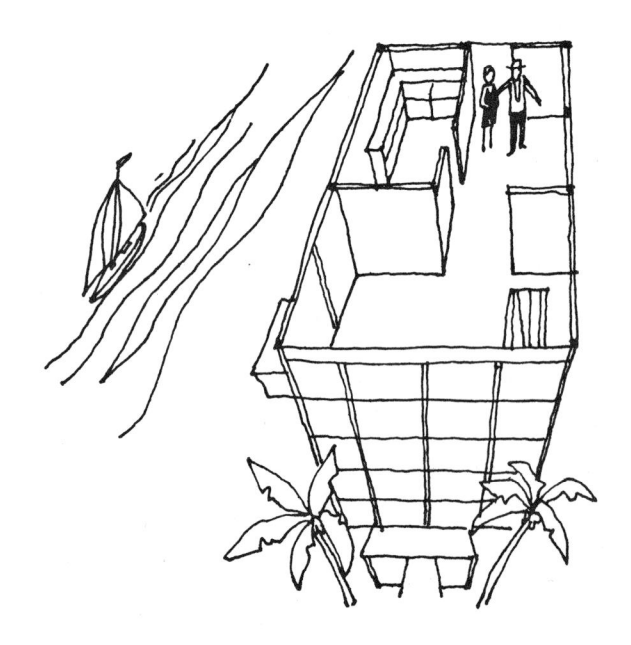

Contracts

(See also CREDIT AND INSTALLMENT BUYING; DOOR-TO-DOOR SELLING)

CONTRACTS ARE BINDING legal documents, and **sales contracts** are no exception to this rule. Their function is to describe the exact obligations of the signers — the parties to the agreement — to one another.

Sales contracts require the seller to provide a service or to deliver a product in exchange for a specified amount of money to be paid by the buyer under specified conditions.

Important factors to remember in regard to sales contracts are:

- **A contract generally cannot be broken or changed unless both parties agree.** Unless refund or cancellation privileges are part of the contract, or unless the sale was made through outright fraud or misrepresentation (both of which are hard to prove), the terms and conditions set forth in the contract are final. The exception to this rule is the "cooling-off period" established by the Federal Trade Commission in regard to door-to-door sales of merchandise costing $25.00 or more (see DOOR-TO-DOOR SELLING).
- **Oral promises usually do not affect a written agreement.** They are very difficult to prove. If an appliance salesman says installation of your new dishwasher is part of the deal, make sure this statement is covered in the contract. If installation is not included in the written contract, the seller is under no obligation to provide it and you may be obligated to pay for the service.
- **Warranties and guarantees should be in writing, and they should be clear and explicit** (see WARRANTIES).
- **Read before you sign.** There is no better way to protect yourself than to read and thoroughly understand a sales contract before you sign it. *Read every word.* What happens if you miss a payment when you buy on credit? What penalties are involved for cancellation of the contract? Suppose you sign a contract obligating you to pay for the services offered by a health club and the next day you slip a disk? Must you pay for services you cannot receive?
- **Don't be intimidated by the fact that a contract is already printed.** The only time to change the terms and conditions of a "standard" contract of any kind is *before* it is signed. If a provision

does not meet your satisfaction, it can be changed (even if the provision is "standard") as long as the seller and you agree on the change and both initial it on the contract form. Remove any terms and conditions that are not applicable to your agreement by marking them "not applicable" and make sure any such deletions are also initialed by both yourself and the seller.

☐ **Never sign a contract that contains blank spaces.** This is tantamount to signing a blank check. The seller is free to add terms and conditions you would never have agreed to, had you read them first.

☐ **Never sign a contract under pressure.** If a salesman implies that today's price will not be in effect tomorrow, he could be telling the truth, but chances are that he is applying more pressure. Usually a good buy on the first of the month will still be a good buy ten days later. Keep in mind that reputable businessmen supply complete pre-purchase information to their customers without applying pressure for an immediate decision. Because they want their customers to be satisfied with the merchandise, reputable businessmen prefer to have their customers shop and compare.

Before you sign
If you are in doubt as to the terms and conditions of any sales contract for a major purchase, don't sign until any unclear provisions have been explained. A seller's statement that the contract is "standard" is not enough unless you understand it.

EVALUATING SALES CONTRACTS

To be sure you are satisfied with the seller's part of the agreement, you must verify that everything the seller is to do is covered by the contract. The price, type, style, color and model number of every item, the quality and condition of the materials to be used, service obligations and the date of delivery of merchandise and/or completion of service or installation should be stated precisely.

On installment contracts, interest rates and finance charges must be set forth and expressed as an annual percentage rate (see CREDIT AND INSTALLMENT BUYING).

Remember that a contract noting that a product is being sold "as is" imposes no obligation on the seller — you cannot return the merchandise, and the seller makes no promises in regard to its condition. If the product needs service or repair, you are on your own.

One of the best ways to make sure you will not be cheated is by dealing with a reputable dealer. Responsible businessmen have an interest in maintaining good customer relationships by dealing openly and honestly. When in doubt as to the reputation of a dealer in goods or services, check with your Better Business Bureau.

Cosmetics

ACCORDING TO ESTIMATES of the Cosmetic, Toiletry and Fragrance Association, the American public spent over $9 billion in 1980 to cleanse and beautify itself with various toilet articles and preparations.

Bear in mind that cosmetics advertising is often subjective or unspecific, intended to communicate a mood, an "aura" or a state of mind. Buying decisions can be equally subjective — as frivolous and ephemeral sometimes as the advertising itself.

Medical authorities agree that good health is the best basis for good looks. The skin is nourished by a proper diet, not by vitamins, minerals or hormones contained in cosmetics. Proper nutrition, exercise, the proper amount of sleep and a minimum of exposure to the sun (that summertime bronze can lead to premature aging of the skin) all contribute to long-lasting attractiveness.

Many cosmetics users take for granted the notion of health as the basis for good looks. Then they choose to take another step — to add the color and the fragrance which they feel is important to good grooming.

TIPS ABOUT CERTAIN KINDS OF PRODUCTS

- **Acne preparations.** The treatment of acne, whether mild or severe, should be medical rather than cosmetic. The basic cause is physical, and linked to changes in hormone production. See your family doctor or a dermatologist and follow the *prescribed* treatment. Don't confuse cover-up with treatment.
- **Antiperspirants and deodorants.** Antiperspirants inhibit or control perspiration; deodorants minimize or eliminate odors caused by perspiration. Manufacturers' instructions — to avoid use on broken skin or if a rash develops — are on the labels for a very good reason. Follow these instructions. You may be one of the people who react negatively to one or more of these products.
- **Hair-care preparations.** Shampoos and conditioners, like other personal-care products, are chosen for subjective reasons. If you experience problems with hair and scalp (including dandruff, dryness, itching) consult a dermatologist; don't assume that medicated shampoos or conditioners will solve the problem. Remember that constant indiscriminate application of medicated products of various kinds can be harmful.
- **Moisturizers, skin creams and lotions.** These are generally recognized as helpful in promoting the softening and smoothing of dry skin. A humidifier may also be helpful to counteract the dry heat of many homes and apartments.

    Remember: There are many inexpensive and moderately priced products on the market that are just as effective as the expensive ones. Your judgment and your budget should guide your choice.

> **Promises, promises . . . opinions, opinions**
> Personal care is a personal matter. The cosmetics you use can be expensive or economical, depending on your mood and your budget. Ingredients hardly vary at all, and some critics of the industry cite this as a major reason for the reluctance of manufacturers to provide ingredient labeling of their products. There would be little reason, they theorize, for consumers to buy a moisturizer at $10.00 per ounce if ingredients listed are identical to those contained in a moisturizer that costs $.25 per ounce. The attributes that change most from product to product are fragrance, packaging and price.
>   Downright cheap products can be just as effective as high-priced items. One over-forty, youthful-looking actress has confided to her biographer that she uses periodic all-over applications of petroleum jelly to "moisturize" her skin — a treatment that certainly wouldn't appeal to everyone. If more expensive, fragrant products give you pleasure (and if you can afford them), your options are open. For some people the luxurious feeling is worth the additional cost.

COSMETICS AND SAFETY

The Food, Drug and Cosmetic Act requires that cosmetics be produced in sanitary plants, that they be free of hazardous substances, and that they be packaged in safe and nondeceptive containers.

It is true that cosmetics do not have to be tested for safety before they are marketed, but most manufacturers of nationally distributed products either maintain their own testing laboratories or use the services of consulting laboratories for product development and testing.

According to government sources, some sixty thousand people each year are injured by cosmetics. Injuries range from mild allergic reactions to those serious enough to result in baldness, disfigurement or blindness.

Exercise reasonable care when you use cosmetics. Follow these guidelines:

- ☐ Date cosmetics when you buy them — especially eye make-up and mascara — and discard them after four months. Cosmetics are free of bacteria when you buy them, but they provide a good medium in which bacteria can grow; the longer they are used, the more dangerous they become.
- ☐ The eyes are vulnerable to infections and injuries. Always apply eye make-up — as well as other cosmetics — with clean, freshly washed hands. *The hands carry bacteria which can cause serious infections.* Use mascara applicators with care — severe infections (some causing loss of sight) have resulted from scratching the surface of the eye with bacteria-laden applicators.

- ☐ Keep cosmetics covered to avoid contamination with dust and dirt, and store them carefully. High temperatures, for example, can destroy the preservatives contained in face creams and other cosmetic preparations.
- ☐ Do not borrow or lend cosmetics.
- ☐ Keep a careful eye out for reactions to cosmetics. Discontinue the use of any preparation that causes irritation of any kind. If the rash, itching or whatever persists, see a doctor.
- ☐ Follow manufacturers' directions with care. If the manufacturer of the hair tint or dye you use suggests a patch test before each use of the product, follow this direction. A little care can save you the severe discomfort of an allergic reaction.
- ☐ Remember that a product you have used uneventfully for years can suddenly cause an allergic reaction. It is well known that allergies are unpredictable.
- ☐ The indiscriminate use of medicated products — *especially those including hormone creams* — can be hazardous. Limits are set by the Food and Drug Administration (FDA) on the quantity of hormones that can be added to cosmetics, but there is still the possibility that consumers will use these products in greater-than-recommended quantities. If you use such a product at all, use it in small amounts.

If you have a complaint concerning cosmetics, tell the manufacturer. Describe the problem or the disappointment, and request an adjustment. The manufacturer may or may not ask you to return the rest of the preparation. If your complaint concerns advertising, send a copy of your letter to the Better Business Bureau. If you are reporting an allergic reaction or problem caused by a cosmetic, a copy should also go to the FDA (see IF YOU ARE DISSATISFIED for addresses).

Credit and Installment Buying

(See also CONTRACTS; WARRANTIES)

IN 1945 CONSUMER CREDIT outstanding in the United States amounted to less than $6 billion. By the end of 1971, it exceeded $135 billion. And, as of June 1980, consumers owed some $325 billion for personal loans, credit card accounts, automobile financing and department store accounts.

Many factors have contributed to the growth of the use of consumer credit. Among them are the following: higher incomes; increase in the standard of living; increase in the number and variety of consumer goods appearing on the market; decrease in the size of required down payments; increase in home ownership and its accompanying demand for household furnishings and appliances; and creation of new forms of credit, e.g., credit cards, etc.

Consumer credit is a powerful tool that influences the entire economy. Its effectiveness for the individual depends upon the skill of the user. If wisely used, buying on credit can provide the consumer with:

- a convenient way to pay for goods and services — and the convenience of using merchandise while it is being paid for;
- an accurate record of expenses useful for budget background information and tax purposes;
- a means of budgeting major expenses over a period of time;
- a temporary assistance in meeting unexpected obligations and emergencies, such as heavy, unpredictable medical expenses.

Credit is a service that consumers pay for. In some cases it may cost a substantial amount of money, even though the price of a single installment may seem easily affordable to you. Never let the idea of the convenience of having some desired item immediately get in the way of your giving the added cost of credit or installment buying the sort of close examination it should have.

CREDIT AND YOUR BEST INTEREST

Credit is easy to get — and not so easy to pay for. Studies have demonstrated that families and individuals who use credit for most purchases tend to buy more (from 25 to 35 percent more) than those who use cash. Charge accounts are useful and sometimes necessary for consumers and, because they increase sales volume, they are most

CREDIT AND INSTALLMENT BUYING

useful to retailers.

It is important to remember that credit grantors — department stores, credit card companies, finance companies and banks — are all engaging in business for profit. Money is a commodity. When you borrow it or delay payment for a purchase, a rental fee is charged. Interest is the "rent" you pay for the use of money that belongs to another person, a retailer or a lending institution.

There are two basic forms of credit:

- ☐ **Open-end credit,** offered by credit card companies, department stores and banks (in the form of bank credit cards), frequently bears an annual interest charge of 18 percent, or 1.5 percent per month if not paid within a specified period of time. The customer can, in effect, choose how much of his monthly bill he wishes to pay at any one time. When payment is deferred, additional interest is charged.
- ☐ **Closed-end credit** (installment purchases and loans) is less flexible. This is the form of credit used to finance major purchases such as appliances and automobiles. A specific amount is borrowed and is repaid in monthly installments over a specific period of time.

Finance charges for closed-end credit are variable and negotiable. Since the Consumer Credit Protection Act (Truth-in-Lending Act) requires credit grantors to disclose the finance charges both in dollars and as an annual percentage rate on installment loans and credit sales, it is possible to shop for credit by comparing annual percentage rates. For example:

The car you have chosen requires financing of $3,000.00.

Bank A charges 14 percent interest on a 36-month automobile loan. The cost of the loan is $691.00.

Bank B charges 11.08 percent for the same amount of money for the same period of time. Your cost: $540.00.

Shopping saves you $151.00.

1.5 PERCENT PER MONTH DOESN'T ALWAYS ADD UP TO 18 PERCENT PER YEAR

The annual percentage rate for most charge accounts and credit cards is 18 percent.

Does it follow that you pay 1.5 percent per month on the balance of your account for any given month?

Not necessarily.

It depends on the method used by the credit grantor to calculate your "balance." There are three ways to do it, and consumers should find out which accounts are more expensive as a result of the system used.

109

> **Know the alternatives**
> In general, the selection of source and type of credit by a consumer is the product of a complex set of factors. A variety of competing services is offered by various types of credit grantors, giving the consumer the option of different means of purchasing for any single purpose. Thus, a major item may be financed indirectly by a bank or a sales finance company which purchases the consumer paper evidencing the debt. It may be purchased with proceeds of a personal loan obtained from a bank, credit union, sales finance or consumer finance company. Or it may be financed by the retail seller directly. In the case of the bank, the "loan" may be made in traditional fashion or, perhaps, through the use of a bank credit card or check guarantee or overdraft plan. Most goods, on the other hand, may be acquired with the proceeds of a personal loan, in whatever form, by means of a retail charge account, credit card or by some other form of credit plan.

1. **The adjusted balance method (or closing balance method)** is most economical for consumers. The finance charge is calculated on the unpaid balance of the previous month, less credits and payments made in the current month. For instance:

Opening balance:	$200
Payments and credits:	$100
Monthly finance charge:	1.5%
Actual finance charge:	0.015 × 100 = $1.50
Annual rate of finance charge:	18%

2. **The previous balance method,** used by many retailers, will cost you more. Finance charges are based on the amount owed on the final billing date of the previous month, *before* any payments or credits for returned merchandise have been recorded. The result:

Opening balance:	$200
Payments and credits:	$100
Monthly finance charge:	1.5%
Actual finance charge:	0.015 × 200 = $3.00
Annual rate of finance charge:	36%

3. **The average daily balance method** levies finance charges approximately equal to that of the previous balance method. It is arrived at by a more circuitous route. Finance charges are determined by dividing the sum of the balances outstanding *for each day of the billing period* by the number of days in the period, and then

multiplying by the daily rate of interest. With this kind of account, the longer payment is delayed, the higher the average daily balance and, therefore, the higher — and more profitable to the credit grantor — the finance costs.

All these methods are legal in most states. The credit grantors who use them are, furthermore, in compliance with the disclosure requirements of the Truth-in-Lending Act. They do, after all, tell you that you are paying 1.5 percent per month in finance charges on the balance of your account. All that is left for you to do is get out your calculator and find out what balance is their basis.

BORROWING AGAINST TOMORROW
Today you can charge or finance almost anything you buy. Delayed payment plans, once reserved for major purchases, are now used routinely by many American families for daily purchases and entertainment. Quantities of such "small" expenditures turn into large payments to be made at the end of the month, or into hefty delayed bills accompanied by equally hefty finance charges.

Credit counselors tell us that most people who get into credit problems are families in the middle- to upper-income brackets. They are young families, with incomes likely to increase on a predictable annual basis. But they make one big mistake: they fail to plan their expenditures. They do not agree upon, and live within, a reasonable budget. As a result, they find it easy to overspend or go far into debt.

You and your budget
There is nothing difficult or mysterious about drawing up a family budget. Use this simple procedure:

Take a piece of paper and draw a line down the middle. On the left side, note your take-home income from all sources — salaries, income from interest or stocks, etc. On the other side list the actual costs of living: in addition to house payments or rent, utilities, insurance, taxes, average clothing costs and projected medical expenses, include the children's allowances, amusements, the cost of the children's summer camp, the family vacation cost, the golf greens fees, etc. Add up both sides.

If your income isn't at least 10 percent higher than your expenditures, you're in trouble.

Remember: There are two changes you can expect — higher prices and higher taxes. If your expenditures are equal to or greater than your income, you have left yourself no leeway for unexpected expenses.

Most important is the fact that you are not saving money for the future.

Now comes the most difficult aspect of the budget-drawing process: You must find a way to live with it.

CHOOSING CREDIT, EVALUATING ACCOUNTS

Once you take the time and trouble to find out how much it costs to use the accounts and credit cards you have, you may decide that it is a good idea to close the most expensive accounts. There is no reason to keep those accounts which assess finance charges on money you no longer owe. **Remember:** The *adjusted balance method* is the one you want.

Don't use credit cards indiscriminately for day-to-day purchases. Remember that credit card purchases may cost you money.

If you pay quickly, not just the "minimum" due on a charge card account, but the full total owed, you can avoid additional finance charges.

If you can, try to pay off high-interest loans quickly. But protect long-term low-interest secured loans. If you fall behind in payments, you may have to renegotiate the loan at a higher interest. Be especially careful to keep up with mortgage payments.

If for some reason you cannot make a monthly payment, call your creditor and explain the situation. Don't wait for him to contact you.

DEALING WITH DEBT

If you are swamped by heavy debts, there are several things you can do. One is taking out a debt-consolidation loan through a bank or consumer finance company.

Be wary of getting help from debt consolidators who handle repayment of bills in return for 10 to 25 percent of the amount owed. While some of these firms are legitimate, others will take your money and pay off only a few creditors. Check with your Better Business Bureau before you deal with such a firm. In some states, they are not allowed to do business at all.

Another alternative is to consult with a **consumer credit counseling service.** These nonprofit credit clinics usually charge nothing, or only a nominal fee, to get you back on a pay-as-you-go basis without resorting to bankruptcy.

Usually a detailed budget is worked out between the client and the counselor. The client may be asked to sign an agreement stating that he or she will follow the budget and avoid making additional purchases on credit. The counselor contacts the creditors and negotiates a debt-repayment plan, with smaller monthly payments spread out over a longer period of time.

Credit counseling services usually deal with consumers who are employed. However, very often free counseling services are offered to persons on welfare and social security. For a list of such services in your area, write to the National Foundation for Consumer Credit, 8701 Georgia Avenue, Suite 601, Silver Spring, MD 20910.

Use the following tips for buying on time:

- ☐ Shop for credit as carefully as you shop for products.
- ☐ Read and understand the contract (see CONTRACTS). Make sure it includes, *in writing*, the following information:

- exactly what you are buying — a full description of the product or service must be included in the contract;
- the purchase price;
- any other charges, such as installation fees or shipping costs;
- down payment and/or trade-in allowances;
- total amount due;
- the dollar amount of interest or service charges;
- the annual percentage rate;
- the number, amount and due dates of all payments; and
- *all promises* made by the salesman.

Oral promises in regard to the seller's commitments for maintenance, service or replacement of defective merchandise have about the same value as the air they are written on. Get such promises in writing (see WARRANTIES), or be prepared to disregard them.

Finally, get answers to these important questions before you sign any retail finance or credit agreement:

☐ **What happens if you miss a payment?** Will there be a delinquency charge? Will the balance fall due? Will the seller automatically repossess the item?

☐ **What happens if you pay ahead?** Is there a penalty for prepayment? Will any of the finance charges be refunded?

LAWS AFFECTING CONSUMER RIGHTS

Many states have enacted laws governing credit, including setting ceilings on rates that can be charged. On the federal level, three major laws, in addition to Truth-in-Lending, have been passed to help assure you of your rights as a consumer.

The Equal Credit Opportunity Act prohibits creditors from discriminating on the basis of sex, marital status, race, color, religion, national origin and age in any part of a credit transaction. It applies to all lenders who regularly extend credit.

The Fair Credit Billing Act protects charge account and credit card holders by requiring creditors to comply with rules applying to the correction of billing errors. In some cases, the act also protects consumers who may have problems with an item costing more than $50 and bought on a credit card.

The Fair Credit Reporting Act protects you against the circulation of inaccurate or obsolete information and insures that consumer credit reporting agencies act in a fair manner. It provides steps that you may take if you have been denied credit, or if you believe your credit record contains false or misleading information.

If you are considering entering into an installment contract, ask yourself these questions before you sign:
- ☐ Can you make the payments out of your regular income?
- ☐ Have you any credit or cash reserve to cover an unexpected illness or accident? What would happen to your credit and installment accounts — and your credit rating — if you lost your job?
- ☐ Are you willing to give up part of your income for the specified number of months for the sake of the credit purchase?
- ☐ How far is your credit extended? Credit experts say that no more than 15 percent of your income — after taxes and excluding mortgage payments — should be tied up in time payments.

Day-Care Centers

FINDING SAFE, pleasant day-care centers that will contribute to preschoolers' education is a problem facing many working parents. Parents looking for such facilities, says the Better Business Bureau, should put together a checklist of specific requirements, then visit day-care centers to inspect facilities and talk with the staffs.

With increasing numbers of women entering the work force, the supply of day-care facilities in most areas usually doesn't satisfy the demand. *Parents should start their shopping early, before children reach the age of three (the acceptable entry age at most centers) to help ensure their child a place in the center of their choice.*

For children under three the following arrangements may be made:

- ☐ **Family day-care,** provided in the home of a relative, neighbor or friend who is paid for the care (the latter may or may not run a licensed day-care home); or
- ☐ **Nursery schools,** providing part-day programs charging tuition.

For help in finding reputable day-care centers, call departments of social services, child welfare offices, schools, the YMCA and YWCA, or local organizations that serve as referral and coordinating centers for child care. Take a checklist along when inspecting the centers. Focus not only on the type of care the center offers, but also on the health and safety aspect of each facility.

Your checklist might include the following questions.

- ☐ **Is the center licensed?** Most states require licenses for both day-care centers and family day-care homes, public and private. Licensing requirements vary from state to state, but usually include an inspection for minimum state health and safety requirements. Call your local BBB to check out a day-care center.
- ☐ **Are there adequate facilities and equipment?** The center should be well-lighted, safe and in good repair. There should be adequate fire extinguishers and well-marked exits as well as smoke alarms. If there are windows on upper floors, they should be locked or made secure with screens or bars. Stairways should have handrails. All rooms, bathrooms in particular, should be clean and free of odors. There should be a variety of playthings in good condition, and there should be a well-equipped and well-maintained fenced play area outside.

- ☐ **Is the atmosphere pleasant?** Does the staff listen and respond easily to the children? Do the children seem content?
- ☐ **Is the staff responsible and knowledgeable?** Are they professionally trained? What is the attitude toward discipline and supervision?
- ☐ **Are activities constructive and stimulating?** A good day-care center should have a well-rounded program to give children various learning experiences, helping them develop physically, emotionally, socially and intellectually. Books, records, dolls and toys should help teach children about people different from themselves and about the possibilities open to them. Materials shouldn't cater to one ethnic group or to one concept of family life and male-female roles.
- ☐ **If meals are served, are they wholesome and nutritious?** Are kitchen and dining areas clean and pleasant?
- ☐ **Are charges reasonable?** What is covered in the basic fee? Are there extra charges, such as for transportation? Will parents have to pay on days that the child cannot attend? Parents should be sure each day-care facility explains its fees in full. Tax credit is given for the cost of child care in most cases, so parents also should be sure to obtain dated receipts for each payment they make.

Keep in mind that because children should be cared about and not just cared for, the best day-care centers may not necessarily be the most expensive.

Dishwashers

DISHWASHERS ARE AVAILABLE in many models — with a variety of special features at a wide range of prices. Some have special "energy-saver" controls; some have several special cycles for heavy scrubbing of cooking pots and casseroles plus a gentle cycle for fine china and stemware. It is certainly possible to pick and choose among features that fit individual family needs. The heavy-cleaning cycle is generally likely to be much more useful than the gentle cycle intended for fine china and stemware; such fragile items, which are expensive and/or impossible to replace, are safer washed by hand.

Remember: A major factor in the cost of routine dishwashing is the amount of hot water used. Sink washing does not automatically mean a saving of hot water. Actually, a full load of dishes in a dishwasher generally requires less hot water than the same quantity washed by hand.

You can cut the cost of using your dishwasher still further by eliminating the drying cycle — open the door after the dishes have been washed and rinsed and allow the dishes to air-dry.

Only operate the dishwasher for full loads. It is a waste of energy (and hot water as well) to operate the machine unless it is fully loaded.

When you buy, follow these guidelines:

☐ **Check available options carefully.** Buy the machine that provides only the cycles you really need.

☐ **Choose your dealer carefully.** If you are in doubt about his reputation, check his complaint record with your Better Business Bureau. Be careful of dealers who add to advertised low prices charges for installation and delivery.

☐ **Make the warranty part of your buying decision** — as you should do with any appliance purchase.

☐ **Make safety part of your buying decision.** If at all possible, have the machine demonstrated (by the service or installation technician, if not in the store), and make sure you are familiar with its operation *before* you use it.

☐ **Make sure you know how the interlock mechanism works.** Never risk the hazard of having the door open while the machine is in use.

☐ **Read your owner's manual carefully.** Follow the manufacturer's use and care instructions to the letter.

Door-to-Door Selling
(Direct Selling)

DOOR-TO-DOOR or direct-selling firms distribute their merchandise directly to their customers through sales representatives (usually independent businessmen and businesswomen paid on commission). Door-to-door sales include any transaction completed, according to the Federal Trade Commission, "at a place other than the place of business of the seller."

Firms engaging in direct selling may also have retail stores — the carpet, slipcover or upholstery salespersons representing local retailers are considered "direct" sales representatives.

The Direct Selling Association (DSA), a trade association of direct-selling firms, has about one hundred active members. However, DSA says it is "anybody's guess" as to the number of firms actually using direct-selling methods. In 1980 DSA's estimate of the market share occupied by direct-selling firms was about $8 billion, and an estimated four million sales representatives were operating in the field.

THE COOLING-OFF PERIOD
In 1974 the Federal Trade Commission established the "Cooling-Off Period" Trade Regulation Rule, which sets minimum standards for a three-day cooling-off period for door-to-door sales to consumers involving transactions of $25.00 or more. It applies to sales made in your home and to sales made anywhere other than the seller's normal place of business. (It does not, however, apply to sales made at the seller's place of business, sales made totally by mail or phone, sales under $25, sales of real estate, insurance or securities, or emergency home repairs.)

The ruling stipulates that sales representatives must furnish their customers with a fully completed receipt or copy of any contract in whatever language was used in the sales presentation. (If the sale was made in Spanish or Italian, for example, the receipt must be in the same language.) Furthermore, this receipt must contain:

- ☐ the date of the transaction;
- ☐ the name and address of the seller;
- ☐ the following statement in 10-point type:

> YOU, THE BUYER, MAY CANCEL THIS TRANSACTION AT ANY TIME PRIOR TO MIDNIGHT OF THE THIRD BUSINESS DAY AFTER THE DATE OF THIS TRANSACTION. SEE THE ATTACHED NOTICE OF CANCELLATION FORM FOR AN EXPLANATION OF THIS RIGHT.

DOOR-TO-DOOR SELLING (DIRECT SELLING)

In addition to the receipt or contract, the salesperson must also supply two copies of a completed form attached to and easily detachable from the contract or receipt, as follows:

NOTICE OF CANCELLATION

Date _____

YOU MAY CANCEL THIS TRANSACTION, WITHOUT ANY PENALTY OR OBLIGATION, WITHIN THREE BUSINESS DAYS FROM THE ABOVE DATE.

IF YOU CANCEL, ANY PROPERTY TRADED IN, ANY PAYMENTS MADE BY YOU UNDER THE CONTRACT OR SALE, AND ANY NEGOTIABLE INSTRUMENT EXECUTED BY YOU WILL BE RETURNED WITHIN 10 BUSINESS DAYS FOLLOWING RECEIPT BY THE SELLER OF YOUR CANCELLATION NOTICE, AND ANY SECURITY INTEREST ARISING OUT OF THE TRANSACTION WILL BE CANCELED.

IF YOU CANCEL, YOU MUST MAKE AVAILABLE TO THE SELLER AT YOUR RESIDENCE, IN SUBSTANTIALLY AS GOOD CONDITION AS WHEN RECEIVED, ANY GOODS DELIVERED TO YOU UNDER THIS CONTRACT OR SALE; OR YOU MAY, IF YOU WISH, COMPLY WITH THE INSTRUCTIONS OF THE SELLER REGARDING THE RETURN SHIPMENT OF THE GOODS AT THE SELLER'S EXPENSE AND RISK.

IF YOU DO MAKE THE GOODS AVAILABLE TO THE SELLER AND THE SELLER DOES NOT PICK THEM UP WITHIN 20 DAYS OF THE DATE OF YOUR NOTICE OF CANCELLATION, YOU MAY RETAIN OR DISPOSE OF THE GOODS WITHOUT ANY FURTHER OBLIGATION. IF YOU FAIL TO MAKE THE GOODS AVAILABLE TO THE SELLER, OR IF YOU AGREE TO RETURN THE GOODS TO THE SELLER AND FAIL TO DO SO, THEN YOU REMAIN LIABLE FOR PERFORMANCE UNDER THE CONTRACT.

TO CANCEL THIS TRANSACTION, MAIL OR DELIVER A SIGNED AND DATED COPY OF THIS CANCELLATION NOTICE OR ANY OTHER WRITTEN NOTICE, OR SEND A TELEGRAM, TO __(Name of seller)__ AT __(Seller's place of business)__ NOT LATER THAN MIDNIGHT OF __(Date)__.

I HEREBY CANCEL THIS TRANSACTION.

(Date) _____

_____
(Buyer's signature)

The salesperson must also provide an oral explanation or your right to cancel. He or she is not allowed to ask you to waive this right. Don't be misled into thinking that in order to buy something you really want (or think you want at the time) you have to give up your right to cancel the contract within three business days.

It is interesting and important to note that in many cases state laws have preceded the FTC rule. The function of the FTC provision is to assure every consumer in the United States the same minimum rights in dealing with door-to-door salespersons operating in interstate commerce.

The FTC rule does not, however, preempt state or municipal laws that provide greater protection to the buyer. If your state law provides for a *four*-day cooling-off period, then cancellation notices provided by door-to-door and direct salespersons should carry this information. State law may also provide, for example, that companies involved in telephone solicitation sales must provide written agreements, notice of cancellation rights, etc.

No recommendation is made by the FTC on the method buyers should use to return that all-important cancellation notice to the seller, except that you should "mail or deliver" the notice, or "send a telegram" to the seller. Better Business Bureaus suggest that, for your own protection, you use certified mail (return receipt requested) or a telegram. Either way, your date of cancellation is recorded, as is the date of its receipt by the seller.

Exceptions to the cooling-off rule — transactions *not* covered by the FTC regulation — **include:**

1. Merchandise purchased in a retail store to be delivered to your home.
2. Purchases covered by the Truth-in-Lending Act (the Consumer Credit Protection Act — see CREDIT AND INSTALLMENT BUYING) where the cooling-off period is spelled out for purchases involving a lien or mortgage on your home.
3. Purchases made to "meet a *bona fide* immediate personal emergency of the buyer." (This *"bona fide* personal emergency" might include a malfunctioning furnace in ten-below weather or a leaking water heater which is filling the basement with water. In this case, the merchandise — a part for the furnace or a replacement for the water heater — would be purchased in your home, but you would have called for immediate delivery and installation. Further, the seller may ask you to provide a personal statement in your own handwriting dated and signed by you, describing the situation that requires an immediate remedy and expressly waiving the right to cancel your purchase.)
4. Mail and phone orders that exclude any other contact between the buyer and the seller before the merchandise is delivered (no salesperson has appeared at your house).
5. Purchases made when the buyer has called for them and specifically

asked the seller to visit his home for the purpose of repairing or performing maintenance upon the buyer's personal property (painting the house or repairing the television set would qualify here). However, if additional merchandise is sold to you in the course of such a visit (the painter suggests you need new storm windows or the television repairman sells you an antenna), then the three-day cooling-off right does apply. In this case you would have the right to change your mind about a purchase of materials unrelated to the parts or supplies needed for maintenance or repair of your property.
6. Purchases covered by other regulatory agencies — the sale or rental of real property, the sale of insurance, or the sale of securities or commodities by a broker-dealer registered with the Securities and Exchange Commission.

A wide variety of products and services are sold from door to door or through party plans or sales meetings held in local hotels and motels. These include home improvements (a new roof for the house, surfacing for the driveway, etc), encyclopedias, carpets, cookware, cosmetics, magazine subscriptions, family photographs and vacuum cleaners. Correspondence courses and vocational school courses are also frequently sold through direct-sales methods. Whatever the product or service, it is important that consumers keep in mind the fact that the three-day cooling-off period regulation applies to all these sales.

HOW TO DEAL WITH DOOR-TO-DOOR SALESPERSONS
According to the Federal Trade Commission, consumer complaints on tactics used by some door-to-door salespersons tend to fall into the following five categories:

- ☐ Deceptions used to get into the house ("I'm taking a survey" or "You have been selected to receive a free gift");
- ☐ High-pressure sales tactics ("The price goes up tomorrow" or "Your roof is in really bad condition");
- ☐ Misrepresentation of the quality, price or characteristics of the product;
- ☐ Charging of high prices for low-quality merchandise;
- ☐ The general nuisance created by uninvited salespersons.

Any problems with door-to-door sales representatives who use deceptive or misleading tactics to gain access to your home, who misrepresent their products or, having made a sale, fail to comply with the FTC's requirements for notification of the three-day cooling-off period should be reported to your local Better Business Bureau, the state or municipal consumer protection agency, or directly to the Bureau of Consumer Protection, •Federal Trade Commission, Washington, D.C. 20580.

Use these guidelines for dealing with door-to-door salespersons:

- ☐ Your first and best defense, when you have no interest in the product being sold, is your refusal to let the salesperson take your time.
- ☐ Demand identification. If in doubt about the company a person represents, check with your local Better Business Bureau *before* you let the person in.
- ☐ Reputable business people do not use high-pressure sales tactics. Never buy in haste, especially from a home-improvement contractor who "just happens to be in the neighborhood" or from a salesperson who says the price will be higher tomorrow.
- ☐ Never sign an order for anything just to get rid of an aggressive salesperson.
- ☐ Never sign an order for merchandise until you have had an opportunity to read it thoroughly.
- ☐ Never sign a sales contract that contains blank spaces, and make sure the company hasn't pre-dated the day of the transaction on your receipt.
- ☐ Take time for full consideration of a product or service before you buy. Even though the three-day cooling-off period protects you against occasional bad judgment, it's smarter to take time to compare prices and compare merchandise and services before entering into any sales contract. Tell the salesperson to come back tomorrow or next week. Your time and your money are at stake. Reputable firms will allow time for reasonable buying decisions.

Drugs, Nonprescription

(See also COSMETICS; DRUGS, PRESCRIPTIONS; HEALTH AND MEDICINE)

HEADACHES . . . insomnia . . . an achy cold . . . upset stomach . . . constipation . . . acne . . . muscle pains . . . bad breath — an amazing array of symptoms, it seems, can be alleviated (notice that "cures" are rarely claimed) by over-the-counter (OTC) remedies available everywhere.

OTC remedies (nonprescription drugs, proprietary drugs) are self-medications intended to relieve symptoms of temporary minor illnesses. They do not prevent or cure illness or infections. They are not substitutes for professional medical diagnosis and treatment. And there is a good reason for that familiar phrase on the labels of such products, *If condition persists see your doctor.* When headaches occur and recur, when gargling with some antiseptic solution fails to dispose of the ache in the throat, when a drugstore-purchased lotion can't make a skin rash disappear, medical help — not another brand of OTC — is called for.

Manufacturers of nonprescription drugs are required to provide important information on the labels of their products. This information should be read and understood by anyone who purchases and uses such a medication. Labels will tell you:

☐ the name of the product;
☐ the name and address of the manufacturer or distributor;
☐ the net contents of the package (e.g., 100 5-grain tablets, 6 fluid ounces, etc.);
☐ complete directions for use, including:
— the purpose or purposes for which the medication is intended;
— how much to take;
— how often to take it;
— when not to take it;
☐ identification of the active ingredients;
☐ warnings, when necessary, against misuse of the product; and
☐ storage instructions, when necessary.

A warning you may not find on the label
Never take several OTC drugs simultaneously (or in combination) with prescription drugs without consulting your doctor. Each medication taken individually may be perfectly safe, but several together may produce a chemical reaction which creates problems.

GETTING MORE FOR YOUR MONEY

Wise consumers will pay special attention to dosage instructions and warnings against misuse of the product.

Dosage instructions on the aspirin label are explicit:

ADULT DOSE: 1 or 2 tablets with water every 4 hours, as necessary, up to 12 tablets a day.
CHILDREN, 10 to 15 years, 1 tablet.
CHILDREN, 5 to 10 years, ½ tablet.
CHILDREN, 3 to 5 years, ¼ tablet.
CHILDREN, under 3 years, consult your physician.

The warning is equally clear:

WARNING: Keep this and *all* medicines out of children's reach. In case of accidental overdose, consult a physician immediately.

Warning labels on other over-the-counter medications advise:

Do not apply to broken skin . . .

If redness, irritation, swelling or pain persists or increases or if infection occurs, discontinue use and consult a physician. Should not be used for more than ten days except on advice or supervision of a physician . . .

Do not drive or operate machinery while taking this medication . . .

If rapid pulse, dizziness or blurring of vision occurs, discontinue . . .

Do not exceed recommended dosage . . .

CAUTION: Do not take any laxative when abdominal pain, nausea or vomiting are present. Frequent or prolonged use of this or any other laxative may result in dependence on laxatives. If skin rash appears, do not use this or any other preparation containing phenolphthalein.

If some of these cautionary messages give you pause, and if some of them are new to you, you may not have been reading the labels on the products in your medicine chest with sufficient care. It might be a good idea to review the warnings on all the medications you keep in the house. Then, if you are in doubt about some of the side effects you have been warned to watch for, check with the family doctor before you use the medication again.

Drug containers. Prescription *and* nonprescription drugs come in packages designed to preserve the strength of the product. Always keep a product in its original container. Changing the container may cause the medication to become ineffective or unsafe.

> **Childproof containers** for OTC drugs, required by the Poison Prevention Packaging Act, seem to be effective. Accidental ingestion of aspirin has declined some 20 percent since the hard-to-open packages appeared on the market.
>
> These same well-designed, child-resistant caps can also be adultproof and annoying to people who have no children to be protected by this special packaging. If you live in an all-adult household, you will be interested to know that the Poison Prevention Packaging Act allows manufacturers to market containers with easy-to-open tops. This exception was made for the benefit of the elderly or handicapped consumers, but it is equally beneficial to young, healthy, unmechanical purchasers. If the easy-to-open containers are not available in your drugstore, you still have an alternative to a wrestling match with a recalcitrant aspirin bottle: ask the pharmacist to transfer the medication to a conventional container.

COMMON NONPRESCRIPTION DRUGS

Aspirin is the most common and most consistently used OTC drug (see HEALTH AND MEDICINE). It works, and for most people it is safe in the recommended dosages. (Consumers who are allergic to aspirin should follow their doctor's advice on substitute products.) It is a safe, effective analgesic (pain-killer), useful for headaches, rheumatic pain and aching muscles. It lowers fever and the pain that accompanies colds and flu.

Although there are differences, it is essentially a standardized product and off-brands are usually less expensive. However, some off-brands with a distinct vinegary smell have been on the shelf too long and should not be used.

The largest quantity is not necessarily the best buy. Choose the amount you are likely to use within a two- or three-month period. Moisture and heat can cause chemical decomposition of the tablets, which in turn reduces the effectiveness of the medication and makes it more likely to irritate the stomach.

Acne treatments. Whether these are advertised as cosmetics or as OTC remedies, they certainly will not effect a "cure" and they are not likely to relieve the symptoms. Acne is not fundamentally a cosmetic problem. It is caused by a hormonal imbalance that occurs during puberty in both men and women. Skin problems caused by this hormone imbalance may occur more frequently for women going on or off the Pill, during pregnancy, after childbirth and, perhaps, during menopause.

See a dermatologist for help with skin problems. Medical aid is a *must* here.

Cold remedies. Colds are caused by viruses. They are not caused by wet feet, cold weather or too much time at the beach. Most Americans have two or three colds each year, each of which lasts from three to five days. Antihistamines do not shorten their duration, nor are colds prevented by vitamin C.

The standard medical advice for treatment of the common cold is to use aspirin to reduce the fever and the aches, stay in bed, drink liquids and eat a light, well-balanced diet. As for nose drops or nasal sprays, use them if you must but not more than two or three times a day. Get your doctor's advice on what kind to use.

Sleep-aid drugs sold without prescription — the widely available OTC variety — may not always be effective in the recommended dosages and can be hazardous if directions for their use are not followed. The same basic ingredients are used in a variety of different OTC products sold as sleep aids. They are methapyrilene (an antihistamine) and scopolamine. Both ingredients have very mild sedative properties — and can cause serious ill effects if the recommended dosage is increased.

Some general guidelines
No one — least of all your doctor — would insist that you call for help any time you catch cold or have a mild headache or an upset stomach. Aspirin, rest, perhaps some bicarbonate of soda for the latter should help. But any time symptoms persist, it's important to find out why and to cure the problem — by way of professional diagnosis and treatment.

And remember:

- Never take a drug, OTC or prescription, unless you need it. Frequent use of drugs or nonprescription remedies can render medication less effective when you really need it. This includes the small quantities of hormones and antibiotics used in some cosmetics and OTC preparations.
- Read the labels. Follow the instructions for dosage and recommended use. Pay close attention to the WARNING section of the label. Leaflets enclosed with OTC products are part of the labeling. Read them. Don't discard them.
- Date medications when you buy them. Old OTC products — as well as old prescriptions and cosmetics — can deteriorate, lose their effectiveness or become dangerous. Clean out the medicine cabinet every six months or so. Flush discarded drugs down the toilet and discard the containers.
- Don't overbuy. If you rarely take aspirin — or any other OTC product — buy a small quantity.
- Never combine several drugs, whether they are OTC or prescription drugs, without telling your doctor the full range of medications you are taking.
- Don't mix alcohol with any type of drug, especially antihistamines, tranquilizers or sleeping pills. This can be a deadly combination. Alcohol also cancels out the effect of some prescription antibiotics. Check with your doctor.

Drugs, Prescription

(See also DRUGS, NONPRESCRIPTION; HEALTH AND MEDICINE)

PRESCRIPTION DRUG prices have become a consumer issue in recent years. More people are needing regular medication for chronic ailments of "old age," as the median age of our population continues to rise. In addition, medical research has found drugs for conditions previously untreated or treated less effectively.

It's no secret that drug prices vary widely, even within a given city. One government study showed a price difference of $16.50 to $2.95 for one drug. Comparison shopping for drugs is therefore very important. Be sure to ask for price information before buying the drug that has been prescribed for you.

In 1976 the Supreme Court resolved a legal debate that had lasted more than two years when it ruled that *no state may prohibit pharmacists from advertising the prices of prescription drugs.*

Competitive pricing of prescription drugs is becoming more and more frequent. In many states it is now possible, and indeed mandatory, to find comparative pricing of the most popular ethical drugs wherever they are sold. If they are not posted, you have every right to demand the store's pricing schedule before you decide.

GENERIC VS. BRAND NAME DRUGS

What does it mean when your doctor writes a prescription for a "generic" rather than a "brand name" drug? "Generic" refers to the scientific name given to a drug; "brand name" is the name chosen by the company that distributes the drug. One drug may have several brand names.

Buying a drug by its generic name rather than brand name may mean a substantial saving to the consumer. Yet, some critics of this idea, including pharmaceutical companies and some physicians, say that generic drugs can be just as costly as brand-name drugs.

It is possible that the same drug may vary in quality from one manufacturer to another. Also, say advocates of brand names, even though two drugs are chemically equivalent, containing the same amounts of the same active ingredients, they may not be therapeutically equivalent. Because of *inactive* ingredients, it can be argued, all generic drugs are not equally effective.

A drug's therapeutic equivalence is measured by its "bioavailability," the amount of the product's active ingredient that is absorbed into the bloodstream to perform its function. Critics of generic labeling claim that buying a drug under a generic name is risky, because that drug may differ in bioavailability from one manufacturer to another.

In addition to the comparisons of brand-name drugs and generics, there are great variations in the costs of the exact same brand-name drugs from store to store. The fluctuations can be significant, so it is worthwhile to check the costs at your local drug store, and then check others in the community, to get the best buy. (To be fair to the pharmacists, it must be noted that prices can vary enormously not only from store to store, but from brand to brand of the same medicine. Drug pricing is a labyrinth, affected by a wide range of economic and merchandising factors.)

Because the price is not the only reason for choosing to deal with one retailer instead of another, you might choose to stay with the pharmacist you have dealt with for years. His prices may be higher because he provides services you need or want, such as 24-hour service, delivery, charge accounts, etc. Perhaps you like his around-the-corner convenience or the atmosphere of the store. The point is: *With price information available to you, you can make an informed choice between pharmacies. You would be aware that you are paying for additional services which may or may not be available from stores at the lowest end of the price range. In these circumstances, your choice is free.*

On the other hand, choices made without adequate knowledge of available alternatives are not informed.

PHYSICIANS, PRESCRIPTIONS, PHARMACISTS AND HEALTH

In 1910, the ten most important drugs in medical practice were ether, morphine, digitalis, diphtheria antitoxin, smallpox vaccine, iron, quinine, iodine, alcohol and mercury.

In little more than half a century, the development of the chemical treatment of disease progressed with incredible speed. Now doctors are faced with more than four hundred "new" drugs (some are only minor variations on old themes) that enter the market each year.

You can still save money on prescriptions. Here are a few tips:

☐ Ask your doctor if the prescription should be generic rather than by trade name.
☐ Let your doctor know of your interest in price comparisons for the medication you must use. It is true that advertising directed to doctors does not include price information, but there is no reason why your doctor shouldn't assist in your search for the full range of consumer information you need. And there is certainly no reason that doctors should not be aware of the comparative costs of the medication they prescribe.

☐ If you must continue medication with a specific drug for a long period of time, talk with your doctor about prescribing it in large amounts. Like all other products, the "large economy size" may save you money.
☐ Find out from the pharmacist whether temperature and humidity changes can affect the medication. Ask for advice on storage. And *always* keep prescription drugs — in small or large quantities — out of the reach of children, preferably in a locked storage area.

Dry Cleaning

(See also CLOTHING)

DRY CLEANING IS A crucial element in the proper care and maintenance of a wide variety of garments, and as such it should be taken into account in the clothing budget. Maintenance of clothing, especially in this era of rising prices, is no small item, but it protects an even larger investment in garments that are likely to be the most expensive in any family's wardrobe. Your own knowledge of dry cleaning can bring you more value for your clothing dollar.

Shopping for new clothing can be fun when you're doing it, when it's associated with special occasions and great expectations . . . but it may bring frustration *later*, if you are so absorbed in selecting just the right outfit or in meeting your budget that you forget maintenance costs.

The time to think about dry cleaning a garment is when you buy it.

LABELS
Look for the care label required by the Federal Trade Commission. When the label says "Dry Clean Only" follow the instructions. Sometimes garments that are both washable and dry-cleanable have only washing instructions on their labels, but keep in mind the fact that most washable items can also be dry cleaned and that dry cleaning can often remove soil and stains that washing does not affect, such as oil-based stains on synthetic fabrics.

Beware of contradictory labels. Imagine buying and wearing a garment whose two sets of instructions caution you against dry cleaning for one part of the garment and washing for the other. This has happened — resulting in consumer complaints and frustrations — when incompatible fabrics are used in the same garment. Look for special instructions on dress and suit linings or, for example, on wool coats with leather trim.

FABRICS
Technology has greatly increased the range of fabrics, textures and colors of natural and man-made fabrics (see CLOTHING). Manufacturers have improved permanent press materials, pile fabrics, bonded fabrics,

double knits and fun/fake furs so that they are durable, cleanable, and present few problems to dry cleaners — as long as they are accurately labeled with clear care instructions. Nevertheless, there is much the consumer should know about the cleanability of fabrics.

- ☐ Many **luxurious fabrics** lack durability and should be purchased only if the consumer is aware of their limitations. These include cashmere, camel hair and lightweight, loosely woven wools, which have a tendency to snag and sag.
- ☐ **Suede and leather garments** must have special processing to preserve the finish, feel and color. Suede, which has a tendency to fade, spot and develop uneven color, should be handled only by cleaners equipped to cope with this fragile leather.
- ☐ **Imitation suede and leather,** though much improved, are still often accepted for dry cleaning only at the owner's risk. Imitation products often become stiff when dry cleaned.
- ☐ Take special care with **fake furs.** For example, some types of imitation Persian lamb disintegrate in the cleaning process if the furry fabric is attached to its cloth background with an adhesive that may dissolve in the cleaning solvent. When the "fur" is sewn into the backing material, however, the garment usually dry cleans successfully.
- ☐ **Bonded fabrics** may disappoint you. Consumer complaints cite cases of partial or complete separation of the face from the lining fabric and of shrinking, puckering, stiffening and adhesive staining.
- ☐ **Polyester knits** often lack the stability of woven fabrics and are susceptible to shrinkage and snagging. **Acrylics** often stretch if they are steamed.

COLOR

There is no way to judge the color stability of a fabric by looking at it. Read care labels carefully and follow cleaning instructions. If the fabric fades in spite of your careful handling, *complain.*
Remember:

- ☐ Colors are either applied as dyes, which are absorbed by the fibers of the fabric, or they are printed onto the surface of the fabric. Usually both processes produce "fast" (nonfading) colors. However, some colors will fade in water and not in dry-cleaning solvent; some will fade in dry-cleaning solvent but not in water; others may be unstable in both water and solvent.
- ☐ **Gilt prints** and some **pigment prints** are only skin deep, held to the fabric with an adhesive, so that loss of color through dry cleaning means loss of design. **Embossed designs** may also be fragile if they are pressed into the fabric; and they may become less distinct with wear and cleaning.

□ **"Fume fading"** is a complex color change that occurs when certain types of dyes in some acetate and wool materials are subjected to combustion gases commonly present in the air of most homes. When this happens, the fabric becomes streaked or changes color. Fume fading is not caused by dry cleaning, but the color change sometimes becomes more apparent after an item has been dry cleaned. Solution-dyed acetate fabrics do not fade in this fashion.

DECORATIONS

Buttons, beads, sequins and other decorations can be troublesome. Keep the following hints in mind:

- □ Buttons or trim made of polystyrene tend to melt in dry-cleaning solvents.
- □ Belts and other items that have cardboard-type stiffeners or adhesives need special attention.
- □ Beads or sequins may be covered with a thin coat of paint or a shellac, which may come off during wear or cleaning. Beads or sequins on a continuous thread may all come off if the thread is broken. Even worse, the coating may dissolve and leave indelible marks on an otherwise wearable garment.

AT THE CLEANER'S

When you take a garment to be cleaned, be sure to notify the cleaner of any special problem spots or potential stains. Stains caused by beverages containing sugar, for example, may not show up until the sugar is caramelized (heated). *Don't expect your dry cleaner to be a magician. The longer a stain is allowed to set, the harder it will be for the dry cleaner to remove it.*

Care labels are intended to be permanent — don't remove them. They are helpful to you and to the cleaner as well. For example, acrylic knits are easily confused with other fibers and are likely to stretch when they are heated in the cleaning and finishing process; if you know an article contains this fiber, notify the cleaner so that he can take action to avoid the problem.

Knits that shrink can be stretched back to size and reshaped if you ask for this service.

Sizing, applied to fabrics during the manufacturing process to give the finished garment added shape or body, may be removed during one or more cleanings. This is also true of water-resistant and spot-resistant finishes. The cleaner can restore sizing and special finishes.

Some wool and synthetic blends in suits and dresses "pill" — that is, they develop tiny woolly balls on the surface of the fabric due to rubbing. Cleaning may increase the problem. Sometimes the cleaner can remove pilling.

Fluorescent brighteners used by garment makers to make colors brighter or whites whiter may become dull or yellowed after continued wearing or exposure to sunlight. Often the owner is not aware of this until a good cleaning removes the soil that may have masked the condition.

Coin-operated dry-cleaning machines can give you satisfactory results on bulk loads — often at considerable savings. Follow the same general rules you use when you do the laundry at home:

- ☐ Clean light-colored fabrics separately from dark ones.
- ☐ Clean fragile clothing separately from heavy clothing.
- ☐ Remove lint from the surface of the fabric and from cuffs and pockets.
- ☐ Check pockets for lipsticks, fountain pens, matches and other articles that might create stains.
- ☐ Read and follow the machine-operating instructions carefully.
- ☐ Never overload the machine.

Remove garments from the machine immediately after the cleaning cycle is complete. Hang them quickly to prevent wrinkling. If cleaning solvent odor clings to the clothes, hang them in the open air or in a well-ventilated room until they are thoroughly dried.

Employment

(See also CONTRACTS)

EMPLOYMENT AGENCIES ARE service companies that charge for services they provide to client companies and to individuals.
  For employers, they:

- interview and screen applicants;
- fill the personnel needs of client companies on a regular basis;
- maintain contact with prospective employers to obtain listings of job openings.

For job-seekers, they:

- provide counseling on preparation of resumés and preparation for interviews;
- provide specific details regarding job openings and information on the employing company;
- schedule personal interviews with employers and, if asked to do so, submit resumés to client firms;
- search for positions to suit the particular needs of the applicants they are most qualified to help.

"Fee paid by the employer..." should mean exactly what it says: that the employer has agreed to pay the entire agency fee and there will be no fee whatsoever to the applicant if he fulfills the conditions of the contract by accepting and keeping the job. The conditions may change and the applicant may be required to pay a fee if:

- The applicant accepts a "fee paid" job and does not report to work, or if he is discharged for cause or leaves of his own accord. (Remember that circumstances beyond your control could make it necessary to "leave of your own accord." Find out whether you are obligated to pay the agency fee if you get sick, if you must leave town, or if family obligations make it impossible to stay with the job.)
- The applicant is offered another job, unlisted with the agency, for which no agreement has been made for the employer's payment of the fee. Before you accept the offer, clarify the fee obligation with the employer and the agency.

> **Fee paid**
> Complaints concerning employment agencies often involve terms of the contract, particularly the amount of the fee to be paid to the agency. These occur because of a job seeker's failure to read and understand the terms of the agreement — or because of failure on the part of the agency representative to explain the agreement.
> Standard advice on contracts applies here: *Never sign a contract you don't understand.* If you have questions about any terms of the contract, make sure they are answered before you sign. If any oral promises are made — for example, granting extra time for the payment of the fee — have them written into the contract and initialed by the agency representative.
> Get and keep a copy of any agreement you sign.

Use these general guidelines:
- State law governs employment agencies; you may want to check.
- Use an employment agency only if you are fully aware of and able to meet the terms of the contract governing fees.
- Accept a job only after careful consideration, so you are sure you want it. An acceptance automatically obligates you to pay the agency fee.
- If you find out that an agency has sent you to a firm that has not requested applicants or listed an opening with the agency, get yourself another agency.
- If the agency wishes to distribute your resumés to potential employers, inform the agency of any restrictions you wish observed as to the firms to whom the resumés may be sent.

If you are in doubt as to the reputation and/or competence of an employment agency, check with your local Better Business Bureau before you sign a contract obligating you to pay for its services. If you have a complaint — if you feel that an agency has been less than fair to you —put your complaint in writing and send it to the Better Business Bureau.

PUBLIC EMPLOYMENT SERVICES

There are alternatives to using a private employment agency, in addition to setting up your own at-home system of distributing resumés. State and local employment services can be helpful. And there is no fee to employer or applicant.

Public employment services often list a wide range of jobs, skilled and unskilled. They may have vacancies for domestic or seasonal farm labor as well as clerical and administrative jobs in public agencies and in business. Serious job hunters should keep these employment sources in mind:

- **Federal civil service:** Examinations are given periodically in many employment areas. Information on vacancies and examinations will be available at the nearest post office.
- **State employment:** Examinations for merit employment are often required for state jobs. Information will be available from the State Department of Personnel, the State Department of Labor, etc., in your state capital or from the local office of the State Employment Service.

These state-supported employment services may be able to provide many of the services of a private employment agency — job counseling, assistance with preparation of the resumé and advice on handling the all-important interview. Services may vary from state to state. You owe it to yourself to check them out.

EXECUTIVE CAREER COUNSELING

Economic changes in the mid-1970s resulted in a dramatic increase in the number of executive-level job seekers. Some executives use the services of public and/or private employment agencies; others turn to career-counseling firms for assistance. Better Business Bureaus around the country have found that inquiries concerning such career counselors have increased dramatically. They have also found that the firms and their services vary widely.

Before enlisting the aid of any counseling firm, executive job seekers should look beneath the label to find out what services are being offered, keeping in mind the fact that the name or self-description of the firm may not define the nature of its services. Sometimes the promotional material of such firms is ambiguous.

A few words of caution for job-hunting executives

Local Better Business Bureaus report that executive complaints have frequently alleged that they did not receive the services promised. For this reason, *it is important that these services be clearly defined.*

Executive clients should demand unmistakable evidence of results produced for other clients:

- Ask to see materials prepared for other clients with similar backgrounds.
- Ask for references from clients.
- Get a clear explanation in writing of what the firm will and won't do, what the costs will be, and what period of time is covered by the contract.

Executive counseling firms are *not* employment agencies. They are usually not in a position to guarantee employment, *and the fees charged are not contingent on employment.* Instead, the fee is charged for specific services such as preparation of the resumé and advice on handling interviews. *The client executive should insist that all details, including the fee, be spelled out clearly in writing. It is a good idea for the client to have the contract checked by a lawyer before it is signed.*

Protect yourself. Be suspicious of executive job-counseling firms who, for a substantial fee, promise much, do little and guarantee nothing. You may find that you have bought nothing more than expensive clerical service to do something that you could have done yourself or hired someone else to do for far less money.

Among the abuses uncovered by Better Business Bureaus are high-pressure sales tactics and overpriced aptitude "tests" and letter-writing services. Beware of firms that claim to represent employers and yet want to charge you a fee ranging from hundreds to several thousands of dollars to prepare your resumé and conduct a compaign for you.

Executives investigating career-counseling services would be wise to consider the following:

- ☐ What obligations are being incurred?
- ☐ How long has the firm been in business?
- ☐ How competent is the staff? Who are they and what are their qualifications?
- ☐ What is their record of success? Ask to see a list of satisfied clients who have been placed successfully.
- ☐ What is the service period covered by the contract? What provisions for refund are included?

The contract should cover all aspects of the agreement. Make sure all oral promises also appear in writing (see CONTRACTS).

If you are at all in doubt, don't hesitate to call your Better Business Bureau for a report on the firm.

EXECUTIVE SEARCH FIRMS

Executive search firms are not, properly speaking, employment agencies. They work for and are paid by client companies to identify and appraise executives qualified to fill specific positions. Their fees are paid by the companies that retain them.

Now a highly specialized area of the management-consulting profession, "executive searching" (or "recruiting") was once one of the services rendered by general management-consulting firms. (Management-consulting firms are retained by companies, institutions and government agencies to undertake particular studies and provide assistance with management and operating problems.) Executive search has experienced rapid growth since the end of World War II, both in the United States and abroad. There are hundreds of consultants, most of whom refer to themselves as "firms" that handle executive search either as a specialty or in conjunction with other forms of consulting services.

While these firms are willing to receive resumés from executive job hunters, they are usually not in a position to help executives find jobs.

If you decide to contact an executive recruiter, start with providing a detailed and carefully prepared resumé. The recruiter may have a number of jobs he is trying to fill and you may hear from him if your background reflects the requirements of one of the positions. Or he may file your resumé for future reference.

Whether you contact a recruiter or he contacts you, the procedure is the same. If you are considered qualified for a position, the executive recruiter will invite you to his office for a preliminary interview.

If the preliminary interview is mutually satisfactory, the recruiter will provide you with detailed information about the position and the company.

As you approach the end of the selection procedure, the recruiter will wish to contact people for whom and with whom you have worked in the past. He may also wish to talk with people who have worked *for* you.

The final step is the introduction to the company represented by the recruiter. The intermediary role of the recruiter is not over at this point — he will be asked to discuss with the company representative the results of the direct interview and he will make additional calls for references if these are requested by the client. The recruiter also participates in final negotiations.

Some advice for the job-hunting executive
- ☐ Several self-analytical questions are in order. First, take stock of yourself — your interests, abilities, experience, education, salary requirements, your strong and weak points.
- ☐ Check out the employment picture. Find out where the opportunities are. Study the employment sections of the newspapers to get an idea of the trends. Learn what kind of experience and talents are in demand in the areas in which your interests and qualifications lie.
- ☐ You may want to consider undergoing a battery of tests as a guide to setting future goals and to help you understand (and perhaps re-evaluate) your capabilities. The names of qualified professional psychological testing services can be supplied by professional societies, universities and state agencies.

Encyclopedias

(See also CONTRACTS; DOOR-TO-DOOR SELLING)

ENCYCLOPEDIAS — educational reference books — can be a good foundation for a home library. At their best, they contain solid introductory and background information on people, places, things and ideas as well as study guides and bibliographies of additional sources of information.

They can also be oversold, with the result that they can involve the unwary consumer in a long-term monthly-payment contract for merchandise that fails to meet the needs of the family. Consumers who decide to make the heavy investment required for a set of encyclopedias should consider the long-term needs of everyone in the family who will use the books and base the buying decision on research rather than the sales presentation of a door-to-door representative. Sometimes it is wiser *not* to think too far ahead: an encyclopedia bought to "give your child everything he'll ever need" when the child is two years old will be about ten or twelve years out of date when he is ready to use it.

A good source for impartial ratings of reference books is a publication called *Encyclopedia Buying Guide* (R. R. Bowker Company) available in your local library. Ratings are based on reader age, suitability, price, readability and subject matter. Your librarian will also have access to the American Library Association's reviews of encyclopedias. Read the ratings and reviews and then form your own opinion of the reference books available by checking out the sets in the library.

Prices range widely — from under a hundred dollars for a series of reference books sold in a supermarket to five hundred dollars or more for those sold in your home by a sales representative. The price you choose to pay should be based on the needs of your family and your budget.

The following secondary considerations will affect the price you pay:

- ☐ The binding — plastic, cardboard or leather — and the paper quality.
- ☐ Yearbook service, usually available at an extra charge. Scientific, historical and technical articles do need updating from time to time, but the majority of information contained in most encyclopedias does not change significantly from year to year.
- ☐ Information services. Some publishers offer an information service that allows you to send in cards for additional reference materials on various subjects. They usually respond to such

requests with a bibliography, articles or other reference sources.

SALES METHODS

Before you invite an encyclopedia sales representative to your home, determine the kind of encyclopedia you want and the price range you can afford. If a salesperson arrives without your invitation, ask for identification (including the salesperson's name, and the name and address of the firm he or she represents). If in doubt, check with your local BBB.

Be wary of any representative who misrepresents the purpose of the visit and the nature of the product being sold. These sales methods are condemned by reputable direct-selling firms and should be reported to your local Better Business Bureau and/or consumer protection agency.

Misleading sales practices include gaining entry to your home by way of the "I'm-taking-a-survey" ploy or your being told that the encyclopedias are "free" with your subscription to the company's ten-year updating service.

Another misleading door opener is "You have been selected" to receive something special — perhaps the "free" encyclopedias — because of your position as leader in your community.

Question the sales representative closely on any statement that is not completely clear to you. A sales representative is normally a commissioned businessperson who is paid for every sale.

When you commit to buy

Check your sales contract carefully. Make sure that it contains all the salesperson's oral promises and that it includes:

- ☐ a list of each item you ordered, completely described;
- ☐ the delivery date for the books and any additional items;
- ☐ the total price you will be paying, including the finance charge, the annual percentage rate of the finance charge, the charges, if any, for "shipping and handling";
- ☐ your payment schedule, the length of the payment period — 12, 24 or 36 months — and the amount of each monthly payment;
- ☐ the procedure for cancelling the sale (see DOOR-TO-DOOR SELLING for details on the three-day "cooling-off-period") and how you make your decision to cancel known to the company.

Most important: Read and be sure you understand the contract before you sign. Never sign a contract containing blank spaces. Have the representative write "not applicable" on any lines that are irrelevant to your own transaction, then make sure you and the salesman initial the deletions to show that you have both agreed to any change or deletion in the standard contract.

Energy

ENERGY HAS BEEN THE basis of the labor-saving American life style. Though the United States has only one-seventeenth of the world's population, roughly one-third of the world's energy is consumed here. Once an insignificant item in family budgets, dramatically rising energy costs have now made conservation an economic necessity for many families. A little more than half your energy budget goes toward heating and cooling your home. Why not try to save fuel and money by devising a system of household energy "trade-offs"? Your "energy budget" can be balanced the same way family finances are balanced and allocated — by evaluating your energy "needs" as opposed to energy "wants." Weigh the value of the various energy eaters around your house, decide which ones are most important . . . and spend the energy budget accordingly.

HEATING AND COOLING SYSTEMS

As already mentioned, a little more than half the energy budget of most American families goes toward heating and cooling the home. Here are some seasonal conservation guidelines to keep in mind.

Cold weather conservation:

- ☐ Lower the thermostat to 60° to 65°F during the day and to 55° at night. Wear a sweater or use an extra blanket until you become accustomed to this new, more economical temperature. *If you keep the temperatures 6° lower than during last winter you should save about 15 percent in heating costs.*
- ☐ Have the furnace serviced each year in early fall. Proper service means more efficient operation and about a 10 percent decrease in fuel consumption. Keep air filters clean; check them every three or four weeks.
- ☐ Check heating ducts for leaks. Repair them with duct-sealing tape or with ordinary adhesive tape.
- ☐ Vacuum or dust radiator surfaces often.
- ☐ Use available heat from the sun. Keep drapes and shades open during the day. Close them against cold air at night.

Hot-weather conservation:

- ☐ Set the air conditioner thermostat at 80°. Consider restricting the use of air conditioners to the hottest days. On hot days set the fan speed of room air conditioners at *high*; in humid weather set it at *low* for less cooling and more moisture removal.

- Close drapes and shades in sunny windows. Close the windows and outside doors during the hottest time of the day to keep cooler air inside.
- In summer turn off the pilot light in your gas furnace (unless it also serves as your hot water heater).
- You might consider an attic fan as an alternative to an air conditioner. An attic fan will often do a sufficient cooling job and will save you money.

INSULATION — CONSERVATION FOR ALL SEASONS

Insulation is a good investment — and a relatively inexpensive one (see INSULATION). Initial cost will be offset by smaller heating and cooling bills.

Manufacturers rate insulation effectiveness in terms of "R" (resistance) value. The higher the "R" value, the better the material slows winter heat loss and summer heat gain. When buying, look for the "R" value on the package — do not be guided by thickness.

There is a point beyond which additional insulation is a waste of money. Generally, an adequately insulated home has these "R" values: ceilings R-19 to R-38; floors 0 to R-19; and walls R-11 to R-17. Yet, you may need higher or lower "R" values, depending on the climate where you live. Your local utility company may suggest the best "R" values for your house.

Consider these insulating measures:
- Install storm windows to lower your fuel bills (see STORM WINDOWS AND DOORS). The most convenient type are combination storm and screen windows, because you don't have to remove them in mild weather. If your home is air conditioned, leave them on in summer. Or you can tape clear plastic film to window frames and still get the effect of storm windows, at a fraction of the cost.
- Install insulation in your attic, because a lot of heat is lost there. A depth of six inches or more will cut costs considerably. Then consider the floors over unheated areas, and your walls.

HOT WATER

Next to heating and cooling your home, hot water accounts for the biggest share of the energy budget. To save:

- Keep the water heater thermostat set on *normal* — that's about 140°F. This is the most economical setting.
- Insulate the hot water tank and the water pipes.
- Wash clothes in warm or cold water and rinse them in cold. Always wash a full load, unless your washer has lower water-level settings for partial loads.
- Take showers instead of baths to save hot water.
- Repair any leaky faucets, especially when hot water is dripping. One drop per second wastes water at the rate of 700 gallons a year.

☐ Fill the dishwasher to capacity when you use it. Each load uses about 14 gallons of hot water. A half-full load drains your dollars needlessly. If you feel you have to rinse dishes before loading them, use cold water. To save even more, let your dishes air-dry after the final rinse — turn off the dishwasher and open the door.

Energy Labels on Appliances

In December 1975 Congress passed the Energy Policy and Conservation Act which replaced an existing voluntary appliance industry energy program with a mandatory government program. Its objectives are to encourage appliance manufacturers to produce more efficient home appliances, and encourage consumers to buy these more efficient appliances. The Appliance Energy Labeling Program, approved by the Federal Trade Commission in 1979, requires that appliance manufacturers provide labels containing energy information on their products. These labels started to appear on appliances in the summer of 1980.

Appliances and equipment covered by the labeling programs are: single door refrigerators, combination refrigerator-freezers, freezers, dishwashers, water heaters, clothes washers, air conditioners and furnaces. The following are not required to be labeled: portable space heaters, television sets, kitchen ranges and ovens, clothes dryers, humidifiers and dehumidifiers.

All labels have the same heading in large, black letters: "ENERGYGUIDE." Air conditioners and furnaces have an EER (energy efficiency ratio) rating (for a fuller discussion of energy efficiency ratings, see entries for specific products, e.g., APPLIANCES, AIR CONDITIONERS). The other appliances, which are not climate-control, are labeled with an estimated yearly operating cost. All labels have to show the lowest to highest range of operating cost of EER rating for a certain product class. Additionally, labels giving operating cost are required to have a cost/use format to help consumers determine their specific individual costs.

So when you shop for appliances, look for the labels that tell the EER rating (the higher the EER, the more efficient the appliance) or an estimate of what its use of energy will be over a specified time. Then compare these figures to those for other brands or models. Remember that you'll be paying the cost of operating an appliance over the years in addition to paying the amount on the price tag. Keep in mind, too, the long-term economy of buying energy-efficient equipment, even though the initial cost may be high.

COOKING

☐ Use pans that fully cover the heating element when cooking on

top of the range. Use pots with tight-fitting lids. More heat will enter the pot and less will escape to the surrounding air.
- ☐ Make the most of your oven heat. Try to plan all oven-cooked dishes for a meal, or fill the oven with extra foods that can be reheated for later use.
- ☐ Turn off the oven thirty minutes before roasts are done; enough heat will remain in the oven to finish the job.
- ☐ Don't open the oven door to check foods. Every time you do this you lose as much as a quarter of the heat.
- ☐ If the seals around the oven doors are not airtight, your money is being wasted. Replace the seals, if necessary, or adjust the latches. (The same advice holds for refrigerators.)

LAUNDRY
- ☐ Wash in warm or cold water. Fill the washer to capacity.
- ☐ Separate drying loads. Light items take less drying time and lower temperatures.
- ☐ Fill the dryer to capacity to avoid wasting heat.
- ☐ Don't dry clothes any longer than necessary.
- ☐ Clean the lint screen in the dryer after every load or two.

YOU CAN SAVE IN OTHER WAYS
- ☐ Lights left burning in unused rooms waste your money and unbalance your energy budget. Turn them off. To reduce electricity consumption further, remove one bulb out of three and, for safety, replace it with a burned-out bulb.
- ☐ Don't skimp on light for reading, study or work areas. Where plenty of good light is a necessity, one large bulb is more efficient to use than several smaller ones; a 100-watt bulb gives you more light than two 60-watt bulbs.
- ☐ Fluorescent lights are more efficient than incandescent lights. A 40-watt fluorescent bulb not only gives you more light than a 100-watt incandescent one, but it lasts ten times as long and uses less than half the energy as well.
- ☐ Use long-life incandescent bulbs only in places that are hard to reach — these bulbs give less light than ordinary bulbs of the same wattage.
- ☐ Dust light bulbs and fixtures regularly. Dirt absorbs light.
- ☐ Light colors for walls, rugs and other furnishings reduce the need for artificial lighting.
- ☐ Instant-on television sets use electricity even when you're not using them. Color sets use more energy than black and white.
- ☐ Save energy by turning off your television set when you're not watching it. Unplug the instant-on set when you are going to be away from home. (This is a good safety idea as well as an energy saver.) And when you're watching an old movie, why not use the black-and-white set?

- ☐ If you own a power lawn mower, you can save energy by cutting the motor when it is not in use. Don't let it idle for considerable periods of time.
- ☐ Make sure to turn off all power tools when they are not in use.

SWIMMING POOLS

- ☐ Try reducing filter operation time to between six and eight hours each day. Watch the water clarity to see if this amount of time is adequate. (Remember, though, that the filter should be running whenever the pool is used.) Clean the skimmer and pump strainer baskets frequently.
- ☐ If the pool is heated, operate the heater only when the pool is being used, allowing for a short warm-up time. Keep the thermostat no higher than 78°F.
- ☐ Use pool and patio lights for safety at night, but don't leave them on when the pool area isn't in use.

THE FAMILY CAR

Cars are a necessity for suburban and rural living. However, carpooling, public transportation, bicycling and walking do save energy and cut transportation costs.

When you do use the car, keep good gas-mileage practices in mind:

- ☐ Regular tune-ups will make your car run more efficiently.
- ☐ Check the tire pressure frequently; under-inflated tires are not only dangerous, but they cut gas mileage.
- ☐ Drive smoothly. Accelerate gradually and anticipate changes in the traffic ahead to avoid quick stops and starts. Don't ride the brakes.
- ☐ Drive at the most efficient, economical speed. Stay within the 55-mph speed limit.
- ☐ When you're waiting in your car, turn off the engine instead of letting it idle.

Once these energy-saving methods become ingrained habits in your family, household fuel consumption will decrease. This does not mean, however, that household energy expenses will decrease to the level of previous years, since utility rates continue to increase; but conservation practices, the purchase of the most efficient available appliances, and perhaps an increase in the use of person-power instead of electrical power will help keep growing energy costs within reasonable bounds.

Fire Protection Systems

(See also SAFETY)

EVERY YEAR ALMOST ten thousand persons in the United States die as a result of fires in their homes. Most of these deaths result from exposure to smoke rather than flames. And most of these fatal accidents occur in the late evening hours when most people are asleep.

Adding to the tragedy of these deaths is the fact that many of them are caused by carelessness and could be prevented. Consider these major causes of fatal residential fires:

Careless smoking — 56%
Faulty or improperly used heating systems — 13.8%
Faulty electrical wiring and equipment — 7.5%
Hazards caused by cooking stoves — 7%

Fire prevention is often a matter of carrying out a few simple precautionary measures to reduce or eliminate home fire hazards. General advice concerning your own home is available from the fire prevention unit of your local fire department. You can also contact the National Fire Protection Association, 470 Atlantic Avenue, Boston, Massachusetts 02210, for copies of their publications on the subject.

There are two basic types of fire detectors: **smoke detectors,** which sound an alarm at the first trace of smoke; and **heat detectors,** which sound an alarm to warn of an abnormally high temperature in the immediate area of the detector.

Smoke detectors. Presently there are two types of smoke detectors on the market, ionization and photoelectric. Smoke entering the area of an **ionization detector** impedes the flow of electric current, causing the alarm to go off. The ionization detector responds particularly well to fast-burning, almost smokeless fires, but is not as sensitive to visible, slow-rising smoke from a smoldering fire. Because this device requires very little current, it can be powered effectively by batteries and installed almost anywhere. Keep in mind, however, that batteries run down and must be replaced periodically.

Photoelectric detectors emit a beam of light that is scattered by smoke particles and then picked up by a light-sensitive photocell when a fire occurs. The typical photoelectric detector is relatively sensitive to smoke from smoldering fires, but reacts rather slowly to flaming fires. This device must be connected to an electrical outlet (AC powered) which limits its installation possibilities. Should a power failure occur, the photoelectric detector would be rendered inoperative.

Ionization and photoelectric smoke detectors can be equally effective in the home. When weighing the strengths and weaknesses of each, consider purchasing both types for maximum home safety. Their different sensitivities and characteristics will supplement each other. Smoke detectors should be installed outside each bedroom area and on each additional story of the house. For extra protection, be sure to install smoke detectors inside the bedrooms, dining room, furnace room, utility room and hallways. Heat detectors should be considered for added protection in kitchens, dining rooms, attics, basements, integral or attached garages, and furnace and utility rooms.

Without minimizing the very real concern each homeowner should have in regard to fire prevention, a warning note should be sounded. Homeowners should be wary of high-pressure, scare-selling tactics used by some salesmen of fire protection and detection systems.

If a door-to-door sales representative brands your house a firetrap and shows you pictures of death and destruction in residential fires in an attempt to induce you to install an expensive fire protection system, report him to your local Better Business Bureau and to local authorities as well. If you're concerned that your house may contain fire hazards, call on the fire-prevention unit of your local fire department for advice.

A second illegitimate sales method is used by the sales representative who offers to install the system "absolutely free" if you refer him to other homeowners who will buy the equipment. The notion that you get anything free for participating in a referral sales scheme is nonsense. More than likely, you will find yourself with no referrals and the obligation to pay the full price for an overpriced system.

SHOP FOR THE SELLER

If you are considering investing in a protection or detection system, get competitive bids from at least two companies. Find out whether the necessary maintenance of the equipment can and will be carried out by the firm that installed it, and under what conditions. Are there additional costs for maintenance?

Ask for references. Ask the firm selling the equipment for the names of former customers you can contact. If they refuse to provide references, refuse to do business with them.

FIRE EXTINGUISHERS

There are four basic types of fire extinguishers:

- ☐ **Type A,** used for fires in common cellulose materials such as wood, paper and some fabrics;

FIRE PROTECTION SYSTEMS

☐ **Type B,** designed for use on flammable liquids such as grease or paint;
☐ **Type C,** used on electrical equipment;
☐ **Type D,** for use on metal fires.

Read the labels. Fire extinguishers can be designed for use on one type of fire or on several. An extinguisher with the designation BC on its label, with a small A underneath, will serve the purposes of an average home. This is multipurpose equipment, which can be used on flammable liquid fires as well as on wood, paper and some fabrics. *Look for a label showing that the extinguisher has been tested by Underwriters Laboratory or Factory Mutual Laboratories for greater assurance that the device will perform.*

Read the instructions. Your purchase of a good fire extinguisher is worthless if you don't know how it works. Make sure that you and every member of your household are familiar with how and when to use it.

Food Shopping

(See also NUTRITION)

SMART FOOD SHOPPING begins at home, with careful attention to meal planning for nutritional value and a shopping list shaped to family needs. The following general strategies apply to shopping for any number of people.

When you plan meals:
- ☐ Plan menus for a week in advance.
- ☐ Watch for midweek "food specials" advertised in newspapers and on radio and television. These "specials" fall into several categories:
    - **Items available in large quantities** for lower-than-usual price.
    - **Seasonal specials:** Fresh fruits and vegetables in season, grown locally, are usually less expensive than out-of-season foods shipped long distances.
    - **Foods in abundant supply:** Meat prices, for example, fluctuate with the season and with the supply. Look for special prices on beef, lamb, pork and poultry.
    - **Special "promotion" prices** offered by manufacturers to improve slow sales, introduce new products or prompt new business.
    - **"Quick-sale" specials:** Look for special prices on items that your neighborhood store or supermarket can't keep overnight or over the weekend, such as fresh seafood, produce and bakery goods.
    - **"Close-out" specials:** These are products that will no longer be available and which are reduced in price to clear shelf space for faster-moving products.
    - **Damaged packages or cans specials:** Examine these carefully before you buy. A dented can may not change the quality of the contents, but *never eat anthing from a can that has bulged* — the contents are definitely spoiled. Buying unmarked cans (labels removed) is risky. You have no way of knowing whether you will want what you get or whether the product is worth the money.
- ☐ Consider the needs and appetites of family members. **Remember:** Everyone needs the same basic nutrients, but the quantity of

calories required changes with age and the amount of physical activity of the individual.
- ☐ Don't buy extra just to have leftovers unless you have a specific plan for the extra portions. This practice is often wasteful or fattening — or both.

Build your shopping list around carefully planned menus.
- ☐ Don't overbuy. Buy only the amounts and foods you can conveniently store.
- ☐ List your needs in relation to the shopping pattern you prefer to follow in your favorite store. If you haven't evolved a pattern of your own, try this one:
  - — Heavy, bulky staples go into the cart first, so that fragile items are not damaged by canned goods, potatoes, detergents, etc.
  - — Next come fresh fruits and vegetables. Make sure you put the "squashables" (tomatoes, berries, etc.) together, with nothing heavy on top of them.
  - — Meats, frozen foods, dairy and delicatessen items should be chosen last.

Follow your own system in supermarket shopping — not necessarily the one laid out for you by the merchandisers. Remember that floor plans and displays in the stores don't just happen. They are the result of careful market research geared to maximize sales in general and to boost "impulse buying" of maximum-profit items. If you train yourself to buy only the items on your shopping list, you will resist the colorful displays calculated to sell you more than you had planned to buy.

Use unit prices. Check the price per measure (per ounce, per pound, per quart, etc.) of products in different sizes or brands.

Is packaging important to you? Individually packaged single-serving containers of food (such as dry cereal) usually cost more per pound of product than the larger sizes. Is the packaging worth the price?

Make sure "specials" are right for you. Before deciding to cash in on what seems to be a bargain, do a little double-checking:

- ☐ Does the ad list the "regular" price *and* the "special" price?
- ☐ Is the "special" price available only on a large quantity of the product?
- ☐ If the reduced price applies only to one package size, is that amount practical for your family?
- ☐ Does the store offer a "raincheck" if they are out of an advertised special?
- ☐ Are special conditions attached to the special price? For example, must you spend a minimum amount in a store to take advantage of a reduced price on sugar? Must you make a special trip to the store to take advantage of a price reduction offered for a limited time? Is the trip worth the projected saving?

GETTING MORE FOR YOUR MONEY

☐ Some "special offers" — such as two-for-one packs and cents-off coupons — may influence you to buy more than you had planned. *Make sure any special offer makes sense to you, applies to a product you can really use, and actually saves you money within the framework of your planned expenditures.*

Read the labels. Many packaged items contain combinations of foods or ingredients. Everything in the package listed in the ingredient line must be in a designated order: *the first item listed is the most plentiful and the list continues in diminishing order down to the smallest quantity.*
For example:

WHAT'S IN IT?

VEGETABLE & BEEF STEW
water, potatoes, carrots, peas, beef, onions, spices

BEEF AND VEGETABLE STEW
beef, water, potatoes, carrots, onions, peas, spices

Federally regulated meat and poultry products such as "Beef with Gravy," "Chicken Soup" or "Pizza with Meat" must contain a minimum percentage of meat, poultry or other ingredients.

Certain products have a standard recipe (Standard of Identity) established by the Food and Drug Administration. Products that conform to these standards do not have to carry ingredient labeling. For this reason, you will not find ingredients listed on mayonnaise, though they *will* be listed on the labels of the low-fat "imitation" mayonnaise products.

FOOD SHOPPING

Nutrition labeling is required for products labeled "Fortified" or "Enriched." "Fortified" means that the quantity of one or more nutrients, naturally present in a lesser amount, has been increased. "Enriched" describes the addition of one or more nutrients which are not naturally present.

The following information, for example, appears on a nonfat dry milk product:

INSTANT NONFAT DRY MILK
FORTIFIED WITH VITAMINS A AND D

Nutrition information per serving
(8 FL. OZ. OF RECONSTITUTED NONFAT MILK)

Serving size: 6 tablespoons (22.7 grams)
reconstituted to 8 fluid ounces

Servings per container	12
Calories	80
Protein	8 grams
Carbohydrate	12 grams
Fat	Contains less than 1 gram

PERCENTAGE OF U.S.
RECOMMENDED DAILY ALLOWANCE (RDA)

Protein	20
Vitamin A	10
Vitamin C	2
Thiamine	6
Riboflavin	25
Niacin	*
Calcium	30
Iron	*
Vitamin D	25
Vitamin B6	4
Vitamin B12	20
Phosphorus	25
Magnesium	6
Pantothenic acid	8

*Contains less than 2% of U.S. RDA
of these nutrients
INGREDIENTS: NONFAT DRY MILK
VITAMIN A PALMITATE,
VITAMIN D2

You can see at a glance that one eight-ounce glass of this product provides 80 calories, a minuscule amount of fat, 20 percent of the amount of protein you need each day, 10 percent of the vitamin A you should have, and 25 percent of the vitamin D, in addition to varying amounts of other necessary nutrients.

Nutritional labeling, then, provides a basis of comparison of the nutritive values of the food you buy.

Label reading can be a challenge, especially when unfamiliar ingredients must be identified. Standard ingredients must be listed by their common names (salt, for example, instead of sodium chloride), but there are no common names for some ingredients which are added to keep foods fresh or to stabilize the texture, enhance flavor and color.

MEAL PLANNING AND FOOD PURCHASING

The overall objective of meal planning and careful attention to food purchasing is to arrive at a system that fills the nutritional needs of the family with the least damage to the budget. For this reason, the following suggestions and information are centered around what have come to be called the Basic Four Food Groups (see NUTRITION).

1. Milk and dairy products are best buys for protein and calcium and vitamins A and D. When fortified with vitamin D, milk is the major source of this important nutrient in the diet.

Nonfat dry milk is fine for drinking as well as for cooking. Serve it well chilled or mix it, half and half, with fluid whole milk.

Compare the price of proprietary (store or chain brand) dry milk with the price of nationally advertised brands. House brands often cost less while providing equally high quality.

Butter or margarine: The difference between them is in the *source* of the fat they contain. The fat quantity is the same — both spreads contain 80 percent fat, from sweet cream or selected sour cream for butter, and from vegetable oil (sometimes with added animal fat) for margarine. Compare prices: whipped butter and margarine are usually more expensive than the conventional type packaged in quarter-pound sticks.

Eggs are more plentiful — and therefore less expensive — in the winter, but they are among the best buys for nutrition the year round. They are excellent sources of high-quality protein.

When you buy eggs, remember that the **grade** and the **size** are not related to one another. Grade is a measure of quality. Grade AA eggs have a large amount of firm white and rounded, high-standing yolks. Grade A and B eggs have thinner whites and flatter yolks, *but they are identical in food value to the more expensive grades.* If the appearance of poached or fried eggs is important to you, Grade AA eggs are the ones to choose. Use A and B grades for scrambling, omelets, and cooking and baking, particularly in recipes that do not require the whites and yolks to be separated.

In some areas, brown eggs are cheaper than white. Buy them. Nutritional value, taste and quality are exactly the same as white eggs. The color of the shell is irrelevant.

FOOD SHOPPING

Before you buy eggs in the store, open the carton to make sure none is broken.

Cheese. Always compare prices and packaging when you buy. You may decide to invest in a cheese slicer and buy the product in three- to five-pound blocks when you find out how much more you pay for elaborate packaging.

Keep a covered container in the refrigerator for storing leftover cheese. Use it on hot sandwiches or sprinkle it, grated or diced, over salads and casseroles.

Yogurt. For the greatest economy, try making your own. It is not necessary to invest in an electric machine for this purpose. Glass jars and warm water also work well.

General notes on dairy products. When you buy dairy products, *always check the "pull date"* (that is, the stamped date on the product indicating the last date on which the product may be sold as fresh). Remember that the date does *not* indicate that a product marked May 12 will be spoiled or stale on May 13. You will still have time to store and use the product at home.

If you buy a dairy product that has not been properly stored and find that it is spoiled or stale when you open it, **do not hesitate to return it to the store for a replacement or refund.**

Dairy products are excellent choices for nutritious desserts. Make custards with milk and eggs, serve yogurt or cheese with fresh fruit, and try your hand at making homemade ice cream. These will be better for the family than empty-calorie, nonfood dessert products.

2. Meat, poultry and fish provide high-quality protein — a necessity in the diet. Nutritionists recommend two or more servings of this important food group each day, but the recommended serving size is much, much smaller than the average portion consumed at each meal in our meat-and-potatoes, steak-and-salad society. The recommended serving size is *two to three ounces;* the routine restaurant portion is anywhere from eight to sixteen ounces (see NUTRITION).

When you buy meat, remember that *the price per serving,* not the price per pound, *is the most important consideration.*

- Many **boneless meats** yield four (or five) servings per pound. These include ground meat, cubed steak, stew beef, variety meats (liver, kidneys, brains, heart, tongue, sweetbreads), center-cut ham, veal cutlet, fish steaks and fillets.
- **Bone-in cuts** yield two to three servings per pound. This includes most roasts, chops and steaks, poultry and some fish.
- **Meat with substantial fat and bone** yields only one or two servings per pound. This includes short ribs, spareribs, chops of lamb, pork or veal, rib roast, brisket, porterhouse and T-bone steaks, and chicken wings and backs.

Look for special prices on the boniest cuts of meat in the

supermarket (such as beef neck bones and chicken backs and wings) and use them for nutritious soups, broth and stock.

Large cuts of meat, which you can cut into usable portions at home, are generally economical, but *never* buy more than you can use, store or freeze conveniently.

Use less tender cuts of meat and learn to vary methods of preparation to suit them. Chuck, flank and some cuts from the round contain less marbling (flecks of fat in the lean) than the more tender cuts, and though they may require more time and care in preparation they are flavorful and nutritious. Ask the butcher to trim these cuts for you.

"Variety" meats are often a bargain, both economically and nutritionally. Look for supermarket specials on tongue, tripe, heart, kidney and liver. These can be used in a wide range of main dishes.

When you buy **poultry,** remember that the whole bird is usually a better buy than its ready-cut parts. *Learn to cut it yourself.*

The tenderness of poultry depends upon the age of the bird. Young birds are good for roasting, frying, or broiling; mature birds for stewing, making stock and for use in soups and salads. Always use fresh-killed poultry within one or two days or freeze it for storage.

When you buy **turkey,** remember that the bigger birds are the better buy. They have a larger proportion of meat to bone and usually cost less per pound.

Fish is an excellent source of low-calorie protein. **Fresh fish** should be served as soon as possible after it is caught. When you buy it, look for clear, bright, slightly protruding eyes, firm flesh and shiny, unfaded skin. When you buy **frozen fish** check for solidly frozen, tightly sealed packages.

Fish can be almost as expensive as beef if you insist on serving only sole, striped bass and salmon. Look for the less expensive varieties: flounder, haddock, mackerel and codfish are often better buys.

Never overbuy fish — allow three or four ounces per serving of cooked boneless fish, or a half-pound per serving of dressed or pan-dressed fresh fish.

Canned tuna is often a "best buy" for food value. Choose flaked tuna for sandwiches, chunk style for casseroles. The solid-pack style is more expensive.

Do you care how bright your **canned salmon** is? The price varies with its color. Pink salmon costs less — use it for loaves and croquettes. The more expensive red variety is attractive in salads, but there is little difference in flavor.

Use meat substitutes once or twice a week for economical, nutritious meals. Supplement the protein value in an all-vegetable meal by serving milk, eggs or cheese.

Textured vegetable proteins can be used to extend ground beef. The most economical way to use meat extenders such as soybeans is to buy the beans and cook them yourself. The packaged prepared meat extenders are expensive. Make your own.

3. Fruits and vegetables. Fruits and vegetables in season and locally grown are usually your best buys in this important food group. Use the greatest variety available to supply a wide range of important nutrients in the family diet (see NUTRITION). One serving of citrus fruits, strawberries, cantaloupe, sweet peppers or brussels sprouts will provide the day's supply of vitamin C — as will two servings of tomatoes, raw cabbage, potatoes, kale or turnip greens. Dark green and yellow vegetables and fruits are good sources of vitamin A. **Remember:** The wider the range of foods within this group your family enjoys, the better their chances of having a fully balanced diet. In addition to vitamins A and C, this food group supplies generous amounts of other vitamins, minerals (especially calcium and iron), some protein and carbohydrates.

Try these suggestions:

- Don't overbuy fragile perishables such as berries, summer fruits or melons. *Food the family does not eat is no bargain.*
- The size and shape of vegetables and fruits does not affect the flavor. You may want to use picture-perfect specimens for an edible centerpiece, but you don't need them for fruit salad.
- You can usually store fresh seasonal vegetables for two days. The exception to this is root vegetables (onions, potatoes, etc.), which can be stored in a cool, dry place for several weeks.
- Baked or boiled potatoes are a natural convenience food. Ounce for ounce a potato has no more calories than an apple, and it is a nutritious, inexpensive food. Buy whole potatoes and prepare them yourself for greatest economy and flavor.
- Preserve the important nutrients in vegetables by steaming or cooking them in a very small amount of water until they are just tender. *Save the cooking liquid for use in soups, stews and sauces.*
- Vary salads for flavor, texture and economy. Use spinach instead of lettuce (combine fresh spinach with sliced mushrooms, croutons and a sprinkle of pecans with a homemade oil and vinegar dressing); or try adding a variety of fresh raw vegetables, such as cauliflower, broccoli, brussels sprouts or zucchini, to a standard lettuce salad.

4. Breads and cereals. Breads and cereals, whole grain or enriched, supply protein, the range of B vitamins, vitamin E, many minerals and fiber to the diet. Nutritionists recommend two or three servings daily for each family member. The recommended portion is one slice of bread, one serving of ready-to-eat cereal, 1/2 to 3/4 cup of cooked cereal, or 1/2 cup of pasta or rice.

- Buy bread by weight, not size of loaf. The popular large, soft loaf often used for sandwiches is frequently bigger because it contains more air than the more compact firm breads.
- Homemade yeast breads may not be more economical than the

store-bought variety, but the flavor is incomparable.
- ☐ Look for reduced prices on day-old baked goods at "thrift stores" operated by producers of national-brand products or on house-brand merchandise at the supermarket.
- ☐ If you choose to buy breads that do not contain preservatives, use them within forty-eight hours or store them in the refrigerator. Breads made with preservatives can safely be stored for a week at room temperature.
- ☐ Learn to make pancakes, quick breads and muffins from scratch. Mixes are expensive, and the recipes for these homemade treats are simple, requiring little more time than it takes to use a prepared mix.
- ☐ When you buy prepared cereal, buy for nutrition. Study nutrition information on the package to make sure the product provides the nutrients cereals are *supposed* to provide. Heavily sugared or empty-calorie cereals may not be the best bet.
- ☐ Check or compute the unit price (the price per pound, per ounce) of cereals. Price differences directly attributable to packaging may surprise you. The unit cost per ounce of individually packaged servings is usually far greater than the cost per ounce when you buy in bulk.
- ☐ Preflavored, single-serving packets of cooked cereals can also cost more than twice as much per unit as the unflavored "old-fashioned" variety, which takes a little longer to cook than the add-hot-water-and-stir style. Add your own fresh or dried fruits and spices.
- ☐ It is also much more economical to buy plain, unprocessed rice instead of the parboiled or preseasoned products. Follow the directions in a basic cookbook or on the packages. You will find that the unprocessed rice is easy to cook — and just as easy to season yourself with stock and spices and herbs. Leftover rice can be used in a variety of ways — add it to soups or casseroles, or use it in stuffed peppers, tomatoes, cabbage, etc.
- ☐ Pasta is the umbrella term for a wide variety of shapes and sizes of macaroni, spaghetti and noodles. For best nutritional value, buy the enriched variety. Combine this versatile food with meat, fish, poultry, cheese or eggs to make any number of entrées or side dishes.
- ☐ If the family feels deprived without snack foods, cookies or desserts, make them yourself. Read the ingredient labels on supermarket desserts and learn to avoid nonfoods which add only empty calories to the diet, such as "lemon" pie that has no trace of real lemon in it. It is easy, economical and usually more nutritious to make wholesome peanut butter, oatmeal or wheatgerm cookies, etc., from scratch.

FOOD SHOPPING

> **Budget carefully and spend only what you can afford**
> If you feel this is easier said than done, you're right. Nevertheless, it is important to the family's financial stability and your own peace of mind to create a budget you can live with and stick to. Know the limits of your spending power *before* you make up your menus for the week. When you make up your shopping list, price it out to see if it matches your budget. If you spend more than you planned to spend for food, you will inevitably have less to spend elsewhere.
> Remember these basics:
>
> ☐ Organize your meals for nutritional value.
> ☐ Shop the ads.
> ☐ Plan your shopping trips.
> ☐ Don't shop when you are hungry — that's when you are most likely to overspend.
> ☐ Read the labels.
> ☐ Check your receipts at the check-out. Mistakes are always possible.
> ☐ Return defective items quickly.

NATURAL FOODS

There are several reasons for the renewed interest in "natural" foods, organic foods and foods without additives. Many people prefer fresh foods in season because they are more flavorful than, say, an out-of-season, picked-before-it's-ripe version of the same food. Other reasons often stem from confusion about the relationship of food-production methods to food value. And this question is often still further clouded by the current controversy over the risk-benefit ratio of food additives.

Whether or not you believe that organically grown, organically processed foods are better for you, you can be absolutely sure of this fact: *You will pay more for foods sold as organic.*

And, regardless of the cost, you usually have no real assurance that the natural or organic foods for which you pay a premium price are actually organic in the real meaning of the term. There are as yet no controls and no standards for food sold as "natural" or organic. If you want to make sure your family's food is free of materials to which you object, your best bet is to grow it yourself. If you lack facilities for a garden of your own, you must:

☐ Find a market or health food shop that you trust. Make sure that the foods come from ethical suppliers with strict production standards of their own.
☐ Expect to pay more for your special selection of foods than you would pay at the ordinary vegetable stand or supermarket.

- ☐ Don't expect greater nutritional value from organically grown and processed foods.
- ☐ Never assume that a "chemical-free" diet will cure or prevent health problems. Medical problems require medical treatment.
- ☐ Never neglect the overall picture of total nutritional needs in favor of a special, limited group of organically produced foods. That way lies malnutrition — and more health problems than you bargained for.

Some definitions, naturally

There are no precise, official, universally accepted definitions for such terms as "natural" or "health foods" or "organically grown" or "organically processed" food. The terms are used loosely by self-styled nutritionists and by the producers of so-called natural foods as well. Firm definitions have been proposed, however, for legal use in the formulation of standards and regulations for certifying foods claimed to be organic or natural:

- ☐ **Natural foods** do not contain synthetic or artificial ingredients and may not be more than minimally processed. "Minimal processing" is defined as including washing, peeling, canning, bottling, freezing and grinding.
- ☐ **Organically grown** refers to food grown without pesticides or "artificial" fertilizers. Organically produced meat would be from animals fed on organically grown pasture and feed containing no growth stimulants, antibiotics or synthetic materials.
- ☐ **Organically processed** means organically grown food which has not been processed with preservatives, hormones, antibiotics or other synthetic additives of any kind.

The term "health food" resists definition. It could refer to any or all of the above, but it is often used by food faddists to mean some food or combination of foods claimed to have some special supportive effect on good health or some special virtue for the prevention or treatment of disease.

Franchises

FRANCHISE, observes the Bank of America's *Small Business Reporter* (Volume 9, No. 9), is a term without a firm definition. Essentially, the buyer of a franchise purchases a "packaged" business that is to be operated under contract with the parent company, says the *Small Business Reporter,* and "as far as the public is concerned, the business is indistinguishable from a company-owned outlet." But, the article continues, "lawyers, economists, legislators and marketers have devised their own definitions of franchising, each reflecting group concerns and separate viewpoints. The courts, in dealing with franchisor/franchisee disputes, do not appear to attach any particular weight to the term *franchise* but look beyond it to the facts of the business relationship involved."

Anyone interested in going into business for himself by buying or entering into a franchise relationship would be well advised to follow the court's procedure. Look beyond the term and carefully evaluate the business relationship.

Thousands of people have profited from franchise arrangements . . . and thousands more have not only failed to make a profit, but have lost their investments.

Before you make any investment in a packaged business, thoroughly investigate what you are getting into.

The franchisee's capital investment must usually cover equipment, supplies, labor, operating and reserve funds *plus* the franchise fee. In addition, the franchisee must be willing to invest large quantities of time and hard work to open and build the business.

Potential franchisees should get answers to the following questions before signing any contract:

- ☐ How long has the parent firm been in business?
- ☐ What is its financial strength?
- ☐ What are the background and experience of the company officers?
- ☐ What is the source of the company's earnings? If they make their profits from selling products to franchisees or from royalties (instead of simply selling franchises), they are more likely to be interested in your staying in business.
- ☐ How well is the product selling? How well has it sold in the past? *Assess the product on its merits.*

☐ Is your sales territory well-defined and exclusive?
☐ What is the level of competition in your sales area?

Effective October 21, 1979, franchisors and franchise brokers are required to furnish prospective investors with a disclosure statement and documentation for any earnings claims at the time of the first meeting to discuss a franchise purchase. In all cases you must receive these statements at least ten business days in advance of signing a franchise or related agreement, or ten business days before paying any money in connection with the purchase. The disclosure statement contains detailed information on the following:

— business experience of the franchisor and its key management personnel;
— litigation and bankruptcy history of the franchisor and its key management personnel;
— financial information on the franchisor;
— costs, both initial and recurring, which will be required to be paid by the franchisee;
— statistical information on the number of franchises and company-owned outlets;
— termination, cancellation and renewal provisions of the franchise agreement;
— number of franchisees terminated during the past year and the reasons for their termination;
— training offered by the franchisor;
— restrictions imposed by the franchisor on the manner in which the franchisee may operate his business (this includes restrictions on such things as the types of goods that can be sold, suppliers that can be used and the geographic area in which the franchise may operate).

Consider your need for ongoing assistance.

☐ Does the franchisor provide continuing assistance? You will probably need personal guidance and support in your new business, especially during the first year. Find out how many field representatives the company maintains, and how often they would visit you.
☐ Is training offered for franchisees and key employees?
☐ How and where is the product advertised? What will be your share of advertising costs?
☐ Examine the contract carefully. Does it cover all aspects of the agreement? Have your lawyer read it.

If a franchisor makes any written or oral earnings claims, they must be relevant to the area where you would be doing business, and they must be stated clearly in a special document you must be given. Also, if you ask for substantiation of earnings claims, the franchisor must give it to you.

- ☐ Can the contract be renewed, terminated or transferred?
- ☐ Is there an additional fixed payment each year? Or do you agree to pay the parent company a percentage of your gross sales?
- ☐ Must a stated amount of merchandise be purchased? From whom?
- ☐ What is the geographical territory in which you are authorized to sell?
- ☐ What is the exclusive territory awarded to you?

Ask for references. Investigate the operations of other franchisees of the chain under consideration. Ask for their advice or complaints.

CAUTION

Move slowly. Many franchisees have lost their investments by dealing with fraudulent operators who used the following tactics:

- ☐ wildly improbable claims about potential products and/or the ease with which the product "sells itself";
- ☐ sound-alike names, where the company name of the franchisor is very similar to that of a well-known company;
- ☐ pyramid distribution schemes which involve you in selling additional distributorships much like the operation of a chain-letter scheme;
- ☐ demands that you sign a contract immediately so that you can "get in on the ground floor";
- ☐ promises of large incomes from work-at-home or spare-time efforts.

WHERE TO GET HELP

For assistance in your investigation, contact your local Better Business Bureau or the regional office of the Small Business Administration in your area for general information on franchising.

Fraud and Deception

OUTRIGHT FRAUD and deception in the marketplace have existed even before *caveat emptor* became the wise buyer's rule in the marketplace.

Despite the fact that the schemes and the schemers constitute a minority in the marketplace, and despite the fact that the schemes themselves rarely change, they are important enough to warrant attention.

Beware of the following potential problem areas, among others.

BAIT AND SWITCH
Better Business Bureaus have warned against this sales method for more than half a century. This is how it works: Some fabulous bargain is advertised as "bait" — to attract customers to the store; the retailer and his sales staff have no intention of selling the item at the advertised price. Instead, they are willing to demonstrate any number of shortcomings in the advertised merchandise in order to sell — "switch" to — a higher-priced item.

One product that has frequently fallen into the hands of bait-and-switch sellers is the vacuum cleaner. A "reconditioned" model of a well-known cleaner made by a reliable manufacturer is advertised at a remarkably low price. The shopper goes to the store and asks to see the cleaner. The salesperson brings it out and proceeds with a demonstration. The machine operates erratically. It starts, stops, starts again and wheezes on. The salesperson drops some ashes and dust on a section of carpet and moves the cleaner over it; the cleaner fails to collect the mess. The demonstrator looks puzzled and tries again, with no better success. The customer at this point gets fed up and probably says, "I wouldn't take that thing if you *gave* it to me!" — which is just what the salesperson is waiting for.

He quickly demonstrates another machine which works well. The price is far higher than that of the advertised model. But the customer, who is in the store anyway and *does* need a vacuum cleaner, may very well buy it.

The "bait and switch" scheme has worked. And the customer is likely to discover at a later date that the machine he or she has purchased is available — same model, same efficient operation — at a lower price at a reliable merchant's store down the street.

This is just one example of bait and switch. The technique has many variations and they are used to sell many kinds of merchandise — appliances, carpets, cars and furniture.

> **Selling up** should not be confused with bait and switch. The difference between the two practices is that in selling up, the salesperson is perfectly willing to sell the advertised merchandise but, *without disparaging the item,* he may call your attention to a higher-priced model and explain why it may suit your needs better. The choice is up to you.

Any time you find a bait-and-switch scheme in operation, report it. Tell your local Better Business Bureau or the city, county or state consumer-protection agency. Guard against the practice by using these guidelines:

- ☐ Don't do business with "bait" advertisers. Bait and switch advertising is an unfair practice and is against the law.
- ☐ Be wary of all offers that appear to be too good to be true; they usually are.
- ☐ Compare prices to find out what similar merchandise sells for in other stores.
- ☐ Always do business with merchants who are interested in having you buy from them again. Wise retailers know that satisfied customers are the most valuable form of advertising.

LAND SALES

You are invited to dinner or perhaps to spend the weekend at some delightful place. The dinner or the vacation is absolutely free. All you are asked to give in return is your attendance at a private showing of a color film or, perhaps, the time it takes to tour mountain or shore home sites.

This "free" entertainment may contribute to one of the most costly mistakes you will ever make. A sales meeting is involved, and high-pressure sales tactics are used to convince you that you need and want a very special piece of land for a second home. If you get in on the ground floor of this great investment opportunity, you are told, you can buy the property for a bargain price. Later, as the land is developed, your land's value will appreciate. You can sell, if you wish, for a triple-your-money profit.

Reputable, reliable real-estate professionals do not use such high-pressure sales tactics. Nor do they encourage their clients to purchase property without seeing it.

Nevertheless, tens of thousands of unwary buyers have been enticed by unscrupulous land-development companies to buy worthless land — perhaps a piece of the desert, a home site that turns out to be under water at high tide or land on which no one can build because zoning regulations make development impossible.

Never invest in land without thorough investigation (see guidelines listed under LAND PURCHASES).

ITINERANT SELLERS

Itinerant sellers of various goods and services should be readily distinguishable from legitimate door-to-door salespersons. Legitimate door-to-door sales representatives tell you that they are calling to sell you something. They have identification and are willing to have you check it, and they do not use high-pressure sales tactics.

Some itinerant sellers, on the other hand, misrepresent the purpose of their visits, using less-than-honest techniques to gain entrance to your home. They then proceed to attempt to sell you shoddy merchandise.

Beware of the following opening lines from strangers at the door:

I am a city (county or state) inspector and I'm here to check your furnace.

I'm from the gas (or electric) company, here to check the heating system (wiring).

I am taking a survey . . .

I've just finished a job down the street and I have just enough material to repair your roof.

Any of these lines should cue you to *demand identification and check it.* Call the local utility company or the local government agency the person at the door claims to represent. Find out whether such inspections are going on. (Be advised that it's hardly likely that door-to-door inspections are *ever* carried out like this.) Or call the local Better Business Bureau, consumer-protection agency, the Chamber of Commerce or even the local police to alert them to the presence of the "inspector" or "contractor" in your neighborhood and ask advice. In short, *do anything necessary to check the identity and operation of such callers at your door before you admit them to your home.*

Chances are that a bogus inspector, contractor, or poll-taker will have disappeared before you have a chance to complete your check. That would be all to the good for you. Otherwise, you risk wasting your valuable time with a "pollster" who really wants to sell you some product you neither need nor want.

Wise buyers deal with reputable companies they know and can trust. One immediate clue to identification of a fake contractor should be your own experience. After all, you know that appointments for major home improvements and repairs must be made well in advance of the time they become a necessity. Good contractors, plumbing and heating specialists, roofers and such have all the work they can handle without soliciting more on the grounds that they are "just in the neighborhood." If a contractor is good, he's moving quickly on the way to his next job.

And wasted time could be the least of your problems. Fake "inspectors" and "contractors" have been known to:

- ☐ dismantle furnaces or damage wiring or plumbing, then offer, for *immediate* sale, totally unnecessary goods or services to replace the damaged equipment;
- ☐ frighten householders with notions of fire in the night from a supposedly damaged flue or chimney;
- ☐ damage roofs or driveway surfaces with the shoddy material they use to "repair" them.

MODEL HOMES AND REFERRAL SALES

Another hardy perennial sales pitch is the "model home" or "referral sale." This involves an appeal to the householder-victim's vanity. The seller (of aluminum siding, burglar alarms, encyclopedias, vacuum cleaners, you name it) is clearly a person of perception. He or she has immediately identified you as a "leader in the community," someone with a model personality and a "model house" — a person whose many friends are eager to follow your lead in the purchase of goods and services. Therefore, the merchandise about to be offered to you will cost you little or nothing. All you have to do is give the seller the names of others who might buy the merchandise. You get a discount, a commission or some other financial consideration for each sale made through one of your referrals.

Don't fall for the "model home" or any other type of referral sales scheme. The commissions you are promised never materialize, and the initial price you pay to fix up your house as a "model home" is likely to be much more than what you would pay a reputable contractor. If you think you have encountered a referral selling scheme, get in touch with the Better Business Bureau or local consumer-protection agency. And remember: *Referral selling is illegal in some states.*

Other deceptive activities in the marketplace attempt to involve you in "profitable" schemes of one kind or another. Almost everyone could use supplementary family income, and unwary participants in a scheme preying on this fundamental need can lose quantities of money while attempting to earn money.

Multilevel marketing techniques. The term "multilevel selling" is usually applied to a sales program that relies on independent distributors who buy a product at varying discounts from "list price" for resale to distributors and independent agents they, in turn, have recruited and sponsored. Usually, the higher the monthly purchase volume, the greater the discounts from "list price."

There is nothing illegal or unethical about multilevel selling plans. Reputable firms that use independent distributors at various levels do not promise the proverbial pot of gold at the end of the rainbow. Nor do they indicate that the way to profit and prosperity is an easy one.

They stress that the only way to earn commissions is by selling the products, establishing repeat business and providing the kind of service that keeps customers happy. Selling is not easy. This is one of the reasons that even legitimate door-to-door sales operations suffer a high turnover of personnel.

"Pyramid" schemes. Their dishonest counterparts, however, concentrate mainly on the quick profits to be earned by recruiting others to invest . . . who, in turn, will recruit still others and so on. Commissions and bonuses are paid for recruiting other investors, other distributors. The merchandise or service to be sold is largely ignored, and little or no mention is made regarding market saturation resulting from the ever-increasing number of participants attempting to recoup their investments in products by recruiting from the ever-decreasing number of potential investors in a given area.

Consider the results if one person recruited six distributors, each of whom, in turn, recruited six others, and carry the process through nine steps as follows:

	1
1	6
2	36
3	216
4	1,296
5	7,776
6	46,656
7	279,936
8	1,679,616
9	10,077,696

At more than ten million people for every nine steps in the distribution program, the distributors would soon be recruiting one another.

The tragic aspect of these rackets is that they concentrate on and exploit people with limited means and limited knowledge of business — people who cannot afford to lose the "small" first investment they put into the program. Thousands of unsuspecting and trusting investors have lost millions of dollars by investing in multilevel selling schemes. Even worse, the schemes have robbed some retired persons of their life savings.

Guidelines for prospective investors:

- ☐ The basis for any company's sales promotion should be the retail sale of its products, *not* the unending recruitment of distributors.
- ☐ The firm should acknowledge that it is not necessarily easy to sell or recruit and train other sales people. This requires time, effort and personal commitment.
- ☐ Investors should be wary of promises of high potential earnings.
- ☐ The firm should provide a market for its products.

- Distributors should be assured of a continuous supply of quality products.
- The recruitment of additional distributors or sales personnel should be based upon the potential market, the population of the specific community or prior sales competition. Limiting the number of distributors in a state on the basis of the entire state population may not be adequate protection for a distributor in any given community within the state.
- The company should set standards for advertising local business opportunity meetings and also for all sales recruitment literature.
- The company should accept the responsibility of checking the qualifications of potential distributors and remove those who violate company policies or local laws.
- No more than a minimal initial inventory should be required to become a distributor or dealer.
- A reliable firm should guarantee in writing that any products ordered but not sold will be bought back by the company within a reasonable period of time for a certain percentage of the original price.

By honest evaluation of any prospective venture into the sales field in light of these guidelines, a potential investor can avoid the shady multilevel sales operator.

Remember: If you are approached to attend an "opportunity meeting" ... if you are encouraged to make an investment in a distributorship ... if you are promised quick, high returns on your investment ... check the company's record with the nearest Better Business Bureau, your local consumer protection agency or the attorney general's office in your state.

Funerals

FUNERAL DIRECTORS ARE vendors of consumer services. Like other retailers they operate profit-making businesses. However, most purchasers of their services are under stress and, as a result, frequently do not know what they are buying and rarely compare prices.
 A study by the Federal Trade Commission indicates:

- ☐ Funeral prices vary substantially.
- ☐ Price information *is* available, but must be sought aggressively by the purchaser.
- ☐ Many options are available to purchasers of funeral arrangements.

The cost for an average funeral these days is approximately $2,000. This includes such items as the casket, vault or liner, and grave marker, as well as basic services, depending on the funeral. Because the costs of funerals are so high, many funeral homes are beginning to provide simple "graveside" services. Often the body is interred within twenty-four hours, without a viewing, thus eliminating the need for embalming and other extras adding to the funeral's expense.
 Consumers who are interested in the preservation of family resources for the use of their survivors would do well to investigate alternatives, and make an independent choice in regard to funeral or memorial service arrangements and disposition of the body.

Leaving instructions for your own funeral
NEVER include instructions for funeral arrangements in a will, which is usually read after burial. A separate statement should be prepared and notarized, and its contents and location be made known to relatives and, perhaps to the family attorney. DO NOT file this statement in your safe deposit box, which may be sealed after death until the probate process begins.

Alternatives to traditional funeral arrangements include:

1. Donation of the body to a medical school. After the cadaver has been used for instruction, it is cremated and the survivors may, if they wish, claim the ashes for burial or interment in a columbarium.

2. Cremation or burial followed by a memorial service. The difference between a traditional funeral and a memorial service is that the body is not present in the latter. (Some people believe that the presence and "viewing" of the body is a necessary adjunct to "the grief experience" without which the fact of death is not accepted by the survivors.)
3. Burial or memorial societies often offer alternatives to traditional funerals as well as information on low-cost traditional services. They also may work out special rate arrangements for their members with local funeral directors.

The Council of Better Business Bureaus suggests that preliminary funeral arrangements be made by someone who is *not* directly involved with the person who has died — for example, a close friend of the family. The survivor(s) can then approve the arrangements before they are completed. This way the most vulnerable people will not be exposed to a difficult and stress-filled series of decisions which may result in needless expenditures, and the best arrangements can be made in keeping with the family's resources.

If you must assume responsibility for a funeral (either as a helpful friend of a family or as a survivor), get answers to these questions:

- ☐ Is the funeral home you are considering reliable? Try, as with any other consumer service, to find people who have dealt with the funeral home under consideration. Find out whether the bill was in line with the original estimate for services.
- ☐ How many "traditional" services are actually optional? If you feel you are being pressured into purchasing services that are neither needed nor wanted, feel free to refuse them.
- ☐ What is the least expensive arrangement available? What is the most expensive? What is the difference between them?
- ☐ If one price including all arrangements is offered, find out exactly what is included. Get specific information about services or goods that may result in extra cost. Again, feel free to refuse them.
- ☐ Ask for the price of the casket, funeral service and other fees before disclosing the amount of insurance, pension or government death benefits due the family of the deceased. Don't let death benefits influence the funeral director's prices.
- ☐ Local laws vary. Find out if a casket for cremation or embalming before cremation is *really* required in your state. Find out whether the cemetery requires that the casket be placed in a vault for burial. (Many consumers believe that burial in a vault of some sort is required under state law. This is not true. Instead, vaults are required by most cemeteries because they prevent the earth from settling over and around the casket. Don't hesitate to inquire: higher maintenance fees for nonvault burials may still be considerably more economical than the price of a vault.)

Watch out for schemes
As in any business providing a service, the funeral industry is not without its swindlers. Watch out for the "free plot" offer, for example. The victim may receive a phone call indicating that a "free" cemetery plot has been won. The caller then asks if it is agreeable for a salesperson to visit the person's home in order to get a signature on some papers. The papers turn out to involve a high-pressure sales pitch encouraging the customer to buy an expensive cemetery plot.

Furnaces

(See also AIR CONDITIONING; ENERGY; INSULATION; WARRANTIES)

FURNACES, like air-conditioning systems, should be installed and serviced when you don't need to use them. Heating contractors are more readily available (and likely to charge less for their services) when they are least in demand.

The most convenient and inexpensive time to install a furnace or forced-air heating system is when a house is under construction — when heating and cooling capacity can be planned, and ducts and registers placed for maximum efficiency. New houses, it goes without saying, are likely to come equipped with central forced-air heating/cooling systems, or with forced-air heating systems to which air conditioning can be added with relatively little difficulty.

Purchasers of older houses, on the other hand, may find a more traditional heating system still in use, and it is likely to fit into one of these three categories:

- **The hot-air gravity system** (still being installed in many homes today): A system in which cold air is heated in a furnace and rises through the registers to the living areas above through a number of vertical ducts. The problem with this system is that the heat is sometimes unevenly distributed.
- **The floor furnace:** A second form of gravity system in which the furnace is suspended below the floor and hot air rises through a large floor grille. This system has no ducts and is inexpensive to install. Its major disadvantage is that the grille grows hot enough to burn the unwary and is very likely to be dangerous to children.
- **The hot water (hydronic) system:** A system in which water is heated in a boiler and then pumped through radiators. Steam heat uses a similar but necessarily more powerful system, in which steam is forced by pressure from the boiler into radiators.

Whatever kind of heating system you are currently using, an annual inspection, adjustment and cleaning by a heating contractor is a must. To operate efficiently, any heating system must be properly maintained.

GETTING MORE FOR YOUR MONEY

Choosing a contractor may be the most important aspect of heating-system maintenance, repair or replacement. Choose a contractor before you need one — *before* the heating season, so that there is ample time to check the reputations of several firms (with friends, neighbors and your local Better Business Bureau). In a case where extensive repair or replacement of an older heating system is necessary, you will want to secure bids from two or three contractors, have enough time to analyze them, make your decision, and — most importantly — have the work executed before the cold weather sets in.

Follow these guidelines:

☐ Bids for extensive repair or replacement of heating systems should be submitted in writing. Estimates should always include a full description of the repairs required. If the heating system is to be replaced, the estimate should include a full description of the system to be installed, plus a full description of additional work required for the installation of ducts, registers and electrical wiring.

☐ When you compare bids, compare more than cost. Check the size of the equipment each contractor recommends. If the sizes vary significantly, something is wrong. Ask each contractor to explain how the estimate of the required heating capacity and equipment was determined.

☐ Compare warranties (see WARRANTIES).

☐ The contractor you choose should provide at least one "call back" free of charge after installation to check the system. See that this is written into your agreement. Find out if a service contract is available providing you with an annual furnace inspection and maintenance.

Beware of scare specialists. Your heating system is an expensive, long-term investment, to be purchased from and maintained by a reputable local heating contractor. If you have followed the guidelines on choosing a reliable contractor, you will probably protect your investment in heating by using the same contractor for annual or semiannual cleaning, inspection and repair.

But you still need to beware of hazards to your heating system represented by unscrupulous individuals who may gain entrance to your home by telling you they have been sent — by some city department or local utility company — to inspect the heating system, or by claiming that they have finished a repair job close by and "just happen to be in the neighborhood." Whatever the opening line, you are then presented with a demand or an offer for a complete inspection of the furnace.

Once in the basement, the representative completely dismantles the furnace and proclaims that it is in an extremely dangerous condition and is beyond repair. Such scare tactics are used to induce homeowners to sign a contract for a new furnace — immediately.

FURNACES

Protect yourself against door-to-door "inspectors"
- ☐ Demand identification from any so-called "city inspector" or representative of the utility company. Don't let anyone in the house until you have checked his identification with the firm or department the person at your door is supposed to represent.
- ☐ Call or write the Better Business Bureau to let them know of the approach being used.
- ☐ Reputable, reliable heating contractors do not solicit business door-to-door, nor do utility companies or local government departments send "inspectors" door-to-door for random inspections of heating systems.

Furniture

(See also ANTIQUES)

ANYONE WHO HAS EVER lived for a time in surroundings planned and furnished by someone else (summer sublets or motel rooms, for example) knows the effect of an incompatible atmosphere on one's overall emotional state. When you plan your home and make major purchases of furniture and accessories, you are establishing an atmosphere for years to come — unless you can afford to redecorate each year.

Planning. The best planning, therefore, is slow and careful, and should be based on a list of your own priorities. If entertainment is basic to your life style, you may decide to furnish bedrooms with the simplest basics and put a large share of your home-furnishings money into the rooms in which entertaining takes place. Or perhaps you need to focus on a good library and work area, or whatever. Set your priorities and stick to them.

Starting with floor plan (on graph paper) and templates (cut-to-size furniture shapes), try visualizing several different arrangements for the top-priority rooms. When you have an idea of what size objects in what style (traditional, country casual or modern) and color would be right for the atmosphere you want to create, it's time to shop.

When you shop:

- ☐ Always carry a wooden or metal ruler (the kind that folds up) or metal tape measure. One of the most prevalent errors in buying is choosing a piece of furniture that will not fit the space reserved for it. In a huge department store, the seven-foot sofa can look smaller than it is.
- ☐ Don't choose a color — for upholstery, carpet, drapes or accent chair — without securing a swatch of the fabric to take home. The light in your room will be very different from the light in a department store's display room. The bigger the swatch of fabric you take home, the better you can judge its harmony with your color plan. Don't forget that colors change with morning and evening light.

JUDGING QUALITY

You want quality in construction and materials. But quality is often hard to judge. There is no way to look at a wing chair in a furniture store and somehow sense that springs will stay firm, that cushions will stay flat and comfortable, and that the frame is as sturdy as it looks. The manufacturer's literature will tell you how upholstered furniture is constructed.

Do not attempt to judge quality by price alone. There are too many variables in furniture construction and upholstery that affect price without reflecting quality. For instance, the upholstery fabric, expensive and luxurious, can cover slipshod construction.

Read the labels:

- ☐ Filling and cushioning materials will be identified (as required by law) on that ubiquitous tag headlined "DO NOT REMOVE UNDER PENALTY OF LAW." Shredded, flaked or ground foam must be so identified. A tag reading "Polyurethane Foam" should mean that the foam rubber is in solid sections. "Shredded Urethane Foam" means what it says — the cushioning material is in bits and pieces.

The Federal Trade Commission's guidelines on identification of furniture materials have been revised. Revision was necessary, the FTC explained, because "major changes in technology and materials used in furniture construction have occurred so rapidly . . . Plastic can look like wood. Vinyl may look like leather and marble dust may appear to be slate." As a result of all this, the FTC was convinced that there had been widespread misleading advertising and other deceptive practices in the furniture industry.

Now, under FTC guidelines (which became effective March 21, 1974), furniture advertised as maple or walnut must actually be made from that type of solid wood. Veneered construction (where a layer of superior wood covers a less expensive wood base) must also be disclosed.

When wood names are used merely to describe a color, grain design, or other simulated finish applied to the exposed surfaces of furniture, it must be made clear that the names describe the finish only. Terms such as "walnut finish" or "fruitwood finish" are no longer acceptable.

Look for labels that read "walnut color" or fruitwood finish on birch solids and veneers," etc. These tell you what you are buying.

Guidelines also call for "affirmative disclosure" (statements of identification) of such materials as plastic, vinyl, marble dust, etc., "when the lack of such identification . . . could have the capacity and tendency or effect of misleading or deceiving." *This means all advertising, catalogs, brochures, hang tags and other labels must be clearly worded.* A trade name such as "Durahyde" (a fabric-backed vinyl upholstery covering which simulates leather) must be followed by a statement of the composition of the product (e.g., fabric-backed vinyl) or a statement that the product is not leather (e.g., "simulated" or "imitation" leather).

The guidelines also provide that:

- ☐ Manufacturers may still label products with terms such as "French Provincial" and "Mediterranean" when appropriate, because the FTC believes most consumers understand that these terms denote furniture styles, as opposed to places of origin.
- ☐ Manufacturers may *not* use the name of a country on its own unless the merchandise originates from that country. If a piece is called "Danish," it must be from Denmark; otherwise it must be referred to as "Danish style," "Scandinavian design" or a suitable equivalent.
- ☐ Any advertised performance tests on upholstery fabrics must have been performed by "qualified persons in a proper manner so as to constitute a reasonable basis for evaluating the fabric as a furniture covering." Furthermore, test results must be communicated in layman's language.

Administer your own performance test. After a careful reading of identifying labels, you should administer your own performance test as an aid to determining quality. Try using these hints as guidelines:

- ☐ Furniture should stand firmly and flatly on the floor. Try shaking it gently — does the table tip? Are the dining room or kitchen chairs unstable in the store? They will be even less stable at home.
- ☐ Check to see how pieces of wood are joined. The strongest joints are dovetail, mortise and tenon, and dowel. The least satisfactory are those that have been simply glued or nailed.
- ☐ Drawers should slide effortlessly and have center guides or treads. Look for stops that prevent you from pulling the drawer all the way out. When closed, drawers should fit flush to the furniture surface.
- ☐ Drawers should have reinforced corners and dovetail (interlocking) joints.
- ☐ Make sure the degree of finishing on a piece of furniture meets your expectations and needs. Are the undersides well sanded and smooth? Is this important to you? If a piece of furniture is to be

used in an area where the back will be exposed to view, is it well enough finished, or — as in the case of some self-assembled bookcases — is it made of heavy cardboard or unfinished low-quality wood?

Upholstered furniture, as already mentioned, presents a special kind of problem. If the hang tags have been removed from pieces that interest you, there is really no way for you to know what materials have been used in construction. Look for labels that identify:

- ☐ **The wood used in the frame:** Kiln-dried hardwood will provide lasting stability.
- ☐ **The construction of the frame:** Is it corner-blocked (fitted and glued) and doubled-doweled for extra strength?
- ☐ **The kind and number of springs:** Construction of top-quality furniture is still identified by hand-tied coil springs (a minimum of eight or, better, twelve per seat). Durable springs are oven-japanned — if the furniture is well constructed, you may never see them, but look for identification in manufacturers' information brochures.
- ☐ **The nature of the webbing base:** Quality furniture once featured a jute webbing base for the springs; now steel webbing is often used.
- ☐ **The cushioning materials:** Applied directly over the springs and frame, cushioning can be made of a wide variety of substances, including curled hair, cellulose, cotton batting, rubberized fibers, polyester fibers, down (found only in expensive upholstered pieces and now mostly 75 percent feathers, 25 percent down), kapok, foam rubber, polyurethane foam.

    The synthetics have a great deal of natural resilience, and are often combined. The identification label will always signal this: e.g., latex foam rubber, 30%; polyester fibers, 25%, etc.
- ☐ **The kind of fiberfill:** This is the protective padding between cushioning materials and the outer upholstery fabric. Materials include polyester and combinations of polyester and down, foam or cotton (used in less expensive furniture).

After you are fully informed on material content and construction materials of upholstered furniture, you will want to do your own consumer-testing in the store:

- ☐ Gently push and pull at the arms of sofas and chairs; a well-constructed piece of furniture will be firm.
- ☐ Be sure to sit on upholstered furniture. Bounce on it. Move about. Does the upholstery fabric shift easily? Do the lines stay firm?
- ☐ Remove the cushions from their supporting platform (called the *deck*). The deck material should be made of a tightly woven fabric.

Cushion care

The reason that cushions on upholstered furniture have zippers is that it simplifies the manufacturing process. *The covers are not to be removed for cleaning,* but unless you read the care booklet supplied with upholstered furniture from cover to cover, you might never know this. Buried midway through one manufacturer's material is a clear statement that cushion covers must not be removed for separate washing or dry cleaning. The zipper is only there, they say, to make the covers fit well. They warn: *Washing or dry cleaning cushion covers separately from the total piece can result in shrinkage, change in color and damage to the backing.* Furthermore, if you don't heed the warning (which you may not have seen), you risk cancelling the warranty (if there is one) on your furniture.

Some manufacturers and retailers include care instructions on their deck labels, out where you can see them when you turn the cushions. Keep an eye out for them.

One reads like this:

CARE INSTRUCTIONS
Keep away from direct sunlight.
Vacuum upholstery weekly.
Turn cushions monthly.
Do not remove cushion covers
    for cleaning purposes.

Extension of care-labeling regulations (see also DRY CLEANING) to include upholstery and decorating fabrics is under consideration by the Federal Trade Commission. *For your own protection, until these care-labeling rules go into effect, read all the way through manufacturers' information booklets.*

Upholstery fabrics change constantly — new synthetics, new blends, new finishes to guard against stains and watermarks — and the market can be confusing.

Read the manufacturers' consumer information material thoroughly. You will find that warranties (see WARRANTIES) are extended on construction, but that there is no guarantee as to the durability of the fabric. Some manufacturers go so far as to classify fabrics as to wearability standards of their own. Check the deck label for fabric information.

Look for a manufacturer's warranty. (If you buy a house-brand piece of furniture from a national retailer, the upholstered furniture may carry a retailer's warranty.)

Check:

☐ What is warranted and for how long? Construction, for example, may be warranted for five years, upholstery fabric for one year.

☐ Are there any warranty limitations? Warranties must be designated "full" or "limited," and limitations must be clearly defined.

Wearability tests you can carry out yourself. Have the salesman supply you with a swatch of the upholstery fabric, and do the following:

☐ **Hold it close to a light.** A tightly woven fabric will show no light through the threads.
☐ **Rub the fabric surfaces together.** There should be no sign of wear and no pills should form.
☐ **Press the fabric as hard as you can,** gripping both edges, pressing with your thumbs. If the fabric is durable, it will not be forced apart; the weave will stay firm.
☐ **To test colorfastness, repeat the rubbing treatment.** If the print smudges, don't expect it to be colorfast. Dye should go all the way through printed fabrics. Check this by holding the fabric up to the light. If the design is literally "printed" on the fabric on one side only, you can expect it to wear off.

PROTECT YOURSELF
Use these guidelines when you shop:

☐ "Bait and switch" (see FRAUD AND DECEPTION) is still a prevalent furniture-selling scheme. This is the practice of advertising merchandise at a low cost without intending to, or wanting to, sell it. The customer is "baited" with a low price, then "switched" to higher priced merchandise. If you encounter this selling scheme, leave the store.
☐ Know how much you want to spend when you walk into a store. It's amazing how quickly you can forget that you were interested in a $99 chair when your attention is drawn to a specially-priced living-room set.
☐ If you buy something on "discount," make sure you know what you have to give up to get the lower price. Delivery? Installation? After-purchase service?
☐ Before you take advantage of a "discount" offer, compare prices of similar merchandise at other stores.
☐ Find out the store's return policy.
☐ If you buy on the installment plan, check the contract very carefully. If there is any part of it you don't understand, ask questions or take it to someone you trust who can help you understand.
☐ Before you sign a contract or sales agreement, make sure it contains accurate descriptions of the items you bought.
☐ Buy only from reputable merchants. Check with neighbors and with the Better Business Bureau.

Furs

IF A FUR COAT, jacket or stole is high on your "want list," you have probably been looking them over for years. You have an idea of the cut and color you want, and a good idea of when and where the best "fur sales" are scheduled. But you need more information for your final buying decision.

Look at the labels; read them carefully. They must contain the following information:

- ☐ Type of fur (muskrat, rabbit, mink, etc.);
- ☐ Whether it has been bleached or dyed or otherwise artificially colored;
- ☐ Whether the garment is made of used furs, or paws, tails, bellies or waste fur;
- ☐ The country of origin, for imported furs.

HOW CAN YOU EVALUATE THE FUR?

It should be soft and silky, with thick, glossy hair and a soft texture. Brush the hair backwards — against the grain — to judge the density. Lower-quality fur appears sparse and may feel stiff.

Animals from colder areas, for obvious reasons, have thicker fur. Their pelts will produce a warmer garment. Check the country of origin listed on the label. Alaskan beaver and seal, for instance, have dense, silky coats. If your coat's label lists a more southerly origin, expect a thinner, less luxuriant fur.

Check the workmanship. When you look at the underside of a coat, you may well be surprised at the number of seams. It is not the number of skins used, but the way they are put together that is meaningful here. The skins should be combined so that you can't tell where one ends and another begins. The overall design should give the impression that the entire coat came from one animal.

Consider fit and style carefully. You should be able to move comfortably in your coat. Unnecessary stress and strain on a fur, even a carefully constructed one, will cause rips and faster wear, shortening the life of a major clothing investment.

PRICE CONSIDERATIONS

Storage and maintenance. Even inexpensive furs require summer storage and seasonal cleaning by a professional. Check cleaning and storage costs. **Remember:** Clothing maintenance can be expensive; be sure to make this a *pre-purchase* consideration.

Insurance. This is a must for major investments. In connection with storage, make sure to find out whether the quoted price includes *adequate* insurance.

The furrier and you

When you shop for a fur, remember that *only the merchandise*, not the salesperson and the selling method, should be smooth and glossy. Reasonable questions deserve reasonable answers, and your questions in regard to the merchandise that interests you should be answered fully and courteously.

If the salesperson is vague, if your questions are glossed over on the grounds that they are irrelevant because all the merchandise in the store is "guaranteed," ask to be served by someone who can provide the information you want. You may need a clear explanation of label terminology or of the store's ninety-day payment policy, etc. If you don't get the answers you need, find yourself another store.

Follow these guidelines:

☐ Check with your Better Business Bureau to find out the dealer's consumer complaint record. If a number of complaints have gone unresolved, you are forewarned.

☐ Be suspicious any time a salesperson offers to cut the price "just for you." The price, no doubt, will have been inflated so that such offers can be safely made.

☐ Fur sales are traditionally scheduled in January and August, and you can save money by shopping a reputable retailer's offerings during those months. **Remember:** A sale is not a sale when it goes on . . . and on . . . and on. Avoid stores that advertise "last ten days of sale" for weeks or months at a time.

☐ A retailer who offers furs "below cost" or at "wholesale prices" either (1) has decided that he no longer needs to make a profit or (2) is lying. The former is unlikely; the latter is probably the case. Avoid the store.

☐ Be wary of anyone who tells you it's your "last chance" to buy such a fabulous fur at "this special price." This is a high-pressure sales tactic, unworthy of being taken seriously. The salesperson is much too eager to get your name on a sales agreement. Don't be rushed into an ill-considered purchase.

> **Consider alternatives**
> Fake and "fun" furs, made of synthetics or (if real) of rabbit skin, often come in bright colors and different patterns. Some are dyed to look like ocelot, zebra and other skins.
> The synthetics need no storage and they dry quickly if you get caught in the rain or snow. They are warm. And they cost a fraction of the price of real fur.
> If you prefer rabbit fur to synthetic — on the grounds that it is, after all, real, you may be able to find it at prices competitive with the synthetics. *But be warned:* Rabbit fur molts. It also becomes brittle when it dries and may wear less satisfactorily than synthetics. And if you can't wear a fur in bad weather, when you need it, why have it?

If you are in the market for expensive furs, remember that the long-haired varieties are generally less expensive than the flat furs. They also give you more warmth, and are more durable.

Mink, it appears, is still high on the popularity list, and prices of some mink garments are remarkably reasonable. Furs produced in the United States and Canada (ranch-bred, commercially produced) are of excellent quality. The wide range of colors is a result of cross-breeding for color variation though mink, like other furs, is often dyed.

Long-wearing, sturdy furs include:

- **Beaver:** relatively expensive, very warm.
- **Fitch:** moderately priced, moderate warmth.
- **Krimmer:** moderately priced, good warmth.
- **Mouton:** one of the least expensive furs, good warmth.
- **Muskrat:** moderately priced, good warmth.
- **Nutria:** moderately priced, good warmth.
- **Persian lamb:** expensive, good warmth. (Check the label; a much lighter-than-usual version comes from South Africa. Much of the heavier "Persian" lamb has its origin in Russia.)
- **Sheared raccoon:** moderately priced, good warmth.

Gardening and Lawn Care

GARDENING AND LAWN CARE are comparable to dieting. They are all long-term projects which require planning, attention to detail, determination and plenty of exercise.

In considering the source of seeds, seedlings, bedding plants, trees and shrubs, wise consumers will choose nursery-stock suppliers as carefully as they choose the source of the furniture for their homes. Ask veteran gardeners what their experience has been with local garden centers and nursery-stock suppliers. Check with the Better Business Bureau as well for the complaint records of local firms and mail order suppliers.

Plants by mail. Catalog and advertisements of mail-order nurseries should indicate the regions to which advertised plants are well adapted. Specific planting and care instructions should be furnished. If plants are "guaranteed," the guarantee should be specific (see WARRANTIES).

"Mary, Mary, quite contrary . . ."
Common garden-variety nonsense is a hardy perennial. As sure as spring follows winter, misleading nursery-stock advertising will feature claims like "grows 20 feet in one year"; "supplies bushels of fruit from summer to fall"; "produces thousands of exotic blooms in a few weeks." The immediate clue to virtually all misleading nursery-stock advertising is grossly exaggerated claims.

A second garden pest is the fly-by-night promoter who creates exotic names and descriptions for whatever he is selling. Very common trees and shrubs are advertised as "revolutionary" discoveries and/or "an unheard-of value." The value is questionable and the reason the plants are "unheard of" is that the promoter has just coined the name. In this way, the common silver maple becomes "The Silver Acer" and the thornless honey locust is transformed into "The Flowering Umbrella." *The Federal Trade Commission requires that when a nursery product has a generally recognized and well-established common name, that name must be used in all advertisements.*

TOOLS AND EQUIPMENT

Necessary *hand tools* such as leaf and lawn rakes, spades and hoes are often offered at "low, low" prices in a set. Check such items carefully before you buy. Sturdy, well-finished tools may be more expensive than the 4-for-$5.98 "bargain" offer, but they will be durable and, in the long run, easier to use because they will be better balanced, better constructed and made of a higher-grade metal.

When you buy **power lawn and garden tools,** look for designs featuring double insulation, protective shields and easily accessible controls. Follow the manufacturer's use and care instructions to the letter. If you are thinking about buying a power tool that you are relatively unfamiliar with, why not rent it first to try it out? You may find that power models are less practical than you thought.

The lawn mower. For people with a small or moderate-sized lawn, the traditional reel-type person-powered lawn mower is both economical and efficient. Consider these advantages:

- ☐ **Safety.** Although greater attention to built-in safety features has been given to rotary power mowers, their high-speed blades make them inherently dangerous. Prospective purchasers should carefully consider both risk/benefit and cost/benefit ratios before they buy.
- ☐ **Efficiency.** The simpler the mechanism of any piece of equipment, the easier it is to operate and maintain. The simple, well-cared-for hand mower is virtually maintenance-free. It is also constantly under control and easily maneuverable in use.

Power mowers, reel or rotary, may be considered a necessity by owners of homes surrounded by large lawns. They should be chosen with careful attention to safety maintenance factors. Check product-rating publications for evaluations in regard to efficiency and safety.

When using power mower equipment, follow the detailed use and care instructions provided by the manufacturer. Take special note of the standard list of precautions contained in the manufacturer's instruction booklet, including these commonsense practices.

- ☐ Precheck the area to be mowed and remove sticks, stones, wire or any other debris.
- ☐ Do not mow when the grass is wet.
- ☐ Keep children and pets away from the mower. (Injuries have occurred to people in yards across the street from rotary mowers because the high-speed blades can throw stones with the speed and effectiveness of bullets.)
- ☐ Refuel out of doors and when the engine is cool. A hot engine can ignite gasoline.
- ☐ Always keep feet and hands well away from the blades. Never mow in sandals, sneakers or with bare feet.

HIRING PROFESSIONALS: LAWN MAINTENANCE

Lawn care for hire is available. Some lawn specialists offer such services as bulding a new lawn from scratch or rebuilding and maintaining the lawn. The agreement might call for lawn preparation, fertilizing, seeding, liming and aerating, plus weed, disease and insect control.

The contracts signed by homeowners for such services should, like all other contracts, be carefully examined before they are signed. Always:

- ☐ Check the reputation of the firm with the local Better Business Bureau. Some maintenance contracts have gone unfulfilled while demands for money continue or, worse, no service may have been rendered despite money paid in advance.
- ☐ Check the contract: What services are specified? For how much? How does the price compare with the cost of weekend, pay-as-you-go services provided by a local lawn-care professional? What happens if specified services are not delivered? Are all oral agreements written into the contract? Are all inapplicable items deleted?

Common "lawn pests." Never, never buy sod or topsoil from an itinerant who "just happens to be in the neighborhood" with "exactly the amount of material you need for your lawn." Homeowners have often been sadly disappointed in the quality of sod, and many have made the serious mistake of buying topsoil by the bushel at an exorbitant price. **Remember:** Topsoil is sold by the *truckload*, unless you're buying it for a flowerbed.

Don't be taken in by fast-talking, self-styled tree surgeons who might also "just happen to be in the neighborhood." If you are contacted by a tree surgeon, it's a signal to be wary. Reliable professionals are too busy to need to drum up business this way. Don't let anyone work on your valuable shade trees or your lawn without checking his reputation with neighbors and with the Better Business Bureau.

If you need information from a local professional in regard to lawn care and maintenance, check with your county agricultural extension office.

For safety's sake . . .

Be fussy about the use and storage of all lawn and garden equipment. Rakes and hoes left on the lawn "just for a moment," sharp points upward, pose an immediate safety hazard. Any tool not in use should be left leaning, points or edges inward, against a wall. When you take a lunch break, take time to put the tools in the storage shed. Sharp tools of all kinds should always be kept out of the reach of small children.

Gasoline and Gasoline-Saving Devices

(See also AUTOMOBILES; ENERGY)

USING THE CORRECT GRADE of gasoline in your car can increase your engine's efficiency and save you money. Current federal regulations require that all gasoline pumps show a bright yellow sticker that tells you the octane rating of the gas in each pump. The octane rating or grade of gasoline is a measure of its resistance to engine knock, a noise that indicates that your engine is burning gas unevenly. Knocking decreases engine power and fuel economy, and can damage engine parts over a period of time. The higher the grade, the more the gasoline will resist this problem.

Even if you don't hear any knocking, you may still be using the wrong octane level — that is, gas with too high an octane rating. That doesn't help your engine any or your wallet; it also wastes energy and puts more lead pollutants into the air.

Check your car's operations manual to find out what octane is right for your car. Then wait until the gas tank is almost empty and fill it up with the recommended grade. Drive a few miles until the car is warmed up and then come to a complete stop. Next, accelerate hard. If the engine knocks, use up the tank and fill up with the next higher grade. Repeat the test. If the engine doesn't knock, this is the correct octane.

If the engine is not knocking at the recommended grade, try the same test but decrease the grade you fill up with instead. If the engine knocks, the lower grade may be inadequate and you should go back to the recommended level.

BE WARY OF EXAGGERATED OR FALSE CLAIMS
Along with rising gasoline prices and attempts to reduce American dependence on imported oil have come advertisements claiming that a variety of devices and additives will dramatically increase automobile fuel economy.

Among products commonly advertised as gas savers are devices that attach to a car's crankcase, ventilation line or carburetor, and additives put directly into the gas tank. In an effort to be thrifty, people are spending money on special values, replacement distributor rotors, air jets, pre-agitators, hydrocatalysts, "miracle" spark plugs, pellet or liquid additives and vapor, foam or liquid injector systems.

GASOLINE AND GASOLINE-SAVING DEVICES

The Environmental Protection Agency has tested and evaluated many devices and additives for which fuel savings claims have been made and with few exceptions has found little significant improvement in gas mileage. Some of the gimmicks do nothing at all. Others actually increase gas consumption. One device requires advancing the timing of the engine spark, an illegal action that can upset the emission control system and result in engine damage and a stiff fine. Two others do increase gas mileage, but at the same time produce exhaust emissions that exceed emission standards. Using them violates the anti-tampering provisions of the Clean Air Act and one of them actually causes marked deterioration of vehicle driveability.

Despite the fact that advertisements for these products have appeared and that at least one internationally famous American has endorsed such a device in commercials, many of the claims made for these products are exaggerated and misleading. Data offered to substantiate gas-saving claims under normal driving conditions have often been inaccurate, outdated, or otherwise insufficient. The Federal Trade Commission has issued complaints against a number of companies because their gadgets don't work. None gives the 28 to 35 percent increase in fuel economy that ads promise. And none adds 100 extra miles between fill-ups. In short, the large majority don't provide enough improvement in miles per gallon to justify the cost of purchase and installation. Check with your BBB for information on specific devices and additives.

If you want to improve your automobile's fuel economy, follow these well-documented energy saving tips to get better mileage:

- ☐ Check tire pressure frequently. Underinflated tires can cut down gas mileage more than you think. Make sure the wheels are properly aligned.
- ☐ Keep your engine well tuned. Some estimates say that proper tuning, oil changes when needed and engine cleaning can increase fuel efficiency by as much as 10 to 20 percent.
- ☐ Instead of letting your engine idle for more than a minute or two, turn off your motor whenever possible. An idling engine gets 0 miles to the gallon.
- ☐ When you're driving in town, anticipate the traffic ahead so you can brake sparingly. Accelerate smoothly and avoid quick starts and stops.
- ☐ On the highway, don't exceed the 55 miles per hour speed limit.

Hair Dryers

THERE ARE TWO BASIC MODELS of home hair dryers:
- **The stationary, hooded appliance,** adapted from the machines used for years in beauty salons; and
- **The hand-held model** — blow-dryers and dryer-styling devices, which are used with comb and brush attachments.

Hooded dryers are useful for hairstyles which must be "set" with curlers, rollers or pincurls. Hand-held models are useful for drying and shaping long, straight hair and short, casual styles.

Carefully inspect the range of equipment available before you make a selection. Unless you have seen an identical model in operation — or tried it for yourself in a friend's home or in your beauty shop — insist on a close look at the demonstration models in the store. If necessary, have the salesperson remove the appliance from its carton for your inspection. This may not endear you to sales personnel, but you need to assure yourself that the equipment you buy has the attributes you want.

A few words of caution
Overuse of overheated electric hair dryers can damage the hair, making it stiff, dry and brittle. Use your dryer with caution and with careful attention to the manufacturer's use and care instructions, so that the end result is healthy hair with the soft texture, body and shape you're looking for.

Many hand-held stylers have only two settings: "DRY," which produces intense heat, and "STYLE," for moderate heat and gentler air flow. Others can be set for "HIGH," "MEDIUM" and "LOW"; still other models have as many as nine settings.

Shop carefully for the features you need. Weight, balance and the extent of vibration will be important factors affecting efficient use of these appliances. Before you make a final decision on which styler or blow-dry appliance is for you, hold it in your hand to feel for yourself how easy or difficult it is to manipulate. Keep in mind the fact that *you must keep it moving,* otherwise you scorch your hair with high heat concentration on one area.

For example:

- ☐ Make sure that the power and temperature controls are easily accessible.
- ☐ Check table-model hooded dryers for stability. See for yourself that the model you buy is well balanced when it is in use.
- ☐ Some hooded dryers allow you to move about while your hair is drying. Check the length of the cord and, again, the accessibility of the control mechanism.

Before you buy any dryer or styler:

- ☐ Check consumer research and reporting publications (available in your local library) for the product you are considering.
- ☐ Recheck with friends and with your hair stylist for their personal evaluations of several products.
- ☐ Make the warranty a key part of your buying decision (see WARRANTIES).

Note: In the early part of 1979 the U.S. Consumer Product Safety Commission conducted an investigation to identify hair dryers containing asbestos materials and to determine any hazard associated with those products. To obtain a list of hair dryers that do and do not contain asbestos, write to Hair Dryers, Consumer Product Safety Commission, Washington, D.C. 20207.

Consider safety

- ☐ Hair dryers, like other pieces of electrical equipment, should carry the UL safety seal (the seal of Underwriters Laboratories, Inc.). This means the article (or the part of the article to which the seal is attached) has been tested for fire, electrical shock and related accident hazards.
- ☐ Dry and style your hair in a dressing room or bedroom, *not in the bathroom* where the risk of dropping the equipment into a water-filled basin or sink is too great. You could risk a fatal shock.
- ☐ Never attempt to clean the combs, brushes or air vent while the dryer/styler is plugged in, even though the power switch is off.
- ☐ Dryer/stylers should be unplugged and stored away when they are not in use, well out of reach of children.

Always check use and care manuals for all electrical appliances, large or small, before you use them. Follow manufacturers' instructions to the letter for use, care, cleaning and storage. This is important both for maximum efficient use of the product and for your own safety when you use it.

Health and Medicine

(See also DRUGS, NONPRESCRIPTION; DRUGS, PRESCRIPTION; INSURANCE, HEALTH; NUTRITION)

> *Good health is not merely absence of disease; it means mental and emotional health as well as the normal functioning of the body, sometimes called "physical health." Health . . . is an attribute of a human being which enables him to live with the greatest satisfaction to himself within the framework of the society to which he belongs.*
>
> —Justus J. Schifferes, Ph.D.,
> *The Family Medical Encyclopedia*

MEDICAL KNOWLEDGE, technology and treatment methods have made great strides forward in the last half-century.

Unfortunately, quasi-medical misinformation has kept pace. There seems no limit to the number of health frauds and fads that promise quick cures for what ails the American public. Some are dangerous, such as the remedies for cancer used, in lieu of professional medical treatment, by thousands of people. Arthritis "cures" ranging from copper bracelets to diets and massage may be equally harmful by delaying treatment of a degenerative disease which, although it cannot be cured, can be arrested in its early stages.

Other fads, such as diets promising miraculous results for the aging, the obese and, again, for arthritis victims, may or may not be actively harmful, but neither are they likely to produce the long-term positive results that adopting a simple, well-balanced diet would provide.

Good health habits are logical and fundamental to good health. Good health requires good nutrition, common-sense hygiene and adequate exercise balanced with adequate rest and relaxation. Add to these routine checkups by a good dentist and that annual checkup by the family doctor, and the result is likely to be, for most people, generally good health.

HOME HEALTH CARE, FIRST AID AND THE FAMILY MEDICINE CHEST

Though the family is healthy and wise, you still need to guard against accidents in the home and know what to do when they occur (see SAFETY). There will also be times when a mild headache or a cold sends you to the medicine chest in search of a remedy.

Your medicine chest should contain:

- ☐ **Aspirin.** This simple item is the major active ingredient in a variety of proprietary (nonprescription, over-the-counter) remedies. You can pay a lot or a little for aspirin in products that fizz, in "buffered" products, and in "time-release" preparations.

    Although there are differences, it is essentially a standardized product and off-brands are usually less expensive. *Just take this simple precaution:* Check to see if the contents smell like vinegar. If they do, the tablets have been on the shelf too long and you should ask for a fresh package.

    If you buy flavored "children's aspirin," be sure to keep it out of reach of youngsters who might mistake it for candy. Aspirin in large doses is poisonous. Instead of children's aspirin, the standard 5-grain tablet can be cut into halves or quarters, crushed, and the taste disguised by mixing the proper amount with a spoonful of jelly or a gelatin dessert.
- ☐ **Adhesive bandages and patches** in assorted sizes.
- ☐ **Sterile gauze pads,** separately packaged, in 2"×2" and 3"×3" sizes.
- ☐ **Sterile absorbent cotton.**
- ☐ **Antiseptic,** such as hydrogen peroxide, for cleansing minor cuts and scrapes.
- ☐ **Elastic bandage,** about three inches wide, for treating sprains.
- ☐ **Scissors,** for cutting bandages and tape.
- ☐ **Tweezers** (the fine-pointed type), for removing splinters.
- ☐ **Clinical thermometers,** one rectal, one oral.
- ☐ **Bicarbonate of soda** (ordinary baking soda), for simple indigestion or "hyperacidity." This simple home remedy is as effective as the expensive, much-advertised proprietary remedies sold for the same purpose.

For safety's sake

The medicine chest should have a locked section for storage of potentially dangerous prescription drugs and over-the-counter remedies, *especially if there are children in the house.* Often, pills and preparations look and smell good enough to eat and drink, with the result that unsupervised youngsters are likely to do just that. And *all* children are unsupervised sometimes.

> **A good first aid manual is a must**
> It will tell you how to treat minor injuries at home and — equally important — what to do for more serious injuries until medical help is available.
>
> A "best buy" is *Standard First Aid and Personal Safety* published by the American Red Cross and available from local Red Cross Chapters. Buy two — one for home, one for the car.

Budgeting for medical care may be virtually impossible. The need for extensive medical (or dental) care is unpredictable, and the cost of care has been steadily rising.

Make sure your budget includes medical insurance fees, the cost of the annual complete physical for each member of the family, and those necessary visits to the dentist, eye doctor, etc. Base your estimate for medical care on last year's expenditure — then, if possible, add a 5 percent margin.

CHOOSING THE FAMILY DOCTOR

It isn't easy to become a well-informed consumer of medical services. The people who provide such services are often authoritative, "too busy" to spend time answering questions or, much worse, fail to take a complete medical history on which diagnosis and treatment must be based.

To choose a doctor, apply the same wise-consumer logic you apply to the choice of goods and services. Use these guidelines:

- ☐ Select a doctor while you are healthy. A good place to start is with the routine annual checkup.
- ☐ Ask family or friends for recommendations, or check with the local medical society. (Organization membership only means that the doctor is licensed to practice and that he paid his annual dues; it is not necessarily a measure of competence.)
- ☐ You might also start with a referral from a hospital, preferably a teaching hospital associated with a medical school. Doctors who practice in a teaching environment must stay abreast of current medical knowledge and treatment methods. Secure a list of three or four general practitioners (likely to be found in rural areas) or internists (specialists in disorders of the internal organs) who have completed at least three years of training beyond the basic four-year medical course. You should, when you visit these doctors or when you phone to make an appointment, inform them that you are interested in selecting a family physician. *Do not hesitate to inquire about fees and services:* e.g., what arrangements are made for back-up care when the doctor is away? What is his or her policy on house calls?
- ☐ Evaluate the physician's general attitude toward patients. Your

own reaction to the doctor is also very important.
- ☐ Consider the atmosphere of the office. If it is apparent that some patients have been waiting several hours for an appointment scheduled at 10:00 (and if this sort of thing annoys you), cancel your appointment and look for another doctor whose scheduling procedure is more efficient. There *are* doctors who manage to maintain reasonable schedules.
- ☐ Consider group practice. Doctors who work in groups are likely to consult with one another on evaluations and diagnoses and, furthermore, are likely to have been screened by their peers for competence.
- ☐ Evaluate the initial examination. Personal and family medical histories are important diagnostic tools. Questions should be thorough and specific, and answers should be carefully recorded. In some cases doctors have the history recorded by an assistant, and this is fine — if it is reviewed by the physician in the course of your complete physical examination.
- ☐ That "complete" physical should be complete. Routine blood and urine tests, a digital rectal examination, and for women, a Pap smear and pelvic examination.

Do you feel comfortable with the doctor?
A good doctor/patient relationship must be based on confidence and mutual respect. If you have doubts or reservations about being able to develop a long-term relationship with the doctor you have just seen for the first time, you should feel free to ask to have your records transferred to another physician on your "try" list.

Before your initial appointment with any physician — whether general practitioner, specialist in family practice, internist or specialist — make a list of specific questions that concern you. Note recurrent symptoms, however mild, which might signal a problem. Don't assume that sudden blurred vision, for instance, means that you need an immediate appointment to have your glasses changed. Mention the problem to the family doctor. Blurred vision could be caused by high blood pressure, diabetes or other problems. Evaluate the doctor's attitude toward preventive medicine. Advice on diet, exercise, smoking habits and so on are very much in order. Women should be advised by family physicians or gynecologists on how to perform routine self-examination of the breasts. Patients should be regarded by physicians as active participants in health care.

> **About surgery**
> The American public has become increasingly concerned about reports of unnecessary surgery — and the concern is well founded. A Cornell University study indicates that surgeons in the United States perform an estimated 2.4 million unnecessary operations each year. And some 11,900 patients die each year as a result of complications arising from surgery.
>
> One indication that such studies have been taken seriously was Blue Cross/Blue Shield's decision that the costs of second opinions on the necessity for surgical procedures would be covered by insurance in the interest of reducing the number of unnecessary operations.
>
> **Remember: A second opinion on the need for surgery will be much less costly in terms of time, pain, possible complications and money than rushing into unnecessary surgery would be.** Any reputable physician should understand your interest in having his diagnosis and recommendation confirmed. Laboratories have been known to make errors on tests which form the basis for diagnosis. The best-intentioned doctors are human and capable of errors in judgment, and even the most routine surgical procedure can become complex. So get additional opinions.

CHOOSING A DENTIST

A good dentist can save you pain, problems, and — most important — your teeth.

Look for a dentist who is prevention-oriented. You will have to work with him or her to promote dental hygiene and prevent dental disease, but the prevention-oriented dentist will show you how by explaining how to brush with maximum efficiency, how to use dental floss, etc.

A good dentist views the removal of a tooth as a major disaster and will do everything possible to help you save all your teeth. It might seem more economical to remove a tooth instead of going to the expense of saving it, as with root canal work; but the long-range consequences of extractions can be even more expensive and uncomfortable.

When you go to a new dentist, expect a full examination, complete with medical history and, if you haven't brought records provided by your former dentist, a full-mouth set of X-rays. *The dentist, not the hygienist, should make a complete oral examination.*

Find a dentist who explains what is being done and why. Don't be afraid to ask questions. Your mouth shouldn't be a mystery to you. A good dentist explains alternative treatments for specific dental conditions as well as their possible benefits and complications.

He or she will also:

☐ Participate in continuing education programs to keep up with

new developments in the field;
- ☐ Have a clean, well-organized office (as with doctors, be wary of dentists whose offices are always crowded and who spend little time with their patients);
- ☐ Give you emergency treatment when it's necessary.

The question of fees is important. Your complete treatment plan should include a cost estimate as well as a complete and comprehensive discussion of the examination and an evaluation of the X-ray findings. Make sure you understand the explanation. If the work is going to be expensive and extend over a long period of time, you may want to request a written summary of the work to be done and the fees to be charged.

Remember: Modern dentists do not just "fix teeth." They are concerned with your complete oral health — gums, bones and palate. Your diet — and whether you smoke — is of concern. If you want a healthy mouth and sound, lasting teeth, you should be equally concerned.

Consider a dental clinic

If you are lucky enough to live near a medical/dental school, you may find that dentists-in-training, *under the supervision of their professors,* staff a dental clinic. Because the services are offered by a teaching facility, they are likely to be thorough — slower, perhaps, than the services provided by the dentist in private practice — but well-supervised and competent.

Hearing Aids

(See also CONTRACTS; WARRANTIES)

IT IS IMPORTANT TO remember that no one hearing aid is suitable for every type of hearing loss, and also that some hearing difficulties can be corrected by medical or surgical procedures. For these important reasons, accurate diagnosis of the source of a hearing problem is vital.

If you suspect a hearing loss, the first step is to consult your family physician. If your family doctor cannot help you with your hearing problem, he may refer you to an ear specialist. The ear specialist, called an otologist or otolaryngologist, is a physician who specializes in the diagnosis and treatment of hearing problems. He will seek to determine the cause of your hearing problem and may be able to help you through medical or surgical treatment.

If a hearing aid seems indicated, the otologist may refer you directly to a hearing aid dealer. In this case, the dealer will test your hearing with an audiometer, demonstrate the aids he sells, help you select a particular aid, determine your need of an ear mold, assist you in getting used to your aid, help you learn to care for your aid, and have repairs made afterward as they are needed. In most states, licensing regulations establish qualifications and standards for hearing-aid dealers.

Your doctor or ear specialist might also refer you to an audiologist. An audiologist has been professionally trained and specializes in the prevention, identification, and assessment of hearing impairment. Among the specialized services audiologists provide are screening and evaluation of hearing in infants and young children; auditory habilitation including lip reading; counseling; and assistance in choosing the appropriate hearing aid, if necessary. Licensing laws in many states have established professional requirements for audiologists.

There are two major types of hearing loss:

1. **Conductive hearing loss** originates in the outer or middle ear. Its first sign may be that sounds are not as loud as they used to be, though the *quality* of sound may be about the same. This problem may come from any number of causes: wax may be blocking the ear

canal; the tissue lining the inner ear may be infected; the eardrum may be punctured; or the tiny bones in the inner ear may not move properly. These problems are often treated successfully through medical or surgical procedures.
2. **Sensorineural hearing loss** (often referred to as "nerve" hearing loss) is the type most commonly assisted by hearing aids. Here the problem is in the inner ear and results from cell or nerve damage with accompanying loss of volume and sound distortion. *More than 95 percent of all hearing aids are worn by people who have this type of hearing loss.*

Some hearing impairment results from a combination of conductive and sensorineural causes — **"mixed" hearing loss.** This can often be helped by the use of a hearing aid following medical or surgical procedures.

Watch for the following indications of hearing loss in family members, especially in the very young, the elderly, and in those who are exposed to a great deal of noise for extended periods of time:
- ☐ Frequent requests for repetition of spoken material;
- ☐ Inconsistent response to sound — now you hear it, now you don't;
- ☐ Ear infections, constant ringing in the ears or dizziness;
- ☐ Inattentiveness;
- ☐ Failure to develop speech (in children) or faulty speech (among the elderly);
- ☐ Excessive frustration with communication followed by gradual withdrawal, especially among the older members of the family.

When you and your doctor have determined that a hearing aid can help you, and when your doctor has referred you to a dealer or audiologist, the next step is to select the equipment best for you.

Here are some questions you should keep in mind when making your evaluation:

- ☐ How is the quality of the sound?
- ☐ Does the aid help you understand speech in quiet places? In noisy places?
- ☐ Is it comfortable to wear?
- ☐ Are the controls (tone control, volume control, telephone switch) easy to operate?
- ☐ If it is to be worn by a child, is the aid sturdy?
- ☐ Does the price include the ear mold?
- ☐ What are the upkeep costs?

> Hearing aids are simply miniature amplifying systems. They consist of:
> - ☐ A microphone, which picks up sound waves and converts them into electrical signals;
> - ☐ An amplifier, which increases the strength of the signal;
> - ☐ A battery, which supplies operating power;
> - ☐ A receiver, which changes the electrical signals back to sound waves; and, usually,
> - ☐ An ear mold, which connects the receiver to the ear canal.

It is quite likely that you will be able to arrange a **trial or rental period,** and within a few weeks you should know whether the equipment is right for you. Even though you may have to pay a rental fee (which is often applicable to the purchase price of the aid and the cost of the ear mold), a trial period is undoubtedly the best way to make an informed decision on the type of equipment you can use effectively — and on the dealer as well. The dealer you choose should have the patience, skill and experience to help you adjust to the equipment and to help you adjust the equipment to your needs.

CHOOSING A DEALER

Hearing aid dealers fit, sell and service hearing aids. Reputable dealers do not engage in bait advertising (see FRAUD AND DECEPTION), high-pressure sales methods or other unfair practices.

Find out and use the answers to the following questions as an aid to evaluating dealers in your area:

- ☐ How long has the dealer been in business?
- ☐ Does he have an established office?
- ☐ Is he a member of the National Hearing Aid Society? Is he a member of the State or City Hearing Aid Dealers Guild or Society?
- ☐ If your state licenses hearing aid dealers, does he hold such a license?
- ☐ Does he provide a clear, comprehensible *written* warranty or guarantee? (See WARRANTIES.)
- ☐ Does he represent and promote his products openly and honestly? (Check with friends who have dealt with various dealers and with your local Better Business Bureau.)
- ☐ Can he provide rapid and efficient repairs when your aid needs service?
- ☐ Is his representative able and willing to answer questions concerning the sales contract? (See CONTRACTS.)

By law, a hearing aid dealer may not sell you a hearing aid unless you have a physician's statement that your hearing loss has been medically evaluated and you may be considered a candidate for a hearing aid. However, *if you are 18 or older and have carefully considered the state of your own health, you may waive the medical evaluation,* in which case the dealer:

1. Must inform you that the waiver is not in your best health interest;
2. Must not in any way actively encourage the waiver; and
3. Must afford you an opportunity to sign a written statement of waiver.

The dealer should also provide you with a copy of a user instructional brochure before you buy, and review it with you.

Financial assistance is sometimes available to people who need hearing aids and cannot afford them. Your doctor, dealer or a local speech and hearing center may be able to tell you if assistance is available to you. Or you may write to or call:

☐ Your local United Fund or other social service organization.
☐ Your state vocational rehabilitation or public health department.
☐ Medicaid, whose program offers assistance to those who qualify in some states.

The Veterans Administration provides hearing aids to eligible veterans. For further information, contact the nearest VA office or hospital.

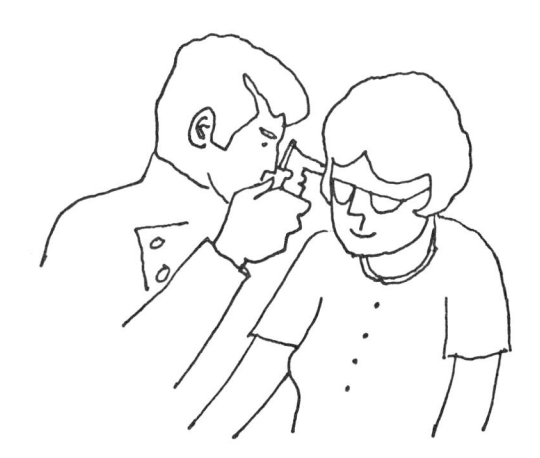

Home Maintenance and Improvement

(See also CONTRACTS; FRAUD AND DECEPTION; GARDENING AND LAWN CARE; INSULATION; PAINTS AND PAINTING; ROOFS AND ROOFING; WARRANTIES)

HOME MAINTENANCE — getting and keeping your house in top-notch order from roof to basement and all around the lawn — not only helps to create a comfortable and safe environment for you to live in but also maintains the value of your house.

Maintenance and repairs are best, and most economically, made as soon as they are needed. If the attic or basement feels damp, check for condensation, seepage, a clogged gutter or downspout. Don't wait until a leak in the roof or a drainage problem becomes more apparent. Locate the problem immediately before a small amount of moisture becomes a trickle and then a stream. Otherwise, a heavy rainstorm can result in costly damage.

Some maintenance problems develop slowly, and families tend to somehow become acclimated to them until they grow more complex. One such problem is reduced water pressure: the long time it takes to fill the bathtub somehow doesn't seem especially annoying, but the day the washing machine doesn't fill properly because someone flushed the toilet upstairs makes it clear that the plumbing system needs an overhaul.

Major plumbing problems constitute a hazard; a clogged line or a septic tank untended for too long can affect and possibly contaminate your water supply.

THE LIVED-IN LOOK VS. SLOPPY MAINTENANCE

Lived-in is nice, but torn, threadbare or worn can be a hazard (see SAFETY). There is a big difference between the homey look of an oriental carpet faded to soft, harmonious colors and a kitchen floor covering that should be replaced. Worn linoleum or loose tiles in the kitchen can mean accidents waiting to happen: a nasty fall or slip. Either condition also poses a hazard to property. Spilled water can seep down to the subflooring causing wood rot and providing household pests with a warm, moist haven.

Consider these points in your periodic home maintenance checks:

☐ Check for loose stones in the steps and wooden sections in porch

stairs or flooring which should be replaced. Make sure handrails on outside stairs are sturdy.
- ☐ Gutters and downspouts should be inspected and cleaned twice each year.
- ☐ Adequate storage space for tools and lawn equipment is a must. Storage areas should be well lighted. Tools should never be left helter-skelter, sharp points upward, indoors or outdoors. In either place they present a safety hazard.
- ☐ The lawn should be free of leaves, debris and rubbish.
- ☐ Indoors, floor coverings should be firm, neither loose nor worn.
- ☐ Stairs should always be maintained — no loose steps, no loose carpeting — with good light and sturdy, reliable handrails.
- ☐ Both for fuel economy and maximum efficiency, all household systems should be checked periodically. This includes heating and cooling systems, the water heater and all appliances.
- ☐ Keep basement, attic and other storage areas clear of useless debris such as broken furniture, old clothes and rags.
- ☐ Never leave greasy or oily rags lying about. If you must store them, keep them in a tightly closed metal container.
- ☐ Do you have a safe storage area for flammable fuels and solvents such as gasoline, benzine and naphtha? All these liquids give off vapors that can be readily ignited. Some can be ignited by a spark from the water heater. If you don't have a safe storage area for these, don't keep them around.

The all-round handyman for hire has vanished from many areas of the country, but many of us remember him with affection. Once a month or so he would appear, tool kit in hand, and he would be given a list of chores — trim the japonica, oil the basement door hinges, fix the loose stone in the patio, etc. Today homeowners have been left holding the tool kit, so it is even more important to keep track of the home maintenance tasks to be accomplished. Otherwise the squeaky hinge or the loose stone will become a fact of life.

Remember to take care of small maintenance chores before they become major problems.

Home improvements — the major jobs that make it necessary to hire a contractor for building, rebuilding, finishing, repairing or replacing the roof — add to the size, comfort and value of your home. They are usually expensive and they can be messy. If done by a professional, however, such jobs should be relatively painless. The reliable contractor can give you a reliable estimate of how long the job will take and how much it will cost. And the contractor you hire had *better* be a professional — or you can be in big trouble.

This is not to say you shouldn't hire a student to build your wall-to-wall bookshelves. Your student can have a professional attitude toward his work though he does not spend all his time at carpentry and painting.

You can get an estimate of the professionalism of anyone you hire — from full-time contractor to part-time worker — by insisting on references from other customers. This is important to you, your budget, your peace of mind and the condition of your home.

Standards of advertising and selling practices for the home-improvement industry have been developed by the Council of Better Business Bureaus, with technical assistance provided by the National Home Improvement Council. The basic principles of these standards are similar to those of other industries (see ADVERTISING).

These principles establish that advertising should mean what it says, that prices advertised or quoted should be accurate, that "bait and switch" tactics are frowned upon, that homeowners' decisions on goods and services should be made upon a basis of factual information, and that contractors and their sales representatives "should not speak with forked tongue." Elementary.

Most people who make home improvement their business are honest, reliable, skilled professionals. Some are not.

How do you identify the reputable professionals? Use these guidelines:

- ☐ Get references. Contractors should be able to give you the names of previous customers for whom they have performed similar work. Call them or, preferably, visit them to inquire about the quality of work.
- ☐ Another source of reference might be merchants who are known to you, at the lumber yard or the hardware store where you trade.
- ☐ And you can always check them out with the Better Business Bureau.

Get estimates from three contractors:

- ☐ Never pay for an estimate. A reliable contractor will provide a free estimate in writing, complete with specifications for materials to be used.
- ☐ Estimates are likely to be higher than advertised prices for similar work. These advertised prices may also be estimates or they may be come-ons for a "bait and switch" artist (see FRAUD AND DECEPTION).

Make this your rule when pricing home improvements:

Be wary of contractors who quote you a flat price for anything without visiting your home and inspecting the site of the work to be done.

This applies to aluminum siding, remodeling kitchens, installing air conditioning, resurfacing driveways — anything at all that varies from one house to another.

The contractor who claims that he can put aluminum siding on your house (sight unseen) for a low, low price, and give you a free television set besides is misleading you.

Beware the model-home come-on. One of the most troublesome frauds in the home improvement field is the model-home approach. It is a variation on the widespread referral scheme (see FRAUD AND DECEPTION) and it works like this:

A salesman appears at your door to point out that your home could use some specific improvement or repair. Then he lets you in on a secret (perhaps because you are a sterling character and an opinion leader in your community). He represents a well-known manufacturer who is moving into your area. As part of a major advertising program, the company would like to undertake the necessary improvement job on your home at a minimum cost. Yours will be the "model home" to which the company will refer other prospective customers as an example of excellent workmanship. And that's not all. For every sale to someone who comes to view the improvement on your house you will get a substantial commission. The commissions will reduce the amount you pay for the improvements.

It all sounds fine. In the meantime you are asked to sign a contract for the full price of the work — which, of course, you sign. You are secure in the knowledge that those promised commissions will bring the cost down to a minimum, if not clear the account entirely. You may feel you have made an excellent bargain.

But there are two catches.

First, it may turn out that there are no commissions. Many of your neighbors may have made the same "model home" deal that you did — the same neighbors who would have brought in those commissions. Often a salesperson will have blanketed the entire area, offering the same opportunity to everyone. If *everyone* gets the "model home" deal, there will be no customers to view your own "model" and no commissions for you to look forward to.

Second, you may discover — too late — that a reputable local contractor would have done the same job, or a better one, at a lower price.

SIDING

Aluminum and the newer synthetic plastics have much to recommend them as siding materials *when they are of good quality and applied by a reputable contractor who knows his business.* The materials are durable and require a minimum of maintenance. (Check product-rating publications for information on comparative quality.)

The quality of either type of siding will be no better than the quality of the workmanship. It is best to buy from a reputable local contractor whose reputation is known to you — and who will still be around next year.

Siding is often advertised in newspapers at very low prices, with the added implication that a small quantity will serve for the average house. *Don't be misled.* The cost of siding on a home is usually designated in terms of "per square." One "square" of aluminum siding is equal to 100 square feet.

When you are given a price quotation per square, it should include all costs — labor for installation as well as materials. Make sure your contract includes this stipulation. Also make certain that you are given the whole price — not only per square, but for the number of squares your house will require.

When you buy siding, beware of:

- the model-home scheme;
- bait and switch (see FRAUD AND DECEPTION);
- unrealistic guarantees (see WARRANTIES);
- prices quoted in linear feet (aluminum siding is not sold in linear feet);
- prices that don't include the cost of materials *and* labor.

LUMBER

The price difference between good lumber and bad may be very small, depending on the quality involved. You can be sure that the cost of good lumber is worth the price when you compare that price with possible future replacement and/or repair costs and the added inconvenience of having to replace materials that should have been better chosen in the first place.

In an average-size ranch house, paying the comparatively small difference in price between good lumber and green lumber for the entire structural part of the house — that part which holds it together and will be hidden from view — could save you thousands of dollars later on.

Always buy "dry" wood — that is, wood in which the sap has dried up. It is the drying of sap that "seasons" wood. **Remember:** As lumber dries, it shrinks; so that if the lumber you buy is not well seasoned, it still has some shrinkage left in it. Warpage (bending) as well as shrinkage in unseasoned lumber can create some serious problems.

Lumber comes in many stock sizes and is graded 1 through 4. The highest grade is 1. Whatever grade is recommended will be the minimum grade required for whatever job you have in mind. Don't settle for a lower grade on the theory that you will save money.

Make sure that any lumber that is to come in contact with concrete (this lumber is called *plates*) is treated with a wood preservative for protection against moisture and termites. Also, make sure that the ground beneath the concrete slabs is chemically treated with pesticides (this is a job for a professional). This will provide double protection against such insects as termites.

DRIVEWAYS, CONCRETE AND ASPHALT

A concrete driveway for your home? It will look neat and clean and it

HOME MAINTENANCE AND IMPROVEMENT

can last as long as the house. Or it can crack and crumble and make you wish you had forgotten the whole thing.

As with other home improvements, the quality of the workmanship will affect the durability of the finished product. Unless you are an experienced builder or mason, you will need a reputable contractor for this kind of job. Preparation of the underpinnings of the driveway will be important. If the climate in your area is subject to extreme temperature changes, reinforcing rods or mesh will be a *must*. Preparation of the surface to be covered will entail:

- ☐ cleaning the area of all debris, weeds, trash and sod;
- ☐ setting and anchoring the forms into which prepared concrete will be poured;
- ☐ applying reinforcing rods or mesh (take your contractor's advice on whether this is necessary for the climate you live in).

For a driveway, you will want a skidproof brushed surface.

Remember: The final strength of concrete will depend on preparation *and* on the way it is cured. The contractor should take this into account. For example, concrete should not be poured on an extremely hot, dry day because the surface moisture will evaporate too rapidly. New concrete should be kept damp for seven to ten days (covered with a layer of canvas, straw, dirt or building paper, and wet down occasionally). Rapid drying or freezing during the curing period will result in a short-lived surface.

Driveways — a favorite target of fly-by-nights

". . . I was just in the neighborhood and I noticed your driveway needs a coat of sealer. There's enough on the truck to take care of it. I'll do it for close to nothing."

If you fall for that tired old door-opener and accept the offer, what you might get for your money is used motor oil. Whatever substance is used, you'll be lucky if it washes off in the next rain without harming the azaleas or ruining the hedge.

Contractors — good ones — are too busy to solicit business this way. Do business only with reputable local contractors who are known to you. If in doubt, check with the Better Business Bureau.

Find out whether your contractor will guarantee a concrete driveway — many builders do not. Builders often state that the crumbling of concrete is due to the use of salt or de-icing compounds used for melting snow. They're right. For a concrete surface that is (partially) resistant to de-icers, have the contractor air-entrain the concrete during the installation process. (Air-entrained concrete contains billions of tiny air bubbles and is necessary in all concrete subject to freezing and thawing.) *Do not use a chemical de-icer on any new concrete surface for at least one year. Try sand.*

Asphalt driveways, like concrete ones, involve a major construction job, complete with the use of rollers and other heavy equipment. The construction must be carried out according to rigid specifications.

There are three major types of asphalt surfacing for driveways:

☐ **Surface treatment** consists of a thin "wearing course" usually less than an inch thick, composed of two or more applications of liquid asphalt, covered with mineral aggregates. This surface has limited durability, but it does provide a watertight surface for light traffic. The treatment may also be used as a stage for a cold-mix or hot-mix installation. In any case, it must be laid on an adequately prepared base.

☐ **Asphalt cold mix** is a combination of asphalt materials and aggregates, usually applied in layers at least an inch thick.

☐ **Asphalt hot mix** ("hot top") is the most durable form of asphalt driveway and will give the best service with the least maintenance. This consists of well-graded aggregates and asphalt mixed in a central plant and laid while hot in layers at least an inch thick.

The surfacing for residential driveways will vary from one to three inches in thickness, depending on the subgrade soil. Heavier thicknesses — when properly installed — should be more serviceable.

Driveways should be at least eight feet wide, and the base should be wider than the asphalt layer. *Any kind of driveway should be wide enough and strong enough to support heavy service trucks which will use it from time to time.*

A light coat of sealing material should be applied to the asphalt driveway to renew and waterproof the surface. It is best to have this done at intervals of five to ten years.

A contract for a driveway should include these specifications:

☐ kind and depth of base;
☐ thickness of the surfacing to be applied;
☐ exact dimensions of the finished driveway;
☐ a completion date.

Make sure that your guarantee is clear, specific and in writing (see WARRANTIES).

ADDITIONS TO THE HOUSE

Playroom? Family room? A greenhouse? A sunroom? The sensible reason for making an addition to your home should be to make it more livable, more comfortable for the family.

It's best not to make an addition if you plan to sell the house and just want to add to the resale value — you will not be likely to recoup the cost. (*If you're selling, concentrate on maintenance, not improvements.*)

You will want to plan any additions carefully, but before you even begin the planning process, find out what sort of restrictions apply to the remodeling you may want to do. The size and structure of the house, the size of the lot, local zoning regulations and building restrictions all govern the kinds of additions you can make.

Contact a reputable contractor, one who has done business in your area and whose references you can check. If you know nothing about building — even if you know a little about building — you will have to rely on him. Explain your needs and your budget, and let him give you an estimate. Then contact two or three other reputable local builders and get estimates from them.

Whenever remodeling or home improvement involves a large expenditure, it may be advisable to have your lawyer draw up a contract for your protection. The contract must be specific, including details of the work to be done, the materials, and starting and completion dates.

Watch it: Never sign a completion certificate until all the work called for in the contract has been completed as specified. When you sign the certificate, you are telling the contractor (and the lending institution that supplied the remodeling money) that the job has been completed according to the provisions in the contract and to your satisfaction. *Be careful not to sign a completion certificate along with a sales order. Never sign anything without reading it.*

When the improvement project you have contracted for has been completed, you will, obviously, be expected to pay the contractor. Before you pay him, you should secure from him a sworn statement (again, you may need the services of your family lawyer) listing all persons furnishing materials and labor and the amount due to each. Secure a waive of lien from the contractor, and have him provide you with a waiver signed by every person who furnished labor or materials covered by your payment. This should include all persons listed in the sworn statement. *This is important. If the contractor does not pay these people, each supplier and subcontractor can file a lien against your property, even if you have already paid the contractor.*

Finally, the importance of the contractor's reliability cannot be overemphasized. **Use this checklist to summarize your knowledge of any contractor you are considering:**

- ☐ If you are dealing with a salesperson intent on selling a contractor's services, do you have complete, verified identification? Do you know his name, and the name and address of the company he represents?
- ☐ Before you sign the contract, have you checked on the reputation, dependability and reliability of the firm? Get and check

references. Call the Better Business Bureau.
- ☐ Has the salesperson used high-pressure sales tactics to get you to sign a contract?
- ☐ Has the company or salesperson said your home would be used for advertising purposes? As a model home? Have you been promised a special discount for displaying the company's identification on your property?
- ☐ Have you been told that the company is a direct-selling agent for a manufacturer? Again, check with the BBB. Such statements are nonsense.
- ☐ Have you obtained more than one bid?
- ☐ Does the company provide liability and compensation insurance to protect you in the event of an accident?
- ☐ In reference to long-term guarantees, have you reason to believe that the company will still be around to fulfill the guarantee some ten, fifteen or twenty years from now?

Any guarantee or warranty must be in writing (see WARRANTIES). Make sure you find out the following:

— What is warranted? The entire project? Workmanship? Labor? Materials? For how long?
— If only the materials are warranted, who pays labor costs if repair or replacement is necessary?
— Who stands behind the warranty? The dealer or the manufacturer?

Remember: A warranty is only as reliable as the company that provides it.

- ☐ Do you know how much the entire job will cost including interest and service charges?
- ☐ Have you shopped for your home-improvement loan? Have you compared the cost of borrowing money from different sources by comparing the annual percentage rate? **Remember:** Banks and lending institutions offer FHA loans for home improvements that make your home more livable and useful.
- ☐ Have you been told that the FHA "guarantees" the performance of the company or the quality of the work to be done? *The stark fact is:* Anyone who makes such a statement is lying. The FHA does not guarantee either quality of work or contractors. FHA only requires that the lender approve any dealer who arranges for an FHA-insured loan.
- ☐ If the work is to be subcontracted, will the contractor post a bond to protect you against liens on your home?
- ☐ If your home improvements are necessitated by damage that is covered by insurance, have you checked with the insurance company before signing the contract?

HOME MAINTENANCE AND IMPROVEMENT

- ☐ Does the written contract include all the oral promises made by the salesman?
- ☐ Does the contract include exact specifications for materials? Quality or grade, brand name, weight, color and size of materials should be included in the specifications.
- ☐ Have you read and do you understand the contract? Do you have a complete copy signed by the company's representative?
- ☐ Do you know whether your contract covers labor and materials? Materials only? Labor only? It is very difficult to hold a contractor to any commitments unless they are in the written contract. You and the contractor are both bound by the terms of the contract. Read it and understand it thoroughly. And *never* sign a contract that contains blank spaces.
- ☐ Are you asked to pay cash to a salesman instead of by check or money order to the company itself?
- ☐ Do you know whether you will have to pay to cancel the contract? If there is a cancellation penalty, how much is it? Under what circumstances is it due? See your lawyer if you don't understand this.

Housing, Home Buying

(See also APARTMENTS; CONDOMINIUMS AND COOPERATIVES; CONTRACTS; MOBILE HOMES)

HOUSING AND HOME OWNERSHIP are not the same thing at all. Housing is shelter, and many a confirmed apartment dweller would be acutely uncomfortable with the responsibility for maintenance that accompanies home ownership. Home owners, on the other hand, choose a life style — a commitment to a kind of nesting instinct operative in them, whether their houses are in an urban, suburban or rural setting.

There are practical benefits that go with owning a home. For instance, mortgage loan interest and property tax are both deductible for federal income-tax purposes. But at least one study indicates that home owners are motivated more by life style than economic factors. Tax advantages and building an equity in real estate were strong factors considered by prospective home owners looking for a hedge against inflation, but the interest in privacy and in a specific kind of environment for the children as well as a desire for space and freedom to develop the property all entered into the buying decisions of the home owners surveyed.

HOW MUCH SHOULD YOU PAY FOR A HOME?

Budget considerations will play an important role in your choice of a community as well as of a home. In the past, home buyers have used the following rules of thumb:

- ☐ The price of the home should not exceed 2 to 2½ times the annual family income. A young couple should stay on the low side of this estimate. If income is substantial and job prospects promising, the upper level (2½ times the annual income) will be reasonable.
- ☐ A home owner should not pay more than 25 percent of income for monthly housing expense, which includes payment on the mortgage loan plus the average cost of heat, utilities, repair and maintenance.

Additional considerations in budgeting for home ownership are:

- ☐ the kind of mortgage you will use (VA, FHA or "conventional" financing); and
- ☐ the size of the down payment (with a "conventional" mortgage, you will need up to one-third of the purchase price).

These should be related to the second general rule above, that not more than 25 percent of the monthly income should be earmarked for housing expenses. Keep in mind that there is no substitute for examining your own budget carefully; these general rules are only guidelines and may not apply to everyone.

CHOOSING A COMMUNITY
When the budget has been planned, when you know how much you can afford to spend for housing, the next step is to decide upon the community you want to live in and the neighborhood that appeals to you. If you are looking for the right house in an area that is known to you, conducting the search on your own makes sense. If you are moving to another state, you would do well to let a real estate representative help you search. The real estate agent will also want to know a good deal about your family and its interests. It would be a good idea to ask yourself the same kinds of questions the real estate representative might ask.

- ☐ The budget question is basic. You have already answered that one for yourself before you started to look for a house, and certainly before you contacted a real estate representative.
- ☐ Review the family's interests and needs. Consider priorities: the quality of the schools, the convenience of shopping areas, public transportation, houses of worship. Will a house, pleasant as it might be, mean that someone will have to drive the youngsters to school, to music lessons, to basketball practice and to friends' homes? If the someone who must be responsible for the driving has a number of outside interests, this sort of thing can become a burden.
- ☐ If you want to own a house with a lot of land around it, you will need to check zoning regulations. Will your large lawn and the privacy you are searching for be in jeopardy when the city grows in your direction? What if your home turns out to be on the outskirts of an area zoned for industry?

A good real estate broker, informed on the amount of money you want to spend for your home and given a good idea of your family's needs and interests, can screen and choose a number of homes that should interest you.

The broker can also provide general information about communities and neighborhoods, as well as specific information about schools, public transportation facilities and stores. Remember, however, that the broker is usually working primarily for the seller of the home. Do not rely heavily on oral promises or agreements.

NEW HOUSE OR OLD?
Two out of every three buyers select a used house. One advantage of older houses used to be that they were likely to offer more space for

the money. Things changed in the 1970s, however, when fewer new houses were constructed and a tight housing market forced the prices of existing houses to unheard-of highs in many parts of the United States. This does not mean that new houses were bargain-priced since construction costs also soared.

When you shop for an existing house, you will be seeing homes that are furnished and livable. Landscaping will have been done for you. *Don't* let the comfortable warmth and attractiveness of the operating home distract you from a thorough inspection of the house and its condition. Visit the house in daylight. Make several visits, in fact, and take a knowledgeable friend with you.

Pay special attention to these aspects of the homes you consider:

- ☐ **General appearance:** Never forget the resale value. Even though you plan to put down roots in this community, this neighborhood and this particular house, the fact is that this is a mobile society and your company might transfer you again two years from now. Remember that a modern, well-equipped kitchen will increase resale value. Watch out for the ill-proportioned gable, tacked-on porch, etc. They may not bother you, but they could make the house hard to sell later.
- ☐ **Check the floor plans for convenience.** Ideally, bedrooms should be separated from the living and working areas of the house so that a late party or card game doesn't keep the children from studying or sleeping.
- ☐ **Go over the structural features.** Check for sturdy uprights, floors supported by two-by-fours, and a good strong foundation. (It's at this time your knowledgeable friend or professional appraiser will be most helpful. Many people have no idea how to tell whether a foundation is strong.) Make sure the doors open smoothly. If they stick, it might mean that the house has begun to settle out of plumb. This condition can only get worse; be assured it won't get better. Take a good look at the walls and ceilings, particularly if they are plaster. Check the wallpaper — you're looking for stains, cracks and streaks that could signal leaks in the plumbing or roof.
- ☐ **Wall-to-wall carpet sometimes covers cheap, softwood floors.** If you prefer the look of polished hardwood floors, check under the rugs.
- ☐ **Check for indications of termite infestation and wood rot.** The importance of a check by a reputable termite specialist cannot be overemphasized and should be a requirement in the offer to buy.
- ☐ **Look carefully at the exterior walls.** Lines should still be straight. If you are not sure of your ability to judge this sort of thing, it's time to call in your knowledgeable home-owning friend.
- ☐ **Check for inadequate wiring.** Make sure that there are enough

conveniently located electric outlets in each room and that there is enough amperage to operate all your appliances without overloading. Make sure all the outlets work. Ask a local inspector to assess code compliance to make sure the wiring is not aging, exposed or dangerous.
- ☐ **Check the furnace, the general condition of the heating system, as well as the central air-conditioning system.** How old are the furnace and air-conditioning units? Are repairs needed?
- ☐ **Insulation** is important both to family comfort and to the efficiency and economy of the heating system. Find out whether the attic and walls are insulated. What material was used and how was it installed?
- ☐ **Plumbing:** A home connected to a public sewer system is preferable to one served by a septic tank or cesspool. Check with the plumber who services the house to find out the condition of the plumbing. Ask him to test for water pressure.
- ☐ **Hot water heater:** What is the capacity? Will it provide enough hot water for family needs? Look for any signs of rust or leaks. Ask for the warranty held by the previous owner. Is the warranty still in effect?
- ☐ **Roof and gutters:** What kind of roofing material was used? How old is it? Check inside the attic for water stains and discolorations.
- ☐ **Wet basements:** Look for watermarks on the basement floor and around the walls. Check the foundation for water penetration.
- ☐ **Check storage space.** Are there enough closets? Are they conveniently located?
- ☐ **Check the fireplaces, if any.** They should have workable dampers.

If the house you want to buy is structurally sound but needs a few repairs here and there, you may find that noting the needed repairs (and offering a lower bid than the owner's asking price) can get you a good buy. Many home owners prefer to have control of the repairs themselves instead of buying on condition that improvements will be made by the previous owner.

But remember: Never sign an offer to buy until the price is firm and the necessary repairs have been effected or compensated for by lowering the asking price of the house. Once you have signed an offer to buy, you are committed.

MORTGAGES

A mortgage is a special loan for purchasing a piece of property. The lender supplies cash to buy or build the house. The borrower (mortgagor) signs a contract that obligates him to repay the lender (mortgagee) regular payments, including interest, for a specified number of years. House and lot serve as security and the mortgagor promises to pay the taxes, keep the house insured and maintain the property in good condition. Should the mortgagor default (fail to make payments), the mortgagee has the legal right to take over the property and the mortgagor may lose any equity in the property he has acquired. (Check for information about new **variable mortgage plans** that allow you to pay less in the early years and more later on when you are more financially secure.)

Opinions differ on the size of the down payment and the amount of time home owners should choose:

☐ Should you make the largest down payment you can afford and obligate yourself to the smallest mortgage you can get?
☐ Should you make the minimum down payment and elect a longer-term, larger mortgage?

The answer to both questions is *maybe*.

Should you have to move to another part of the country, you will find that the greater your equity, the larger the amount of cash you must recoup, the harder it may be to sell your home.

Also contrary to the "smallest mortgage, shortest term" philosophy, there is a good deal of opinion that the largest mortgage and longest term may well be the most economical in the long run. If the United States continues its inflationary trend, the value of the dollar twenty or twenty-five years from now will be considerably reduced. Under this reasoning, it may be wise to borrow "expensive" dollars now and pay back with "cheap" ones later. Be sure to consider how much money you want to put into real estate and how much you want to put into other areas of investment, such as stocks or mutual funds that might hedge against inflation.

Sources of mortgages include:
☐ savings banks;
☐ commercial banks;
☐ savings and loan associations;
☐ mortgage bankers;
☐ insurance companies.

From each of these financial institutions, you may secure:

☐ a conventional mortgage loan;
☐ a loan insured by HUD—FHA;
☐ a loan guaranteed by the Veterans Administration, if you are an eligible veteran.

To secure a mortgage, you must have:

☐ an acceptable credit record;
☐ cash for the down payment and closing costs;
☐ enough income to meet monthly mortgage payments *and* the maintenance and operating cost of the home.

Types of mortgages

Below is a short listing of the typical types of home mortgages now available on the market. Some realtors can take parts of the different mortgages and build a completely new financial structure. In this event, make sure that you are dealing with a reputable real estate broker and mortgage lender. If in doubt, check with your local Better Business Bureau.

- **Conventional loan:** The terms of a conventional loan can be variable, worked out between the mortgagor and the mortgagee. No third party "backs" or insures conventional mortgages; they are, therefore, more conservative. Your own credit and the value of the mortgaged property secure the loan.
- **FHA-insured mortgage:** Your loan is insured by the U.S. Department of Housing and Urban Development — Federal Housing Administration (HUD—FHA). This additional insurance factor allows the lending institution to lend you a higher percentage of the appraised value of the house than would otherwise be granted.
- **Veterans Administration Guaranteed Mortgage (GI Loan):** The Veterans Administration (VA) guarantees the lender a percentage of the loan. If you are a veteran, you may be entitled to a mortgage with little or no down payment.
- **The Assumable Loan:** This usually is an initial VA loan that second, third, fourth, etc., buyers can assume by paying the difference between the selling price and the outstanding balance on the loan. These loans are somewhat rare, but there are still some available. The rub here is being able to meet the pay-off and closing costs. Sometimes the money "difference" can be financed separately or rolled into one loan with a lower interest rate. The loan then becomes a "Wrap-Around" loan. The borrower usually gets a break in the interest rates if the VA loan interest is lower than current interest rates. In short, the borrower "assumes" the lower rate mortgage and finances the "difference money" at higher interest rates. The rates, then, are "averaged" into a lower rate.
- **The GPM Loan:** GPM stand for Graduated Payment Mortgage. Here, the borrower pays back the loan at a lower rate at the start of the loan and at a higher rate at the end of the loan — or at a specified time down the installment payment line. The borrower is assuming that his/her earnings will be larger 5 years or so from the date the papers are signed.
- **The VRM Loan:** VRM stand for Variable Rate Mortgage. As the interest rates change, so does the interest rate on the mortgage. If the rates go up, the borrower pays more. If the rates go down, the borrower pays less. Some lenders will let the borrower transfer the loan to another home if the first home is sold.

GETTING MORE FOR YOUR MONEY

Sometimes the borrower can refinance the loan if the prepayment isn't too much. The interest rate can fluctuate as much as 2 to 3 percent. This loan is often a good one for a borrower subject to transfer.

☐ **The Rollover Mortgage:** The borrower can renegotiate this mortgage. Sometimes the mortgage can be reworked at an interest rate below the initial interest cost. The time span for renegotiating usually varies from 3 to 5 years.

☐ **The Take Back Loan:** The seller is willing to "finance" part of the mortgage at a "reasonable" rate of interest for a 1 to 5 or more year time period. This reduces the borrower's initial loan from a commercial lender and, therefore, "qualifies" the buyer for the commercial money he might not be able to borrow. However, the borrower has to make two payments each month: one to the seller and one to the mortgage lender.

No matter what type of loan you obtain, you should request the right to repay at a faster rate than the mortgage specifies (or prepay it), without having to pay a penalty to the lending institution.

At first most of your monthly mortgage payments go for interest on your loan, a smaller percentage actually repays the loan (amortization). As your equity increases, the amount required for interest goes down and the sum for amortization goes up.

You may elect to have bills for taxes and insurance included in your mortgage payments. You may also choose:

☐ **Package mortgage:** This type of loan includes payments for home appliances, such as a dishwasher, washer, dryer or built-in stove.

☐ **Open-end mortgage:** At the discretion of the lender, during the term of the loan the borrower may borrow again — up to the amount of the original loan or more. The interest rate for the new loan will reflect the current mortgage charges.

☐ **Second mortgage (trust deed):** If the down payment is more than you have available or more than you wish to pay, it is sometimes possible to get the difference through this loan method from the previous owner or another lender.

A second mortgage or trust deed means that the borrower carries a tremendous burden for amortization, since this form of loan is usually short-term. The interest rate is usually higher than the first mortgage, and there is frequently a "balloon payment" at the end of the three-, five- or ten-year terms.

BUILDING A NEW HOUSE

After weighing the advantages and disadvantages of existing houses on the market, perhaps you decide to build the house that will be absolutely right for your family. You select the site, you plan for unique family needs, and your brand new house is built to order.

Choosing a builder. Your dream house could become a nightmare if you fail to choose a reliable builder. Check with the Better Business Bureau for the complaint records of builders under consideration, and talk with people who live in homes constructed by local builders. Find out how long a builder has been in business; a reputable builder has a valuable local reputation to maintain.

Then consider these guidelines:

- Is the model home impressive? It was meant to be — it is a major selling point for that new subdivision. Find out exactly which features come with the house and which are optional extras. Don't wait until later to find that the fireplace and the patio were optional.
- The contract must be complete (see LEGAL SERVICES). It must specify *exactly* all the features and all the extras included in your purchase. There must be agreement on every detail of the transaction. Don't sign until you understand every section of the document.
- Services such as water lines, sewers, streets and sidewalks will be important to you. Don't neglect to find out whether such services will add to the cost of the home.
- Lots look spacious until houses are built on them. If the land around your house is important to you, be very sure to know how much — or how little — land you are buying. Look at land plots with houses superimposed.
- If there are trees on the property, make sure the builder knows which ones you want to keep. Obviously it's easier to build on a clear site. Find out whether the builder you have chosen is one who clears without consideration.
- **Zoning:** Check it yourself or have your family lawyer do it for you. The wooded area in back of your home could be zoned for commercial use at a later date. (*This factor can affect property values in the future and cannot be overemphasized.*) If you do the legwork yourself, the city, county or township clerk's office can tell you where to inquire about zoning. Talk with long-term residents and with business associates whose judgment you trust. Zoning can change. Get an idea of the way your community is growing. A semicommercial or overcrowded, overbuilt area a block or two away can also affect property values.
- Make sure your contract with the builder stipulates the completion date of your new house — including penalties for late completion. Don't hesitate to check the progress regularly while your house is under construction. (The biggest complaint is a house not completed on time.)
- Before you take title to the house, inspect it thoroughly. Is all the equipment installed as specified in the contract? Check windows and doors. Try out the heating and cooling systems. *It is too late to make changes after the closing process.*

- When you take possession of your new house, you should receive:
    - manufacturers' warranties for all attachments;
    - certificate of occupancy;
    - all applicable certificates of code compliance.

The Home Owners Warranty Corporation (HOW)

An insured warranty program for home owners was established in 1973 by the National Association of Home Builders (NAHB). It is now an independent mutual company, which administers a voluntary program for builders that provides ten-year protection backed by insurance on newly constructed homes, including condominiums and townhouses. The program is found in 47 states and in 1981 covered more than 30% of all new homes sold.

HOW's objectives are:

- To provide a means for customer assurance that new homes are produced at acceptable standards of construction workmanship and materials, and are backed by an extended insured warranty.
- To establish a program for identification of reliable, competent and ethical builders authorized to provide an insured warranty agreement to their buyers.
- To provide a quick, effective and free complaint-handling mechanism for consumers.

HOW's insured warranty program adds a modest but very worthwhile fee, ranging from $2.60 to $3.90, for every $1,000.00 of the final selling price. Here are its warranty provisions:

- During the first year, the builder is responsible for correcting problems caused by faulty workmanship and defective materials due to noncompliance with nationally approved standards. The builder is also responsible for correcting any major structural defects in construction.
- During the first two years, the builder is responsible for correcting defects due to faulty installation of plumbing, heating, cooling and electrical systems, as well as for defects in construction.
- During the third through tenth years of the warranty, the home is protected against major construction defects through insurance coverage arranged by HOW; however, the home owner must pay a one-time deductible amount equal to 1% of the original selling price of the house.
- During the first two years, HOW's insurance coverage assumes the builder's responsibilities if for any reason he cannot or will not meet his warranted responsibilities, but this is subject to a one-time $250 deductible paid by the home owner.

Participating builders must be registered with HOW, and registered builders must agree to observe guidelines set by HOW's quality standards, in which workmanship defects, acceptable tolerances and methods of repairs are listed.

Builders must meet professional standards — ethical, technical and financial. Their HOW registrations must be renewed annually. Builders who fail to make good on their warranty responsibilities can be expelled from the program.

HOW's complaint-handling system requires the home owner to present his complaint in writing and deal directly with the builder during the first two years the warranty is in effect. HOW believes most complaints will be resolved at that level. However, if the home owner feels that a problem is being neglected or has not had adequate attention from the builder, he may file a written complaint with HOW's dispute settlement procedures. Under these expedited procedures, a neutral third person is appointed to mediate and, if necessary, arbitrate the dispute. The resulting decision is binding on the builder but not on the home owner who is free to pursue other remedies.

For more information, see your state or local home builders association or write to the Home Owners Warranty Corporation, 2000 L Street, N.W., Washington, DC 20036.

Better safe than sorry
Better Business Bureau studies indicate that home owners list seven principal reasons for regretting the purchase of a home:

1. They initiated the purchase with insufficient funds.
2. The house turned out to be more expensive to maintain and operate than they expected.
3. The house proved to be poorly built.
4. The property decreased in value over the years.
5. The family income decreased, making the house a burden.
6. They did not examine the house carefully enough before buying.
7. They grew dissatisfied with the neighborhood.

Since buying a home for many people is the most important financial investment they make, it's wise that you be fully informed and plan wisely before you buy. Ask your lender for a copy of the booklet on settlement costs, which is given out at the time of application as required by the Real Estate Settlement Procedures Act (RESPA). Once you have purchased a home, make sure you are immediately and adequately insured against fire and liability.

GETTING MORE FOR YOUR MONEY

The vital importance of shopping for a builder cannot be overemphasized. You will have given careful thought to the house you want to live in and the life style it will provide. You will have given serious consideration to the needs and interests of your family. *Make sure your builder can deliver on time the home you have in mind at the price you want to pay.*

Your biggest buy of a lifetime should also be the best buy you can get.

Insulation

(See also ENERGY; STORM WINDOWS AND DOORS)

IN THESE DAYS OF rising utility and fuel costs, insulation should be considered an investment. Homes insulated with the right materials in the right places will make more efficient use of fuel used for both heating and cooling systems.

DO YOU NEED INSULATION?
To find out, make a thorough inspection of your home. Is there insulation in your attic? How thick is it? (Under six inches usually is not enough.) Next, in cold weather, place your hand at several places on an interior wall (one that separates rooms) and compare its temperature with that of an exterior wall (facing outdoors). If your home is adequately insulated, the exterior wall will feel only slightly cooler. Air drafts around cabinets, baseboards, windows and doors mean you could use weatherstripping, caulking, or storm windows or doors. Finally, cracks or gaps on the outside of your house, especially in the chimney or where pipes or wires enter the house, may need caulking.

"R" VALUE — THE KEY TO EFFECTIVENESS
Manufacturers rate insulation effectiveness in terms of "R" (resistance) value. The higher the "R" value, the better the material slows winter heat loss and summer heat gain. *When buying, look for the "R" value on the package. Do not be guided by thickness.*

There is a point beyond which additional insulation is a waste of money. Generally, an adequately insulated home has these "R" values:

Ceilings	R-19 to R-38
Floors	0 to R-19
Walls	R-11 to R-17

You may need higher or lower "R" values, however, depending on your climate. Your local utility company will probably be able to suggest the best "R" values for your house.

TYPES OF INSULATION AND INSULATING MATERIALS
Insulation is made from various materials in three basic forms: blankets, boards and loose fill. Before buying, consider the area to be

insulated, the "R" value needed and your budget. No one type is best for all applications. Materials vary according to quality, thermal resistance ("R" value), safety features, dimensions, and where and how they are applied.

The following are among the most common materials:

- ☐ **Mineral fiber:** This is made from mineral substances such as rock, slag or glass, and is processed from a molten state into a fibrous form. Most commonly known as "glass fiber" (fiber glass) or "rock wool," it comes as blankets (rolls or batts) or loose fill.
- ☐ **Cellulose fiber:** This generally comes in loose fill form, and is made from recycled paper or paper stock that has been defibered. It should be treated for fire resistance and other conditions by the manufacturer.
- ☐ **Foamed plastics:** As polystyrene and polyurethane, these are preformed into boards or blown (foamed) into wall cavities by contractors. Before having plastic foam insulation installed, be sure to check local building codes and fire regulations to determine if the material complies with them, or if it requires a fire-resistant covering. Foamed plastics usually have a higher "R" value per inch than other materials, but they may be relatively expensive.
- ☐ **Expanded materials:** These include vermiculite and perlite, and they usually come as loose fill. They can be poured into odd-shaped spots or smaller areas. This is sometimes a more expensive insulating material for a given "R" value than other types.

PROFESSIONAL SERVICES . . . OR DO-IT-YOURSELF?
If you are hiring an insulation contractor, follow these suggestions:

- ☐ Ask your local utility company for names.
- ☐ Solicit names from friends and neighbors.
- ☐ Call the Better Business Bureau for a reliability check.
- ☐ Make sure all materials identify "R" values.
- ☐ Be sure either you or the contractor has adequate insurance in case of injury on the job.
- ☐ Get at least three estimates on work over $200.
- ☐ Get the contract *in writing*, down to the details of "R" value, type of material, areas to be covered and, in case of loose fill, the number of bags to be used (in fact, count them when the job is done).

Do-it-yourselfers must take safety precautions. Here are a few suggestions:

- ☐ Provide good lighting while you work.
- ☐ If the attic is not floored, lay boards or plywood sheets down over the tops of joists or trusses to make a walkway (the ceiling cannot be trusted to support the weight of even a slightly built person).

- ☐ Be careful of roofing nails protruding through the roof sheathing.
- ☐ Wear gloves and a breathing mask.
- ☐ Keep the insulation material wrapped until you are ready to use it.
- ☐ *Be fire-conscious.* If you are installing insulation around electrical wires, do not pull or twist those wires. Carefully handpack insulation around electrical cables. Make sure there are at least three inches between insulation and any recessed lighting fixture or any kind of heat-producing equipment, and a space of at least two feet above an electrical unit.
- ☐ Use only materials certified as resistant to all types of corrosion and infestation.

SPECIAL CONSIDERATIONS

Roll and batt insulation can be bought with a "vapor barrier" on one side — a kraft (paper) or foil-like covering protecting the material from moisture. It is important to keep the vapor barrier facing in the right direction. If new insulation is not covering old insulation, face the vapor barrier toward the living area of your home.

When adding new insulation over existing insulation, use unfaced material to avoid creating a condensation problem. If batts or blankets without facings are not available, use the vapor barrier type, but remove the vapor barrier.

Fire safety. According to the National Bureau of Standards, many insulation materials are combustible, which means that they will burn and release heat, smoke and gases, especially when exposed continuously to large fire sources. There are two fire safety factors you should consider about insulation: the flammability of the material itself and the area in which it is applied.

Some materials, such as cellulose, must be treated during manufacturing with flame retardant chemicals (generally boric acid). Others, like polyurethane and polystyrene, must be enclosed in a flame- and heat-retardant structure, such as gypsum board. Improperly treated and installed materials can produce fire risks. You should check with your local authorities to make sure the insulation you are considering meets the fire-safety requirements of building codes.

Fact sheets. The Federal Trade Commission has rules that require disclosure of pertinent information about insulation both on product labels and in "fact sheets" that retailers and installers must show or provide to customers. The fact sheets and labels must contain a table which, depending on the type of insulation, shows "R" value, dimensions, thickness, coverage, etc. for the product. Fact sheets must also disclose the type of insulation and who made it.

Insurance, Health

(See also HEALTH AND MEDICINE)

HEALTH INSURANCE IS a necessity. Consider these statistics:
- ☐ The early 1980s saw the average cost of care in community hospitals rising to more than $245 per day, *twice as much as the cost of care in the mid 1970s.* Other hospitals charge as much as $300 a day.
- ☐ The total cost of "fairly routine" surgical procedures such as appendectomy, gall bladder surgery and hernia repair ranged from $1,500 to $2,500.
- ☐ The total cost of care during catastrophic or prolonged illness was estimated to exceed $10,000.

In a typical year, about forty million persons in the United States (one in every five) suffer illnesses or injuries serious enough to warrant medical attention. One out of every eight of these spends some time in a hospital.

So who needs insurance to cover medical expenses and hospitalization?

Everyone.

Sources of health insurance include insurance companies, local hospital and such medical service plans as Blue Cross and Blue Shield, Medicare and Medicaid and through various organizations such as fraternal societies, employer and labor unions, college health departments, rural and consumer health cooperatives and other private organizations.

Normally, premiums are significantly lower under group insurance plans, 15 to 40 percent less than similar coverage on an individual basis. When many individuals are insured under a single contract, the insurance company realizes significant savings in sales and administrative costs. There are other advantages to group health insurance: your coverage can't be canceled, unless and until you leave the group. You don't have to take a medical exam to qualify, and a pre-existing illness won't disqualify you, although it may mean you'll have to wait in order to qualify for maternity benefits.

BLUE CROSS AND BLUE SHIELD
A word about Blue Cross and Blue Shield. It is not one "company," as many people assume, but a large number of independent groups that operate under the same name. The benefits and rates vary around the country. Blue Cross generally pays all hospital costs for a semiprivate room for 70 or 120 days, according to its most widely held national contract. Blue Shield plans pay certain medical costs other than hospitalization — surgery, diagnostic examinations and the like.

Usually, the physical condition of the insured person does not have a bearing upon his eligibility for a group plan. The insurance company is concerned with the health of the entire group, not any individual, in underwriting the plan. Under group policies the individual's coverage cannot be canceled. It normally terminates when he leaves his job or drops out of the organization. However, many groups offer continued coverage for an individual at higher premium rates.

MEDICARE
At the present time, persons over 65 are entitled, without premium payment, to certain health insurance benefits under the U.S. government's Medicare program, which went into effect in 1966. Set up under the Social Security Administration, the program provides both hospital and doctors' services in and out of a hospital. In 1980 hospital benefits provided for ninety days of semiprivate coverage after the patient paid the first $160.00 of the hospital's charges. The first sixty days of hospitalization are then fully covered. The last thirty days are covered except for a daily deductible. These ninety-day hospital periods can be renewed if the patient is discharged from the hospital for a full sixty days. There is also emergency lifetime coverage of sixty days which can be used between regular ninety-day periods. This emergency time cannot be renewed and has a daily deductible of $80.00.

In addition, Medicare pays for up to twenty days confinement in a nursing home after at least three days of hospitalization and thereafter assumes part of the cost up to the hundredth day. Also covered are part of the costs of diagnostic tests, such as X-rays and cardiograms, and a certain number of home-care visits by nurses, physical therapists and other health-care specialists.

Check with your local Social Security office to see if there are any changes in the provisions or coverage since 1980.

INSURANCE FROM YOUR EMPLOYER
Many employers provide health insurance for employees through group plans, paying all or most of the premium. Such coverage is considered part of the worker's salary — and the worker's dependents are covered by the same policy.

How much coverage do you have?

If you know your employer carries health insurance, but you have no idea about the amount and extent of coverage available to you, you would be wise to find out. Don't wait until you need medical care to learn that you need more coverage than you have. Find out how much it would cost to increase your insurance and base your decision on the number of dependents you have, your income and the quality of your health.

In most group insurance plans the employer or organization is issued a master contract. Certificates of insurance are provided to each participating member of the group. Study this carefully. If you find your own policy or certificate of insurance incomprehensible, get an explanation from your insurance agent, personnel office or union representative.

Acquaint yourself with the nature of the policy by answering these questions:

☐ Is dental-care coverage included or available?
☐ Are such services as eye examinations, prescription eye glasses and hearing aids covered?
☐ Can you choose your own doctor, or must you use a doctor associated with the insurance plan?
☐ Does your insurance cover the cost of a second medical opinion in regard to recommended surgery? (*This is important — see* HEALTH AND MEDICINE.)

TYPES OF HEALTH INSURANCE

There are five basic types of health insurance:

Hospital-expense insurance, logically enough, pays the hospital bills. Benefits are provided for hospital care for varying lengths of time. Usually this insurance pays all or most of the charges of a hospital stay up to a stated maximum number of days (thirty, seventy, etc.). In addition to daily room and board, these charges include services such as routine nursing care, laboratory tests, anesthesia and the services of an anesthesiologist, use of the operating room, drugs and medications, minor medical supplies and local ambulance service.

The average hospital stay, according to the American Hospital Association, is about seven days. This is important to know because some policies do not provide coverage for the first seven or eight days of hospitalization. Check your coverage.

In these, and all other types of health insurance policies, the benefits you receive, the number of days covered and the amount of money paid by the insurer depends upon how much coverage you have. The more coverage, of course, the higher the premium.

Surgical-expense insurance helps pay the doctor's fee for operations. The various surgical procedures covered and the maximum amount the insurance company will pay for each are listed in each policy. Note, however, that in some cases the allotted amount will not cover the surgeon's fee. For example, a policy may allot $500 for a certain procedure for which most surgeons would charge from $1,500 to $2,500.

Some policies cover minor surgery which is performed in the doctor's office. Other policies cover only operations performed in the hospital. *Be sure to check your policy.*

Physicians'-expense insurance helps pay the physician for services other than surgery, including visits to the doctor's office, house calls and some hospital visits. The services covered vary from policy to policy, so be sure to check exactly what is included.

Major medical insurance helps limit the cost of very serious or prolonged illness. Like automobile collision insurance, most major medical policies call for a "deductible" — you pay all your medical costs up to a stated amount before the insurance company begins to pay. You are also expected to pay a specific percentage of the balance of the medical fees, usually 20 to 25 percent.

This is the way it works: If your major medical policy calls for a $100 deductible, and the insurance company pays 80 percent of the balance, then on an illness costing $3,300 you will pay $740 ($100 + 20 percent of $3,200) and the insurance company will pay $2,560. With a $500 deductible on a similar policy, you would pay $1,060 and the company would pay $2,240. The lower the deductible, the higher the premium.

These policies cover a wide range of treatment, in or out of a hospital, as long as it is provided by a licensed physician. Coverage includes such services as private nursing care, ambulances, surgical appliances, drugs, tests and X-rays.

Disability insurance is designed to protect a worker from total loss of income. It generally requires that the worker be totally disabled before any benefits are paid. Check your policy. "Total disability" can mean any of these:

☐ inability to perform any job requirement;
☐ inability to engage in any gainful occupation to which you are fitted by education, training or experience;
☐ inability to engage in any occupation.

Cash benefits usually range from half to two-thirds of regular income, depending upon the policy selected. The duration of the payments also varies considerably — from thirteen, twenty-six or fifty-two weeks or for an entire lifetime. As in major medical policies, there is a deductible in the form of a waiting period ranging from one week to two or three months or more. (Usually, there is no waiting period in the case of accidental injuries.) The waiting period eliminates payment of a large number of small claims, since most illnesses last only a couple of weeks. Therefore, the longer the waiting period, the lower the cost of the insurance.

HOW MUCH AND WHAT KIND OF HEALTH INSURANCE DO YOU NEED?

Because there is virtually no way to budget accurately for the cost of medical care, there is no simple formula for determining the amount of insurance an individual or family should have. In general, the best family or individual program is one that prevents undue financial strain from an unexpected illness or injury — and is not too expensive to maintain.

Take these factors into account to get some idea of the amount of coverage you need:

- ☐ How much money do you have available for emergencies?
- ☐ Is your income large enough to absorb some of the financial burden of illness?
- ☐ How much do hospitals and doctors charge in the community?
- ☐ If you or a member of your family should become ill, are community health services in the form of low-cost or free clinics available to you?
- ☐ Are there any unusual health hazards associated with your job? Your life style? Your community?
- ☐ How good is your family's health history? Many illnesses? Few? The length of illnesses should also be considered.

Finally, what protection do you already have? Check into benefits under Workmen's Compensation, Social Security benefits, the medical benefits under liability insurance, and your life-insurance disability provisions.

Use this checklist for help in planning your coverage:

- ☐ Does the policy cover everyone in your immediate family? Until what age are children insured?
- ☐ Can the policy be canceled by the company? If so, under what conditions?
- ☐ What is the policy's effective date?
- ☐ How many hospital days are covered per year and how much will the policy pay for each day? Are hospital services (nursing, lab tests, X-ray, medication, use of the operating room) covered? How does the maximum coverage compare with current per diem hospital costs in your community?
- ☐ How long is the waiting period before benefits are payable by the company?
- ☐ Are surgical payments allotted by your policy in line with surgeon's fees in your community?
- ☐ What conditions are *not* covered?
- ☐ What is the maximum amount payable under major medical? How large is the deductible? After recovery from an illness, is there a waiting period before the maximum amount of benefits again become available?

- ☐ Before acquiring disability insurance, determine the total amount your family can get from all sources (Workmen's Compensation, Social Security, sick pay from your employer) if your income should cease.
- ☐ Read a disability ("loss of income") policy carefully for the exact definition of "total disability."
- ☐ Have you investigated the reliability of your insurance agent and the company he represents?
- ☐ Is the company licensed by your state department of insurance? (Do *not* assume that such licensing exists just because policies are sold by a local agent or because policies are advertised in local newspapers.)

Beware of high-pressure sales tactics by an agent and/or glowing promises contained in an advertisement. Neither sales representatives' promises nor advertised promises are meaningful if the policy contains limitations and/or exclusions that contradict them. Study the policy with special care before you sign it.

Insurance, Home

THERE ARE SEVERAL DIFFERENT packages of homeowner's insurance available. Here are the most common forms:

Basic form offers you the minimum protection and covers the following perils: fire or lightning; loss of property removed from premises; windstorm or hail; explosion; riot or civil commotion; aircraft; vehicles; smoke; vandalism; theft and breakage of glass constituting a part of the building.

Broad form insures your property against the above listed perils as well as falling objects; weight of ice, snow, sleet; collapse of building(s); sudden and accidental tearing asunder, cracking, burning or bulging of a steam or hot-water heating system or of appliances for heating water; accidental discharge, leakage or overflow of water or steam from within plumbing, heating and air-conditioning systems and appliances; and sudden and accidental injury from artificially generated currents to electrical appliances, devices, fixtures and wiring.

Comprehensive form insures against all of the above perils and many more. The exceptions are listed in the policy.

Special form provides broad-form coverage on personal property and comprehensive-form coverage on a house. This is the most popular form of homeowners insurance.

Tenants form is for those who rent an apartment or house. It insures household contents and personal belongings against all perils included in the broad form.

Flood insurance is offered only in communities that have passed and enforce government-approved zoning restrictions on future flood-plain development. Ask the insurance representative for more information on its availability.

Earthquake insurance is usually written as an addition to a fire or homeowner's insurance policy, with minimum premiums.

Home insurance policies were once considered protection against fire and theft, with liability available as a separate policy. Newer homeowners' policies often are sold in a package, thus:

1. **Property coverage**, including:

    ☐ The "dwelling" (the house and its supporting equipment, such as furniture, lawnmower, air conditioners and the like);

- ☐ "Appurtenance private structures" (other buildings on the lot, such as the garage, tool shed, playhouse, etc.);
- ☐ "Unscheduled personal property" (contents of the household such as carpets and clothing which are not specifically named in the policy);
- ☐ "Additional living expense" (monies payable for living expenses if you are unable to stay in your house while it is being repaired).

2. Liability
   - ☐ "Personal liability" (coverage for suits filed by a visitor or neighbor injured on your property);
   - ☐ "Personal medical payments" (expenses of people injured by you, your pets or a member of your family, on or off your property);
   - ☐ "Physical damage to property" (damage to the property of others).

Homeowners' policies are often sold with a "deductible" — that is, the homeowner is responsible for the first $100 or $500 worth of repairs or replacement, and the insurance company pays the rest (or a percentage of the additional amount) up to a stated amount.

Expect premium rates to vary with:
- ☐ the amount of your deductible;
- ☐ the amount and extent of coverage;
- ☐ the type of house (wood costs more to insure than brick or stone);
- ☐ the condition of the house, the heating system, etc;
- ☐ the degree of availability of community fire protection;
- ☐ the security of the neighborhood.

It is important to get sufficient coverage without getting oversold on a policy. The more dangers you insure your house against, the more this special coverage will cost you. It's a good idea to discuss special coverage with the insurance representative. Make a realistic decision on those risks (fire, flood, hurricane, snow/rain damage, etc.) that are a significant threat to your home. Then decide what types of special coverage you need. *Remember that you shouldn't overinsure your house but you should consider the inflated value and replacement costs of today's homes.* Do not include the value of the building site, foundation or underground pipes and wiring in making your evaluation.

If your home insurance protection, purchased when you bought your home, has not been recently reviewed, it should be. If your home and its contents were lost to you, you can assume that yesterday's coverage will not meet today's replacement costs.

Perform the following preliminary precautions, which will greatly simplify both revision of your current policy and evaluation of loss, if it should occur:

- ☐ Take an inventory, room by room, of all your household goods. List furnishings and possessions such as jewelry, silverware, art objects and so on. Note the date of purchase or acquisition.
- ☐ Have the inventory notarized and keep it in your safe deposit box, your attorney's files or a similar equally safe place. This will provide documentary evidence on which insurance claims can be based. The inventory will be especially important if your home and its contents are totally destroyed.
- ☐ Some policy holders take the additional precaution of filing photographs of their rooms with the written inventory.

INSURANCE PROBLEMS

There are few other businesses or occupations in which absolute dependability is of such vital importance as it is in the field of insurance. **Remember:** The first thing to do when you are approached (by mail or in person) with an offer of insurance of any kind is to *find out whether the insurer is licensed to operate in your state.* Insurance firms that are not licensed are not subject to the laws of those states, and they cannot maintain agents to do business there.

Check with your Better Business Bureau.

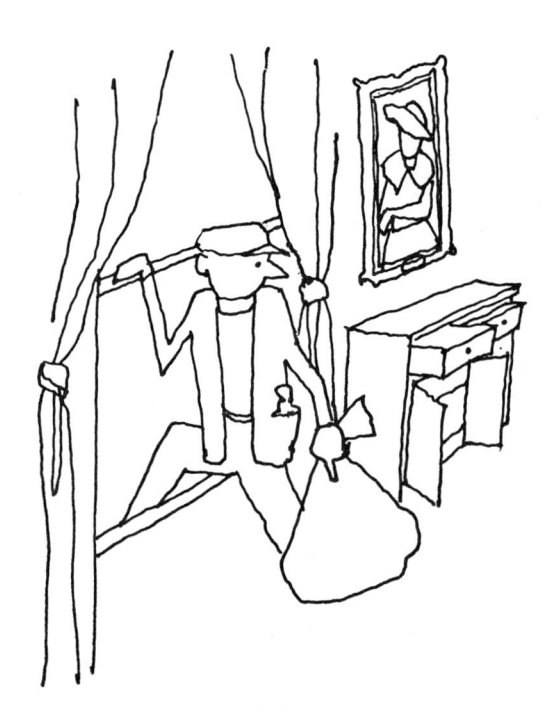

Insurance, Life

THE FIRST THING TO DO when shopping for life insurance is to evaluate the life insurance companies in your area. Check the reputation of insurance companies in your state — call the local Better Business Bureau. You may also contact your State Insurance Department to determine licensing requirements and to find out whether a company under consideration is licensed to operate in your state.

Compare the cost of similar policies offered by a number of firms. Premiums vary substantially.

In addition to comparison shopping in regard to price, however, compare policy provisions, such as reinstatement rights.

CHOOSING A REPRESENTATIVE
In all states a life insurance representative must be licensed to sell policies to consumers. Qualification is based upon a written examination and often representatives will have had further training in various insurance areas such as financial planning. An insurance representative may receive extensive training through the company he or she represents or the National Association of Life Underwriters and may have received a certificate as a Chartered Life Underwriter (CLU) from the American College of Life Underwriters after completing a college-level course of study. You, as the policy buyer, must be assured that the representative you select has the knowledge and experience to advise you and, equally important, will provide the time and service to advise and assist you in the future with questions you may have about your insurance program.

THE INSURANCE ESTATE
The major purpose of life insurance is to secure financial provision for dependents if the breadwinner should die. A second use — and more important now than ever, because people are living longer — is to add to retirement income.

Life insurance is available in individual or group plans. As is true of group health insurance plans, premiums are lower for group life insurance policies. Group plans are available to employees through company, union or organization policies.

These are the three basic types of coverage available:

1. Term insurance is pure insurance. **Renewable term** insurance can be renewed at the end of the term, at the option of the policyholder and without evidence of insurability, for a limited number of successive terms. **Convertible term** insurance can be exchanged, at the option of the policyholder and without evidence of insurability, for another plan of insurance.

For a stated, limited term, this type of insurance will provide protection over a set number of years — usually five- or ten-year periods. At the end of this term the protection ends. Usually there is no cash value for the premiums paid over the years. That is, no money is returned to the buyer. Premiums for a renewed term are higher than the original payments. However, term insurance usually is the least expensive kind and many term policies can be converted to whole life or endowment policies (*see below*) at any time during the term of the insurance. Term insurance can be the most economical way for a wage earner with a limited income to provide adequate protection for a family or for a single person to provide for his own death costs and payment of any debts outstanding at the time of death.

2. Whole life insurance provides protection for the lifetime of the buyer. At the buyer's death the amount of the policy will be paid to a beneficiary (the person named by the policy buyer). Payment of the premiums can be set up in a variety of ways: annual premiums as long as the buyer lives; annual premiums for a set number of years or to a certain age; or one single payment for the full cost of the policy at the time of purchase.

There are two kinds of whole life policies, depending on the way premium payments are set up, and each offers specific advantages: straight life and limited payment life.

Straight life, sometimes called "ordinary life," calls for payments for the lifetime of the buyer. The payments remain fixed and cannot be raised. In addition, these policies build a cash value after a certain number of years which the buyer may use for loan purposes during the years of the premium payments. These policies usually offer other options that allow the buyer to cancel the policy, receive either a cash payment or an income for life or for a stated, limited time; they can also be converted to reduced paid-up or extended term insurance. Their flexibility and the fact that premium costs are the lowest of whole life policies make these policies among the most popular.

Limited payment life is the same as straight life, except that the premiums are paid for a limited period of time, such as twenty or thirty years or until the buyer reaches a certain age. This limited payment period means that the buyer pays up to the value of the insurance over a shorter period of time than for straight life and, therefore, the premiums are somewhat higher. These policies also build a cash value faster than straight life which the buyer may use for the same range of options.

3. Endowment policies enable a buyer to accumulate an amount of insurance that is paid in full to the buyer at a specified date or is paid out as annual income. When an endowment policy matures, the owner has four options: leave the money at interest; take it periodically (proceeds and interest) for a specified number of years; take it for a fixed amount of money periodically until the proceeds and interest are exhausted; or take a life income.

An owner can take the lump sum from any permanent life policy, including endowment, and purchase a lifetime income from an insurance company. This is the same thing that happens with a single premium immediate annuity purchase. This can be for life only, or life and ten or twenty years certain, and it can be for one or more lives.

There are variations on these four basic themes:

The family income policy is a combination of straight life and term insurance, intended to meet the protection requirements of a young couple with growing children. The straight life portion of the policy provides permanent life insurance; the term portion provides additional temporary protection while the children are young.

If the insured dies when the children are young, the family would receive an income while the children are growing up. Some policies provide that the face value of the permanent insurance will be paid at the end of the family protection period. Others make this payment immediately.

Disability benefits written into insurance policies provide the policy holder an income if he becomes completely and permanently disabled. An alternative method dictates that premiums are waived while the policy holder is disabled.

Accidental death/double indemnity policies provide beneficiaries with twice the face value of the policy in case of the accidental death of the insured.

Annuities, which are not life insurance policies at all, are also sold by life insurance companies. These contracts guarantee a specified income for life with, in some cases, an additional guarantee for a certain number of years. Annuities are used to provide retirement income.

Discrimination?
If you're having trouble getting insurance coverage that you think you have a right to, get in touch with the state insurance commission. It will take action on cases involving unfair discrimination, whether it's sex or race; it is also concerned with other illegal insurance practices. Some state insurance offices offer to sit down with you and answer any questions you have about your coverage. This is a good way to double check what the insurance representative has told you about your policy.

One type of annuity provides that, if the policy holder (the annuitant) should die before he receives all the money invested in the annuity, his beneficiary would receive the balance. A second plan — a **joint survivor annuity** — can be purchased by a husband and wife; when one partner dies, the annuity would continue to provide an income for the other as long as he or she lives.

The cost of an annuity depends upon the type purchased and the age and sex of the annuitant. Annuities cost more for women than for men because women live longer and are likely to receive more payments than men. No medical examination is required for an annuity, but the person who applies for one must supply proof of his or her age. Annuities may be purchased with one lump-sum payment or over a number of years on an installment plan.

Retirement income policies have annuity-like features in that should the policy holder die before retirement, his beneficiary receives the proceeds of his insurance *or* the cash value, whichever is greater. (To provide this annuity, the policy builds large cash values.) In this case, when the policy holder retires, the cash value of his policy is used to provide a lifetime income.

Special discounts may be available through clubs, associations, place of employment, etc. and for certain personal attributes such as not smoking or drinking.

Mail order life insurance

From time to time you may encounter an offer to buy life insurance through the mail at an attractively low price and, often, without a physical examination and regardless of age.

Be careful! Never purchase such a policy until you have read and understood every word of it. Do not rely solely on the advertising. Check with state insurance regulatory authorities to find out if the company is licensed to sell insurance in your state. If an unlicensed company should refuse to pay a claim on your policy to which you feel you are entitled, you may have no recourse to the insurance department or commission of your state since it does not have supervision over that company.

LIFE INSURANCE, SAVINGS AND INVESTMENT PLANS

The best way to spend your money depends on what your needs are and the extent of your resources. Every family should set funds aside for all three — insurance, savings, and investments.

In considering life insurance, some people may argue that it is better to buy the least amount necessary to protect dependents and to put one's money over the years in such things as stocks and other investments. The usual reason given for this is that the cash value of life insurance does not automatically go up to keep pace with inflation, and for a buyer to increase insurance protection at a later date means higher premiums to the buyer.

Those considering straight life insurance, for example, should keep in mind that twenty or thirty years from now the cash value of the policy could depreciate in terms of current dollars; however, bear in mind that a straight life policy provides guaranteed lifetime protection at a guaranteed lifetime level price. While it is true that in inflationary times you will pay your premiums in "inflated" dollars, your final insurance payout could be adversely affected by inflation to some extent.

Be sure to consider how much you want to put into insurance, and how much you want to put into other areas of investment, such as stocks, mutual funds or real estate, that might hedge against inflation. A low cost term insurance policy may be the best bet for some; it has no cash value build-up, but offers protection for your family in case of death. Because term insurance costs are much less than straight life, you will have more money on hand, money which can be invested in more extensive term coverage or in apparently safe and sure assets that will appreciate over the next twenty or thirty years. Keep in mind, however, that if you follow this "buy term and invest (save) the difference" path, you must exercise a degree of self-discipline and acquire the expertise to systematically and prudently invest or save. Otherwise your protection/savings program might not produce the results you have anticipated.

Jewelry

(See also PRICES AND SALES)

JEWELRY CAN BE A good investment, an elegant gift, something special to receive, a delight to wear for years.

It can also be an expensive mistake.

How do you know which is which?

Wise buyers will follow BBB advice when they invest in jewelry of any kind: *If you don't know the merchandise, know the merchant.*

CHOOSING A JEWELER

Check the establishment's complaint record with the local Better Business Bureau. It's true that any business firm is likely to have received its share of complaints, so find out how consumer complaints have been handled.

- ☐ Beware of merchants who have a record of misrepresentation in advertising or sales.
- ☐ If complaints have resulted from a misunderstanding of some sort, the issues should have been clarified and the problems resolved by way of good clear explanations.

Any time a salesperson cannot or will not answer reasonable questions about merchandise, ask for another salesperson to supply the information you want. If you can't find the kind of help you need, leave the store.

Reputable, ethical merchants stand behind their products and services. In addition to basic ethical principles, there is a good business reason for this: people who stay in business rely on repeat customers. Having sold you an engagement ring, the reputable jeweler would like to sell you birthday and anniversary presents for years to come. It follows that his or her merchandise will not be misrepresented and that your questions about prospective purchases will be answered as carefully, fully and intelligently as possible.

But in this specialist field, how do you know what questions are (a) important and (b) reasonable? Familiarizing yourself with the following terms and definitions will help.

> *Classic,* purrs the copy, *is forever, like the diamonds in this candlelight setting. Two perfect stones highlight simple elegance.* $450.00
>
> What's a "candlelight setting"? How much of what kind of precious metal does it contain?
>
> "Perfect" stones? The word "perfect" will not be found in ad copy placed by jewelers who follow the Federal Trade Commission's *Trade Practice Rules for the Jewelry Industry* — unless the stones meet specific standards:
>
>> It is unfair trade practice to use the word *perfect,* or any other word, expression or representation of similar import, as descriptive of any diamond which discloses flaws, cracks, carbon spots, clouds, or other blemishes or imperfections of any sort when examined in normal daylight, or its equivalent, *by a trained eye* under a ten-power, corrected diamond loupe or other equal magnifier.
>
> Italics have been added: Few jewelry clerks and even fewer consumers could even begin to judge the quality of a diamond. And, in fact, most diamonds have flaws; perfection is hard to come by and — for most purchasers — impossible to buy.

GEMSTONES

The value of a **gem** is determined by the extent to which it possesses certain qualities. Gemstones are minerals which, because of their color, transparency or other qualities, are considered beautiful. Other factors affecting value are rarity, durability, portability and fashion. A few gems are not classified as minerals since they are of organic origin. These are pearl, coral, amber and jet.

Diamonds, like humans and snowflakes, are unique individuals. They are the hardest and most brilliant of gemstones, "universally recognized," according to the *Encyclopaedia Brittanica,* "as chief among precious stones." Most other commodities, from iron to gold, are relatively easy to assess and evaluate.

There are well-defined grades of quality and well-established market prices for each. But this is not true of diamonds. Buying a diamond is comparable to buying a work of art, because its value is not determined simply by size or weight any more than the value of a Rembrandt or Cezanne is determined by the number of square inches of canvas. Only an expert can judge the true value of a diamond; judgment will be based on four factors: color, clarity, cutting and carat weight — commonly known as "the four Cs."

Color: Fine color usually means the absence of color — a pure, clean, colorless or "white" transparency. Color is virtually impossible for the layman to identify, but a reliable jeweler will tell you frankly where

> *October's stone is the opal . . .
> the stone with fire in its heart.*
>
> 10K setting, hand carved
> OUR PRICE SEPTEMBER 15 TO
> OCTOBER 31 ONLY — $54.95
> ABC WHOLESALERS . . .
>
> There is a fact in this copy: October's birthstone *is* the opal. All other implications are pure fantasy. Not all opals are fire opals. There is something peculiar about the advertised price. And if ABC Wholesalers is selling to you at retail prices, is it really a wholesaler? It is extremely unusual for a consumer to be able to buy at wholesale prices (see PRICES AND SALES).

each stone stands on the color scale. A stone may take color from the room or from the setting it is in.

Bluish diamonds are extremely rare and are very expensive. Only one out of five hundred high-grade diamonds examined by the Gemological Institute of America was found to have any trace of blue, and fewer than ten did not have some tinge of yellow. Clever tricks of the trade have been used by unscrupulous jewelers to change or disguise the color of stones. If you are in doubt as to the value of a diamond, insist on securing an independent appraisal.

Finally, color can be a matter of taste — you can get a larger stone for your money if you do not insist on the "whitest" white.

Clarity: refers to the physical structure and condition of the diamond — that is, the relative absence of impurities, inclusions, internal cracks and tiny bubbles. A tiny inclusion, imperceptible to the naked eye, may not appreciably mar the stone's brilliance — but it does prevent the stone from being labeled or sold as "perfect" or "flawless."

Most diamonds have flaws. They are products of nature and each is likely to have some degree of imperfection. As a general rule, the less the degree, the smaller the flaw, the more valuable the stone. **But remember:** a so-called "flawless" or "perfect" diamond may still be a bad buy because of poor color or workmanship.

Cutting: In the rough, a diamond is homely. A piece of quartz is more appealing. Only highly skilled and laborious work reveals a diamond's color, clarity and brilliance (as much as a month may be required to finish a one-carat stone). A properly cut diamond catches all the light that enters the top, breaks it into all the colors of the spectrum and reflects it back through the top of the stone. A full-cut round diamond has at least 58 facets (or surfaces), including the "culet" facet or point, all in proper geometric relation to one another. Some special or novelty cuts have more than 58 facets, but it is very difficult to measure any increased brilliancy claimed for such stones.

Carat: Diamonds are weighed in "carats" and "points." There are 100 points to a carat. A quarter of a carat is 25 points (usually written with a decimal point: .25 carat).

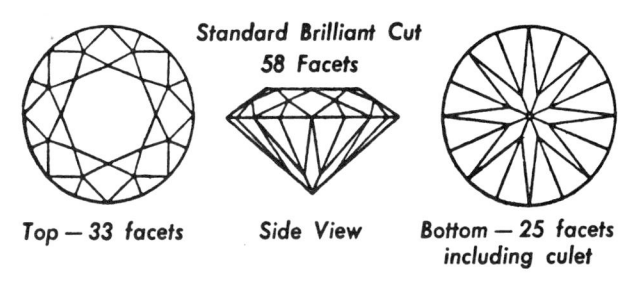

**Standard Brilliant Cut
58 Facets**

Top — 33 facets   Side View   Bottom — 25 facets including culet

Carat-weight representations are occasionally misrepresented or exaggerated: however, carat-weight should not vary more than 1/200th of a carat (1/2 "point") from the actual weight.

Remember: When you choose between two diamonds of the same color, clarity and cut, you must expect the larger of the two to be worth much more than twice the value of a one-carat stone. Why? Because larger stones are rarer and rarity inevitably increases value.

If a piece of jewelry containing several small diamonds appeals to you, bear in mind that the phrase "total weight" (which may be used in advertising or in a sales talk) can be misleading *unless you remember that small diamonds cost much less per carat than large diamonds.* For example: ten diamonds at .10 carat each have a total weight of one carat — but should cost considerably less than a single one-carat diamond of the same quality.

> Small diamonds, usually under .05 points each (one-twentieth of a carat), often have only 18 facets and are worth much less per carat than the 58 facet full-cut stones.
>
> *A sidelight:* In the South African diamond mines, more than twenty tons of rock, sand and gravel are moved and processed to yield one carat of finished gems — regardless of the size of the individual stones. However, a "diamond in the rough," large enough to be polished into a single one-carat gem, requires some 250 tons of rock, sand and gravel to be mined.

Emeralds are the green variety of the mineral beryl. The finest quality stones have a velvety grass-green color. The emerald is a hard stone, but it fractures easily and requires special care when being worn or handled.

Rubies are a transparent to translucent variety of the mineral co-rundum, red with only traces of other tints or hues. Expect natural rubies to contain what appear to be angular-shaped bubbles.

Sapphires are transparent or translucent and come in a variety of colors: blue, yellow, green, orange, purple, pink, etc. Like the ruby, sapphires are varieties of corundum.

Pearls
Produced "naturally" by certain kinds of oysters, pearls are as individually unique as diamonds. No two of them are ever exactly alike. They are judged (by experts) by their luster, absence of blemishes, color, size and shape (round or perfectly spherical, irregular "baroque" pear, drop, button and mabe — which is half-round).

"Natural" or Oriental, are produced by a certain type of oyster found in a number of oceanic waters, generally areas of the Pacific Ocean, South Sea Islands and the Persian Gulf. They are extremely rare.

Cultured pearls have almost completely replaced the natural or oriental variety. Developed in Japan, cultured pearls are also "natural," inasmuch as they are also produced by oysters, but their production is scientifically controlled. The process begins with the insertion of a mother-of-pearl bead inside the living tissue of the oyster. The oyster coats the bead with nacre and thus produces a cultured pearl over a period of from one to three years, depending upon seasonal conditions and water temperatures.

Cultured pearls are reasonably priced as well as beautiful. Again, no two are exactly alike. Most pearl necklaces are the result of careful matching of pearls which *appear* to look alike in color, luster and size. Pearl matching is considered a fine art.

Other Gemstones — a wide range from amethyst to zircon must be judged and evaluated by experts. Each has its own character, and a reliable jeweler can help you choose from among them for value.

If you are in doubt as to the value of any stone offered for sale by a seller, you would be well advised not to buy it unless you can secure a second opinion as to its value.

PRECIOUS METALS
The eight precious metals are: gold, silver and the six members of the platinum family: platinum, palladium, rhodium, ruthenium, iridium and osmium. The last five are very rare and generally are used more for industrial purposes than for jewelry.

Gold. A karat is the unit used to measure the amount of gold any article contains — pure gold being 24 karats fine. 18 karat gold has 18/24 or 3/4 gold by weight and, in alloy with other metals, is stronger and more durable than pure gold.

A karat measure used for gold should not be confused with the carat weight used for measuring diamonds. You rarely see the unqualified term "gold" used when jewelry is advertised — the karat designation must be identified.

Karat gold designations are 10K, 12K, 14K, 18K, 22K and 24K fine. The gold alloy most commonly used in jewelry is 14 karats, or 14 parts of gold mixed with 10 parts of one or more other metals. Karat gold articles are stamped with the exact karat designation, beginning with 10K. Articles containing less than this carry no karat designation.

Colored gold is alloyed with other metals to produce variations in color. (The karat designation does not change, however.) A gold/copper alloy produces a red-gold color, and white gold is produced by combining gold with nickel or palladium.

"Gold-filled" refers to articles made of base metal on one or more sides or surfaces to which there is affixed by mechanical means, a sheet(s) or shell of karat gold which has been rolled, drawn or pressed.

"Gold-plated" refers to an article having a plating of gold alloy of not less than 10 karat fineness and substantial thickness, and the plating is at least 1/20th of the weight of the metal of the entire article.

Except on watch cases, the quality of gold must be identified by a phrase stamped onto the metal. For example, "1/10 12K Gold-Filled" means that one-tenth of the weight of the article is 12K gold. To qualify for description as "gold-filled," the gold component must be at least one-twentieth of the total weight of the finished article. "1/30 10K Rolled Gold Plate" indicates that one-thirtieth of an article is 10K gold.

Gold-filled jewelry usually contains more gold than gold-plated pieces and can be expected to wear better. Articles designated **"gold electro-plated"** contain a very small quantity of gold applied by an electrolytic process that results in a gold coating measured in millionths of an inch. Jewelry termed **"gold-washed"** contains even less.

Silver is very soft in its pure state, and must also be combined with other metals for general use. The standard for **sterling silver** has remained unchanged since 1300, when Edward I of England established an early trade practice rule for silversmiths, decreeing that sterling must consist of 92.5 percent pure silver alloyed with 7.5 percent copper. The word "sterling" refers, therefore, to the composition of the metal, never to the weight of a finished article — which can be thin and light (when used in a bangle bracelet or chain) or very heavy.

Some silver articles, such as candlesticks, may have bases loaded with another material which gives the articles weight and balance. In such a case, they are marked "weighted" or "loaded."

Jewelry made of part silver and part gold must carry quality designations such as "sterling and 10K."

"Silver-plated" flatware and jewelry is produced by an electrolytic process whereby a layer of silver is plated to a base of metal. The thickness of the silver on such articles may be as low as 1/100,000 of an inch.

Platinum Metals. The six platinum metals are the least abundant of the precious metals. In fact, the world's annual production of precious metals, valued at more than a billion dollars, consists of approximately 7,500 tons of silver, 1,500 tons of gold and a mere 35 tons of the platinums. The most plentiful of these is platinum itself. Next comes palladium. Even less abundant are rhodium, ruthenium, iridium and osmium.

Like pure silver and gold, platinum and palladium are alloyed for the production of jewelry. Unlike silver and gold, which are alloyed with base metals (usually copper), platinum and palladium are alloyed with other precious metals (iridium and ruthenium). The resulting alloys contain little, if any, base metals.

About flatware

Sterling flatware is produced in varying weights. There is no legal requirement governing the weight, for example, of a sterling silver spoon. Trade custom, however, has evolved weights known as **trade medium, heavy** and **extra heavy,** and the difference in weight between them — on sterling spoons — is about two ounces per dozen pieces. When you choose a sterling pattern for lifetime use, shop the "feel" of the pieces as well as the pattern. It is a pleasure to use well-balanced flatware.

On **silver-plated flatware** the weight of the pieces will bear no relation to the silver content. There are no regulations governing the thickness of the coating of silver applied to the base metal. FTC trade regulations state only that the article must be *completely* covered by "silver which is of substantial thickness." Quality markings from "A1" (the lowest amount of silver) to "XXXX" (or "Quadruple") have not been consistently used. And from the lowest to the highest silver content, these markings may indicate an amount of silver plating weighing two ounces per gross of teaspoons in the "A1" classification up to eight ounces per gross of teaspoons classified "XXXX."

Platinum jewelry is usually produced from an alloy of 90 percent platinum and 10 percent iridium. Sometimes a softer alloy of 95 percent platinum and 5 percent ruthenium is used. Expect to find platinum used in jewelry set with large diamonds in which the cost of the metal would be a minor item.

Palladium, discovered in 1809, is lighter than gold and all the other platinum metals. Jewelry craftsmen use this when they need to eliminate excess weight from earclips, brooches, etc. The usual alloy is

95.5 percent palladium, 4.5 percent ruthenium. Expect the cost per piece of palladium jewelry to be a little higher than 14K gold.

There is no national stamping regulation for the platinums as there is for gold and sterling silver, but the above proportions are most frequently used in alloys. When other metals are more extensively used, the combinations are called Iridium—Platinum, Irid—Plat, or by fractions indicating the proportions of the alloys. *Such terms as "Platinum effect," "Platinum finish," "Iridium finish," "Palladium finish," etc. should not be used to describe articles which do not contain these metals. Read advertising carefully and question the jeweler closely to make sure you know what you are buying.*

Land Purchases

REAL ESTATE — a good investment? A hedge against inflation?

Prospective purchasers of real estate should move with care and make sure they have complete information of the land under construction before they sign *anything*.

There are more than five thousand land developers in the United States, ranging in size from very small to corporate giants. The land they sell also covers a wide range of uses — resorts, theme parks, vacation retreats, "second home" locations, retirement home sites and recreational camp sites. Much of the land sold is undeveloped and most of it is purchased for investment.

Land is difficult to buy wisely. Many prospective purchasers haven't a clue to the kind of information they need to make an informed decision. Unscrupulous firms and individuals in land sales can easily take advantage of this lack of knowledge for several reasons:

- ☐ The present value of any given piece of land is normally unknown to prospective purchasers. It is virtually impossible to know when a salesman is making gross exaggerations or telling outlandish lies.
- ☐ Comparative shopping techniques don't apply to shopping for real estate. No two pieces of land are exactly alike. In addition to variables such as location, topography, water supply and soil composition, equally important factors such as zoning make each lot, tract or parcel of land unique.

CAN YOU AFFORD TO BUY LAND?

This fundamental question is often overlooked. A study of complaint case histories by the Council of Better Business Bureaus indicates that the ability to keep up with monthly payments and the need to raise cash to meet financial crises are major complaint sources. If you buy land for investment purposes, you will want to sell when the value has increased (*if* the value grows at all), not because you need cash.

Choosing a developer. It's most important that you deal with a developer who is well regarded and financially sound. Remember that the size of a development company is not necessarily a good yardstick for measuring reliability. Make sure you talk with people who have done business with the developer before. This may be the best, cheapest and easiest way to determine a company's reliability. If you have a question, get in touch with the Better Business Bureau.

Many developers and builders perform certain basic engineering and survey work, install preliminary improvements through a portion of the subdivision and start the first phase of development. Then, in anticipation of success and continued financing, the developer begins a sales program which in turn permits the planning of further phases of the development. Make sure you consider that the developer could misjudge the marketability of the development; the prospects for substantial development of an area consisting of thousands of lots may be remote.

Don't be rushed. Some land developers use a variety of techniques to afford you the opportunity of seeing their developments. Make sure you take the following precautions.

- ☐ Be skeptical of lavish dinners or get-togethers which offer free gifts or a reduced-rate "vacation" to attract you. The same advice applies to dealing with those land salespeople who call you on the phone or knock on your door. Don't fall for high-pressure sales tactics.
- ☐ NEVER sign a contract if you feel pressured. Any reputable land company wants you to know exactly what it offers. So when you receive the promotional materials, a copy of a contract and a copy of the Property Report or offering statement (which in most cases must be filed with the federal government), tell the salesperson you want to study these documents at your leisure. *Really study them:* discuss them with your attorney. Contact the local Better Business Bureau.
- ☐ NEVER buy land without seeing it yourself, whether it is three miles away or three thousand. But don't buy because it looks good either, without a thorough check of local zoning, the legal status of the land and prospects for development.

LAND AS AN INVESTMENT

The most frequently cited complaint against land developers in recent years has been alleged misrepresentation by salespersons of the quick and substantial profit to be made from the purchase of land. Much of the fantastic growth in the sale of subdivided lots has been generated by the claims of many developers that buying land on an installment contract basis provides a opportunity for people of average incomes to get themselves "a piece of the action." Tens of thousands of lots have been sold on the premise that they can be held for a few years and then sold at a big profit. With few exceptions, this notion is nonsense. Although it is true that people have made fortunes from buying and selling land, the fortunes have not come on a lot-by-lot basis.

If you are considering purchasing land from a developer primarily for investment, consider the following.

- ☐ You usually pay a premium price for the lots that are part of a development with promised improvements.

- ☐ If you purchase land by means of an installment contract, you will be *paying* interest for the life of the contract — as contrasted with *receiving* interest that other investments would provide. It's a peculiar "investment" on which the owner pays interest.
- ☐ Developers must pass along their promotional costs to buyers, adding about 40 percent or more to the cost of the lot. This is one more factor that makes it questionable that you will sell your lot for as much as you paid for it.

Property Reports are important to you. The Property Report is based on and is part of a detailed filing called a Statement of Record filed by the developer with the Office of Interstate Land Sales Registration (OILSR) of the U.S. Department of Housing and Urban Development (HUD). Such filing is required by the Interstate Land Full Disclosure Act, a federal law passed by Congress for the protection of lot purchasers. These reports contain detailed information on the availability of such basic necessities as electricity, water, gas, waste disposal systems and telephone service. They also tell you how far it is to the nearest hospital, to public schools and to shopping facilities. The Property Report can tell you more about the present characteristics of the property and its future prospects than the salesperson will. *But you must read it. When you buy property registered with OILSR, you must be given a copy of the Property Report. If you do not get a copy before you sign the contract, you can cancel the contract and get your money back. If you are not provided with the Property Report at least forty-eight hours before you sign, you may still be able to reconsider your decision and get your money back (as long as you didn't waive this right when you signed the contract).*

OILSR does *not*:

- ☐ verify the quality of land offerings or the fairness of the selling price;
- ☐ inspect subdivisions or verify statements made in the Property Report unless it believes them to be inaccurate;
- ☐ require subdividers to post the bonds guaranteeing improvements.

Except in cases where subdividers fail to register or otherwise fail to comply with the law, OILSR cannot prohibit sales of land — no matter how overpriced, or unfair the offering may seem.

Finally, the agency does not approve advertising.

Before you invest, investigate. Use this checklist:

- ☐ Never rely on the oral promises of a salesperson. If they are not included in a written contract, the developer is not bound by them.
- ☐ Take your time. Never allow yourself to be pressured into signing a contract without reading and studying it thoroughly.

LAND PURCHASES

- ☐ Read the Property Report. If you find a section that is especially technical or hard to understand, get it clarified. But read *all* of it. It contains vital information.
- ☐ Check on the land-development company by contacting your Better Business Bureau and by writing directly to the Office of Interstate Land Sales Registration, Department of Housing and Urban Development, Washington, D.C. 20410.
- ☐ Visit and inspect the property before you enter into any agreement to buy. See for yourself whether the property meets your personal requirements and expectations. Misunderstandings as to the desirability of property are much more likely to occur if you don't see what you're buying. *But don't forget that there are a number of important matters that a look at the land will not tell you.* You can't tell by looking at it whether the land is selling at a fair price. Building restrictions, zoning regulations, title clearance problems, etc., should all be known to you before buying.
- ☐ Consider retaining a lawyer who is knowledgeable about the local real estate if you are considering making a sizable financial commitment.
- ☐ Many projects are termed "Planned Developments." These generally include common areas and common facilities that will be operated by an owners' association. These associations usually have the right to levy assessments against you for maintenance of the common areas and for other purposes as well. Your control of the operations and expenses is almost always limited to your right to vote at meetings. In these developments, there could be a current or future obligation to pay water and sewer "availability" fees as well. Find out what these extra fees are and consider them along with your monthly payments to see if the investment fits your pocketbook.
- ☐ If you are buying land primarily as an investment you should compare the risk factors and profit potential with those of other investments such as stocks, bonds, mutual funds, and savings accounts.

Legal Services

FEE SCHEDULES — PROFESSIONAL CODES OF ETHICS — PRICE-FIXING

In 1972 a couple of young marrieds found the house they wanted to buy in Virginia. Unlike most home buyers, they tried comparison shopping for an attorney to handle the necessary title examination required for title insurance, which in turn is required for mortgage financing.

On the theory that there is no reason to pay more than necessary for such standard service, the couple communicated with thirty-six local lawyers to ask for price information. Nineteen lawyers responded, *unanimously:* the minimum fee would be one percent of the property value, as set by the County Bar Association.

This set of responses introduced an interesting question: Was the County Bar Association's minimum fee schedule (and all other bar associations' fee schedules as well) tantamount to price-fixing? If so, then the associations would be in violation of the Sherman Anti-Trust Act.

The resulting test case made its way to the Supreme Court, and on June 16, 1975, Chief Justice Warren Burger's opinion, reflecting the unanimous decision of the Court, held that fee schedules constitute a classic illustration of price fixing and as such were in violation of the Sherman Act.

Prices are easily controlled if no one knows what they are. The Federal Trade Commission has been active in its efforts to change the classic codes of ethics of several professional groups on the grounds that they inhibit competition because they prohibit advertising of prices and professional specialties.

As professionals' codes of ethics are changing and advertising of legal services is becoming more prevalent, the following results could ensue (or have already come into practice):

- ☐ The cost of standard professional services (in law, such items as fees for handling adoption, bankruptcy, debt collection, divorce cases, etc.) could become more variable, making it worthwhile for a consumer to shop around for the best buy.

☐ Consumers now can obtain an up-front price tag on many professional services before they buy. This, of course, has long been considered a consumer right in the purchase of goods, but insofar as professional services are concerned, most people have tended to fly blind.

The legal advertising issue has now been resolved in most parts of the country; quite a few lawyers have actually advertised their services. Prices for legal services are variable and competitive, and purchasers of *all* professional services — medical, legal, etc. — are well advised to comparison shop. *Before* meeting with a lawyer, find out what he'll charge for whatever it is you need — title search, uncontested divorce, drawing a simple will — and check with a few more lawyers before you purchase his services.

Expect to pay for the first consultation period. (There is no reason why you shouldn't ask, before you make the appointment, how much this initial consultation will cost.) Lawyers, like doctors and dentists, should be able to provide a reasonably accurate estimate of fees and other costs for a given piece of legal work. A common way of charging

---

Choosing a lawyer

It's smart to choose a doctor before you need one. It is equally wise to choose a lawyer at leisure. Face it: every family needs a lawyer sometimes, and it is clearly best to use the services of one who is known to you and whom you know to be competent, qualified and considerate — someone you can trust for advice and clarification of terms.

You will need a lawyer when:
   ☐ You buy or sell a home.
   ☐ You consider buying real estate for investment purposes.
   ☐ You go into business.
   ☐ You buy a franchise.
   ☐ You are involved in an injury or damage suit.
   ☐ You plan your estate.
   ☐ You make a will.
   ☐ You enter into a major contract — home improvement, for example, or an insurance plan.
   ☐ You need assistance on tax matters.

You can choose a lawyer about the same way you choose a family doctor:
   ☐ Check with the local bar association's referral service — the way you contact the nearest teaching hospital for the names of several general practitioners or internists.
   ☐ Consult with friends and business associates whose judgment you trust.

for professional fees, in most larger law firms and in more unusual situations requiring a lawyer, is by the hour. If you are shopping around for a lawyer, you may find this is the least expensive way of obtaining legal services, especially in the settlement of an estate, for example. If you are involved with a lawyer or firm that is charging by the hour, get an estimate of the number of hours, the amount of time to be charged to "partners" at a higher rate and to "associates" at a lower rate.

Don't stay with any professional you don't like. The relationship between family and family lawyer should be one of compatibility and mutual respect. If you feel that, for any reason, you are not getting an adequate return in service for the money you spend on legal fees, take time to find a lawyer with whom you feel secure.

Legal clinics

A legal clinic is a new, special type of law firm that handles routine cases for people of the middle-income range at relatively moderate cost. Services include simple divorces, real estate transactions, estate planning, consumer complaints, bankruptcies, etc. These clinics can cut costs because they use specialist lawyers, paralegal assistants and streamlined work systems. Fees are usually posted in the office, and are generally lower than other lawyer fees. Since the advertising of legal services has been approved, legal clinics are becoming commonplace around the country.

Magazine Subscriptions

(See also CONTRACTS; DOOR-TO-DOOR SELLING)

THERE ARE TWO SIMPLE, logical reasons for subscribing to magazines: you like them so much that you want every issue delivered to your door, and you pay a little less than you would pay at a newsstand.

There are also several nonsensical reasons, to which many consumers are easy prey. For instance, they feel sorry for the salesperson, who says he or she can win a "scholarship" by selling quantities of magazines. (What kind of school awards scholarships on the basis of salesmanship?)

Many people who engage in direct sales of magazine or book subscriptions state the purpose of their visit or phone call to you directly and attempt to sell their merchandise on its merits.

Others don't.

There are always a few salespersons who use high-pressure tactics or appeal to your sympathy in order to make sales. Protect yourself against such less-than-honest salespersons by refusing to buy from or discuss the merchandise with people who use the following solicitation methods at your door or over the phone:

- ☐ **"Free."** This word should sound an immediate warning. At some point in the sales presentation you will be presented with a sales contract and asked to sign it. Never sign anything you have not read. The piece of paper will most likely be a written agreement stating that you will pay a stated amount of money for any merchandise you order. It will *not* be your acceptance of free merchandise (see DOOR-TO-DOOR SALES).
- ☐ **"I'm taking a survey...doing consumer research":** Some sales representatives make this claim in order to gain access to your home. Always ask for identification or credentials that support this claim. And remember: legitimate researchers or surveyors *never* have anything to sell.
- ☐ **"You can cancel any time...":** This is nonsense unless it is written into the contract (see CONTRACTS).
- ☐ **"You can help me by buying...":** Unfortunately, these appeals to sympathy are very effective. This popular approach is often used

by magazine salespeople claiming that they are working their way through college . . . that they are scholarship contestants . . . that they are helping victims of some obscure disease, and so on. Don't let these appeals to your emotions influence you. If you want to give to charity, then give to charity. If you want a book or magazine, buy it. If the salesman is working under a genuine incentive program, he should be able to produce documents to prove it — but check them with your local Better Business Bureau.

☐ **"Only a few cents a week..."**: This is likely to be misleading. The contract you will sign obligates you to pay on a monthly basis — perhaps for two to four years, and those dollars add up.

☐ **"Save more by bulk subscriptions"**: Perhaps you don't want the magazines or books for your own use, but you are a willing contributor for materials to be sent to a hospital, nursing home or educational institution. Don't — unless you send them to a specific person at that institution so that you will have a way of checking on delivery.

☐ **"You have been selected..."**: because you are a community leader and the publishers hope your enthusiasm about the product will increase the sales all over town. You *may* be a leader in the community, but the approach is still nonsense — good for the ego, bad for the budget.

☐ **"Your child needs this publication (these books) for school..."**: Does he really? Then why haven't you been notified by your child or his teacher? Since when has curriculum and cultural development been the province of door-to-door selling? Check with the school before you buy the story or the merchandise.

If the salesperson claims to be a teacher, or that he or she is connected with a particular educational institution, ask for some identification. Then verify the claim with the institution involved. Or call your Better Business Bureau.

☐ **"This is a final offer at this special price..."**: Watch for this one. Chances are you will find the same special price quoted in the subscription blank enclosed in next month's copy of the magazine. Never be rushed into making a purchase.

SIGNING THE CONTRACT

As with any written agreement, be sure to read the contract before signing. Make certain that all important information, such as a list of the items you ordered as well as their total cost, is contained in the agreement.

The contract should also provide information on how you can cancel the purchase should you change your mind. If you decide to sign a contract for magazines for more than $25, the three-day cooling-off regulation may apply (see DOOR-TO-DOOR SELLING). This means that you have a three-day period during which you may change your mind and cancel any magazine order made in your home, provided you notify the company *in writing* within three business days of signing an order or sales contract.

Be sure to find out, too, what you must do to cancel the magazine subscription at a later date should you decide to stop receiving it.

When and how to complain

If you write your check for x number of subscriptions...or sign a sales contract and receive a bill...and the magazines fail to arrive, *complain*.

Your receipt or sales contract should have the address of the subscription service. Send your complaint there. Include a copy of your canceled check or your receipt for cash payment, but *never* mail the originals of these important documents. If you receive no answer to your complaint — and still have no merchandise — send your second complaint (with a copy of your original letter and accompanying documents) to your local Better Business Bureau.

Such complaints are a public service. In addition to helping you get the merchandise you paid for, your call for help will alert the Better Business Bureau to the activities of unscrupulous salespersons and inefficient or less-than-honest companies.

Mail-Order Shopping

(See also PRICES AND SALES; WARRANTIES)

MORE THAN SIX THOUSAND firms share the United States mail-order market. Their annual sales are estimated at more than $40 billion. Hundreds of thousands of consumers shop by mail: some because their mobility is limited by age or illness; some because they live in remote or rural areas; some because they believe they save money by shopping at home; and still others because the variety or uniqueness of mail-order merchandise is appealing.

Many reputable firms have provided efficient, convenient and reliable service to their customers over the years. They have demonstrated a very real interest in keeping old customers and acquiring new ones by maintaining high standards in the quality of both their product and service.

As in any field, however, there are unscrupulous operators who engage in misleading advertising, make spectacular, something-for-nothing offers, don't bother to keep advertised merchandise on hand, fail to deliver merchandise within a reasonable time, and sometimes even fail to deliver at all.

Wise consumers can avoid such unpleasant encounters by carefully choosing mail-order retailers. Follow these guidelines:

- ☐ Beware of exaggerated claims for products or unrealistically low prices for merchandise.
- ☐ Read catalogs carefully. They are your best guide to ordering.
- ☐ Always keep a copy of the ad, brochure or catalog from which you order.
- ☐ If you are in doubt about a company, check with your Better Business Bureau *before* placing your order.
- ☐ Find out whether the merchandise is offered on a "satisfaction guaranteed or money back" basis.
- ☐ Always allow six to eight weeks for delivery. Always — especially around holidays — check for a cut-off date for orders.
- ☐ Never send cash through the mail. Pay by check or money order and be sure to include any shipping or handling charges.
- ☐ Be sure to *write your name and address clearly* on the order and, when you order a gift to be sent to someone else, clearly indicate where it is to be sent.

> **Address, please...**
> You would be surprised at the number of people who forget to include their names and/or complete addresses on their orders to reputable mail-order firms. Before you mail your order, check to see that it is complete with your full name and address; that items are fully identified and order numbers accurately recorded; and that your check or money order is for the right amount, including any applicable sales tax, postage and handling charges.

- ☐ Keep a record of your order, including the name and address of the company and the date your order was placed. Keep your canceled checks. Record the number of your money order or bank check for future reference.
- ☐ When your order arrives, check it promptly to make sure you received the right merchandise in satisfactory condition. If there is a problem, notify the company immediately.

Try adapting this policy to your own needs. If you were looking at the merchandise in a store, what information would you expect to find? You would look for care instructions in clothing, check the construction, read hang tags and study warranties, now that warranty information must be available at the "point of sale" (see WARRANTIES). For instance:

- ☐ **Fiber content:** e.g., "Woven cotton and polyester," "100% Acrylic."
- ☐ **Care instructions:** e.g., "Machine wash gentle, tumble dry — low heat."
- ☐ **Information about furniture materials,** required for hang tags in the store, should be equally clear in catalog descriptions: e.g., "Pine veneer on solid hardwood."
- ☐ **Furniture construction:** In the store, you would open drawers to see how they are assembled. Check the catalog for construction information - e.g., "Dovetailed drawers with wood center guides; fiber-board drawer separators."
- ☐ If any item is not fully assembled, the catalog should say so: "Not fully assembled — instructions included."
- ☐ Look for warranty information. For example, "ABC Company Full 1-Year Warranty. Within one year of purchase, we will repair or replace... if defective in materials or workmanship."
- ☐ Sale merchandise should be clearly identified (see PRICES AND SALES). If there is a time limit on the reduced price, the catalog should say so: "Reduced from Fall catalog, see page 405. ORDER NOW. Sale ends September 15."

> **How to choose a catalog**
> A spokesman for a major mail-order company says that it is company policy to consider the catalog as its "point of sale." It follows, then, that the company's objective is to provide mail-order customers with as much information as they would have if they were shopping in the store.

Whenever catalog copy leaves questions in your mind try to get those questions answered *before* you place your order. If for any reason your questions go unanswered or ignored, spend your money elsewhere.

CAN THEY GET IT FOR YOU WHOLESALE?

Not if they plan to stay in business. Beware of merchandisers who advertise "wholesale" or "below cost" prices in their catalogs. Such claims are frequently untrue.

Also, watch out for other potentially deceptive savings claims. For example, a catalog entry reading "List price $42, your price $32" implies a potential saving of $10. But the current retail price of the item in other retail catalogs or in local stores may well be closer to $32 than $42. "Manufacturer's suggested retail prices" and "list prices" are often substantially higher than the amounts for which merchandise is commonly sold in the area. Always compare prices.

And remember: If an offer seems too good to be true, it probably is.

MAIL-ORDER REGULATIONS

If you have a problem involving a mail order company's *failure to make shipment*, a Federal Trade Commission rule may apply. Here briefly is what the rule requires;

> A company must ship mail-order merchandise within thirty days from the time it receives your order, *unless*, in making the offer, the company clearly and conspicuously stated some other time for shipment. NOTE: the rule applies from the date your *properly completed* order is received by the company to the date it is shipped, *not* from the date you sent in the order to the date you receive it. You must allow for shipping time.

If the company cannot ship within a thirty-day period, or within the time it advertised, it must notify you of that fact and permit you to cancel or agree to the delay. If you cancel, it must provide you with a full refund of any money you have paid within *seven working days* from a receipt of your notice of cancellation, or a copy of a credit memorandum showing your account cleared of any related charges within *one billing cycle* if you charged your purchase.

In notifying you, the company must provide a *cost-free* means (such as a postage-paid card) for you to reply if you wish to cancel.

If you do not respond to the notice, the company has the right to assume that you agree to a delay of up to thirty days. The company may not, however, delay shipment beyond an additional thirty days without your express consent. If the company cannot ship within that thirty additional days, or the agreed upon time, it must again notify you and always get your positive agreement to any further delay, or cancel and refund any payment you sent with your order, or credit your account.

The rule does *not* apply to COD (Cash on Delivery) orders or orders with which you send no advance payment and for which you are not billed nor your account charged until shipment is made.

Also not covered are mail-order services such as photofinishing; seeds and growing plants; magazine orders (except initial delivery); "negative option plans" such as those used by some book, record and tape clubs.

Many reputable mail-order firms had served their customers well following these procedures for years before the trade regulation rule was considered or promulgated. One significant function of trade regulation, which is apparent here, is to establish procedures that make it possible to see that all mail-order firms play by the same rules.

Consumers should not, however, assume that trade regulation rules, though they are undeniably important, protect the individual consumer throughout the marketplace. The wise buyer's best protection will continue to be the judgment and care he or she uses in every transaction.

UNORDERED MERCHANDISE
If you receive merchandise in the mail that you did not order, you may consider it a gift. You do not have to pay for it, and it is illegal for the company to bill you for it.

Only clearly marked free samples and merchandise mailed by charitable groups with a request for a contribution can be mailed to you without your consent. And you can still, if you choose, consider such merchandise a gift.

HOW TO GET YOUR NAME OFF A DIRECT-MAIL LIST
If you want to stop receiving unsolicited mailings, there is a way to take your name off nationwide mailing lists. Get in touch with the Mail Preference Service, Direct Mail Marketing Association (DMMA), 6 East 43rd Street, New York, N.Y. 10017, ask for a form, fill it out and return it. DMMA will advise its member companies (over 2,000) of your request, and your name will be deleted from their mailing lists. Keep in mind that this process takes several weeks from the time you send in your form. (If you wish to discontinue receiving unsolicited, sexually oriented mailings, there is a form you can fill out at the Post Office.)

Mattresses and Foundations

MATTRESSES AND BOXSPRINGS are among the most consistently used pieces of household equipment you will ever buy. Because they are used eight hours out of every day, 365 days a year, and because they should last for ten to fifteen years, depending on the quality of the merchandise, you should buy for maximum quality and comfort.

Prices for identical products will vary from store to store and from season to season. Watch for sales in January and February, and be sure to compare the labels of similarly priced items for information on construction and materials used.

Make the warranty part of your buying decision. Most mattresses are warranted for ten to fifteen years and pro-rated (proportioned to the amount of time the owner has had the product) after the first year. Remember that the federal Warranty Act will not allow the manufacturer to make the terms of a mattress warranty conditional upon your purchase of a matching boxspring made by the same manufacturer.

Foundation construction. Box springs are coils that are mounted on a wooden base, topped by padding and covered with fabric. A type of foundation made with a layer of *foam* is relatively new on the market.

Mattress construction. The primary type of innerspring mattress used is made of open coil units, coil springs joined by steel wire. Check the consumer information accompanying these mattresses for details

CHART OF RECOMMENDED SLEEPING SPACE

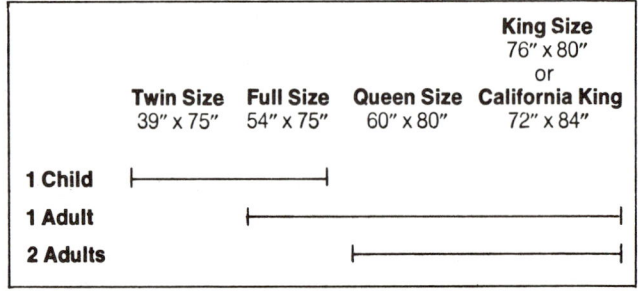

	Twin Size 39" x 75"	Full Size 54" x 75"	Queen Size 60" x 80"	King Size 76" x 80" or California King 72" x 84"
1 Child	├─────────┤			
1 Adult		├──────────────────────────────────┤		
2 Adults			├──────────────────────┤	

Note: Two adults sleeping on two twin beds can find them more comfortable if used "dual twin" style—attached to one king-size headboard.

on the gauge of steel used in the coils and how they are attached to one another, and the materials used in insulation and padding. Coils are covered by a cushioning material made of cotton, felt, polyester, foam or a combination of cotton and foam. An innerspring mattress should ideally have reinforced borders for durability and a strong outer fabric.

Foam mattresses are made up of a core of cushiony plastic foam within a colorful cover. There are two types of urethane foam available: standard foam and the new high resiliency foam, which provides excellent support. In addition, combinations of foam may be laminated together producing different density and support features. For maximum comfort and durability, foam mattresses should be at least six inches thick and made of high quality foam. The cost will be about the same as a comparable innerspring mattress.

When you shop for new bedding, test it in the store.
Lie down. Stretch out. Make sure that it has the degree of firmness most comfortable for you. Look for the right degree of softness on the surface combined with firm support inside.

Most bedding comes in these standard sizes:

Single (youth)	30" × 75"
Twin	39" × 75"
Twin (extra long)	39" × 80"
Double	54" × 75"
Double (extra long)	54" × 80"
Queen	60" × 80"
King	76" × 80"
California King	72" × 84"

One final tip: It's a good idea to buy a mattress and foundation that are designed for each other. Recent research has shown that you'll get better support if your mattress matches the foundation. That means if you're in the market for a new mattress, you may want to buy a new set of matching boxsprings, too. Without it, your new mattress may not provide the service you paid for and not last as long as you would like.

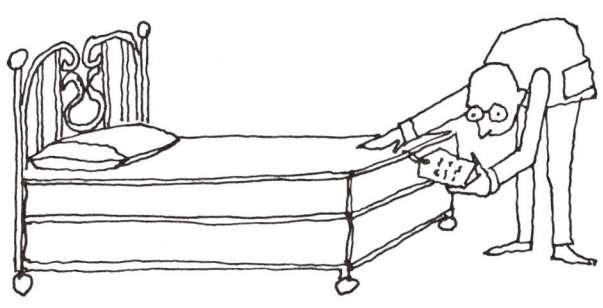

Mobile Homes

MOBILE HOMES are instant housing. They are usually purchased completely equipped with furniture, carpets and drapes, and appliances.

For all practical intents they are *not* really mobile. Unlike travel trailers, they cannot be towed behind the family car from one location to another. They must be moved by professionals and their mobility is often limited to the trip from the factory to the retailer and then to a permanent dwelling site.

Mobile homes offer a pared-down life style in a compact space, and more than nine million Americans live in them. Both the initial cost and maintenance costs are significantly lower than those for conventional housing, and this is probably the most important factor contributing to their growing popularity. Remember, however, that this price does not include a site for the home which has to be rented or purchased separately. You should also consider that appreciation for a mobile home may not be as great as for most conventional housing. However, when permanently affixed to land owned by the home-owner, a mobile home is subject to similar variables as any realty: location, general condition and area availability of housing. Depreciation of any home can be minimized by the careful selection of location and its proper maintenance.

Types and sizes include:

- **Single-section** mobile homes vary in size: 35-90 feet long and 14-16 feet wide (this overall length includes the length of the towing hitch, so 3 or 4 feet should be excluded from the measurement of the actual living space).
- **Multi-section** mobile homes are two single units, built and towed separately and combined at the dwelling site into a single unit. Extra attention is required for the leveling and blocking process at the homesite to assure proper joining of the roofs and heating ducts. (Some multi-sections have separate furnaces for each section.) A typical model has 24 by 60 feet of living area — 1,440 square feet.

The price you pay for a mobile home will vary from one geographical area to another and will be dependent upon several factors, including the model, the number of appliances you choose to buy and the type of furniture you select.

Expect extra costs. The basic price may *not* include the following extras which are required by most mobile home parks and which will add approximately 15 percent to the total price:

- ☐ **Steps with handrails** must be purchased separately for every outside door.
- ☐ **Concrete strips (runners)** or a **base slab** provide necessary underpinning for mobile homes. This foundation will be supplied by most mobile home parks, but if your dwelling site is on private property, be prepared to pay for this extra.
- ☐ **Skirting** is used to conceal the wheels and cover the foundation materials. This must be constructed to allow necessary ventilation and to allow access to crawl space. *Get estimates from more than one supplier for this equipment.*
- ☐ **Anchoring systems** are important for protection against high winds, and many state laws require that mobile homes be anchored to the ground. You, the home owner, are responsible for seeing that the system is secured to ground anchors or footings. Anchoring systems vary — the right one for your home will depend upon local soil and climate conditions.
- ☐ **Transportation and "set-up" costs** are usually included in the basic purchase price, but it is always wise to double-check. Have the salesman write this — as well as any other oral promises — into the sales contract.

FINANCING AND INSURANCE

Most young families and some older ones find it easiest to make a down payment on a mobile home and finance the balance due. Before financing a mobile home, a home buyer should shop around and compare financial arrangements available from commercial finance companies, banks, credit unions, savings and loan associations in addition to the mobile home retailers. In some situations, the Federal Housing Authority or the Veterans Administration will back a loan for the mobile home as well as for a site purchase (if needed) and preparation costs.

Before signing any contract, make certain the finance costs are clear. Do you understand exactly what you will get and what it will cost? Always get any promises in writing and save a completed copy for your records.

Remember that insurance is required by lending institutions and is usually included in the financing package. Don't assume, however, that the insurance required by the lender is all that you need for your own protection. The required insurance may be just enough to protect the lender's interest in your property; you may want to add on extra protection to cover its full value.

WHERE WILL YOU LIVE?

This question is so important that Better Business Bureaus advise prospective mobile home owners to check available locations before the home is actually purchased. **Remember:** The initial cost of the home does not include purchase or rental of a dwelling site, and the placement and use of mobile homes is often severely limited by zoning regulations. Check zoning regulations before you buy, especially if you plan to live on private property.

If you opt to live in a **mobile home park,** you will find that rental costs vary widely. Services provided are equally variable. Find out in advance whether you must pay an additional amount for such services as yard maintenance and trash removal.

Check park regulations. There may be rules regarding children, pets, home appearance, etc. Some parks have a long list of restrictive regulations. Others may have none at all. In either case, it is best to know of their presence or absence before you move in.

The lease you sign is important. Sometimes, when a park is filled — possibly with the help of attractively low rental fees — the owner will sell the facility to a management company, which may then raise the rent. If you do not have a lease, there may be nothing you can do to avoid the increase.

Protect yourself by seeking out an established park or one being developed by a company for long-term investment purposes. Make every effort to secure a long-term lease, though this may be more difficult than it sounds. Some states require written leases for tenants of mobile home parks, but most do not.

Remember:
- ☐ Carefully consider the location of the mobile home park in relation to important goods and services you will need. Is it near public transportation, stores, schools and recreational facilities?
- ☐ Don't make your decision to rent on the basis of one brief visit on a sunny day. Make an effort to find out how well the drainage works in wet weather, and visit the park at night to see for yourself whether it is adequately lighted.
- ☐ Talk to residents to find out what they think of the living conditions and services provided by park management.
- ☐ Don't accept a park owner's oral promises of future facilities such as a recreation building or swimming pool. If promises are made, get them in writing in your contract — and don't forget to find out whether the standard rent will cover the cost of using the facilities.

Mobile home standards have been established covering requirements for the construction of the body and frame and for the plumbing, heating and electrical systems. All mobile homes built after June 15, 1976, for sale in the United States must be built to the National Mobile Home Construction and Safety Standards Act of 1974 established and enforced by the Department of Housing and Urban

Development (HUD). Every home built after the June date must bear a seal indicating that it was built to HUD standards.

Prior to June 15, 1976, 46 states required compliance to the Mobile Home Standard as established by the National Fire Protection Association (NFPA) and the American National Standards Institute (ANSI). All members of the Manufactured Housing Institute were required to build to the ANSI/NFPA standard from the time it was established well over a decade ago until the federal standards became mandatory.

The HUD Home Construction and Safety Standards require that all mobile/manufactured homes sold in the United States today must include the following:

- ☐ two exterior doors, remote from each other;
- ☐ one egress (pop-out) window in each sleeping room;
- ☐ smoke detectors and audio alarms wired into the electrical system;
- ☐ a foundation anchoring system;
- ☐ an electrical system that conforms to the National Electrical Code; and,
- ☐ fire retardant ratings for furnace and hot water heater surfaces and other interior surfaces.

Warranties vary both in length and coverage (see WARRANTIES). Look for a full-year warranty — a ninety-day warranty is virtually useless if, for example, you purchase your home in the spring and discover a problem with the heating system in the fall.

Individual warranties are furnished by the manufacturers of the furniture and appliances. File all warranty certificates in a safe place. If the manufacturers require that the certificates be registered at company headquarters for validation, do this promptly to protect your investment.

Read all warranties carefully. If you don't understand the difference between the manufacturer's and the retailer's responsibilities, ask for clarification. Have these defined at the time of the sale and *have them put in writing* as part of the sales contract.

Mobile home owners should report any problems to the manufacturer or retailer as soon as they occur, depending on which one has responsibility for correcting them under the terms of the warranty.

WHAT ABOUT SAVING ENERGY WHILE LIVING IN A MOBILE HOME?

Requirements for making a mobile home energy-efficient are the same as those for a house. Make sure the mobile home has adequate insulation, weatherstripping, storm windows, etc. (see INSULATION), and that heating and air-conditioning units are the right size. Costs to operate the home will vary depending on the geographical area and the home's location on the site.

Motorcycles

MOTORCYCLES are a source of inexpensive transportation to some riders and an enticing outdoor sport to others. Their growth in popularity and public acceptance has been phenomenal.

Buying considerations for a motorcycle should combine the factors used in judging a bicycle and an automobile. Whether a motorcycle is used as a trail bike or as transportation, handling and maneuverability will be important to the rider. Stability — the sense of balance and structural integrity required by the rider — is equally important.

As you would when buying a car, it is important to consult all available sources of information in an effort to compare the attributes of various makes and models. A good place to start would be with performance data (on braking ability, passing acceleration, etc.). Check the local library for consumer publications offering this information. Compare fuel consumption, safety features, operating factors such as ease of "pick-up," efficiency of the steering and braking systems, and the availability of optional equipment. Compare printed material from manufacturers — give special attention to specifications for construction, braking, etc.

Test driving several models is absolutely necessary to make an informed buying decision. Potential buyers need to know which vehicles best fit individual driving styles, sizes and "reach."

Check these factors:

- ☐ The seat should be comfortable and stable, big enough for stability, well shaped and padded for comfort.
- ☐ All controls should be easily accessible.
- ☐ Check the view from the driver's seat. Rear-view mirrors should be both easily adjustable and stable when adjusted.
- ☐ Test drives should be long enough to give the rider an accurate feel of the steering and braking systems and the vehicle's stability. *Once around the dealer's lot is no way to judge a motorcycle.*

Questioning friends and motorcycle hobbyists on the good and bad aspects of their motorcycles and on the after-purchase in-warranty service provided by local dealerships will help. This is a way to learn about design and operations problems which — as in cars — are likely to arise only after the vehicle has been in use for a few weeks or months.

Take time to check with your local Better Business Bureau on the complaint records of local dealers. Your motorcycle warranty, like the automobile warranty, will be only as good as the dealer responsible for carrying out service under its terms (see WARRANTIES).

Compare prices, but don't base your buying decision on price alone. Dealers who offer the lowest initial prices may not offer the kind of after-purchase service you may need.

MOTORCYCLES AND SAFETY

Did you know that the danger of a fatal motorcycle accident is four times as great as the chance of an accident in a car? Each year more than 325,000 motorcycles, motor scooters and mopeds are involved in accidents; many of them are fatal.

A major cause of motorcycle accidents, according to National Highway Traffic Safety Administration statistics, is the inexperience of the cyclist. Many of those involved in motorcycle accidents are riding for the first or second time. Nearly seven out of ten motorcycle drivers involved in accidents are between 16 and 24 years old. Accidents result from lack of knowledge of the machine, the inability to recognize and deal with potential road hazards, and lack of knowledge and experience in carrying passengers.

For your own safety:
- ☐ If you ride a motorcycle, wear a helmet. Motorcycle deaths dropped considerably when many states adopted legislation requiring helmets for cyclists.
- ☐ Use headlights and taillights *all* the time to increase the likelihood that other drivers will see you. Wearing bright colors should also help increase visibility.
- ☐ Wear heavy protective clothing and boots.

LAWS AND LICENSES

Many states require that motorcycle riders pass a special test before they can be licensed to drive. Be prepared to take a test that's a lot tougher than the one required for automobile drivers. Make sure, too, that you find out the rules of the road if you have to travel from one state to another. These may or may not include wearing a helmet, having a rear-view mirror or driving with the lights on in the daytime.

MOTORCYCLE INSURANCE

You should keep in mind that because of the accident statistics involving motorcycles it is hard to get adequate insurance at a reasonable price. You may find that you will be forced into paying big premiums in order to get liability coverage from insurance companies. To get the best coverage for the money, be sure to compare prices. You may find that you can do better with one of the companies that specializes in motorcycle coverage. Remember, too, that state insurance laws sometimes differ, and that car and motorcycle insurance will vary. In addition, many policies don't cover your motorcycle if you lend it to a friend to drive. Liability coverage may become invalid if you receive a speeding ticket. Be sure to check with your insurance agent to find out what is and what is not covered in the policy you choose.

Mopeds . . . Mopeds . . . Mopeds
The late 1970s saw a rise in the number of mopeds sold to Americans concerned with the high prices and dwindling supplies of gasoline. This lightweight motorized bicycle can travel up to 150 miles on a single gallon of gasoline. A moped is basically a bicycle with a small engine, having a top speed of anywhere from 17 to 30 miles an hour and a price tag of $300—$600.

Even though mopeds may be fun and inexpensive to drive, certain safety rules and state laws still apply. Be sure you know what the licensing, registration and inspection restrictions are in your state. Find out if insurance is required. In addition, keep in mind that helmets and protective clothing can be just as important for mopeds as they are for motorcycles.

Moving

"MAKE THE MOVE AN adventure and a learning experience," suggests one consumer information brochure on the moving of household goods. And a fine idea it is.

But here's a better idea: Learn as much as you can about moving long before moving day. This will help you avoid several kinds of misadventures and learning experiences you'd be better off without. For instance:

- ☐ You felt secure in the belief that your shipment was insured, that the mover was liable for damage. During the move, your antique porcelain bowl is broken. Its value would be $120.00 in an antique shop. The mover's liability is $1.20. This is the worst possible time to learn the mover's liability is limited to $.60 per pound per article. You should have declared the value of your shipment and paid ($.50 per $100.00) for more protection.
- ☐ You meet the mover at your new house. You have your checkbook and are prepared to write a check for moving expenses. This is the wrong time to learn that you should have prepared to pay the driver in cash or by money order, traveler's check, cashier's check or bank treasurer's check. He refuses to unload the furniture. The children enjoy the unexpected adventure of another night in a motel.
- ☐ You arrive at your new home and the van does not. Now you learn that if you really wanted your household goods to arrive on August 12, you should have paid more for "expedited service." Right now everything you own is in Kansas City, where another family's goods are being unloaded from the van you shared. Camping in the new house with neither cooking facilities nor a bed to sleep in is certainly an adventure. The alternative: more motel expenses.

INTERSTATE MOVING

Summer, when the children are out of school, is the time most families move. And one out of five families in the United States moves every year. If this is your year, your first steps in choosing a moving company should be to:

- ☐ Discuss the various companies with friends and business associates whose judgment you trust. (This can be depressing —

most people have horror stories to tell you.) Call the Better Business Bureau for information on complaint records of several firms.
☐ Get estimates, but remember that *your actual cost will depend on distance, actual weight, and any special services or insurance.*
☐ Take advantage of the Interstate Commerce Commission (ICC) regulation requiring moving companies to give each prospective customer a copy of its performance record for the previous year. The record should be provided when the salesperson comes to your home to estimate the cost of your move. Among other things, the moving company must tell you:

—the percentage of shipments picked up and delivered later than originally promised;
—the percentage of shipments whose costs were underestimated by more than 10 percent;
—the percentage of shipments which resulted in damage claims of $50.00 or more;
—the average length of time required to settle damage claims.

Prospective customers should demand, inspect and compare performance records from each moving company under consideration.

Regulated estimates. Because the ICC approves rates on interstate moving, the actual charges from different companies are not likely to vary a great deal. **Be suspicious of any salesperson who gives you an estimate much lower than the others.** The actual charge may be much higher and you will have to pay it. Better Business Bureau records include complaints citing actual charges double or triple the estimated cost.

It is in your best interest to help the salesperson make the most accurate possible estimate by going with him through the house and letting him know exactly what is to be moved — including items stored in the attic, basement and garage. Also specify the additional services you need, such as packing, wardrobe service, "expedited" delivery service, etc.

The ICC publishes a booklet called "Summary of Information for Shippers of Household Goods," which moving companies must provide to potential customers. The booklet lists "major sources of misunderstanding" among which, the ICC says, are the following:

Liability. It's important that you fully understand how much the mover is responsible for in the event your goods are lost or damaged. You have two choices of protection in an interstate move:

1. **$.60 per pound per article:** This means that unless you are being reimbursed for losses by an employer or your goods are of very little value, this will *not* provide you with full protection. Your recovery for any loss or damage will be subject to a maximum of $.60 multiplied by the weight (in pounds) of the article involved.

2. **Full value for lost or damaged items:** This means you must declare a lump sum value for the entire shipment and pay an extra charge depending on the value you declare. In this case, the mover's responsibility is full and not limited to a pound per article basis. In addition, the mover is responsible for liability for claims arising from an act of God and for the loss of or damage to goods packed by you.

Keep in mind, however, that under any protection option you select, the maximum liability of the mover is the *actual value* of any lost or damaged item. Actual value is *not* the new cost of your goods, but the depreciated value at the time of shipment. Make sure you fully understand the maximum liability of the mover; and remember: you are *not* buying insurance; no policy will be issued.

Also note that certain items — documents, currency, jewelry, watches, precious stones, etc. — are excluded from liability. It's best to carry such things with you. Check your household insurance for special provisions on coverage during moving.

Storage. If storage is required before shipment, the goods should be held on a *storage-in-transit* basis. The mover may hold the goods on this basis up to 180 days. After this time, the responsibility for the goods passes to the local warehouseman, over whom the ICC has no authority.

Damages. A mover who damages one of a set of items will only be liable for the single item — not the set.

The mover will not accept liability for mechanical failure of an appliance unless there is evidence of external damage or unless evidence clearly indicates that the mechanical failure was due to the mover's negligence.

Inventory. The mover is required to deliver household goods in the same condition and quantity as they were at pick-up. The inventory is the receipt showing condition and quantity. Do not sign the inventory until every bit of damage and loss has been noted. The ICC prohibits a mover from telling you that you must sign any statements which release the mover from liability. *Be especially careful about the description of antiques.*

Inspection at delivery. It is standard procedure to pay the driver before the goods are unloaded. (It is best to have a cashier's check or traveler's checks with you.) Inspect all your belongings thoroughly, including those that are concealed, and make complete notations of damage on the documents before signing any delivery papers, receipts or inventories. *Notations of indicated loss or damage will be the basis for any claim of loss or damage against the mover.* The ICC says notations such as "subject to further inspection" or "subject to concealed damage" are not effective.

INTRASTATE MOVING
Moving within the state can be as traumatic and problem-filled as

moving across the country. If you move within the state, the basic cost is determined by the time involved.

It is extremely important to check the complaint records of local moving firms with your Better Business Bureau. Ask the company for references. And be sure to check these references.

Should you move yourself? You need several strong backs, a degree of expertise in packing and balancing your household goods, the ability to drive a truck or to compensate for the difference in the way your car will respond to towing a heavy trailer.

You will use a great deal of your own time, strength and energy. But you will probably save money and you will know that your household goods will arrive at your new home when you do.

Shop for truck and van rental services. You will need to check the rental agreement carefully. Be sure to find out:

☐ What is included in the rental charge?
☐ Who is responsible for liability insurance?
☐ What happens if the truck or van develops mechanical difficulty halfway through your move? Do you pay for repairs? How and when will you be reimbursed?
☐ What is the estimated gas consumption of the rental truck — 6 to 10 miles per gallon? More? Less?
☐ Is your car capable of towing a van (trailer) containing three to four rooms of furniture? (Expect gas consumption to increase.)
☐ How will you pay for rental? What is the basic flat rate per week, day or hour? Is there a deposit? An additional charge for collision insurance? What is the deductible on the insurance? Is there a "drop-off" charge for one-way rental? How much?

Make sure to check the availability of insurance on your furniture in transit when you move yourself. See your insurance agent to check the status of your coverage. Find out whether your belongings are insured in a do-it-yourself move. Is a "floater" policy available for this special purpose?

Whatever the moving method you choose, plan your move well in advance. A month or six weeks is not too much time for planning.

☐ Dispose of things you will not need in your home *and* any high-weight, low-value items you can replace. Sell them, throw them away or give them to charity (and don't forget to get a receipt for charitable donations for income tax purposes).
☐ Ask your doctor and dentist whether they can recommend professionals in your new area. And why not take medical and dental records with you? *Make sure you have the children's immunization records.*
☐ In addition to medical records, there are other items you should either carry with you or for which special transportation should be arranged: jewelry, currency, coin or stamp collections, legal

documents, receipts, guarantees and warranties. Moving companies are not liable for loss or damage to such property. Two other items you must carry with you: plants and pets.
- ☐ Whether you are doing your own packing or having the mover do it for you, remove any curtains, shelving and other attached items you are taking with you.
- ☐ Disconnect major appliances. Get advice on special precautions for transporting television sets, freezers and the like.
- ☐ Defrost the refrigerator. Clean and dry it thoroughly and allow it to air — with the door open — the day before the move.
- ☐ Arrange to have the utilities disconnected in your old home and connected in your new one.
- ☐ Notify the post office of your change of address.
- ☐ Also notify: the bank, creditors, insurance company, utilities, magazines and newspapers, book and record clubs, brokers or financial advisers.

Musical Instruments

(See also WARRANTIES)

MUSICAL INSTRUMENTS of all kinds should be tried and tested thoroughly before they are purchased. Whether you are investing in a band or orchestral instrument for a preteen student or in a family piano (a major purchase that will be used for years), it is important to remember that even mass-produced products in this field differ widely from one another.

If you are neither musician nor music buff, there will be no way for you alone to judge the quality of an instrument. *It is necessary to find a dealer whose judgment is sound and who will stand behind the products he sells. If you don't know the product, know the retailer.*

Fine musical instruments, like furniture made of fine wood, age well. Acoustic guitars, acoustic basses, pianos and even brasses (well maintained, of course) become resonant. The better the instrument, the easier it will be to play.

Consider these factors:

- **The "action"** is the feel of the instrument's movable parts (the keys on a piano; the strings on guitar, bass or violin; the valves and keys on a clarinet or trumpet). Action can be stiff or soggy — either way it can pose an unnecessary problem for the player. A student may be convinced that he simply can't play if he must struggle with the instrument he's trying to learn, and when the struggle fails to produce a "right" sound. A poorly made acoustic guitar, for instance, may have strings set so far above the fingerboard that holding them down is painful. The wooden body is likely to lack resonance.
- **The mouthpiece mystique of brass players is real,** and is based on the musculature of the musician's mouth. The mouthpiece must "fit." So, do not be surprised if your student musician comes home with instructions to get a size so-and-so mouthpiece made by such-and-such a firm. The student may also have to try several mouthpieces (even in a given size) before he or she finds one that feels right. These important pieces of equipment — like the instruments themselves — only *appear* to be the same. However, they are not.
- **Woodwinds** were once made almost entirely of wood, but today many are made of other (synthetic) materials, including plastic.

> **Should you buy or rent?**
> Most reputable music stores have two types of "rental plans": first, a rental-purchase agreement, which allows the use of new instruments for a specified period of time at the conclusion of which the renter has the option to apply the rental toward the purchase of the instrument (or trade up to a higher grade instrument); and second, a pure rental plan, in which the renter has no equity in the instrument at the conclusion of the rental period. You may wish to weigh the costs of a rental-purchase agreement against those of purchasing the instrument on a revolving credit plan.
>
> Be sure to read the rental (or rental-purchase) agreement carefully before you sign, since such an agreement is subject to the disclosure requirements of either the federal Consumer Leasing Law or the Truth-in-Lending Law.
>
> You should fully investigate all your options as well as the quality of the instruments for rental and the service/repair policy and reputation of the store. Check with friends, your music teacher or band/orchestra instructor who have dealt with the same music store.

They are still fragile, however, and vulnerable to cracking (except clarinets). The resulting leakage can make the instrument extremely difficult to play. Oboes and other woodwinds must be carefully maintained.

PRICES

In a highly competitive market, list prices on musical instruments may differ. A trumpet that retails in Saskatchewan for X dollars (manufacturer's list price) might easily be purchased in a specialty music store in Toronto for only a fraction of the recommended list price. Such a store may not offer service or on-premise repairs; it is, however, *not* a discount house.

Prices and services will vary from region to region, from city to city, and from store to store. Comparison shopping is the best basis for your best buy.

Remember: *When you shop, compare available local service as well as prices.*

WARRANTIES

Make the warranty part of your buying decision. Find out whether the local retailer offers in-warranty service. Find out whether the local retailer provides a written warranty of his own in addition to the manufacturer's warranty.

Manufacturers supply use and maintenance instructions for their instruments. Follow instructions carefully or you may void the warranty. Drums, woodwinds, pianos, acoustic guitars and basses are vulnerable to damage from too much or too little humidity, improper storage, and improper cleaning. But a well-maintained instrument can last a lifetime.

In accordance with warranty legislation (see WARRANTIES), manufacturers' warranties carry the designation "full" or "limited." A spot check of standard written warranties indicates that most are limited. For instance:

> The XXXX Limited Warranty is granted to the original purchaser of an XXXX instrument when purchased from an authorized XXXX band-instrument dealer. This limited warranty covers defects in workmanship and materials for designated period (e.g. one (1) year) from date of purchase ... XXXX fiberglass sousaphone bodies and plastic bells are warranteed against breakage or cracking for five years from date of purchase. If, within a period of five years, the fiberglass body or plastic bell breaks or cracks for any reason other than malicious destruction, XXXX will replace the affected part free of charge. XXXX will be the sole judge as to the cause of damage or defects and be responsible for repairs under the provisions of this limited warranty only if the instrument is returned to XXXX, prepaid by the owner or authorized dealer. Owner or authorized dealer should write for return authorization and instructions for returning to _____, giving model of instrument, serial number and date of purchase if known.

A percussion instrument manufacturer provides this warranty:

> XXXX drums, timpani, mallet instruments and accessories are guaranteed for five years against breakage from normal use or defective material and workmanship.
>
> This guarantee does not apply to sticks, brushes, beaters, springs, straps, slings or heads.

Do not be surprised if your student musician tells you that he or she is changing instruments. Band directors do not always recommend the "right" instrument to every student. Frequently, too, they are limited with respect to the instruments they *can* recommend. Parents can sympathize with the band director's plight, but sympathy is no reason to deprive a youngster of the instrument of his or her choice. On the other hand, a student may begin with a trumpet, later decide that he or she needs to play a clarinet, and finally settle on the drums. Short-term rental agreements, it seems, would be a logical choice for parents who feel that no learning experience is wasted.

Nursing Homes

(See also HEALTH AND MEDICINE)

NURSING HOMES (sometimes called convalescent homes) provide nursing care and related services to residents. Patients are accepted who need care because of chronic physical disability or age, or during periods of convalescence from illness or injury. Nursing homes do not accept patients suffering from communicable diseases, alcohol or drug addiction, or anyone suffering from a condition — such as mental illness — that may affect the comfort and well-being of other patients.

In general, nursing homes provide three levels of care:

☐ **Simple nursing care supervised by a registered nurse or licensed practical nurse,** with medication and services ordered by a physician; an attendant is on duty at all times.

☐ **Skilled nursing care supervised by a full-time registered nurse;** a practical nurse or registered nurse will be on duty at all times. Personal services include help in walking, bathing and dressing the patient, as well as the preparation of special diets.

☐ **Intensive nursing care supervised by a registered nurse.** A registered nurse is on duty around the clock, every day of the week. Intensive care includes procedures ordered by a physician such as injections, catheterizations, etc. Specialized medical care is available to the patient, as are consultations with a dietitian and a program of physical rehabilitation.

The best nursing homes make every effort to restore patients to the maximum degree of independence.

Good nursing homes are expensive; poor ones are not so cheap.

Conditions vary widely, and purchasers of nursing home services should investigate several before making a final decision.

Consider alternatives. Supportive services for the aged in their homes may be available through community service programs, whose services might include "meals on wheels" and provision of transportation. Counseling and emergency services from psychologists and social workers may be available. Another alternative might be hiring a trained nurse to treat the patient at home, or a homemaker to help with cooking, laundry and cleaning. Care at home could be less expensive than care at a nursing home, and better for the patient.

Medicare and Medicaid. Find out whether the homes you are considering participate in Medicaid and Medicare programs. At the present time, persons over 65 are entitled, without premium payment, to certain health insurance benefits under the U.S. government's Medicare program, which went into effect in 1966. Check with your local Social Security office to see if there are any changes in the provision or coverage.

Careful inspection of nursing home facilities is a "must." Insist on getting answers to the following questions:

- ☐ Do both the home and the administrator hold current state licenses?
- ☐ Will the patient be provided with a special diet or therapy if he or she needs it?

If the answer to the first two questions is no, keep looking.

- ☐ What are the daily charges? What are the extras? (Some homes charge extra fees for wheelchairs, special mattresses, bedpans and even tissues.)
- ☐ Does the home employ a full-time staff physician?
- ☐ Are there facilities and staff for rehabilitation and/or physical therapy? Are they being used?
- ☐ Do patients share rooms on the basis of their preference and compatibility?
- ☐ Do the patients look happy and alert? Or drugged and docile?
- ☐ Are there odors or other indications of unsanitary conditions?
- ☐ What is the attitude of the staff toward the patients? Does the staff appear interested? Or apathetic and overworked?
- ☐ Does each bed have curtains for privacy? A call bell for the nurse?
- ☐ Are hallways, stairs and bathrooms well-lighted? Unobstructed? Equipped with handrails?
- ☐ Does the home meet fire code standards? Does it hold periodic fire drills? Are exits clearly marked and not locked on the inside? Are fire doors kept closed? Is there an automatic sprinkler system?
- ☐ How is the food? (You should sample it yourself.) Does the meal match the printed menu? Try making an unannounced visit at mealtime.
- ☐ Are there planned recreational programs and outings for the patients?
- ☐ How do the patients and their relatives feel about the home?
- ☐ How do the home's actual conditions compare with its advertising and promotional materials?

For information about homes in your area, as well as for information on the qualifications for Medicare and Medicaid, check with local welfare and Social Security offices, county medical societies and the Better Business Bureau.

Read the contract carefully. Discuss it with your attorney. Never sign a contract you don't understand. Be wary if a home insists on your signing a life-care contract. These contracts generally cannot be canceled — and you may find that the home cannot provide intensive care that may be needed in the future.

Beware of institutions that require the payment of a large deposit. This may have the effect of "locking in" a person who, by making such a payment, divests himself of his resources. He may not be able to leave the home because he no longer has funds of his own.

If a deposit must be made, explore the possibility of arranging for monthly payments instead of liquidating the patient's assets to pay for care. If you can, retain a lawyer to supervise these arrangements. Some nursing homes will accept a patient only if he signs over all assets (real estate, jewelry, stocks and bonds, etc.) to become the property of the home after his death. This is most likely to happen if it appears that the patient will not be able to pay the full cost of his care. Make sure you fully understand any such stipulations before you make any commitments.

Nutrition

(See also FOOD SHOPPING; HEALTH AND MEDICINE)

THE UNITED STATES' FOOD supply is varied, plentiful and nutritious, but the diets of many Americans lack important nutrients.

Recent studies show that an estimated 25 percent of households in the United States do not have nutritionally balanced diets because of any one of the following reasons: (1) lack of knowledge about the type and amount of nutrients needed to make up a balanced diet and the food sources rich in these nutrients; (2) too little time to prepare balanced meals; (3) loss of vitamin content while food is being prepared; (4) taste preference for less nutritious foods; and (5) lack of knowledge about individual nutritional needs.

This does not mean that room must be found in the family budget for a major investment in vitamin pills. What it *does* mean is that many families would benefit from a more varied diet, planned to include a range of fresh fruits and vegetables plus a new emphasis on milk and milk products.

The essential components of a balanced diet are the Basic Four Food Groups, as follows:

1. Milk and milk products include cheese, yogurt, ice cream, cream soups and sauces, buttermilk and nonfat dry milk enriched with vitamins A and D, in addition to fresh whole milk.

☐ Recommended allowances:

Children	3 to four cups daily
Teenagers	4 or more cups
Adults	2 or more cups
Pregnant women	4 or more cups
Nursing mothers	6 or more cups

Milk is the leading source of calcium in the diet, and calcium is the important nutrient that builds bones and teeth, maintains muscle and aids blood clotting. It is important to remember that if the body does not receive an adequate supply of calcium, it steals the amount it needs from bones — and this calcium drain can be a source of problems in later life. Milk is also the major source of vitamin D (necessary for the utilization of calcium) and a source of vitamin A, riboflavin, complete protein and other nutrients as well.

Dieters would be wise to use nonfat dry milk or skimmed milk products (again, enriched with vitamins A and D) instead of excluding milk from the diet.

2. The meat group includes the range of meats — beef, veal, pork, lamb, poultry, eggs and fish — plus excellent meat substitutes such as eggs, dried beans and peas, nuts and peanut butter.

- ☐ **Recommended allowances:** 2 servings daily
- ☐ **Recommended portions:**
  2 to 3 ounces cooked meat, fish or poultry
  2 eggs (unless you are on a low-cholesterol diet prescribed by your doctor)
  1 cup cooked dry beans, peas or lentils
  4 tablespoons peanut butter

These foods supply protein, necessary for building and repairing all body tissues — muscle, organ, blood, skin and hair — for energy, and for the formation of antibodies which fight infections. Meats and meat substitutes also contain iron, varying amounts of the B vitamins, and trace minerals. *Keep in mind the fact that the serving size recommended by nutritionists is only 2 to 3 ounces* — well less than half the home cook's or restaurateur's notion of a portion. Most Americans consume more protein than they need.

Adequate quantities of complete protein can be garnered for the family diet at a lower cost in both money and calories by combining cereal or vegetable foods with milk, cheese and eggs. Combine cereal with milk, rice with fish, spaghetti with meatballs — or simply add a glass of milk to each meal for complete protein.

3. The vegetable-fruit group includes a wide range of foods capable of providing a delightful variety to the family diet as well as an important array of nutrients.

- ☐ **Recommended allowance:** 4 servings daily
  Include tomatoes or one portion of citrus fruit daily, one serving of a dark green leafy vegetable, deep yellow vegetable or yellow fruit 3 to 4 times each week.
- ☐ **Recommended portion:**
  ½ cup fruit or vegetable
  1 medium apple, banana or potato
  ½ grapefruit or cantaloupe

This is one of the food groups likely to be missing from the diet. Rediscover the special flavor of fresh vegetables in season, from artichokes to zucchini. And if you haven't tried fresh fruit with yogurt or cheese for dessert, try them now. They add a gourmet touch to any meal.

4. **The bread-cereal group** includes breads, cereals, cornmeal, grits, crackers, pasta, rice and quick breads. These products should be made from whole grain, enriched or restored cereals.

- ☐ **Recommended allowance:** 4 servings daily
- ☐ **Recommended portions:**
  1 slice bread
  ¾ to 1 cup ready-to-eat cereal
  ½ to ¾ cup cooked cereal, rice, macaroni, noodles or spaghetti

Water, though not included in the Basic Four Food Groups, is an important substance, necessary for all digestive processes and for regulating body temperature. Drink four to six glasses of water daily *in addition to* the water contained in coffee, tea, soft drinks, fruit juices, and the like.

NOTES TOWARD A WELL-BALANCED DIET

You don't need to be a nutritionist or a biochemist to see that you and your family get the proper nutrients. Small portions of a wide variety of foods, instead of large portions of a limited variety, selected from the Basic Four Food Groups, will meet the needs of all family members. Use the Food Groups as a basic guide, and consider these general guidelines:

- ☐ **Vitamin supplements?** Check with your doctor. Americans spend about $400 million each year on vitamin and mineral pills and preparations despite the fact that most professional nutritionists and the medical profession agree that a well-balanced diet is easily available and much less expensive.
- ☐ **Changing poor food habits may not be easy, but it is certainly worthwhile.** As in any other area of life — sports, music, books, social activities or what have you — the greater the variety you try, the more you find to enjoy. The examples set by parents will be valuable to children in food selection and enjoyment.
- ☐ **Nutrition quackery** has been produced in sufficient amounts to fill bookshops, libraries and too many minds with misinformation.
  Very simply, there is no single food or combination of foods capable of curing any illness or solving any physical problem. Guard against fad diets promoted as cures for obesity, arthritis or any other ill the flesh is heir to.
- ☐ **Plan ahead for nutrition and economy.** Check newspaper ads for advertised specials; plan menus for the week around these specials (see FOOD SHOPPING).
- ☐ **Learn healthy cooking techniques.** Using the right temperature, avoiding too many fats and oil (as in frying), and steaming vegetables instead of boiling them can stretch food dollars and maximize nutrition.

Painting and Paints

PAINTS HAVE CHANGED A great deal in the last twenty years. Painting hasn't. Durability of a new coat of paint still depends to a great extent on the preparation of the surface to which it is applied. And the preparation process is still a tedious chore.

Preparation. Indoors or out, all loose, flaking and blistered paint should be removed with a scraper or with sandpaper. If the old paint has cracked, ridges between sound paint and bare wood should be sanded smooth. Larger cracks and uneven areas should be smoothed and filled with spackle, caulking compound or putty. The surface should be scrubbed clean of oily residue, smoke stains and mildew.

Outdoors there is an additional step to take: check for "chalking" as you would test for dust inside — with a sweep of the hand. The white powdery substance (the "chalk") must be washed away with detergent and a stiff brush. Then rinse with the garden hose. If, after this treatment, the chalky substance remains, you will have to use a primer coat (under latex) or an oil-based paint.

If Tom Sawyer had been scraping and scrubbing on that sunny Saturday morning, chances are all his helpers would have escaped to the woods. Painting, compared to preparation, is hardly work at all.

This could be one of the reasons that hiring a painting contractor is often an appealing alternative.

Be sure to take these precautions before you sign a contract:

- ☐ Ask for references and check them. Check complaint records for the contractors you are considering with the Better Business Bureau.
- ☐ Especially for big, complicated and expensive jobs, get bids from three contractors — with matching specifications as to the type and quality of the paint to be used, the areas to be painted, the number of coats to be applied.
- ☐ When you sign a contract for the work, the same specifications should be included and a date of completion added.
- ☐ Finally, find out whether the contractor is adequately insured. Even if he is, check your own home insurance for the extent of your liability coverage.

If you decide to do the job yourself, you'll need to know something about types of paint.

Latex (water-based) paints are available in three varieties: vinyl, acrylic and oil-emulsion. All of these dry very rapidly, are virtually odor-free and can be applied during humid weather. Spills can be cleaned up with water. Vinyls and acrylics are naturally mildew-proof; oil-emulsion types are not, but they can be treated for this quality. Latex paint should not be used for painting over old wallpaper.

Oil-based paints must be thinned with turpentine, linseed oil or a commercial oil-base thinner. Drying time will be twelve to forty-eight hours — sometimes more. The greater the amount of oil used for thinning, the longer the drying time will be.

Oil-based paint is often recommended for hard-use areas. It is washable and durable — depending, of course, on the quality of the paint selected. One should not put an oil-based finishing coat on top of a latex primer or base coat.

Exterior oil-based white paints, as noted above, are available in high- and low-chalking formulations.

About chalking

"Chalking" is a built-in characteristic of oil-based paint that allows dirt and sometimes mildew to be washed away by rain. White paints are available in high- or low-chalking formulations. The one you choose should depend upon the area you live in — the cleaner the air, the lower-chalking paint you need.

Colored paints, which do not show dirt so easily, are not usually made to chalk.

If you are painting masonry, do not use a high-chalking formulation.

METHODS OF APPLYING PAINT

In order to do a good job with relatively little toil and trouble, be sure to choose the right tools and learn how to use them properly.

Using a brush. A medium-priced brush may be your best bet if you do only occasional jobs of painting. When you use a brush, you can make sure the paint gets into pores, cracks and crevices. Brushing is especially effective when you want to apply a primer coat or exterior paint. Keep in mind that a good brush is an expensive tool; it really pays to take the necessary time and effort to keep it in good condition. Make sure you follow any provided cleaning instructions to the letter.

Using a roller. For large, flat surfaces, painting by roller is usually easier and faster than painting the same area by brush. It's important to choose a roller that has a comfortable handle. Again, be sure to follow all instructions for using and cleaning the roller.

PAINTING AND PAINTS

The Better Business Bureau warns . . .
Some false claims are made for modern "miracle" paints. It is true that only one coat of some products will be sufficient, *if* the surface to be painted is in excellent condition and *if* a primer has been used. Otherwise, as with any other paint, you may need two coats.

The following claims for new paint formulations are usually true:

- Some exterior paints last nearly twice as long as paints that were manufactured only a few years ago, *if applied according to the manufacturer's directions*.
- The present-day outside whites are brighter, cover more thoroughly and do not yellow as much as lead and oil paints will.
- Some paints dry into porous films which "breathe." This allows moisture to escape and reduces the tendency to blister and peel.
- Fading and color change have been eliminated or greatly reduced.
- Some of the new paints dry so quickly that a second coat can be applied in less than an hour.
- Clean-up is easier with water-based paints. Plain water will clear away spots and spills — but clean them quickly, before the paint has a chance to dry.

Always follow manufacturers' instructions carefully, especially when using spray paints.

Finally, check product-testing and rating publications for information on product performance.

Using a sprayer. If you need to paint a large area, a paint sprayer may be the best tool to use. Spraying is faster than either brushing or rolling, however, some paint may be wasted if you overspray. If you plan to spray paint, remember that the paint must be carefully prepared. Be sure to follow the manufacturer's instructions on the label for the type and amount of thinner you should use. And before you start, check with the paint dealer for tips on how to best use the sprayer. Find out, too, what you have to do to clean the sprayer. And no matter what type of paint you're dealing with, be sure to wear a respirator to keep you from inhaling paint vapors.

Photographic Equipment

(See also PRICES AND SALES; WARRANTIES)

PHOTOGRAPHY, like sound recording and playback, is a hobby that tends to grow. From inexpensive elementary equipment used for snapshots, the hobbyist can easily move to a sophisticated precision instrument with a gadget bag full of lenses, filters and several kinds of film. It then hardly takes any time at all to reach an acute need for a darkroom.

The "acquisition instinct" can stop anywhere along the way. Equipment is available in such variety that at any point the consumer's options are always wide open.

CAMERAS

New, moderate-priced cameras are so easy to use that amateur photographers can concentrate on composition (balance or dramatic contrast of the people or objects being photographed).

You *don't* have to worry about:

- **Exposing the film when loading:** You use drop-in film cartridges.
- **Focus or shutter speed:** But you must follow manufacturer's recommendations in regard to distance between lens and subject. Distance settings, in most cases, will be limited in the least expensive models.

    Shutter speed is fixed in the least expensive models — bright daylight or the flash attachment is required. Some models, a little more expensive, change the shutter speed automatically when the flash cube is mounted on the camera.
- **Double exposure:** The shutter is automatically locked until the film has been advanced.

On the other hand:

- The negative will be small. Enlargements are restricted in size — big ones lose sharpness.

Instant photographs. Instant snapshots, both in color and black and white, have been available for a number of years. Their major advantage is speed. They are fun on a holiday morning.

The models change rapidly. Ease of handling, sharpness of the finished photograph and accuracy of color reproduction have been

PHOTOGRAPHIC EQUIPMENT

improved since the first models arrived on the market. Product-rating publications available in local public libraries are good sources of information on the advantages and disadvantages of comparable camera models.

35mm cameras are available in several types. Shoppers can choose among those with a **built in rangefinder.** This feature will interest amateur photographers who, for whatever reasons, have little interest in learning to adjust the focus (distance from lens to film), f stop and shutter speed. The range from automatic to manual in 35mm cameras allows some choice; in 35mm single-lens reflex equipment (*see below*), many models allow automatic *or* manual operation. More experienced photographers seek out manual adjustment systems, since they prefer the versatility and precision they can achieve with individual adjustment to distance and special light conditions.

Single-lens reflex (SLR) cameras differ from 35mm rangefinders in that the subject (person or scene) is seen through a viewfinder. The single-lens reflex allows the photographer to focus and "frame" the subject through the lens that will take the picture. *You see what the camera sees,* which greatly aids in the precision of composition.

SLRs also:

- ☐ offer a wide choice of film;
- ☐ provide for a range of choice among sizes, weights and features;
- ☐ position light sensors *inside* the camera so that the light meter measures light as seen through the lens;
- ☐ provide for versatility with the use of a variety of lenses, but be careful here — additional lenses can cost as much as the camera;
- ☐ can be used for black-and-white and color photography equally well.

Are they really bargains?

"List price" . . . "manufacturer's list price" . . . "suggested retail price" . . . are frequently not actual selling prices. There is no substitute for comparison shopping.

What you may find is that cameras with list prices of $400 to $500 really sell for prices starting at about $250, going up to $300 or $350.

The lower prices may not be "bargains." Merchandise sells, in most cases, for exactly what it's worth in the present market. Hobbyists are well advised to patronize retailers who do not emphasize only price as a reason to buy. Much more important — especially considering increasingly complex precision equipment such as today's cameras — is after-purchase service, the extent of the warranty and the ability to back it up, and professional assistance with the choice of equipment such as lenses, filters and film.

Until camera adjustment becomes second nature, it will be important to refer to the information sheet packed with every roll of film. Check recommended exposure and *f* stops for various light conditions.

The degree of automation on SLR cameras varies widely — automatic, semiautomatic, automatic *and* manual, automatic aperture (*f* stop) and automatic shutter speed. The kind of camera you choose and the degree of automation you prefer are essentially personal decisions. It might be a good idea to attend a meeting or two of a local camera club, not for answers so much as to gain perspective. What you will find is that opinions differ, that camera enthusiasts get excellent results with a phenomenally wide range of equipment, *and* that your judgment must be your own.

Twin-lens reflex cameras produce a square (2¼ × 2¼ inches) negative, larger than the 35mm negatives. They are easy to see, easy to crop. Contact prints, made in your own darkroom or in a custom shop, can be culled, marked for cropping with a grease pencil and printed as you choose (or as you direct).

Larger negatives often produce sharper, clearer enlargements than 35mm negatives.

Furthermore, the twin-lens is easy to focus. The photographer sees a full 2¼-inch-square image, which is a great help in composition.

The problem? Color slides. Most slide projectors are made for the smaller 35mm slides. Again, buying decisions will be based on the preference of the individual photographer.

FILM

Always check the expiration date on the film you buy. Fresh film will produce your best results.

Guidance on the right film for your camera is best obtained from your owner's manual. If you are a hobbyist who enjoys photographing fast-moving children, athletes, motorcycle races and such, you may want to try several varieties of high-speed film — again, as recommended by the manufacturer of your equipment.

You may have noticed that professional photographers often carry several cameras — two and sometimes three 35mms to go on assignment. There are two reasons for this: the photographer may want two speeds in black and white, two lenses (perhaps the standard lens which he uses for most shots, plus a telephoto or wide-angle lens). The third camera might contain color film.

Color film comes in two basic types: one for slides, one for prints.

Prints can be made from slides and slides can be made from color negatives, but the processing will be more expensive and there will be an inevitable loss of quality.

Quality of color reproduction for both slides and films is variable from brand to brand. Check consumer product-rating publications for comparisons.

Quality of color reproduction is even more variable among processors. The quality of the processing cannot be overemphasized. Custom processing can be expected to cost more than you would otherwise pay for slides and prints, but for those pictures you *know* you will want to keep — the kind of photography that makes equipment worth the expense — the extra cost of custom processing may be well worthwhile.

Some definitions
- **ASA number** (ASA 64, 100, 500, etc.) refers to the *speed of the film*, determined by its sensitivity to light which, in turn, is determined by its emulsion. The higher the ASA number, the faster the film.
- **Shutter speed** refers to the speed at which the shutter opens and closes again. They are available in a wide range. They can range from "time" through one second and on up to a thousandth of a second. Mid-range (1/500th of a second) is suggested by many camera buffs as the one most likely to be used most of the time.
- **f stop or aperture** refers to the opening of the lens.

SLIDE PROJECTORS

Your superb, beautifully composed color slides were never intended to be kept out of sight in boxes. Now you need a slide projector. There are several types to choose from:

- **The single-slide viewer** is the least expensive. Each slide is inserted manually into the slide holder and manually moved into and out of the viewer. This is good for editing a collection of slides, but inconvenient for longer use.
- **The manually operated projector** utilizes a straight-tray slide carrier (capacity: 20 to 60 slides). Each function of projector and slide carrier is carried out manually by the operator.
- **The semiautomatic projector** removes a slide from the tray, projects it and returns it. Slides are shown in sequential order, but some models allow the operator to skip slides or go forward or backward; some can be operated on a remote control unit.
- **The automatic projector,** the most expensive variety, works without an operator. It operates from a preset timer, changing slides automatically.

Choosing a projector also entails choosing a **slide storage system,** since the slides are best and most conveniently stored in the projection tray, where they are ready for use. Most trays come with storage boxes. Some have pressure-fit lids which keep dust out.

The size and cost of the trays you will need should be a factor in your choice of a projector — especially if you have, or plan to produce, a large number of slides. *To arrive at the cost per slide of the storage system, divide the cost of the slide container by the number of slides it holds.*

Consider the lens. The characteristics of the projector lens will determine how large and how bright a picture you will be able to project. The focal length of the lens (three, four, five or seven inches, etc.) determines the size of the image produced at a given projector-to-screen distance. *The shorter the focal length, the larger the image.* Most lenses for home use are four or five inches.

The brightness of the image depends upon the f/number of the lens. The lower the f/number, the larger the diameter of the lens and the brighter the image: F/2.8 is brighter than f/3.5. *Larger diameter lenses require more accurate focusing.*

Many projectors will accept interchangeable lenses. If you plan to use your projector at a variety of distances from the screen, a zoom lens may be the answer. A zoom lens allows you to adjust the focal length of the lens without changing the lens itself. Thus, a four-to-six-inch zoom lens would provide the flexibility of all the focal lengths in between.

Features and options. Like other consumer products, from automobiles to xylophones, potential buyers of slide projectors may choose among special features and options, such as:

- **Focusing, manual or automatic:** Manual focus models allow the operator to move the lens to achieve the desired clarity of image. The automatics take over after the operator adjusts the first slide. Manual refocusing may be necessary for the automatics.
- **Remote controls:** Useful if you plan to use your projector to illustrate lectures.
- **The projection lamp** (the electric light bulb inside the projector): These vary in brightness, heat generated, length of life and cost. Compare them.
- An additional option on some projectors is an **economy switch,** which makes it possible to reduce the voltage supplied to the lamp. This is useful for projecting "small screen image," and can double the life of the lamp.
- **Editing and previewing devices,** self-explanatory, are also available.

The features above are generally available on slide projectors produced by a number of manufacturers. There are others. Options will change and their number will grow; therefore no attempt is made to list them here.

Buying considerations. Your slide projector will be with you for years, so take plenty of time to make your choice. Decide which features you really need and which ones you can do without. Then stick to your decisions. The more complex and option-filled any product is, the more likely it is to be expensive to repair.

Be sure to check the following important factors:

- ☐ **Image clarity:** Have one of your own slides, sharp and well exposed, projected on the machine you are considering. Is the image evenly illuminated from corner to corner? Is the image itself uniformly sharp from one side of the screen to the other?
- ☐ **Noise level:** Because of the intense heat generated by projector lamps, projectors must have cooling fans that operate continuously during projection. Some of these produce more noise than others. Make sure to check the noise level produced by the projectors under consideration. A high noise level may interfere with your narration.
- ☐ **Heat level:** In the store turn on the projector and let it run for several minutes. Expect the area directly above the projector lamp to get very warm. No external portion of the machine should get hot enough to the touch to pose a burn hazard. *Excess heat can damage your slides permanently. Find out whether the machines you are considering have a thermal overload device which automatically stops operation in case it overheats.*
- ☐ **Handling:** The projector should have a carrying case or cover and a suitably sturdy handle. In some models the machine and carrying case are combined. Check the weight and size factors for convenience of handling and storage.
- ☐ **Electrical circuitry:** Has the electrical circuit been checked for proper grounding and shock resistance? Make sure the machine carries the Underwriters' Laboratory seal.
- ☐ **Slide handling:** Take a good look at the way the projector's slide-transport system works. It should work smoothly so that you do not risk bending or damaging the cardboard frames around your slides. *If you use glass or plastic-mounted slides, make sure the projector can handle them.*
- ☐ **Operating controls:** All the principal operating controls on the projector or on the remote control unit should be easy to reach and use during your slide show. **Remember:** You will have to operate the controls in darkness or, at best, subdued light.
- ☐ **Leveling:** Many projectors come with automatic leveling "feet," which permit you to raise or tilt the projector as required. Check to see whether the machines that interest you have some sort of leveling mechanism, and check the ease of operation.

HOME MOVIE CAMERAS AND PROJECTORS

Easy-to-use movie cameras, like the easy-to-use still models, are available in a wide range of equipment — a range greater in 8mm than in 16mm.

Super 8 equipment uses film packaged in a "drop-in" cartridge which holds fifty feet of film. This eliminates the threading and rethreading process. Super 8 film is less expensive than the 16mm size generally in use a few years ago.

Both cameras and film are changing. Cameras that operate under available light conditions may eliminate the use of additional lights for home movie-making. These are the "XL" ("XL" means existing light) products.

Accompanying the XL cameras (and necessary to their operation) is a high-speed film. The ASA speed (160) is four times faster than traditional movie film.

Movie projectors. The Super 8 variety are, like the Super 8 cameras, simple to operate. There is no substitute for trying the equipment in the store — or renting equipment to use at home, to be experimented with and approved at leisure.

Buying considerations for movie projectors should be similar to those for slide projectors: check the clarity of the image, the noise level, the ease of handling, and the convenience and location of operating controls.

Projection screens are available in two types:

- ☐ **Matt white screens,** with smooth surfaces, provide a moderately lenticular backdrop which provides a bright image in subdued light as well as in darkness, and over a wide angle.
- ☐ **Glass-beaded screens** are best at a narrow angle. The clarity of image is reduced at close viewing distance because the images look "grainy" due to the texture of the screen. If you choose a glass-beaded screen, make sure to choose one treated to resist mildew.

THE DO-IT-YOURSELF DARKROOM

As the hobby of photography becomes more and more popular, many people have decided to set up darkrooms in their own homes. If you're thinking of investing in darkroom equipment, it's a good idea to talk with someone you know who has a darkroom before going to a store. Ask about equipment. What kind of enlarger is being used? What are some of the advantages and disadvantages of having your own darkroom?

Once you have some general information, be sure to visit several photographic equipment stores and compare prices. It may not pay to go to the least expensive source, especially if you don't know very much about darkroom equipment. A store specializing in darkroom supplies may provide the best in equipment, expertise and service. Keep in mind, too, that you will have to go back to the store on a regular basis for supplies, accessories and service.

Be prepared to spend some time in the store talking with the salesperson. Selecting darkroom equipment is not something to rush into. Ask the store you plan to do business with about its return policy. Some stores let you take the equipment home, set it up and then return it in its original packaging if you are not satisfied. Before buying, ask about the terms of the warranties on the products. What do they cover and not cover? Who will make good on them? Once you've purchased the darkroom equipment, don't forget that some of the materials you'll be working with in your home are chemicals. They should be kept out of reach of children and pets.

Know your dealer, learn about the merchandise
Make sure that the equipment you are purchasing — camera, projector, screen — is the same as the one the dealer is displaying and demonstrating. Make sure that the features on the demonstration model are also on the one you will receive.

Also check the service department. Are repairs made on the premises? Are replacement lamps available from the dealer? Replacement parts?

Know your warranty. The warranty will be only as good as the dealer or manufacturer who must meet its terms (see WARRANTIES). New equipment should be warranted against defects in materials and workmanship.

☐ Make sure you know the duration of your warranty. Some last for only 90 days, others for a year.
☐ What is covered? What happens if a problem develops? Must the equipment be sent to a factory service center? Who pays the shipping expenses? Try to get a promise *in writing* from the dealer that he will replace the equipment if it fails to function properly — especially if you are buying newly developed equipment, new to the market, the latest thing. "Lemons" grow more luxuriantly among new products.

Power Tools

WHICH POWER TOOLS are "basic"? Opinions differ, but even for those people whose home maintenance activities are restricted to hanging pictures and making a wallfull of bookshelves will find some not only worth having, but virtually indispensable. These include:

- ☐ **Electric drill:** The best-balanced hammer in the most practiced hand is quite capable of damaging a wall in the attempt to hang a picture. The drill is a much more precise instrument for this activity, among a wide range of others. Electric drills must be used with care. Not even double insulation can protect against severe electric shock if you hit house wiring when drilling into a wall.
- ☐ **Electric hand saw:** From making bookshelves to remodeling, the electric hand saw can add to the efficiency of routine cutting and trimming chores.
- ☐ **Electric saber saw:** This is a versatile tool, capable of cutting straight and curved lines in anything from thin plywood to a two-by-four. Look for versatility provided by interchangeable blades capable of performing scroll cuts, bevel cuts, pocket cuts, etc. Look for high-and-low speed capacities. Try the tool in the store to judge the amount of vibration, which may make precision cutting difficult. Also compare the noise levels of several models.
- ☐ **The orbital sander** is sufficiently versatile to accomplish heavy-duty chores and smooth finish work — simply change the type of paper to suit the job.

These portable power tools reduce the time and effort required for a number of household maintenance tasks and do-it-yourself building projects. There are dangers associated with the use of any power tool. They are powerful because they are supposed to be, and anyone who uses them should respect them for the speed and efficiency with which they operate *and* for the damage they can do.

Hand tools range widely in price from the low-cost "handyman" specials to considerably more expensive tools designed for "commercial use." If you are an occasional user, the less costly tools should suffice, but the tough, expensive commercial varieties are often your best buy for major projects or constant use.

Before you buy, check these safety features:

☐ **Double insulation** provides an extra layer of nonconducting material separate from the primary insulation system. It suffers little of the deterioration caused by abrasion or heat that affects primary insulation, so that even if the primary layer fails, the secondary cover shall protect the user.
☐ **Control mechanisms** should be easily accessible for maximum safety.
☐ Look for **guards** shielding the user from accidental contact with motor, belts and gears, cutting edges and other parts of tools which present a mechanical hazard.

A final safety precaution. Equip yourself with safety glasses — some experts recommend a whole-face shield — for protection when using polishing and sanding tools, which may shower the user with pieces of wire and other debris.

Follow manufacturers' use and care instructions carefully, for efficiency and for the sake of your own and your family's safety.

Prices and Sales

(See also ADVERTISING)

PRICES VARY FROM season to season, from region to region, and from store to store. Wise consumers do not base their buying decisions on price alone. A good buy — a "bargain" — should meet these three standards:
1. It is an item *you need or want*
2. at a *price* you are willing to pay
3. from a *reliable* source.

The first standard rules out impulse buying, a habit that can wreck the family budget. The second and third standards are related. You may choose to buy at Store A instead of Store B because you prefer the services available at Store A.

It is, of course, unrealistic to assume that the price of goods and services should play no role at all in buying decisions. Price should, however, be placed in proper perspective, as *one factor in the decision, and not necessarily the most important one.*

Consider these examples:

1. You and your neighbor buy identical television sets at the same time from different stores, at different prices. You paid $30 more at Store A than your neighbor did at Store B. Both sets need adjustments. Store A sends a serviceman who makes the necessary adjustment quickly and efficiently. Your neighbor must return his set to the store. After a month's delay, it is returned, but it still doesn't work the way it should. Who got the bargain?

2. A tweed coat has appealed to you since it arrived in your favorite department store in September. At its original price you consider it an unwarranted extravagance, so you don't buy it right away. You wear your old coat for another season and, in the meantime, watch the price of the tweed. When the January sale comes around, you buy it for one-third off the original price and are thrilled with your bargain.

Now suppose your neighbor beats you to the store and, on impulse, buys "your" coat because the price is attractive. But she soon regrets her impulse purchase: the color isn't right for her and the coat is relegated to the back of the closet. The same item that would have been a good buy for you is a costly mistake for her.

3. A final example: no one expects to find supermarket prices in a local family-operated grocery store. Nor does anyone expect to find small-store services, such as delivery or credit, at the supermarket. The two kinds of stores use different merchandising techniques, offer different services and have different prices. Each fills different needs for the consumer.

It follows that the price you pay for products depends on where you buy them. This in turn depends on your own requirement — the time you can spend in shopping, the variety of merchandise you seek and the extent of services provided by the retailer.

It is important to remember that the best buy — the "bargain" — may not be the cheapest model, style or service. A bargain-priced item bought on impulse (as in the case of the neighbor's useless tweed coat) can be an expensive error, no matter how attractive the price.

COMPARATIVE PRICE AND SAVINGS CLAIMS

Consumers and retailers alike should use caution in evaluating price and savings claims. Such claims are hard to prove and, for consumers, increasingly hard to believe.

Fictitious comparative price claims teach the public to disbelieve all price claims. They raise questions about the pricing policies of the legitimate manufacturer and dilute the value of its advertising dollar.

A retailer may advertise a price reduction or saving by comparing his current selling price with:

☐ his own former selling price;
☐ the current price of identical merchandise sold by others;
☐ the current price of comparable items sold by others.

In all these cases the advertising should clearly identify the basis of the comparison. When an advertiser offers a reduction from his own former selling price, the former price should be identifiable as the actual price at which he has been offering the merchandise *immediately preceding the sale, on a regular basis* and *for a reasonably substantial period of time.*

This kind of price reduction may be most readily identifiable by consumers who tend to shop regularly in the same stores. Other comparative price claims are often not so easily identifiable and can be misleading. It is usually impossible, for example, for any retailer to be sure that his current price is "the lowest price in town" at any given time.

"List price," "manufacturer's list price," "suggested retail price": These and similar terms are often used to state or imply that customers can save money by buying merchandise at prices far below other retailers' current prices. They are used by many retail stores.

For example, in catalog showroom merchandising, *two* prices are listed. One, the "reference" price, is clearly stated; the second, "your" price, is in code. The catalog description looks like this:

> ADJUSTABLE SHAVER. Five shavers in one with adjustable heads for closeness, comfort and tailor-made shaves! Rotary blades, trimmer, handsome metal travel wallet, on/off switch, 110/220 voltage and coil cord.
>
> 4675333C2577 — Wt. 2 lbs. $39.95
>   A   B

The price marked B — $39.95 — is supposed to be the "reference retail" price. The description implies that you would pay $39.95 for this shaver at local retail outlets. The code price, marked A, is $25.77 — much, much lower. What's more, the coded price is a delightful secret between you and the retailer.

If you don't check the actual selling price of the identical product in your local stores or in other catalogs, you may believe this is a real bargain. If you do some comparison shopping, however, you may find that, without benefits of a coded price and all the mystery, local stores sell the same merchandise at prices ranging from about $24.45 to $32.95. And no one, neither catalog nor retail store, may sell the product at the so-called "list price" of $39.95.

Prices vary from store to store, and catalog showrooms are no exception to this rule of the marketplace. Consumers can choose to make their purchases in a variety of stores for a variety of reasons. Perhaps you might choose to do most of your buying in a store with a relaxed, comfortable atmosphere; perhaps you look for stores whose sales personnel are able to provide product information; perhaps the degree of service your retailers give is most important to you; or perhaps you prefer to be left alone to read product information and make your own decisions. In any case, the choices are available and welcome. What is not so nice is making a where-to-buy decision on the basis of inadequate or misleading information such as "lowest price" claims.

Consider these disclaimers contained in the catalogs of two showroom merchandisers:

> The reference prices shown in our catalog are the suggested list prices recommended to us by manufacturers. Reference prices are not our present or former prices and do not necessarily represent the prevailing prices of any particular product in any one community on any one day.

> The prices shown in the right-hand column on each page of this catalog are for reference only, and no representation is made to the effect that any of these prices is the usual or ordinary price at which a particular item is sold. No user of this catalog should assume that a savings will be effected or realized in an amount equal to the difference between the figure in the right-hand column and our price.

PRICES AND SALES

A thorough reading of these catalogs should alert potential customers to more than coded prices, specifically, that the alleged savings may not apply to you.

According to the National Retail Merchants Association, retailers generally follow a pattern in **sale** and **promotional advertising.** Recognize the difference between the two and be prepared to shop for a variety of items at their traditional sales times.

JANUARY — White sales, storewide clearances, resort-wear promotions, fur sales, furniture sales (third week)

FEBRUARY — Furniture, housewares and home furnishings sales, Valentine's Day and Washington's Birthday sales and promotions

MARCH — Housewares, china and silver, garden supplies, spring and Easter promotion

APRIL— Spring-cleaning supplies, paints, housewares, fur-storage promotions, outdoor furniture

MAY — Mother's Day sales and promotions, summer sportswear, air conditioners, fans, bridal gowns and wedding gift promotions, garden supplies, outdoor furniture

JUNE — Graduation gifts, Father's Day sales and promotions, bridal gifts, sportswear, camp clothing and supplies, vacation equipment

JULY — July 4th clearances, sporting goods, sportswear, furniture sales (fourth week)

AUGUST — Furniture sales, fur sales, back-to-school and fall-fashion promotions, fall fabrics

SEPTEMBER — Back-to-school, fall fashions, men's and boy's sportswear, home furnishings, china and glassware

OCTOBER —Women's coats, suits and furs, men's and boy's outerwear, millinery and accessories, Columbus Day sales, home furnishings

NOVEMBER — Christmas toys, pre-Christmas "value promotions," Thanksgiving weekend sales, china, glassware, table linens, home furnishings

DECEMBER — Christmas promotions, gift promotions, resort wear (fourth week)

WHEN IS A SALE NOT A SALE?

Most people understand the word *sale* to mean that merchandise is offered at a lower-than-usual price. You can buy a new mattress for $69.95 for a specified period of time. Or Brand A air conditioner is yours for $119.95 until next Tuesday. The same merchandise will cost more when the sale is over.

Some retailers advertise "sales" so often and so regularly that the stated sale price can be assumed to be the regular price of the merchandise. When this happens, the advertised sale is not a sale at all.

One Better Business Bureau, with the cooperation of a local newspaper, carried out a six-month study of sale advertising. They found that some "sales" continued for months. For instance:

- ☐ Some items were advertised as "on sale" 26 to 93 percent of the time during the six-month period, according to the time limits specified in the ads.
- ☐ Other ads had no time limits on the duration of the sale. The same items were offered at the same "reduced" prices as many as 20 to 42 times, with a maximum of 13 to 19 days between ads.
- ☐ There were repeated extensions of time limits on some advertised sales.

Better Business Bureaus have established a "Code of Advertising" which states, "The unqualified term *sale* may be used in advertising only if there is a significant reduction from the advertiser's usual and customary price of the merchandise offered and the sale is for a limited period of time. If the sale exceeds thirty days the advertiser should be prepared to substantiate that the offering is indeed a valid reduction and has not become his regular price." With this specific guideline in mind, ask yourself just how much of a bargain consumers would get by purchasing the following items:

A three-piece redwood lounge set, advertised at sale prices twenty-one times in four months. Based on time limits specified in some of the ads, the sale prices were good for at least 44 days out of 125. Savings claims were based upon two different "regular" prices for the set, $20 apart.

An air conditioner, advertised twenty-two times in eleven weeks between April 8 and June 17 under such headlines as "Frozen Price," "Weekend Special" and "Sellout Price" carried the same price tag each day.

An automatic washer, advertised twenty times between January 4 and June 17, with a maximum of sixteen days between sales. Eight of the ads limited sale periods to twenty-three days; twelve ads noted no time limits. A "regular" price $50 higher than the "sale" price was quoted in most ads.

> **Something to think about**
> If Product A is really good, why can't it be sold on its merits? Price gimmicks and false sale advertising not only confuse consumers, they confuse the issue as well. The confused issue is likely to be the question of whether the item is worth buying at all.

It seems clear that, in some cases, advertised "sale prices" are actually the prices at which merchandise is regularly sold. Consumers should be wary of advertising that offers the same item at a sale price over an extended period of time. The practice is misleading.

There are, of course, bargains to be found, just as there are genuine sales. Comparison shopping and judicious comparison of retail catalogs can give you a good idea of the range of "regular" prices.

"FREE" FOR HOW MUCH?
Sometimes advertising of special prices and sales includes a something-for-nothing offer, a piece of "free" merchandise.

For example, a complaint to a Better Business Bureau involved a furniture store that advertised a complete living-room suite. The ad stated that customers who purchased the living-room suite during a particular week would receive a full-size pool table "absolutely free." When the complainant told a salesman at the store she was not interested in the pool table, she was informed that the living-room suite would cost $100 less.

How free was the pool table?

This "free" item was covered by what is known as a hidden charge. To most consumers, the pool table actually would appear to be free. The complainant who brought this ad to the attention of the Better Business Bureau was right to do so. The advertisement was deceptive.

All the terms and conditions of a free offer should be accurately disclosed to prospective recipients — or purchasers. Furthermore, when a store advertises an article as free with the purchase of another article, the offer must be a temporary one. Otherwise it is a package deal, always offered, that negates the idea of the free gift.

Free pictures? The pool table story is an example of one form of deceptive advertising that misleads many consumers. Another example involving unclear wording in an ad but lacking the "hidden charge" is free photo developing with the purchase of a roll of film. The unclear word here is *developing*. What does it really mean?

What it *doesn't* mean is free pictures.

The developing process produces negatives, not prints. Printing negatives is another process, for which you must pay. If you encounter this type of offer, be aware that you will not receive photographs just for the price of the original film. It simply isn't so.

Many free offers amount to little more than a "come-on" — an offer made to entice the consumer to purchase goods or services he or she would otherwise not consider buying. Examples of this type of deception are the "free" dance lessons given in the hopes of selling many, many more such lessons. Generally, the chances of your actually receiving such "freebies" are remote at best. Even if you do receive the gift, it probably will not be of the quality you expected.

SOME GUIDELINES

Better Business Bureaus have established specific guidelines in the area of free offers. Among these are the following:

- ☐ Items offered free without explanation must be without cost or obligation.
- ☐ Free items obtainable by mail must be available upon payment of no more than the actual postage costs.
- ☐ The purchase of another item may be required to obtain the free gift if no element of deception is present in the advertising. The consumer has the right to believe that the merchant will not recover the cost of the free item by marking up the price of the original article.
- ☐ The word *free* cannot be used in advertising unless all conditions, obligations or other prerequisites involved are clearly and accurately disclosed.

When someone offers you a "freebie" make sure there are no expensive strings attached.

Remember: The reason this kind of deceptive advertising is so often used is, simply, that it works. If you are neither deceived by offers of this kind nor willing to accept them by purchasing products with hidden costs, then say so. When you are faced with misleading advertising or misleading free offers, complain. Tell the merchant. Tell the Better Business Bureau.

Radios

(See also AUDIO EQUIPMENT; WARRANTIES)

IN ADDITION TO providing music, indoors and out, twenty-four hours a day, a radio can provide you with the latest news, traffic congestion warnings, and weather reports. Whatever your reason for buying a new radio, it's important to know what's available.

An AM radio receives the standard list of AM stations, both local and distant. The FM radio not only gives you different stations but also a better quality of sound. The radios available today are greatly improved over what they were a few years ago.

Among the types available are:

☐ **AM/FM portable radios:** These usually run on house current as well as on batteries. Most have Automatic Frequency Control (AFC), which keeps a tuned-in FM station from drifting away. Other features include earphone and earphone jack and continuous tone control, which gradually increases or reduces treble. The life of the battery depends on the specific radio; many use 4 AA or C-size batteries.

☐ **AM/FM table radios:** These usually run on house current only. Features include separate bass and treble controls, and terminals for attachment of external AM and FM antennas. The table radio can also come equipped with a clock. Those radios with digital-reading clocks may be easier to read in the middle of the night, but may have alarms which are difficult to set with complete accuracy.

An **antenna** is a necessity for FM reception. FM signals, like television, are emitted in a straight line (they are *line-of-sight* media). The right kind of antenna, therefore, will be as important as the tuner/receiver. AM sets, on the other hand, work well with a built-in antenna.

When you shop for your radio, follow these guidelines:

☐ **Choose your price range.** You can stay within the range you have chosen because there will be a wide variety of models and sizes for the price you want to pay.

GETTING MORE FOR YOUR MONEY

☐ **Listen to several sets.** Compare them for:
— **Sensitivity:** the capacity to receive a wide range of stations. Make sure to check the quality of reception of the stations you want to hear at home. The sound should be clear, with no background noise or distortion.
— **Selectivity:** the ability to reject stations close on the dial. The greater the sensitivity of your set, the better the selectivity should be.

☐ **Listen for distortion.** Then turn the volume up and listen again. Look for a set that is free from distortion throughout the full range of volume control.

Finally — as with any purchase — make the warranty part of your buying decision (see WARRANTIES).

Learn the language
The following terms will be useful to know when you are shopping for an FM set.

☐ **AM rejection:** the set's capacity to reject AM sound and other kinds of electronic noise.
☐ **Impulse noise rejection:** the ability to reject sounds caused by other electric or ignition systems.
☐ **Automatic Frequency Control (AFC):** This feature automatically locks the radio on a tuned-in channel. It is best to choose a set that allows you to turn off the AFC feature, especially if your favorite station happens to be a weak one; AFC will often pull the tuning to a nearby stronger station.

Ranges

(See also APPLIANCES; ENERGY)

RANGES, WHETHER THEY are used a lot or a little, must be relied upon for years. A wide variety of styles is available, so it makes sense to consider carefully which is most efficient and convenient to use.

WHICH FUEL IS MOST CONVENIENT AND ECONOMICAL IN YOUR AREA?

Gas and electricity cook with equal efficiency. If you have no particular preference for one over the other, choose the type that will be least expensive to operate in your area.

Both gas and electric models are available in a wide range of shapes, sizes and heights.

☐ **Built-in ranges** are most economically installed in a new kitchen or when the entire kitchen is being remodeled. One advantage of built-ins is that they can be "tailored" to fit the kitchen. But this is accompanied by a disadvantage: *You can't take it along when you move.*

☐ **Stack-ons** are similar to built-ins, but less expensive to install. They are designed for placement on top of a counter or storage cabinet. Some are designed to look built-in.

Electric vs. gas — know the differences
Electric
  ☐ Require a 220/240V circuit.
  ☐ Cooktop utensils should be flat for maximum contact with surface heating units.
  ☐ The broiler is part of the main oven.

Gas
  ☐ The source is the gas line; some also require a 120V electric circuit. They may also operate on natural, bottled liquid petroleum (LPG) or manufactured gas.
  ☐ The size and shape of cooking utensils is not important to cooking efficiency.

GETTING MORE FOR YOUR MONEY

☐ **Double-decker designs** feature ovens at eye level and at standard floor level, with burners in between. They save space, but they require installation, and many models do not provide adequate work space over the burners.

☐ **Free-standing and drop-in models** can come with (or without) the automatic features of built-ins, without the necessity for installation.

There are variations on these themes, including ranges with two separate ovens and six surface burners instead of the usual four. You can choose ovens that clean themselves and/or turn themselves on and off according to a preset schedule, and ranges that include such features as oven rotisseries, an automatic meat probe and thermostatically controlled units and burners.

MICROWAVE OVENS

These energy-saving appliances continue to grow in popularity every year. Some 12 percent of American homes were estimated to have a microwave oven in 1979. By the mid-1980s, it is likely that nearly 40 percent will be using this modern-day miracle. While microwave ovens do not entirely replace conventional ovens, they can provide remarkable convenience, economy and speed for the busy homemaker. Highly sophisticated models exist that boast computerized timing, browning elements, temperature probes and even whole-meal cooking functions. Multiple settings and variable power controls on many ovens have replaced the simple high-power or low-power capabilities of earlier ovens.

A good deal has been written about the safety of microwave ovens. While much of this is more emotional than factual, it *is* important to make sure that a microwave does not leak radiation. Government regulations concerning the safety and operation of these units are very strict, and all manufacturers are required to design and produce ovens

---

Microwave checklist
Before you buy a microwave oven:

☐ Decide on the type of oven best suited to your needs; compare sizes and features of different ovens.
☐ Check the oven interior for cleanability.
☐ Compare the timing mechanisms. Are they easy to operate?
☐ Check the warranty. Microwave ovens have warranty coverage from one to five years. See whether parts and labor are covered, and check the coverage on the magnetron tube — it's the most expensive part to replace. Take note of any restrictions on the use of the oven that may void the warranty (see WARRANTIES).

RANGES

according to the regulations before the units can be sold. But an abused or tampered-with oven can develop serious leaks, and it is necessary to use the appliance with care. Many serious users of microwave ovens check their appliances on a regular basis, using one of several available inexpensive devices that can detect microwave leakage.

The Bureau of Radiological Health also requires that all microwave units manufactured after September 1975 carry the following warning:

Do not attempt to operate this oven with:

☐ an object caught in the door
☐ a door that does not close properly
☐ a damaged door, hinge, latch or sealing surface.

The warning is not required if the manufacturer can prove to the Bureau of Radiological Health that radiation hazards have been eliminated — that is, designed out of its product.

CONVECTION ("TURBO") OVENS

An increasingly popular home oven, the convection oven has long been used by commercial bakers and restaurants. Foods cook by heat propelled through the oven cavity by a fan. The scientific design of the oven enables food to cook more quickly with less shrinkage and at a lower temperature than in a regular oven. To prevent burns, be sure that any convection oven you may consider is well insulated.

When you consider special features, remember that they add to the initial cost of the appliance. They may also add to the operating and maintenance costs as well.

CHOOSE YOUR APPLIANCE DEALER CAREFULLY

Should your range need in-warranty service, it is best to have a dealer capable of providing it.

Installation service will be important not only to the operating efficiency of the range, but to family safety. Gas and electrical installation should be done by a competent service representative. The electrical circuit must be properly grounded.

Make sure the range is level. If it isn't cakes will not rise evenly and you are likely to get a good deal of spatters from roasting and broiling.

For economy, consider buying last year's model. Design, styling and current gadgetry have nothing to do with efficiency and serviceability.

Refrigerators and Freezers

(See also APPLIANCES)

YOUR REFRIGERATOR IS likely to be one of the most-used appliances in your home, but it can be expected to last about fourteen years.

The cost of operation of a new refrigerator should play an important role in your buying decision. Research has shown that consumers can expect operating and service costs to be almost twice what they paid for the refrigerator over the fourteen-year life span of the appliance:

- ☐ The largest share of the operating cost — some 58 percent — goes for electricity.
- ☐ Only about 6 percent is spent on servicing.

Studies have also shown that the number of refrigerators needing service in their first year has been reduced drastically over the past twenty years: from 60 percent in 1960, to under 30 percent today.

The power consumption of refrigerators, however, has increased steadily over the years. Models marketed between 1925 and 1950 required only 6 watts per cubic foot; from 1950 to 1965 the figure rose to about 10 watts per cubic foot.

A 14-cubic-foot refrigerator/freezer marketed in the mid-1970s was estimated to use 1,137 average kilowatt hours each year, at an annual cost of $39.80, with electricity figured at 3.5 cents per kilowatt hour (the figure is considerably higher today, with increasing rates). A frostless refrigerator/freezer (14 cubic feet) was estimated to use

---

You would be surprised . . .
at the number of people who buy a big, new appliance without making sure that it will fit into the space allotted for it in the kitchen. And, in some cases, today's larger refrigerator/freezers can't be maneuvered through the door without removing the door frame.

Take the simple precaution of measuring the space available for your new refrigerator as well as the doors through which it must be moved. Then figure out beforehand how you will cope. You will save yourself time and trouble.

1,829 kilowatt hours annually with a yearly cost, at 3.5 cents per kilowatt hour, of $64.02.

Proposed design changes which would increase the efficiency of new refrigerators are:

- ☐ replacing fiberglass insulation with polyurethane, and
- ☐ increasing the number of copper windings in the compressor motor.

These changes would add about $65 to the cost of the $300 refrigerator, but they would save an estimated $350 in power costs, or $25 per year over fourteen years.

Look for EER (Energy Efficiency Rating) labels on refrigerators when you shop (see AIR CONDITIONERS, APPLIANCES and ENERGY for a fuller discussion of EER).

Before you shop for a new refrigerator, make these decisions at home:

- ☐ **What size do you need?** For a family of two, fresh food-storage compartments should provide about eight cubic feet of space. Add one more cubic foot for each additional person in the family and two more cubic feet to the total if you do a lot of entertaining. For freezer space, calculate about two cubic feet per family member.
- ☐ **What type of refrigerator do you need?** Choose from the conventional one-door model or the two-door model with separate top or bottom freezer, or a side-by-side model. *(Remember to check the kitchen layout so that you don't buy a left-hand door when a right-hand door would be better.)*
- ☐ **Know the terms used for frost-removal features:**
  - **— Manual defrost:** you do it yourself.
  - **— Semiautomatic defrosting models,** according to the Major Appliance Consumer Action Panel (MACAP), are those in which "the defrost cycle is manually initiated and automatically terminated."
  - **— An automatic-defrosting refrigerator** is a cabinet in which the defrost cycle is automatic. The defrost cycle is automatically initiated and terminated. **Caution:** A few models have automatic defrost in the refrigerator section but the freezer section must be manually defrosted.
  - **— "Cycle-defrosting combinations"** are refrigerator/freezer combinations with automatic defrosting in the fresh food section but manual defrosting in the freezer section.
  - **— "No-frost combinations"** have automatic defrosting in both sections.

The greater number of special features you require on your new refrigerator, the more it will cost to buy and to operate. As with other products and appliances, the wise buyer will balance the convenience with cost and then budget accordingly.

Always make the manufacturer's warranty part of your buying decision, and remember that the warranty must be implemented by your dealer. Check dealers' complaint records with your Better Business Bureau.

FREEZERS

Will a freezer save you money? The answer is a definite *maybe*.

If you plan in advance for maximum use of your freezer, it *can* save you money. If you don't plan its use, it is more of a convenience than an economy. Think of it this way: the U.S. Department of Agriculture has estimated that it costs $80.27 a year to operate a 360-pound-capacity freezer (the operation cost has probably increased in most sections of the country) including the cost of operation, maintenance, depreciation and credit; if you store and use 360 pounds of food in that freezer each year, the cost would be 22 cents a pound. But if 540 pounds were stored and used (in a larger freezer) the cost would drop to 15 cents a pound. Small families are not likely to think in terms of such storage capacity and annual food consumption, but the principle still operates — the larger the amount stored, the lower the cost per pound of storage.

You should install a thermometer in your freezer, to make sure the temperature level is safe and satisfactory. The best thermometer attaches to the outside of the freezer, with a wire leading through the door to an inside sensor. This enables you to monitor the freezer temperature without opening the door.

In case of electrical failure or brownouts, be sure to leave your freezer closed, to preserve as much cold for as long as possible.

What can you do if food becomes defrosted?

☐ **Meat,** if partially or completely thawed, should be cooked immediately.
☐ **Vegetables and fruit** can be safely refrozen if still cold. Otherwise, they should be used right away.

A full freezer is an economical one. The more you fill the storage space with food, the colder the temperature, the less energy required and the better use you will get from your freezer appliance.

Food freezer plans. Better Business Bureau files contain many complaints from consumers who have signed contracts for freezers and the food to fill them. If the idea interests you, you are well advised to proceed with care. "Huge savings" on the cost of food could be compensated for by the inflated price charged for the freezer. *The principal cause for complaint in regard to these plans has been the exorbitant price of the freezer, and sometimes an additional charge of several hundred dollars for "membership" in the food-buying plan.*

REFRIGERATORS AND FREEZERS

Heed this simple advice: *Before you sign up for a freezer plan, shop for freezers — find out how much you should expect to pay for a freezer without the plan.*

Other complaints about food-freezer plans mention companies that failed to deliver food and companies that went out of business shortly after installing the equipment.

Before signing up for a food-freezer plan, wise consumers should:

- ☐ comparison-shop freezers and food prices;
- ☐ check the reliability of the firm. Call the Better Business Bureau and find out how long the firm has been in business and what its complaint record has been.

Be sure to check the length of time various foods can safely be kept in your freezer.

Refunds and Exchanges

(See also CONTRACTS)

REFUNDS AND EXCHANGES of merchandise are actually changes in the contract, or agreement, that has been effected between buyer and seller when money (or a promise to pay) and a piece of merchandise have been exchanged.

The buyer has a right to expect that the merchandise can be used for the purpose for which it is sold and that it is neither defective nor misrepresented. The seller has a right to expect that he will be paid — immediately or within a reasonable time — for the product he sells.

Returning the product for exchange, credit or refund is generally a privilege rather than a right. An exception to this rule (see DOOR-TO-DOOR SELLING) is the three-day "cooling-off-period" allowed for purchasers of merchandise from direct (door-to-door) sales representatives.

Return policies vary from store to store. Some stores have "no return" or "final sale" policies, and it is best to inquire what a store's policy is before you make a purchase. In some states, stores are required by law to disclose clearly what their return policies are. The three types of return policies are:

- ☐ **Exchange:** Merchandise may be returned and another item of the same kind may be taken in its place. This privilege is offered when the buyer has made a mistake, for example, in the choice of size or color of the item.
- ☐ **Return for credit:** When merchandise is returned, the customer is given a credit slip or his account is credited with the amount paid. The customer may then apply that amount to the purchase of any item in the store. This policy is a little more liberal than the simple exchange method and there is nothing in the law which compels the merchant to extend this privilege.
- ☐ **Refund:** Under this policy, the customer gets his money back. Retailers who use and advertise this policy effectively guarantee satisfaction with whatever merchandise they sell. If the returned item had been charged to a credit card initially, the refund may

take the form of a credit charged to the same credit card number. In general, credit cards are a safe, "easy" and widely accepted tool of purchasing today; retailers may also be more likely to credit returns of credit-card purchasers than they would cash sales.

In every case these policies are voluntarily adopted by retailers who wish to provide a high standard of service to their customers; they are *not* compelled to do so under the law.

Return privileges are usually extended with the requirement that goods be returned within a specified time period and be in new condition. Stores often require a sales slip or other evidence that the article was actually bought there and not at some other store.

For some items — such as sales merchandise — and sometimes even for all merchandise in some stores, the policy may be that *all sales are final*. Retailers have every right to do this, but the policy should be clear and "final-sale" items should be clearly identified or so advertised. Expect this policy for seasonal merchandise, floor models and for intimate apparel or swimwear which should be worn or used by only one person.

Don't abuse the privilege. Some shoppers shop casually and return merchandise purchased on impulse, causing an unnecessary amount of sales time and paperwork, both of which are expensive for the store. Naturally, these extra costs are passed on to the customer, increasing the cost of all merchandise in the store to all customers. It also causes some retailers to adopt less liberal return policies than they might otherwise use.

How to use return privileges
- ☐ Any time an item you have purchased is defective or was misrepresented, return it to the store. In either case, even if the store has an announced *no return* policy, you are entitled to a suitable substitute or a refund.
- ☐ Make it a rule to check the store's return policy before you buy. If in doubt as to the policy, have your sales slip marked "on approval."
- ☐ Honest mistakes over items that don't fit, don't match, don't serve the purpose for which they were purchased, or turn out to be inappropriate gifts from a well-meaning spouse or friend *do* entitle you to the use of the store's refund policy — provided the store *has* a refund policy.

If you find that you tend to return merchandise regularly, it is probably a good idea to ask yourself whether or not you are taking advantage of a store's liberal return policy. Exercise good judgment whenever you buy. In the long run it will undoubtedly save you time, aggravation and embarrassment — as well as money.

Roofs and Roofing

(See also HOME MAINTENANCE AND IMPROVEMENTS)

A NEW ROOF MADE OF good asphalt shingles (the 210-pound type) can be expected to last ten to fifteen years. This lifetime is likely to be considerably shorter in extreme climates; extreme heat tends to affect the durability of the shingles and extreme cold makes them become brittle.

It is difficult for anyone who is not a roofing contractor or a skilled handyman to judge the quality of asphalt shingles. If you need a new roof, you need a reliable roofing contractor whose judgment of materials you can trust. Wise buyers will use these methods of selection:

- ☐ Get bids from at least three local contractors.
- ☐ Have all three contractors provide references, and make sure you check the references.
- ☐ Check their complaint records with the Better Business Bureau.
- ☐ Make sure your contract with a roofer includes total cost, specifications for materials to be used and a completion date.

When you have chosen a reliable contractor, you will probably take his advice about materials to be used. Chances are, the material will be asphalt shingles. Asphalt shingles come in a variety of colors, which your contractor can advise you about. White or off-white are popular choices in warmer regions because they reflect heat. With a white or very light roof, you can expect your house to be as much as ten degrees cooler in the summer. In very cold regions, of course, the heat-absorbing black or very dark colors are most practical.

The roof over your head is one of the targets of itinerant "roof specialists" who just "happen to be in the neighborhood" and are willing to offer you a very special price on waterproof roof coating. Many people who have taken advantage of this kind of offer later report to the Better Business Bureau that the roof began leaking *after* the "waterproof" coating was applied, that the sides of the house were splashed with the resurfacing material, and that they could have had a competent job done by a reliable local firm for less money.

Care and maintenance. If you begin a program of preventive maintenance for your new roof, you will extend its life and avoid expensive problems later.

The first step in good maintenance is the semiannual cleaning of gutters and downspouts. Give them an especially good going-over in the fall, when leaves are likely to clog downspouts. Flooding from clogged gutters can cause water to collect on the roof, and this contributes to the creation of weak spots.

Have the roof inspected periodically. If it is relatively new, inspections and minor repairs every two or three years should keep it in shape; if it is ten years old or more, an annual inspection is called for.

The inspector will pay particular attention to flashings, roof penetrations and "distress areas" such as blisters and cracks. Spot patching, coating or reroofing may be called for. (If extensive repairs are needed, be sure to get estimates from several contractors.)

Roof coatings are protective preparations in liquid or semiliquid form. They are applied by roller, brush or spray apparatus. Whatever method is used, a coating can be expected to perform satisfactorily *if it is applied properly before the upper watertight layer (roof membrane) has been weakened by deterioration.*

Asphalt-base, alkyd-base or refined coal-tar coatings may be used.

Asphalt-base coatings

1. **The emulsions type** consists of asphalt particles dispersed in water containing bentonite clay, which acts as an emulsifying agent. Asbestos, glass and/or other fibers are added to provide reinforcement to the dried film. This material is used over asphalt build-up and other composition and metal roofs which have adequate drainage. Application is by brush or spray.

    Advantages: This coating, when applied in proper thickness, chalks slowly and is not subject to "alligatoring" or blistering. It can be applied over a damp surface, will not flow under heat and will not support combustion.

    Disadvantages: Requires specific temperature and humidity conditions which permit thorough evaporation of water content before the roof may be subjected to rainfall, freezing or standing water. Drying time depends upon temperature, sunlight, humidity and wind velocity. A clean, usually primed surface is required for adhesion.

2. **The solvent type** consists of asphalt in a solution of petroleum solvents, usually reinforced with asbestos fibers and, frequently, with mineral fillers. It can be applied over asphalt, composition, asbestos-cement, metal and masonry roof surfaces. Application is by brush, roller or spray.

    Advantages: When applied on a clean, dry surface, this coating has good water resistance and does not require priming for adhesion. It can be applied over a wide range of temperatures and, after a short drying period, resists wash-off.

Disadvantages: Flows under extreme heat and *will support combustion*. It is susceptible to blistering if applied over a damp surface or over any material containing moisture.

3. **The aluminum-pigmented type** consists of flakes and aluminum dispersed in solvent-type asphalt coating. As the coating dries, the aluminum "floats" or "leafs" to the surface where it reflects heat. It is usually reinforced with asbestos fibers and may include fillers. It can be applied over asphalt, composition or metal roofs which have adequate drainage, where a reflective or decorative surface is desired. Application is by brush, roller or spray.

Advantages: The reflective surface helps to reduce interior temperature of buildings; it protects the roofing from deterioration by reducing the surface temperature.

Disadvantages: The cost is higher than for other asphalt coatings. Application over low-melt asphalt roofs can result in discoloration and alligatoring. Susceptible to blistering if applied over a damp surface or any material containing moisture.

Alkyd-base colored aluminum roof coatings

These consist of alkyd resin in petroleum solvents, pigmented with non-leafing aluminum flakes, coloring pigments and mineral fillers. It can be applied over metal, composition or masonry roofs having adequate drainage. Recommended for protection of polyurethane foam roofs. Application is by brush, roller and spray.

Advantages: Performs the same functions as the aluminum-pigmented asphalt-base coating. Used primarily for its decorative values. Will not flow under heat and will not support combustion.

Disadvantages: More expensive than other products. Susceptible to blistering if applied over any damp material. Tends to discolor and/or split when applied over low-melt asphalt.

Refined coal-tar coatings

These consist of refined coal tar reinforced with asbestos fibers and (sometimes) other mineral fillers. These are used for recoating tar and gravel roofs, and must be applied to gravel-free, broom-cleaned surfaces. Proper protection requires approximately seven gallons per one hundred square feet. Gravel may be reapplied over the coating. Applied by spray or brush.

Advantages: Has a self-sealing quality at warm temperatures. Excellent water resistance. Can be used where roof is subject to standing water.

Disadvantages: Material tends to be brittle in cold weather. Its use is restricted to relatively flat roofs. Unless gravel surface is used, walkways must be applied for roof traffic.

ROOF MAINTENANCE DOs AND DON'Ts

DO

- Extend roof life expectancy through a planned maintenance program with periodic roof inspections.
- Apply coatings before serious roof deterioration occurs. Some roof coatings alone, without reinforcing membranes, may not correct serious roofing problems.
- Follow manufacturer's instructions carefully in regard to surface preparation, priming, coverage and weather conditions.
- Make necessary repairs to distressed areas before applying any coating.
- Allow asphalt roofs to weather adequately before applying aluminum roof coating.
- Use reinforcing membrane over badly alligatored roofs, if necessary.
- Use a coating chemically compatible with the roof surface.
- Check the reputation and reliability of any roofing contractor before you do business with him. Ask for references. Check with the BBB.

DON'T

- Use roof coatings on a wood shingle roof.
- Apply aluminum roof coatings over coal-tar roofs or tar coatings.
- Apply emulsion-type coatings over an old roof without priming.
- Wait for the first real leak if all evidence points to the need for repairs or reroofing — it could cause more damage than the job need cost.
- Be taken in by a high-pressure roof-coatings sales representative who knows nothing of the type, age and condition of your roof.
- Sign any contract or work order unless you have read and understood it completely.

Safety

SAFETY IN THE HOME is worth some time and attention, in view of the fact that the National Safety Council has estimated that each year accidents in and around the American home result in approximately twenty-five thousand deaths, with another three to four million persons disabled in some way.

In addition to the serious problems, there are the "little" accidents — those that require some degree of medical treatment, however minor, or result in discomfort lasting only a day or two — estimated at twenty million annually. What causes these accidents?

It's hard to say. Are falls, for example, caused by high heels, slippery shoes, slippery floors, shaky ladders, worn or wrinkled carpets, worn stairs or alcohol? And how about fires? Do they result from faulty heating equipment, matches, misuse of cleaning chemicals or equipment, stoves, faulty wiring, flammable fabrics or careless smoking?

Are accidents caused by faulty or defective consumer products? Or by misuse of those products?

There is probably no firm answer to these questions — one can only surmise that both factors contribute to a lack of safety in the home.

FEDERAL AGENCIES AND PRODUCT SAFETY

The creation of the Consumer Product Safety Commission, with its powers to seize and ban from the marketplace "any product that presents an unreasonable risk of injury," was an important contribution to the safety of the American public in the 1970s.

There is, however, no government agency at any level with the power or the omniscience required to guarantee safety or to oversee all the products that enter the marketplace. The individual consumer must exercise reasonable care in the purchase, use and maintenance of consumer products.

Unreasonable risks caused by defective products should be reported. For example:

- ☐ Your two-year-old has dismantled a toy which contains small or sharp objects which could harm him. Report it to the CPSC.
- ☐ A small appliance gives you a healthy shock when you use it. Have there been other complaints about shock hazards associated

with this product? Ask the Consumer Product Safety Commission.
☐ You've heard that there are hazards associated with the use of power lawn mowers. Ask for consumer information on the safety aspects of this equipment from the CPSC.

Should you suspect a problem with some food or cosmetic, report it to the Food and Drug Administration, Office of Consumer Inquiries, 5600 Fishers Lane, Rockville, Maryland 20852.

THE CONSUMER AND PRODUCT SAFETY

How can you tell whether a product is free from defects that can result in "unreasonable risk of injury"? You can't.

What you can do is buy from a reliable source, use care in choosing household furniture and accessories, tools, appliances, toys and recreation equipment.

Follow manufacturers' use and care instructions to the letter.

Use small appliances, tools, and household equipment for the purposes for which they were intended. Misuse can cause serious injury.

The Consumer Product Safety Commission (CPSC) was created by the Consumer Product Safety Act in 1972 and has the power to:

☐ Set safety standards for all common household and recreational products.
☐ Seize and bar hazardous products from the marketplace.
☐ Ban from the market any product that presents an unreasonable risk of injury.
☐ Order manufacturers, distributors or retailers to notify purchasers about hazardous products and to repair, replace or refund the purchase price of such products.

From air conditioners to zoom lenses, almost everything in the house — except for products regulated by other agencies — is covered by the product safety legislation. The exceptions are: tobacco products; motor vehicles and related equipment; economic poisons (pesticides, fungicides, etc.); firearms; aircraft and related equipment; boats and related equipment; and food, drugs and cosmetics.

If you wish to inquire about or to report a potentially dangerous product, use the CPSC's toll-free hotline. The number to call is (800)638-8326 from anywhere in the continental United States except Maryland; in Maryland, call (800)492-8363; in Alaska, Hawaii, Puerto Rico and the Virgin Islands, call (800)638-8333.

Safety check your home (and your habits) from time to time. Use these guidelines:

Fire hazards

☐ **Smoking and matches:** Careless smoking and careless use of matches are responsible for more than half the fatal residential fires that occur each year.
- Never smoke in bed or when you feel sleepy.
- Use only large, noncombustible ashtrays designed to keep cigarettes from falling out. Empty ashtrays only when you are certain all the cigarettes have been extinguished.
- Before you go to bed, check to make sure no cigarettes are burning anywhere.
- Keep matches and lighters away from children. Keep "strike anywhere" matches in a covered metal container and out of reach of children.
- When you discard a match, be certain it has cooled. It's good practice to break or bend each match before throwing it away.
- Use "safety" matches whenever possible.

☐ **Heating equipment:** Many fires are caused by faulty and/or improperly installed heating equipment. Pushing an old heater beyond its capacity may give you heat, but it can also burn down your home. Have your heating system checked at least once a year by a qualified heating specialist. Unless you are fully experienced, don't try any do-it-yourself jobs on the heating system. If something seems to be causing a problem, don't delay— call a professional.

There are several other potential hazards you should be aware of and guard against:
- All flue pipe connections should be inspected once a year. The connections should be tightly fitted and sealed at the joints. When the flue pipes and heating equipment are near combustible material, the combustible surface should be protected by sheet metal, asbestos or plaster.
- Chimneys should be inspected and cleaned at regular intervals, depending on the amount of use.
- A sturdy fire screen should be kept in front of every fireplace.

☐ **Portable gas or oil heaters** present special hazards. Some tip over too easily. Some have open flames capable of igniting the clothing of unwary users. They also consume oxygen, and in a tightly closed room they are capable of suffocating sleeping occupants. *Make sure there is a fresh oxygen supply wherever these are used.*
- Turn off portable gas or oil heaters before you go to bed.
- Make sure they are placed on a level, metal surface.
- Always be sure the heater is out and has cooled off before attempting to refill it. Use a funnel for refilling, and carry out this operation in the open or in a well-ventilated area.

— Any portable heater, including electric models, should be kept well away from curtains, bedding, furniture and other combustible materials.
☐ **Electrical hazards:** People rely on electrical appliances now more than ever. Wiring and circuits must be able to carry the load — inadequate or frayed wiring has resulted in many tragic fires. If you frequently blow a fuse when you turn on an electrical appliance, assume that the household wiring is giving you a warning: *The circuits are overloaded.* Don't try to install a fuse with a larger capacity. Instead have your wiring or circuit system checked by an electrician.
— Unless you are a qualified electrician, do not attempt to install or extend household wiring yourself.
— Avoid multiple-attachment plugs and long extension cords. If necessary, install additional wiring and outlets.
— Don't run extension cords under rugs, over hooks or through partitions and door openings. Wires can easily become worn and cause short circuits.
☐ **Cooking equipment:** Fire hazards in the kitchen are associated largely with faulty cooking procedures or negligence in the use

---

Defining the unreasonable hazard

The U.S. Commission on Product Safety has developed guidelines for defining "unreasonable hazards." The following statement by Professor Corwin D. Edwards supplements those guidelines and takes into account the fact that one consumer's dangerous product could be another's necessary tool:

> Risks of bodily harm to users are not unreasonable when consumers understand that risks exist, can appraise their probability and severity, know how to cope with them, and voluntarily accept them to get benefits that could not be obtained in less risky ways. When there is a risk of this character, consumers have reasonable opportunity to protect themselves, and public authorities should hesitate to substitute their value judgments about the desirability of the risk for those consumers who choose to incur it.
> But preventable risk is not reasonable (a) when consumers do not know that it exists; or (b) when, though aware of it, consumers are unable to estimate its frequency and severity; or (c) when consumers do not know how to cope with it, and hence are likely to incur harm unnecessarily; or (d) when risk is unnecessary ... in that it could be reduced or eliminated at a cost in money or in the performance of the product that consumers would willingly incur if they knew the facts and were given the choice.

and upkeep of the kitchen stove. Avoid trouble by using precautions:
— Keep the stove clean and free of grease and other combustibles. Never keep cans of cooking oil, grease or boxes of matches on the stove.
— If you must leave the kitchen, turn the burners off.
— Help small children learn — early and well — to stay away from the stove.

☐ **Hazards around the house:**
— Never leave greasy or oily rags lying about. If you must store such hazardous items, keep them in a closed metal container.
— It is never a good idea to store gasoline, benzine, naphtha or similar flammable liquids around the house. They produce vapors that can be easily ignited when mixed with air.
— Keep the basement, attic and other storage areas clear of flammable materials such as furniture, old clothes, rags and paper.
— Keep the yard free of leaves, debris and combustible rubbish.

CHILDREN AND SAFETY

Children under five are most vulnerable to safety hazards in the home. It is best to assume that the youngest explorers in the family, if left unsupervised, will certainly experiment with pushing, pulling and manipulating anything within reach. They will also swallow almost anything, and chew anything they can't swallow.

Toy safety is essential (see TOYS). Wise parents should carefully inspect all toys for sharp edges, pins, removable metal or plastic parts attached to stuffed animals, dolls, etc. Children are clever and curious, and good at dismantling playthings to see what's inside. The contents of the toy shelves should therefore be inspected at regular intervals. Look for pieces of toys small enough to swallow, sharp enough to cut. Search out and remove play equipment too advanced or too elementary for the child's age — these are good candidates for misuse.

Children's furniture can be hazardous. Check the slats on the crib to make sure they are placed close enough together so that the child cannot get his head between them. Carefully inspect the safety catches on cribs with sliding sides to make sure they lock securely.

Make sure the mattress fits closely to the sides of the bed, with no open spaces where a small head, hands or feet could get caught. If you choose to buy **bunk beds** for older children, be especially careful to look for sturdy construction, a steady ladder and a good firm safety bar for the top bunk.

Small chairs should be as well balanced as those constructed for an adult so that they resist tipping to the side or turning over when they are used.

Bouncers, walkers, strollers, jumpers and other equipment should be closely examined *before* being purchased. Reject equipment with exposed springs, sharp edges or construction that allows it to tip.

Sports and recreation equipment, from the toddler's small slide to the high school student's football helmet, should be purchased with care. Compare product ratings in consumer research publications. Use all available consumer information to assure yourself that such products will withstand the hard use that children inevitably give them.

When you shop for outdoor play equipment, use the same careful inspection methods you use for the small child's indoor swing, bouncer and walker. Reject equipment that has sharp edges, exposed bolts or springs. Look for solid construction, and make sure that any equipment made to be installed, hung from a porch roof or set into the ground is installed by a professional. The additional safety is worth the extra cost.

SAFETY FOR THE FAMILY, FROM BASEMENT TO ATTIC

Simple, basic safety rules apply in frequently used areas of every home.

- ☐ Use nonskid area rugs and carpets.
- ☐ See that floors and stairways are free of the clutter that causes those potentially serious falls.
- ☐ Make sure that electrical wiring systems are adequate, with no overloaded circuits or outsized fuses substituting for the safe ones.
- ☐ Work areas — kitchen, workshop and sewing room — should be orderly. They should contain the proper tools for both ease of use and safety as well. For example, sharp knives are actually safer than dull ones, and they are certainly more efficient.
- ☐ Bathtubs and shower stalls should have firm bars to hold to. The tub should be as skidproof as you can make it. And, it goes without saying that nonskid rugs should be used on the slippery bathroom floor.
- ☐ The medicine chest should have a section with a lock, where gaily colored pills and medicines are locked away from the youngsters.
- ☐ Electrical equipment — hair stylers, shavers and the like — should be kept in the bedroom or dressing room, and certainly used *away from* the bathroom basin and other damp surfaces. The shock hazard is too great to risk.

Schools, Home Study

(See also CONTRACTS; SCHOOLS, VOCATIONAL)

THE TERMS *home study* and *correspondence course* are interchangeable. They refer to enrollment and study arrangements with an educational institution that provides materials for study by a student working independently, whose assignments are returned to the school to be corrected, graded and commented upon by a qualified teacher who, in turn, returns the materials to the student. It is a two-way communication between student and teacher, as opposed to a *self-study* course, in which the student purchases books and lesson plans and works completely independently.

There are two major sources of home study courses:

☐ **Colleges and universities,** through their extension divisions, offer a variety of home study courses. Students may earn credits toward high school and college degrees. At some schools, participants may also forgo credit and choose courses to study for pleasure in such diverse subjects as flower arranging, gardening, auto mechanics, etc.

The National University Extension Association (1 Dupont Circle, Washington, D.C. 20036) publishes a "Guide to Correspondence Study" ($3.25) listing courses available through its member schools. (The guide is also available from Petersons Guides, Book Order Department, Box 978, Edison, N.J. 08817.)

☐ **Private home-study schools,** of which there are more than seven hundred in the United States, offer practical, noncredit courses in business, technical and avocational or hobby-related fields. Some also offer academic high school courses.

The National Home Study Council (1601 18th Street N.W., Washington, D.C. 20009) publishes a list of private home-study schools that have been examined and accredited by their Accrediting Commission. The "Directory of Accredited Private Home Study Schools" is available free upon request.

Accreditation means that a school meets certain standards set by professionals in the field. It does *not* mean that the school can offer credits toward a degree or diploma. Nor does it mean that the school can find a job for you when you have completed its course.

The accreditation situation may be confusing: a nonaccredited school may be a reputable one, since applying to the National Home Study Council for accreditation is voluntary; and a school must have been in operation for five years before it can apply for accreditation.

When in doubt, or if you should find yourself under pressure from a sales representative of correspondence courses, check with your local Better Business Bureau for information.

Before you sign an enrollment "application," read it carefully. Applications have a way of turning into contracts when signed by prospective students and returned to the school (see CONTRACTS). Never let yourself be pressured into signing an application or contract for a home-study course — or for any other product or service, for that matter.

Prospective students should find out from the school how well students did in courses previously offered, how many got work in the field they studied, and how much money they are making (see SCHOOLS, VOCATIONAL). Check with your state attorney general's office to determine your rights under state law.

Investigate before you invest:

- ☐ It doesn't make sense to take a home-study course advertised to prepare you to become a licensed practical nurse when all states require at least one year of resident training before you can take the licensing examination.
- ☐ In other fields, such as the airline industry, companies have their own training programs. Check with the employment offices of firms in whatever industries interest you to determine for yourself the kinds of skills and training they look for in the people they hire.
- ☐ **Remember:** No "civil service" or other school claiming to offer courses leading specifically to federal employment is connected in any way with the United States Office of Personnel Management, and no school can promise success in "passing" civil service examination.

Study for credit?
Students who wish to earn credits toward a college degree or high school diploma should be especially careful in choosing correspondence courses. Check with the State Department of Education and/or your high school vocational advisor or guidance counselor — or with your teachers. *Make sure that the course you are considering can provide* recognized *credit toward your degree or diploma.*

Home study schools cannot guarantee jobs
Should a field representative for any home study school assure you that accreditation means not only that a course is worth taking but that the school will find you a job, he or she is either seriously mistaken or is intentionally misleading you.

It is true that many schools maintain placement services, but no reputable school will guarantee that they can definitely find a job for you.

Additional information on home-study courses, vocational schools and adult education resources is available from:

- ☐ Office of Personnel Management
  1900 E. Street
  Washington, D.C. 20415

- ☐ National Education Association
  Division of Adult Education
  1201 16th Street N.W.
  Washington, D.C. 20036

- ☐ National Vocational Guidance Association, Inc.
  1607 New Hampshire Avenue N.W.
  Washington, D.C. 20009

- ☐ Superintendent of Documents
  Washington, D.C. 20402

- ☐ U.S. Office of Education
  Adult Education Section
  Washington, D.C. 20202

In addition, many large industries, insurance companies, and trade and professional associations put out career information. You will find lists of them, as well as other vocational literature, at your library.

Schools, Vocational

(See also CONTRACTS; SCHOOLS, HOME STUDY)

VOCATIONAL SCHOOLS can offer sound training for young people who are not college bound and for adults interested in changing or expanding their technical or service training.

> Education should be purchased as carefully as any other service, and the source of any course of study should be carefully investigated before you invest in it.
> Whether it is a course in automobile mechanics, practical nursing, locksmithing or any of the range of vocational education areas that interests you, *move carefully*. Find out whether the course you want is available from the public school system — many vocational courses are. Tuition may be minimal and the quality of instruction excellent, and courses may be offered in night school or adult education classes so that students are able to work during the day and continue their education simultaneously.
> Check with your high school guidance counselor for information on public vocational schools.

Do your homework *before* you sign up with any private vocational school. If you are approached by a school sales representative, get answers to these questions:

- ☐ How many people complete the course of study? Find out how many were admitted to the school and how many actually graduated.
- ☐ Ask for names and addresses of students who graduated in the past six months. Find out what they think of the course content, school facilities and quality of instruction.
- ☐ Is the school licensed by the state?
- ☐ Is the school accredited by an agency recognized by the U.S. Office of Education or the Council on Post-Secondary Accreditation? (Don't assume that accreditation means that the school is good. Check with your high school vocational counselor or guidance counselor.)
- ☐ If you sign an installment contract for payment for the course, who holds the collection contract? Sometimes your contract is sold to a bank or a finance company, which means that if you have questions about the financial arrangements you will not be able to deal directly with the school.

Move slowly. There is always another time, and another semester. Reputable schools have no reason to use high-pressure salespeople to solicit students. If the school representative says you must sign a contract (which may be labeled *Application for Enrollment* or *Enrollment Agreement*) to reserve your place in next semester's class — forget it. A

Don't rely on the answers received from any vocational school's "field representative" — that's another phrase for *salesperson*. Instead, do your own checking. Contact prospective employers and ask these questions.

- ☐ Does the employer hire graduates of the school you are considering?
- ☐ How many has he actually hired in the past year?
- ☐ Were they hired because of the school's contribution to their training?
- ☐ Did the training make any difference in starting salary?

Also contact high school, military or Veterans Administration counselors for advice. Get in touch with unions and trade and professional associations to find out what the job situation is in the field you want to enter. Find out whether the training you have in mind would be valuable. And contact a Better Business Bureau to find out whether complaints have been filed against the school and how those complaints were handled.

reputable school will give you time to check its credentials.

If you have taken an aptitude test or entrance exam offered by the school and are informed that your score is amazingly high, you should be aware of deception used by some unscrupulous schools. Schools which engage in this practice give virtually everyone high marks simply to get them to enroll.

If you have moved with care, taken all these precautions before enrolling in a vocational school, and still feel that you have a valid complaint involving misrepresentation, contact a Better Business Bureau, your state's consumer protection agency, the state attorney general's office, the state department of education or the Federal Trade Commission.

Sewing Machines

SEWING MACHINES, like fabrics and clothing styles, have undergone tremendous changes in the last twenty-five years. The simple straight-stitch machines are still available, but demand for versatile machines with a variety of stitching styles makes it possible to sew on knit and stretch fabrics, embroider, appliqué, you name it. The features you need will depend upon the kind of sewing you do. Be realistic in the assessment of your needs. The simpler the items you intend to make, the simpler your sewing machine can be. If you make a wide variety of clothing for yourself and your family, a more elaborate model might be right for you.

If you haven't been near a sewing machine since that high school home-economics course, but the high price of clothing tempts you to try your hand at home sewing... *don't buy immediately.* Sewing machines can be rented. The rental costs can often be applied to the purchase price, *if you decide that sewing is right for you.* If, on the other hand, you decide that the time and effort required for making your own wardrobe is simply too demanding, you will have lost nothing but the rental fee, time and experience — as compared to the price you would have paid for equipment of your own.

Once you have decided to buy, don't rush into things. As you should do with any piece of equipment you buy for your home, take time to look over your library's files of consumer reporting publications. Talk with your neighbors. Make every effort to find out which machine will be right for you.

Choose the dealer carefully. Check the reputations of dealers with your local Better Business Bureau, and check the warranty *before* you buy.

Use caution when you buy. The use of "bait and switch" advertising and selling (see FRAUD AND DECEPTION) is characteristic of some disreputable operators in this field. If an ad implies by illustration that a certain machine is zigzag-equipped and you later find out that this feature is not available at the advertised price, make your purchase elsewhere.

Avoid high-pressure sales tactics. Don't let a salesperson rush you into a purchase by making a special offer "good for today only" or "because of the company's anniversary." He or she may be trying to rush you, so that you won't be able to do your necessary, thorough comparison shopping or check the machine carefully.

Be wary of a salesperson who offers some enticement to buy, such as a "free gift certificate" or a check. The price of the machine may have been increased to cover the amount of the certificate or the check.

Another gimmick to beware of is the contest, or a drawing of names, in which there is one first prize. All the other contestants "win" second prize and are entitled to a sewing machine head — *if* they purchase the cabinet (at an inflated price).

Again, some companies have offered a "free" machine if the customer agrees to purchase five years of servicing at a specified price, payable in advance. Because sewing machines do not require much service, the machine in such a case may not really be free.

Always compare prices offered by reputable local dealers. Reputable dealers often offer free sewing lessons and other legitimate inducements to buy. When in doubt, check with your local Better Business Bureau.

Storm Windows and Doors

(See also ENERGY; INSULATION)

STORM WINDOWS AND DOORS are energy savers, useful to the efficiency of both heating and cooling systems. By installing them, you can save money by reducing your energy bills. You may be able to claim a tax credit for their installation on your federal income tax return.

Storm/screen windows and doors are easy to convert from winter storm glass to summer screens and back again. Combination models are available with wooden, treated and untreated aluminum, or baked enamel frames. Treated aluminum or baked enamel frames may be your best bet because they are durable and required maintenance is minimal.

Windows are available in two-track and three-track combinations. The three-track model is considered the most convenient and energy efficient because it can be opened easily when there is no need to run heating or cooling equipment. Other alternatives range from a single-pane storm window that has to be removed every time you want to let in outside air to clear plastic film (which can be taped to the inside of the window frame).

The thing to look for in storm windows is tight construction. A storm window is more effective when it fits across the entire frame of the window, not just the glass.

When you buy, remember that these products represent a major, long-term investment. Both construction and materials can be excellent, but in order for them to be useful as you intend, the quality of the installation must be equally good. *Installation is a job for an expert.* Hanging a door is not easy. Fitting a window so that it is airtight is a demanding task.

☐ Check the reputation of firms you are considering with the Better Business Bureau and with friends and neighbors. How does the firm respond to consumer complaints? Have there been a number of complaints regarding quality of materials and/or installation? Be on guard.

□ Check the sales contract (see CONTRACTS). Never sign a contract that contains blank spaces. Make sure that it spells out in detail the specifications of the doors and windows you are purchasing.
□ Are the products warranted ? What is warranted? For how long? What will the manufacturer and/or retailer do to correct problems caused by defective materials or improper workmanship? Never accept an oral guarantee. Your warranty should be in writing (see WARRANTIES).

The "bait and switch" game (see FRAUD AND DECEPTION) is often played in the sale of storm windows and doors. Here are some of the warning signs:

□ Advertisements featuring an unusually low (sometimes ridiculous) price.
□ Salespeople who attempt to divert your attention from the advertised product to another, higher-priced product. The one you've seen advertised, the salesperson says, is not a product you would want to buy, it wouldn't last a season. Merchants who use this kind of ploy to make sales are not the right people to deal with. The sales tactics leave a lot to be desired, and so, you are likely to find, does the merchandise — sale-priced or not.

Televisions

WHAT KIND OF SET do you want to watch? Color? Black and white? Big set? Little set? You have a wide range of options: you can choose sets with remote controls, sets that can be operated outdoors (on rechargeable batteries), sets with headphones for quiet listening, sets with timers that turn themselves off at the time you choose, etc.

Your choice should be determined by the room or rooms in which the television will be used.

Screen size. The screen size, in inches, is the measurement of the viewable picture diagonally from corner to corner. There is no hard and fast guide to screen size in relation to the size of the room, but sets with screens measuring 18 inches or more are generally considered "family" sets, while those with smaller screens are usually used for "personal" viewing.

Sometimes you will also see television sets advertised by square inches of viewable picture — for example, a set with a 25-inch diagonal screen has a picture measurement of 315 square inches; a 19-inch screen measures 185 square inches.

MODULAR AND SOLID-STATE CONSTRUCTION

Set construction has changed. Tubes are out. Solid-state construction is in. The increasing complexity of the sets being manufactured today, coupled with the demand for compact color sets, has led directly to the replacement of tubes by printed circuitry and modular construction. You will notice that many solid-state sets have longer warranties than tube sets, for the very good reason that they are likely to last longer and work more reliably.

Modular construction also has a service advantage. When a problem occurs in such a set, the technician finds the problem area, removes the defective or malfunctioning module and replaces it with another. This eliminates the chore and the attendant cost of taking the set to a shop for repair.

A second advantage is that solid-state sets require less electricity to operate than tube sets — an important consideration in a time of rising utility costs and increasing concerns about energy conservation.

The television receiver is one of the most complex — and one of the most consistently used — devices in many homes.

Because many families depend on television for daily entertainment, news and other information, this piece of equipment is an important purchase, and extra care in its selection will provide dividends in reliability and satisfaction.

COLOR TELEVISION
Color sets are much more complex and more costly than black-and-white receivers. If you are in the market for a color set, it is particularly important to shop carefully.

All color sets have the same basic controls as black-and-white sets: tuning, brightness, contrast and volume. In addition to these are color (sometimes called chroma or color intensity) and tint (or hue) controls.

Until you are completely familiar with a color set, the simplest way to tune it is to turn the color control down and tune a good black-and-white picture. Then adjust the color control for the proper color intensity (neither too pastel nor too garish). Finally, adjust the tint control until faces appear natural. When flesh tones are correct, other colors are in balance.

Fine-tuning is more critical in color than in black-and-white. If a channel is not properly tuned, the color may be lacking or incorrect. Automatic fine tuning (AFT), also called automatic frequency control (AFC), has been added to many sets to correct this problem. This circuit electronically locks the tuner to the exact center of the channel, thus eliminating the need for manual fine-tuning under most circumstances.

Some manufacturers add automatic or preset color controls for tint or flesh-tone tuning, color intensity and, sometimes, brightness and contrast, all of which may add substantially to the ease of tuning a color picture. However, the automatic controls in most sets can be disengaged if you prefer to tune the set manually to your own exact preference. *For best results, be sure to read the instruction booklet provided with your set.*

UHF
Although most sets are equipped to receive both very high frequency (VHF channels 2 through 13) and ultra-high frequency (UHF channels 14 through 78), many new sets have pushbutton, or other simplified systems, instead of the conventional radio-type UHF dial. *If there are several UHF stations in your area, you will probably want to choose a set especially designed for convenient UHF tuning.*

REMOTE CONTROL
Wireless remote control is an increasingly popular convenience available for both color and black-and-white sets. The cost of this additional convenience increases in proportion to the number of functions that can be performed by the remote control mechanism. The simplest units switch the set on and off and change channels. Other, more elaborate units add such functions as volume, brightness, color and tint.

ACCESSORIES FOR YOUR TELEVISION
If you're thinking of buying accessories that will turn your television

GETTING MORE FOR YOUR MONEY

into a display unit for a home computer, a playing board for a wide variety of games or a screen for home movies, films or recorded TV programs, there's a lot you need to know.

Although many people still prefer black-and-white TV sets, for a home video center you are better off with a color set whose screen measures at least 19 inches diagonally. Look for models with AFC (automatic frequency control) circuits. Be sure to judge the quality of the set by examining the picture and the sound.

There are two types of home TV recording systems: the video cassette recorder (VCR) and the video home system (VHS). They are almost the same. You just insert a cassette and push a button to record or play back a program. However, cassettes from each system are not interchangeable because they record at different speeds. Both types, sold under a variety of brand names, are complex machines. Repairs must usually be made at a factory service center.

Giant-screen TVs are also becoming increasingly popular. This type of television uses an optical lens system to project the picture onto a large screen. You can get a single-tube version which uses a modified small-screen set as the source of the picture, or a more expensive three-tube type which projects red, blue and yellow separately. Be sure to look at demonstrations of several brands and models before you make your decision.

Cable television has come into its own in recent years. Now consumers can pay as little as $12 each month and enjoy a series of recent motion pictures and special entertainment on their TV sets. The service is available through local cable television outlets and programs are broadcast without commercial interruption.

CHOOSING THE SET

- ☐ Look for a crisp, sharp picture, with pleasing color tones and a minimum of distortion.
- ☐ Watch titles and commercials on demonstration sets in the store — a good test for crisp, clear pictures. Written matter should be crisp and easily legible. Titles should not "run off the screen" — the first and last letters of a screen-wide title should be visible.
- ☐ Don't select by picture alone; turn the sound up to determine whether it is well balanced and pleasing. Be especially careful to listen for clarity in music.
- ☐ Although it is often true that the television reception in a store is not as good as it will be at home, where there are fewer sources of interference, the dealer should be able to demonstrate reasonably good picture and sound to help you with your choice.
- ☐ To help you choose the right size set, estimate the distance from which you and your family will watch, and stand at about the same distance from the sets in the store.
- ☐ Insist on tuning the set in the store so that you can see — before you buy — how simple or how difficult it is to bring in a good picture.

- Keep in mind, too, that most TV stores have a sophisticated aerial to which their demonstration sets are connected; if your aerial or reception area is not as good, your final results may not be as good as those in the store.
- Compare several sizes of sets made by several different manufacturers. If a simple set appeals to you, don't be persuaded to buy a more complex model — but be flexible enough to consider alternatives.
- Compare warranties. Warranty regulations require that the terms of the warranty be made available to shoppers so that they can contribute to the buying decision (see WARRANTIES).

Paying for your television — cash or credit?
Once you have selected the set you want and the dealer you prefer, there is another decision to be made: How will you pay for it? Color sets and major "home entertainment equipment" can be costly. You may want to finance it through the store or borrow from a bank. Or you may prefer to pay cash. There are advantages and disadvantages to be considered in each case (see CREDIT AND INSTALLMENT BUYING). If you decide to finance your purchase, select the arrangement that is best for you.

Remember: Credit can be costly. Shop for your financing as carefully as you shop for products. Borrow only as much money as you need and pay it back as quickly as possible.

CHOOSING THE DEALER
The terms of the manufacturer's warranty are often carried out by the dealer. Therefore, choosing the dealer should be an important part of your buying decision. Check his reputation (with friends, neighbors and the local Better Business Bureau). Check his policy in regard to in-warranty repairs and/or replacements of malfunctioning or defective sets, and find out whether he maintains his own repair facility. Is a service contract offered? If so, it's a good idea to get all information in writing.

TV SERVICE
When there is a problem with your set, you may be able to avoid an unnecessary service call by making these simple checks:
- Make sure the power cord is plugged in.
- Make sure the antenna lead-in wires are securely fastened to the terminals at the back of the set *and* that the bare antenna leads are not touching each other.
- If the set has no sound or picture, push the circuit-breaker button at the back of the set. *Refer to your instruction book to locate this switch.*

GETTING MORE FOR YOUR MONEY

- ☐ If the sound is normal but you have no picture, turn up the brightness control and try another channel. The station may be having a transmission problem.
- ☐ If the picture is normal and you have no sound, adjust the fine tuning and volume controls. Try another channel.
- ☐ If there is no color, adjust the color and fine-tuning controls. Change channels — you could be watching a black-and-white show.
- ☐ If faces are green or red or purple, try adjusting the tint control.

If you have to call for service during the warranty period, call the dealer from whom you bought the set. He will either have the repair done by his own service department or recommend an authorized service agent. If you have moved away from the area where your in-warranty set was purchased, check the information booklet provided by the manufacturer (or the Yellow Pages) to find the nearest authorized service dealer for the brand you own.

If the warranty has expired and you need service, be certain to select a technician with a good reputation for reliability. Your neighbors' experiences often serve as a good guide. *Beware of service shops that advertise unbelievably low prices,* such as a dollar or two, for a service call. No honest service dealer could stay in business at those rates.

If your set is portable, you can usually save time and money by bringing it to the service shop. Consoles may require a visit to your home by a technician, although many modern sets are designed (modular construction) so that most repairs can be made in your home.

If, for any reason, the console must be transported to the shop for repair, it would be wise to ask (or insist) that no repairs be made until you have been advised of the extent of the problem, the estimated cost of the repair and when you can expect the set to be returned. *If, having received this information, you decide against having the set repaired, you will still owe the technician for time spent in making any calls to your home and for the diagnosis.*

When the repairs are made, the technician should give you an itemized list of charges for parts and labor and a guarantee on the completed repairs. Upon request, he should return to you the faulty parts he has replaced (except the picture tube).

TV ANTENNAS

Even the best television set will provide a poor picture if it doesn't receive a good strong signal. The function of the antenna is to feed the signal to the set. The kind of antenna you should choose will depend upon the area you live in and the distance of your home from television broadcasting stations. If there are few obstructions, such as tall buildings or mountains, to interfere with reception in your area and if broadcasting stations are close by, the standard "rabbit-ear" or single-pole built-in antenna may be satisfactory. However, an outdoor or attic antenna is often necessary for good reception. If most of your neighbors use outdoor antennas, chances are you will need one.

The difference between antenna models is in the number of elements they contain. The *length* of the elements determines the frequencies at which the antenna will be effective. A design combining both long and short elements mounted on a single mast will provide reception of FM broadcasts and both VHF and UHF television. Prices will vary, but they are proportionate to the number of elements in the antenna design.

Select your antenna on the basis of the range needed for your part of the country. Consider a roof-mounted antenna a *must* for color program reception if your home is twenty-five to fifty miles from the nearest stations. At the same distance, the built-in or "rabbit-ear" antenna will serve for black-and-white reception.

If you are switching from a black-and-white to a color set, your old antenna *may* provide satisfactory reception. But remember that a worn antenna, particularly one designed for black-and-white reception, will deteriorate the picture or cut out some of the color signal. The best solution is to try the color set with the old antenna; if you don't get a good picture, have a new antenna installed. In any case, you will want to get an authoritative opinion from your reputable dealer or service organization. Top-quality picture and sound reception is dependent upon other factors in addition to the type of antenna you choose. Experience with coping with all the variables of reception in your area is essential — this is yet another reason to choose your dealer with care.

Some dealers provide "installation and set up" for color sets at no extra charge. This means attaching the set to an existing antenna, making any necessary minor adjustments and introducing you to the operation of your set. This is an added and worthwhile convenience, *if it is included in the price of the set.*

Tires

(See also AUTOMOBILES)

TIRE BUYING
Changing tire technology is not likely to simplify the marketplace for the consumer. On the contrary, warns one veteran retailer of a large chain-store corporation, there will be more consumer information to absorb about a wider variety of products available in an already varied field.

Wise buyers do not make buying decisions on the basis of simplistic standards such as price alone or the notion of some undefined "best." The former is not an adequate standard for a decision which can affect the safety of the entire family, and the latter often translates "best" into the most expensive product.

Shoppers should consider basing their tire-buying decisions on:

1. Knowledge of the products available and the differences in materials and construction that affect safety, ride quality and wear;
2. A realistic idea of the demands to be made on the product; and
3. An understanding of the product warranty.

The "best" tire for the in-town driver of a compact car will be very different from the product needed by the long-distance driver of a heavily loaded station wagon.

Be sure to:

- ☐ Check your owner's manual, which should give you tips on how to match tires to the car and to the *maximum weight* the car will carry.
- ☐ Make a realistic assessment of the kind of driving you do over what kinds of roads. Interstate highways, rural roads and city streets all make different demands on your tires.
- ☐ Consider your driving habits. High speed, jackrabbit starts and quick stops will tax your tires more than gentle driving.
- ☐ Consider your expectations. How long do you *really* intend to use these tires?

Shop for the retailer as well as for the product. Check consumer-research and product-rating publications. If you need help to choose among several retailers, secure reports on their complaint records from your local Better Business Bureau.

TIRE CONSTRUCTION
The basic types of tire construction are:

- **Bias ply tires,** which have been used since the 1920s, are constructed in layers. The cords in the plies which make up the body of the tire cross one another at about 30° to 40° angles to the center line. Cords may be arranged in two, four or more (even number) plies, depending on the strength desired in the finished product. This design builds strength and rigidity into both sidewall and tread, but bias tires tend to "squirm" on the road and they run hotter than either belted bias or radial tires.
- **Belted bias tires** have the same crisscross cord pattern as bias ply products, but an additional two or more layers of fabric (belts) are located between body and tread.

  This construction method provides sidewall rigidity similar to that of the bias tire, and the belts provide increased strength and stiffness in the tread. These tend to run cooler and therefore are likely to last longer than the bias ply tire.

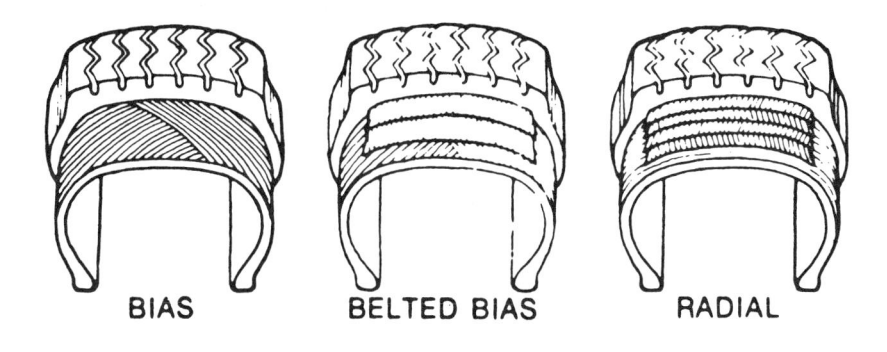

BIAS   **BELTED BIAS**   **RADIAL**

- **Radial tires** have reinforcing cords extending from bead (the point when the tire touches the rim) to bead around the tire, and may contain from one to three plies. Over the radial section is an additional belt, containing up to four plies, with cords angled at about 15° to the center line.

  Radials provide great strength and rigidity in the tread area. Sidewalls are so flexible that even when these tires are fully inflated they look as though they need air. You can expect long wear and greater resistance to damage resulting from impact in the tread area. Because radial tires have lower rolling resistance, they are more responsive than the traditional bias tires and therefore provide a slight amount of fuel economy for long distance open highway driving.

  Remember: Radials should never be mixed with other types of

tires. Differences in construction result in differing road-holding and handling characteristics.

Belt materials used in radials include steel, fiberglass and rayon. A fourth fiber, Aramid, was introduced in 1974 and has replaced steel in some tires. (Aramid is the first fiber developed specifically for use in tires. The others have been adapted to tire construction.)

Beginning with the 1982 model year, the **radial** is the only type of tire available as original equipment on passenger cars sold in the U.S.

BEFORE YOU RE-TIRE

Unevenly worn or bald tires cannot provide adequate traction and are vulnerable to punctures and blow-outs. Check your tires for tread wear on a regular basis. It is easy to do because, since 1968, "tread wear indicators" have been required for all passenger car tires. These appear as continuous bars across the entire tread of the tire when the pattern has been worn down to the last 1/16 of an inch.

You can check tread depth by using a penny (*see below*). If the top of Lincoln's head shows, the tires have less than 1/16 of an inch of tread left and should be replaced.

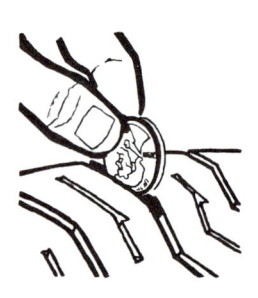

When you install new tires, have your mechanic make sure that:

- ☐ Your car's front end alignment is correct. Improper alignment produces a unique "feathered" wear pattern at the edge of the tread design.
- ☐ The brakes are operating properly. Poorly adjusted brakes can cause tires to wear unevenly. Out-of-round brake drums can cause excessive wear in a single spot.
- ☐ Worn wheel bearings, shock absorbers and ball joints or tie-rods, all of which can cause your wheels to be loose or wobbly, have been repaired or replaced.
- ☐ All wheels are in balance.

When you buy, whether you duplicate the original equipment tires that came with your car or choose among the approved options recommended by the automobile or tire manufacturer, *never* select tires

smaller than the originals. *Information you need at replacement time is molded into the sidewalls or your tires.* For instance:
- ☐ **185/70 HR-14:** The figure "185" is the tire's width in millimeters; "70" is the "aspect ratio" — it means that the height of the tire from the bead to the tread surface is approximately 70 percent of the tire's width. The lower the aspect ratio, the wider the cross section and the wider the tread. "H" is part of a European performance rating system for which, unfortunately, there is no useful American equivalent. "R" means radial construction. The figure "14" simply means that the tire goes on a 14-inch rim.
- ☐ **Load Range B:** The load range designation may be on the inner side of the tire. The letter B indicates a four-ply rating. As letters progress in the alphabet, load range increases. *D*, for example, would be the same as the former eight-ply rating.
- ☐ **Max. load 1,500 lbs. @ 32 psi maximum pressure:** The tire's load limit is 1,500 pounds; 32 psi (pounds per square inch) is the maximum cold inflation.
- ☐ **4 plies under tread (2 nylon + 2 polyester cord); sidewall 2 plies nylon cord.** This identifies the materials used in your tire — they will vary (see "Tire Construction," p. 343).
- ☐ **DOT 000 000000:** The letters DOT certify compliance with U.S. Department of Transportation safety standards. Adjacent to this symbol is the tire identification number including the tire manufacturer's code; the remaining numbers identify tire size, type and date of manufacture.
- ☐ **Tubeless, tube-type** or **radial:** This identifies the construction.

In a product area in which rapid technological change is to be expected, hard and fast rules cannot be formulated for consumers to follow. Wise buyers will be well advised, however, to collect as much current information as possible *before* replacements become absolutely necessary, in order to avoid the necessity of making quick, uninformed decisions.

The following checklist will help with tire maintenance and purchase choice:
- ☐ Maintain the correct tire inflation pressure.
- ☐ Keep your car's front end in proper alignment.
- ☐ Choose replacement tires with care. Shop around, ask for advice, and get the tire that fits your own individual driving needs.
- ☐ Make sure that newly purchased tires are balanced on the wheel before installing them on your car. Have brakes and shock absorbers checked.
- ☐ When you buy new tires, make sure that the seller records the identification numbers of the tire and your name and address. These records are required by federal regulation for use in case your tires are recalled.
- ☐ Check the warranty. Get it in writing and make sure you understand the manufacturer's replacement policy (see WARRANTIES).

Toys

(See also SAFETY)

TOYS ARE SERIOUS business. Just ask any participant in this more than $5 billion-per-year segment of the economy.

At their best, toys are carefully constructed and equally carefully researched to make a real contribution to a child's physical and intellectual development.

"Good" toys need not be expensive. They can be ordinary household equipment such as pots and pans, measuring cups and strong cardboard boxes. Or they can be specially constructed nursery-school equipment or expensive department-store purchases. *The most important objective to keep in mind for toy purchases, however, is that children learn to relate to the world through play.* The play area and its equipment can communicate fun, safety and security. Toys can help youngsters learn to control and manipulate equipment and objects; they can also foster creativity. Toys should be fun, safe and satisfying.

Use age guidelines and child's own interests when choosing toys.

Until the age of about eighteen months, children are so busy learning basic physical coordination that they don't need a great variety of toys. Moving about will be a favorite amusement/learning process — riding, walking and exploring surfaces, textures and tastes occupy the child. At this age children tend to have more toys than they need, simply because toys are fun to buy. Sturdy, washable cuddle toys, nesting boxes (or measuring cups) for manipulating, and soft, safe balls for throwing and retrieving are good at this age.

From eighteen months to two years, the get-into-everything stage occurs, and the play area is wherever the parent-in-charge happens to be at any given time. Use a variation of Murphy's law: Assume that anything that can be pulled, pushed, moved and bitten *will* be. Whether the child *should* pull and bite lamp cords is irrelevant. Pull-and-push toys are good additions to play equipment at this age, as are colorful cloth books. Cuddle toys, dolls and stuffed animals will be carried, hugged, chewed and thrown. The child will begin to imitate adult activities such as reading, dusting, sweeping and gardening.

Between two and three years of age, expect a great deal of "testing" behavior, when the child looks for limits and boundaries in his environment and behavior. Attention span will increase. At this age, add play equipment that can be pounded, hammered and manipulated, such as a pounding board with its own lightweight hammer, nontoxic modeling clay (look for the label) and beads to string. Movable toys such as wagons and riding equipment can be added; blocks, too, though building activity comes later. (At this stage the child will be more likely to place the blocks in a wagon, move them, dump them and start the process over again.) It is important to add books, stories and songs at this age. Listening to simple stories will help the child learn to communicate.

Between three and five, children learn to communicate and socialize with the peer group, use toys cooperatively and share them. They dramatize and imitate adult activities, like to "dress up" in adult clothing and pretend costumes. Introduce creative play materials from about the age of three: water colors, large sheets of newsprint for painting, modeling materials, collage materials, including various shapes of pasta, varied-textured fabrics, old magazines to cut up, colored paper and library paste. Books should still be important.

When you buy games and play equipment, check the manufacturers' recommendations for the suitable age range. Many reputable manufacturers test the toys they sell and label them as accurately as research allows. Don't buy a chemistry set or a mechanical toy meant for a nine-year-old for your brilliant five-year-old unless you are sure your child can handle it, or unless you are sure it will only be used with adult supervision. *Use your own judgment and exercise careful supervision.*

Although the Consumer Product Safety Commission has the power to ban dangerous toys from the marketplace *after they have been proved dangerous,* there is no way to inspect every toy on the market for safety. What is perfectly safe for the older children in the family may be hazardous to the two-year-old.

Safety check all toys
- ☐ For toys bought for younger children, look for wires, pins, buttons in and on stuffed animals and dolls that can be removed and swallowed.
- ☐ Look for sharp edges, points and wires that can cause cuts.
- ☐ Be wary of toys that can be dismantled and improperly used.
- ☐ Look for labels on brightly colored toys that assure you that paints and finishes are nontoxic.
- ☐ Carefully check the stability of all riding toys; these should have a low center of gravity, a side wheelbase and an easy-to-handle steering mechanism.
- ☐ Outdoor play equipment for all ages should be carefully checked and carefully installed for stability. Check swings and slides for sturdy construction and dangerous sharp edges.

Travel, Travel Agents

AMERICANS SPEND BILLIONS of dollars each year traveling in the United States and abroad. Good planning is a factor in making vacation travel a delight, whether you choose to be your own travel agent or to use the services of a professional.

If you use the services of a travel agent, you are buying a service, and the choice of that travel agent should begin with references.

Friends and business associates can tell you—often at great length—of the competence or incompetence, good judgment or ineptitude of people who have helped to plan their vacations. Start with these references, and when you have an idea of two or three travel agencies that interest you, then check with the Better Business Bureau.

These are the services travel agencies offer:

- Arrangements, including reservations, for air, sea, bus and rail travel, cruises, car rentals and car purchases abroad.
- Preparation of individual itineraries and arrangements for package tours and for personally escorted tours or group tours, within the United States and abroad.
- Information on such important details as travel and luggage insurance, visas, passports, inoculations, travelers' checks, currency exchange, the weather, a practical wardrobe, etc.

To provide efficient assistance, the travel agent will need to have a good idea of your travel budget and your special interests.

In order to avoid later misunderstandings, you should be sure to find out which of the agent's services you are expected to pay for. There is likely to be a charge for such complex services as arranging group or individual tours and itineraries. There may be a charge for reservation services, but *only* when no commission is paid the agent by the carrier or the hotel. (Airlines and many hotels pay the agent a commission; most railroads and some hotels do not.)

When you use a travel agent, you have every right to assume:

- That the tour and its accommodations will be exactly as they were represented — the ocean-front hotel will be on the beach instead of a mile away, that a first-class reservation gets you a first-class compartment on the train.

Consider the line that appears (in small print) in many tour brochures: *We reserve the right to change accommodations without prior notice.* No one would mind changing accommodations if the facilities are at least equal to those originally contracted for. But what happens if your luxury hotel has no room for you? If you find yourself in a fourth-rate hotel, do you get a pro-rata refund? From whom? And under what circumstances?

- That the charges you pay will match the charges you expected. Unexpected charges can wreck your carefully planned budget.
- That your charter flight will actually get off the ground at the promised time of departure (barring, of course, impossible flying weather, mechanical difficulties or airport strikes).

Surety and escrow

It is important that you know what these two words mean in relation to air charters.

Surety bonds are required to guarantee that the charter is run and the contractors are paid.

Escrow accounts are deposit accounts in a bank maintained by the charter operator which protect passenger funds until the charter is completed.

Before you make your decision to sign up for a charter, find out if there is a surety bond or escrow account established, and to whom payment is made. If you have to sign a contract, make sure it specifies that you pay directly to the escrow account at the bank, and not to the organizer. Also be sure you know the names of both the insurance company that is providing the surety bond and the bank in which the escrow account is maintained.

AIR CHARTERS

In the past travelers who wanted to take advantage of lower prices for air charter tours were faced with an alphabet soup of different charter plans. That has changed. Now among the charters available are:

- **Advance Booking Charters (ABC)** offer a fixed price and a fixed date for a round trip or one-way charter flight. These are not recurring regularly scheduled flights, therefore signup is usually at least fifteen days in advance. There is a discount if you book early.
- **Travel Group Charters (TGC)** operate similarly to Advance Booking Charters except that in an ABC the organizer takes a risk in meeting costs; on a Travel Group Charter, the organizer earns a set fee. Vacant seats on the plan may increase the price for each passenger.
- **Affinity or pro-rated charters** are designed to serve the needs of organized groups whose members have a prior "affinity" or

GETTING MORE FOR YOUR MONEY

association. If the flight does not sell out, those who do not participate in the flight may absorb the cost of the empty seats.

Your rights as an air traveler are important to you.

- [ ] If an airline overbooks your flight and has to "bump" passengers with confirmed reservations, it is required by CAB regulations to ask for volunteers to give up their seats. If you volunteer the airline must offer to pay you for your cooperation. How much they offer is up to them.
- [ ] If there are too few volunteers and you are involuntarily bumped, the airline must give you immediately *denied boarding compensation* of from $75 to $400, depending on the price of your ticket. If the airline can get you alternate transportation that arrives at your destination within two hours of your originally scheduled arrival time (four hours on international flights), the airline still has to pay you — but at half the above rate. This compensation is in addition to the passenger's ticket, which can be used on another flight or refunded. Compensation is not due you, however, if you are bumped as the result of the need to change to a smaller plane, if the government requisitions space on your flight or you are offered a seat on your original flight but in a different section than specified on your ticket. Also, you get no compensation if you have failed to comply with ticketing, check-in or reconfirmation procedures.
- [ ] If your flight is canceled, the airline is obligated to get you on the next available flight to your destination — using another airline, if necessary.
- [ ] If you are delayed more than four hours or your flight is canceled through the airline's fault, most airlines will provide you with:
    — a free hotel room if the delay occurs between 10:00 P.M. and 6:00 A.M. — unless you are in your home city.
    — ground transportation to your hotel or home.
    — a free meal, if a meal would have been provided on the flight.
    — usually one long-distance call or telegram.

If you have a complaint
If your hotel turns out to be twenty-five miles away from the music festival, the ski slopes or the beach . . . if the quality of the accommodations doesn't measure up to your expectations, bring it to the attention of the travel agent immediately. If you are not satisfied with the response, get in touch with your local Better Business Bureau. If the travel agency is a member of the American Society of Travel Agents (ASTA), you can also register your complaint with them. Their address is: 711 Fifth Avenue, New York, New York 10022.

Typewriters

YOUR TYPEWRITER WILL be a long-term addition to the efficiency of your office or home. Choose it with care.

Try a variety of makes and models in a variety of stores before you make a final decision on which one to buy. Look for the one that "feels" right to you.

Electric or manual? Initial costs vary widely. Some manual models cost as much as some electrics. (The advantage of these price variations is that, within any given price range, there are a good number of options available.) However, electric typewriters cost more to operate and may require more frequent and more expensive servicing than manual models.

The decision between the electric and manual models should be based on two major factors:

- ☐ **How much will you use it?** The electrics are less tiring to operate over long periods of time.
- ☐ **For what purpose?** Material produced by an electric typewriter is likely to have a cleaner, more even and professional appearance.

Some electric typewriters feature a small, globe-shaped element containing all type characters, making typing fast and easy. This type of typewriter has no carriage, and therefore no vibration or machine movement. Type styles can be changed by lifting off one element and replacing it with another, enabling you to choose the type style best suited to each typing job. In using a typewriter equipped with these elements, be sure to follow the use and maintenance instructions provided with the machine and/or elements.

Portable or office size? Some portable typewriters are about as easy to move as the old "portable" television sets — that is, you can move them if you *must*. Many are too heavy (over thirty pounds with case) to be carried easily. If you need a typewriter to travel with you, carefully compare weights and operating efficiency. Consult current product-rating publications for information on comparable models.

If your office at home is in a permanent, organized location, you may find the standard office-size machine is practical and, perhaps, easier to use than a portable.

Consider a used typewriter. Some of the older office-size manual models seem to have been built for the ages. Look for older models on sale in office equipment stores; check the operating action (which is often surprisingly good), the price, the dealer's warranty *and* the dealer's reputation with the BBB.

The major advantage of these older manual models is that they are virtually maintenance-free, aside from occasional professional cleaning.

WHEN YOU BUY
- ☐ Take as much time as you need to make an informed decision. You will want to use the typewriter for years, so be fussy. Insist on trying a wide variety of makes and models in your price range.
- ☐ Compare warranties. Make sure you understand the terms of the warranty: know whether it is "full" or "limited" and what action you must take to have the equipment repaired (see WARRANTIES).
- ☐ Choose your dealer carefully, keeping in mind the fact that your warranty is only as reliable as the dealer who must comply with it. If the typewriter turns out to be defective or needs frequent repair, is the dealer capable of providing the necessary service? (Check with your local Better Business Bureau to determine the complaint-handling record of local dealers.)
- ☐ If you choose a second-hand typewriter, be sure to check it thoroughly (or have it checked by a professional) before you buy.

CARE AND MAINTENANCE
Care of your typewriter will contribute to its long life and help to keep service costs to a minimum. Read your owner's manual carefully (this is especially important if you choose an electric model).

These general care instructions apply to all typewriters:

- ☐ Always keep your typewriter covered when it is not in use. Continued exposure to dust and moisture can shorten the life of both electric and manual models.
- ☐ Keep your typewriter clean. To clean the type face, use a small brush and commercial-type cleaner or plastic cleaning clay. Use *light* strokes; a little effort goes a long way.
- ☐ If you use an eraser to make corrections, move the carriage to the extreme right or left to keep eraser grit out of the mechanism.
- ☐ If you use a correction liquid, make sure the corrected area is completely dry before you type over it. Correction liquid that is *not* allowed to dry thoroughly can form deposits on the platen, type faces and/or rollers and clog the moving parts of the machine.
- ☐ The platen, and the feed rolls below it, need occasional cleaning. Check your owner's manual for instructions.
- ☐ Most manufacturers recommend that typewriters be adjusted, serviced and lubricated by a trained technician at least once a year. If you do a great deal of typing, more frequent servicing may be necessary.

Vacuum Cleaners

(See also WARRANTIES)

VACUUM CLEANERS ARE available in three basic types:

- ☐ **The upright model** is specifically designed for cleaning rugs and carpets. A rotating brush or bar "agitates" the carpet surface, creating vibration which loosens dirt and dust from the pile. The suction (air flow) removes the litter and carries it into the dust bag.
- ☐ **The canister/tank type** uses suction produced by a motor-driven fan to clean. It is effective for thorough cleaning of uncarpeted surfaces, for general floor care and for above-the-floor cleaning. These models are usually lightweight and easy to use.
- ☐ **The combination vacuum cleaner** adds the powered agitator head (powered rug nozzle) to the canister-tank models.

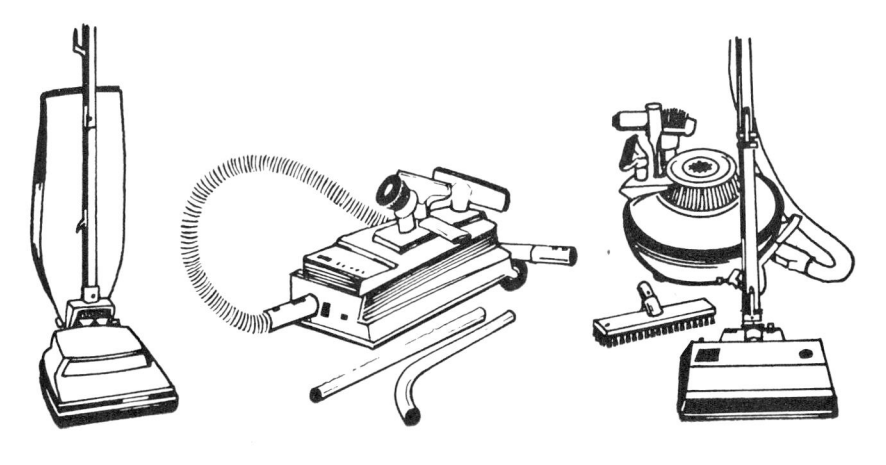

Upright model   Combination vacuum   Canister/tank type

In addition:

- ☐ **Small portable vacuum cleaners and electric brooms** are variations of these three basic models; both are primarily suction cleaners.

For thorough, all-round cleaning the use of two cleaners — upright and canister — may be required for many homes, although the kits of attachments that come with many cleaners add to their versatility and may alleviate the need for two different models.

WHEN YOU BUY

- ☐ Choose the cleaner that suits the kind of cleaning you must do *now*, instead of the model that will be right for the fully carpeted home you will have *some day*.
- ☐ When you shop for an upright model, you should try it out in the store. Push it around on a carpeted surface. Does it feel "right" for you?
- ☐ Take into consideration the amount of storage space it will require, as you should do when you buy any piece of household equipment.
- ☐ How about extra features? Does the cleaner you have in mind come with an automatic cord winder? A headlight to help you uncover dirt in dark corners? Do you need them?
- ☐ Check the size of the disposable bag. Is it large enough so that it will not have to be changed frequently?
- ☐ How about the configuration of the cleaner? Does the dirt fall *down* into the dustbag, or does it have to push *up* under the weight of existing dirt? The downward action saves wear on the motor and enables the bag to hold more.

Always:

- ☐ Insist on seeing the warranty before you buy.
- ☐ Read the instruction book that comes with the cleaner *before* you use it.
- ☐ Choose the dealer as carefully as you choose the appliance. Check his reputation with friends, neighbors and the Better Business Bureau.

SALES TACTICS

- ☐ Beware of high-pressure sales tactics. If a salesperson offers you a "once-in-a-lifetime low price" if you buy his merchandise immediately, he may be hoping to talk you into signing a contract to buy his merchandise before you have an opportunity to compare prices and services in other stores or from other salespeople.
- ☐ Never allow a door-to-door salesperson to leave merchandise you do not intend to buy in your home overnight. He may not return to pick it up, and you may have bought a problem. (See DOOR-TO-DOOR SELLING; FRAUD AND DECEPTION.) Remember your rights under the three-day "cooling-off period" regulations.

Warranties

THE WARRANTY backing a product has always been an important factor in product purchase decisions. Now that the **Magnuson—Moss Consumer Product Warranties/Federal Trade Commission Improvement Act** has redefined the term and set standards for warranties, they may be more important than ever.

This warranty legislation has three basic purposes:

1. To make consumer product warranties easier to understand;
2. To prevent deceptive warranty practices; and
3. To limit the use of disclaimers of implied warranties.

The significance of the new legislation to consumers was well illustrated by the results of a 1974 study by the House Subcommittee on Commerce and Finance. Of the two hundred or so warranties from fifty-one major firms that were examined by the Subcommittee staff, only *one* of the firms offered a warranty free of all exemptions, limitations and disclaimers.

Anyone who has ever experienced the frustration involved in attempting to secure in-warranty service from a reluctant-to-serve retailer or dealer is familiar with the limitations contained in many warranties. The quality of the service provided by a retailer or dealer, as most consumers know, is as important as the quality of the warranty. Nevertheless, it is important to know the basics of the law.

HOW DOES COST AFFECT COVERAGE BY FEDERAL LAW?

1. No-dollar limit situations

Any consumer product, regardless of cost, is sold with "implied warranties" attached to it, unless (in most states) the seller informs the buyer in writing that these implied warranties do not apply and gives no written warranty on the product. Also, any warranty offered to the public on any consumer product is subject to Section 5 of the FTC Act, which prohibits deceptive and misleading business practices

> The terms *warranty* and *guarantee* have been interchangeable, but to reduce the potential for confusion in the marketplace, the Federal Trade Commission suggests (but does not require) that *warranty* be used for the written document that accompanies the products you purchase.

in general. (Examples of deceptive warranties include those that make the warranty applicable at "the sole discretion of the seller" or those that require a service or replacement fee so great as to make the warranty meaningless.)

Any business that offers or serves as a conduit for any warranty or guarantee to the buying public is well advised to review all of its guarantees and warranties to make sure they say exactly what they mean.

Moreover, *no written warranty may disclaim or modify* implied warranties, although any "limited warranty" (not "full") may limit the duration of implied warranties to the duration of the written warranty — if the period is reasonable, the limitation is conscionable and it is plainly stated on the face of the warranty.

Finally, regardless of product cost, any informal dispute settlement procedure or mechanism that is written into a warranty must comply with the FTC Rule 703 provisions, which went into effect on July 4, 1976 (40 Fed. Reg. 60218).

2. Products costing more than $5*

Warranties on consumer items costing more than $5 may not contain a "tie-in" provision — the purchase or use of a service or another product — in order for the written warranty to stay in force. For example:

> "This warranty will be honored only if you use X-46-A motor oil in the motor at all times," or "only if serviced by us."

If the Federal Trade Commission specifically approves such a "tie-in" provision, it may be used. Any such "tie-in" service or product may be required by a warranty if the business provides them at no charge.

When and if the FTC deems it appropriate, it may write additional regulations affecting the over-$5 products. These could include rules for automatically extending warranty periods when products or warrantors have not performed according to the warranty; for the advertising of warranties including point-of-sale information and materials; and for warranty provisions that may be "incorporated by reference" (a shorthand referral to a longer provision) in written warranties. (The FTC may set a higher dollar threshold for these rules on the premise that no substantial consumer harm is caused by the warranties on products costing less.)

---

*NOTE: For all price thresholds under the Magnuson-Moss law, the product must — exclusive of tax — actually cost more than the threshold amount; and if lesser costing items are packaged and sold together so as not to permit a breaking of the package, and for an amount greater than the threshold price, the package is covered by the law. Also, each written warranty on the product falling within a particular threshold must comply with the requirements that apply to all warranties and to any lower threshold requirements, as well as those special requirements for its own threshold level. For purposes of the federal warranty law, the three threshold prices or price ranges to be concerned about are those products retailing for $5, $10, $15 or more.

> A "warranty in writing against defect or malfunction of a consumer product" means:
>
> ☐ Any written affirmation of fact or written promise made at the time of sale by a supplier to a purchaser which relates to the nature of the material or workmanship of a product and affirms or promises that such material or workmanship is defect-free or will meet a specific level of performance over a specified period of time; or
>
> ☐ Any undertaking in writing to refund, repair, replace or take other remedial action with respect to the sale of a consumer product if such product fails to meet the specifications set forth in the undertaking.
>
> It is understood that the written promise becomes part of the basis of the bargain between the supplier and the purchaser.

3. $10 products
Any written warranty issued on a consumer product costing more than $10 must be clearly titled either "full" or "limited," and a "full" warranty must also state its period of coverage or duration in the title (e.g., "Full 10-Year Warranty"). Businesses should note that they will be subject also to all requirements of a "full" warranty if they call a warranty "full" for a product costing less than $10. Even language such as "fully guaranteed" may bring a product under this provision.

4. The $15 threshold
By rule, the FTC has established a $15 threshold that was not specifically set by the law. Warranties on covered products costing more than $15 must follow the FTC's rule on disclosing terms and conditions (*see next section*) and on presale availability. These rules apply to all warranties on products made in 1977 or later.

WHAT WARRANTY TERMS AND CONDITIONS MUST BE DISCLOSED?
The terms and conditions required on a single warranty document covering consumer products that cost more than $15 are:

1. Which parts, products and characteristics (e.g., "fading") are covered and which are not covered;
2. What the company will or will not do if the product does not live up to the warranty;
3. When the warranty goes into effect (if not the purchase date) and how long it lasts;
4. A step-by-step procedure for a customer to get satisfaction under the warranty, including whom to contact, where to go, whether to mail the product or bring it in person, anything else the customer

must do (in addition, the name of the warrantor must be given together with either the warrantor's address, the address of the retail outlet, or a special no-charge telephone number for the customer to get such information on what to do);
5. The statement, which may not be paraphrased or changed, as follows: "This warranty gives you specific legal rights, and you may have other rights that vary from state to state."

Depending on what a business writes into its warranty, the following limitations or disclosures must also be in the warranty:

1. Who benefits from the warranty if there are any limitations, such as a warranty that applies only to the original purchaser;
2. Information on an "informal dispute settlement mechanism," if one is provided;
3. Limitations on the length of implied warranties, if any (such a limitation must also state, without paraphrasing, that "Some states do not allow limitations on how long an implied warranty lasts, so the above limitation may not apply to you");
4. Exclusions or limitations on incidental or consequential damages, if any (such an exclusion or limitation must also state, without paraphrasing, that "Some states do not allow the exclusion or limitation of incidental or consequential damages, so the above limitation or exclusion may not apply to you"); and
5. If an "owner's registration card" or the like must be returned to get warranty coverage, the warranty must state that fact, and conversely, if something like a warranty card accompanies the product and need not be returned for coverage, this too must be disclosed.

WARRANTIES

The trade regulation rules shore up the consumer's right to know the warranty provisions by requiring manufacturers and sellers to make warranty information available at the point of sale. This information can be attached to the warranted product, in a nearby poster or in a special catalog of warranties advertised by the merchant.

WARRANTIES AND RESPONSIBILITIES

Many reputable firms have, for many years, gone farther than trade regulations require in an effort to please their customers. Many firms have, as a matter of course, checked their advertising for accuracy, made product information available, and have not only provided clear, explicit warranties but have lived up to them.

Consumers are well aware that less concerned, less responsible firms have failed to show adequate consideration to their customers.

It is still important to distinguish between these two kinds of operators in the marketplace. Although legislation sets ground rules for operation, information and legal sanctions for those firms that disregard the rules, consumers still owe it to themselves to shop carefully and to choose dealers of goods and services with as much care as they choose products.

Consider the quality of the service department that will be responsible for in-warranty repair of purchases as carefully as you look for quality and as carefully as you evaluate price in relation to service. If a local dealer or service affiliate has been reluctant to or incapable of providing effective service in the past, this factor should play a part in where-to-buy decisions.

Check the record maintained at your local Better Business Bureau. Keep informed on the regulations governing warranties, and follow these guidelines:

☐ Don't wait until a product fails or needs repair to find out how good the warranty is. *The time to become familiar with the terms of the warranty is before you buy the item.*

☐ Comparing warranties should be an important part of the shopping process. Comparing the reliability of the company behind the warranty is equally important. Also, don't be misled by the terms "limited" or "full" on a warranty, because some "limited" warranties will afford more protection than some "full" warranties. For example, a "full" warranty can only be issued on a product when the warrantor can assure service everywhere in the U.S. Some smaller manufacturers may not have this capability but their warranty may be better if you stay in the area where you bought the product.

☐ Warranties should be in writing. A businessman who is unwilling to put his promises in writing is not the person to deal with.

☐ Check written warranties to see whether these key points are covered:

—What is covered? The entire product or only certain parts? Is the warranty *full* or *limited*?
—Whom do you call for in-warranty repairs? The manufacturer? The dealer? A service agency?
—Must repairs be made by a "factory representative" or "authorized dealer" service to keep the warranty in effect? If the answer is yes, is such a repair center located near you?
—Who pays shipping charges for merchandise returned for repair?
—Who pays for parts? For labor?
—How long does the warranty last on the entire product? On parts and assemblies?
—If pro-rata reimbursement is provided, what is the basis for it? The time you have owned the product? Usage? Original cost?
—If the warranty provides for a refund of a defective product, do you get the refund in cash or in credit toward a replacement?
—Will a substitute product be provided for your use while yours is being repaired?

Remember . . .
- Before you use a product, read the owner's manual or instruction sheet. Follow the operating instructions and be sure that any specific routine maintenance or service is done as suggested or required by the warranty.
- Keep your warranty and the sales receipt for future reference. Make a note of the date of purchase and the date of installation. Register your appliance or other purchase with the card provided. Also, keep a record of the dates of all in-warranty repair work.
- Your best guarantee of a good warranty is the care you take in making your purchase.

Watches

(See also PRICES AND SALES; WARRANTIES)

WATCHES ON TODAY'S MARKET run the gamut from inexpensive (and remarkably accurate) work-a-day products to expensive and elegantly designed pieces of jewelry to precision instruments used for special-purpose wear for activities such as piloting aircraft and deep-sea diving.

Whatever kind of watch interests you, especially if you need and intend to pay for accuracy and durability, *check the warranty before you buy.* Look for these key points:

- What is covered? The entire product? Only certain parts?
- How long does the warranty period last? *Make sure the warranty period begins with the date of puchase by you, not the date it was purchased by the jeweler.*
- Is there a provision for replacement of the merchandise if it turns out to be incurably inaccurate? If repeated adjustments are necessary? In short, if you buy a lemon, will the manufacturer replace it?
- Remember that all warranty provisions must be in writing to be meaningful. Oral warranties last as long as it takes to say, "Just bring it back if you have a problem." Anybody who refuses to put a warranty in writing is *not* the one to deal with.

Many of today's modern watches are of the **digital-display variety.** There are two basic types:

- **Light-emitting diode display (LED):** These watches require you to push a button in order to light up the watch dial; they can be easily read in the dark, but are not readable in brilliant outdoor light.
- **Liquid crystal display (LCD):** These watches show the time continuously and don't require that you push a button to check the time. The dial can be seen in normal lighting conditions only and cannot be seen at all in the dark unless an extra light source is built into the watch. This built-in light has to be activated by pushing a button.

Many different kinds of batteries can be used for these watches. Batteries for LED watches usually last about a year; however, the life of the battery depends on how many times the button is pushed to light the dial. LCD watches generally require less battery power, therefore the battery lasts longer. *Be sure to have a jeweler or trained professional replace the battery of an LCD or LED digital watch.* Never put a hearing aid battery in a watch. It's very important that the battery be of the right *type* for the watch. The battery size alone does not necessarily determine the fit. Use these DO's and DON'Ts for watch selection and use:

- ☐ DO check traditional watches for the number of jewels they contain. A good watch has a minimum of seventeen jewels, the function of which is to eliminate and to guard against wear by replacing metal-to-metal contact of constantly moving parts with more durable material. (Watch jewels are synthetic with an intrinsic value of only a few cents each, so that they do not in themselves add to the cost of the watch.)
- ☐ DON'T judge quality by price (see PRICES AND SALES). Good watches range in price from under fifty dollars to thousands of dollars. Special features, such as day-and-date mechanisms, can increase the initial cost of the watch as well as the cost of repair and maintenance as well.
- ☐ DO follow use and care instructions to the letter. Misuse, such as treating a water-resistant watch as if it were waterproof, can nullify your warranty. Manufacturers suggest that all watches — including electronic models — should have a maintenance check at least every two years. This is especially so for watches that are subjected to hard wear and frequent exposure to dust and dirt.
- ☐ DO some comparison shopping before you buy at a "discount" price. Some discounters advertise wildly inflated "list prices" to give you the impression that you are getting the bargain of a lifetime.
- ☐ DO buy from a reputable dealer who stands behind his or her merchandise. Check with the BBB.

Water-Conditioning Equipment

WATER-CONDITIONING EQUIPMENT "softens" — that is, removes minerals — from the household water supply. Before you buy or rent a water conditioner of any kind it is important to make sure you need it. To find out how "hard" your tap water really is, check with the local water company. If you have your own water supply, send a sample to a testing laboratory (or to your state Department of Health) for analysis.

Water softeners remove sediment by filtration. Minerals (usually calcium and magnesium) are removed by a process called ion exchange. Standard water-softening appliances remove sediment, hardness and small amounts of iron from the water supply. Other units are available that are geared to remove chlorine and other taste- and odor-producing substances in addition to performing the standard "softening" functions.

No single type of water-conditioning appliance will cure all water problems. If hardness is the major problem, its extent and cause must be determined because these factors are directly related to the size and type of equipment you will need. For example, high iron content may interfere with the operation of a standard water softener; in such cases a special multipurpose water conditioner or an iron removal unit may be required. If your water supply contains sulfur, the same chlorination equipment used for iron will oxidize and remove this element as well.

The size of the water-conditioning equipment you need is dependent on the amount of water you use. Check your water meter to determine the average week's total consumption in cubic feet. To estimate the average daily consumption in gallons, multiply the number of cubic feet by 1.1.

If you have your own unmetered water supply, estimate about fifty gallons a day total water use for each family member.

To estimate the number of gpg (grains per gallon) a water conditioner must remove each day to provide the degree of "softness" you wish, multiply the gpg figure by the total number of gallons consumed each day. Add half as much again to allow for water used by guests, extra laundry, etc. **Remember:** Undersized equipment can create problems of insufficient flow during periods when large quantities of water are needed.

Be sure to get a detailed estimate of equipment, installation and operating costs, preferably from more than one dealer.

GETTING MORE FOR YOUR MONEY

When you choose a water conditioner, use the following checklist:
- ☐ Buy or rent from a dealer who has an established place of business in your community. Service is very important.
- ☐ Make your decision on the basis of detailed estimates of equipment, installation and operating costs.
- ☐ If you buy equipment, check the warranty. Does it provide for full or limited coverage? Of the entire appliance or only specific parts? How long is the warranty period? (See WARRANTIES.)
- ☐ If installation fees are included in the price of the appliance, make sure there will be no extra charge for by-passing lawn- and garden-watering systems, etc.
- ☐ If you rent equipment, see that the rental agreement includes an option to buy.
- ☐ See to it that the sales representative — in-store or at home — answers all your questions in regard to design, functions and cost of the appliance.
- ☐ Make sure you understand the method and cost of recharging the system.

MAINTENANCE AND SERVICE

Whether you buy or rent water-conditioning equipment, find out in advance whether or not the dealer will service it for you. For example, if you choose soft water service, the water-conditioning company merely hooks up a portable appliance to your water line, and periodically replaces the unit with a freshly recharged one. Service is usually recommended for slightly or moderately hard water supplies, or moderate water usage. Those who buy or rent permanently installed water-softening appliances will find them completely automatic, self-recharging and capable of providing a virtually unlimited supply of soft water. These appliances, however, need salt for recharging. You may want to have your dealer deliver and apply this salt on a regular basis for easy maintenance.

Water hardness is measured in terms of the number of grains per gallon (gpg) or parts per million (ppm). According to the U.S. Department of the Interior and the Water Quality Association, degrees of water quality in relation to mineral content can be designated as follows:

Degree of Hardness	Grains per gallon	Parts per million
Soft	Less than 1.0	Less than 17.1
Slightly hard	1 to 3.5	17.1 to 60
Moderately hard	3.5 to 7.0	60 to 120
Hard	7.0 to 10.5	120 to 180
Very hard	10.5 and over	180 and over

Work-at-Home Schemes

MANY PEOPLE THROUGHOUT the United States have a real need for a supplementary income, but find it impossible to hold even a part-time job because family obligations, illness or age keep them at home. To many of these people, the thought of contributing to the family income by engaging in some sort of craft or service they can manage to carry on at home is very attractive. Unfortunately, ads offering work-at-home opportunities for a price are also attractive to these people.

Earn-money-at-home schemes are very profitable for promoters. The schemes all tend to share this attribute: *They require the purchase of equipment or supplies before you can begin work.* If you answer an ad offering "huge profits" for some at-home-work for which there is a "great demand" and which requires "no experience" you will probably end up losing money instead of earning it.

Beware of ads like these:

"Wanted — ladies to mail advertising for our firm. Good pay. No selling or order taking. Address envelopes at home in your spare time. No typing, no selling, no canvassing. We furnish everything . Earn $40 to $60 weekly."

An ad such as this is placed to sell information. For a small fee, usually $1.00, you receive a booklet explaining the offer. You are given a chance to buy unstamped double postcards which offer some product or service — often names plates, baby-shoe bronzing or cosmetics. You mail the postcards to a mailing list you muster up yourself. If any of the cards are filled in with an order, you receive a commission. No money is paid merely for addressing and mailing the cards.

"Women — $100 monthly for doing assembly work at home."

"Men — We pay you $5.00 per hundred gilding greeting cards. Opportunity for beginners; experience unnecessary; no selling."

Ads like these in "Help Wanted" columns do not tell you that you generally have to sell the item yourself. Ads that state "no selling" trick you by stating that the agreement to buy your finished product depends upon the product's being "acceptable" or "up to our standards." Nothing you make is ever "up to standard." Everything is rejected; you must sell whatever you make yourself.

> "Raise chinchillas — a hobby with fabulous profits. Small space in basement, garage, extra room perfect."
>
> "You can make $1,800 per year raising rabbits in your yard or garage."

The pay-off for the promoter in ads like these comes from the sale of breeding animals at very high prices. If they live and multiply, you have the problem of selling the offspring. After all, the promoter doesn't say *he* will buy them from you.

> "Received $9.80 for his 15 cent local newspaper. Clip news items from your local newspapers, worth $1—$5 each."
>
> "Women — do homework in spare time. All kinds. Pleasant, profitable work. Write Box 00000."

These two ads offer "ideas" for setting up home businesses. They usually suggest that you set up a mail-order business or a home-operated newpaper clipping service.

You can get better ideas and more authoritative advice free. Write to the Small Business Administration, Suite 250, 1030 15th Street, Washington, D.C. 20417, and ask for *Bibliography No. 1, Handicrafts and Home Businesses.*

Take care. Homework scheme promoters will:

- ☐ Promise you huge profits and big part-time earnings, but never offer you regular salaried employment.
- ☐ Insist that you pay for instructions or merchandise before they ever tell you how the money-making plan operates.
- ☐ Assure you of guaranteed markets and a huge demand for your handiwork.
- ☐ Tell you that no experience is necessary.
- ☐ Take your money and give you little or nothing in return — except a lot of disappointment.

Your own mail-order business is likely to turn out to be another work-at-home scheme. The following ads are typical of those that promise to make you rich by setting up a profitable mail-order business in your own home:

Remember: If you have to buy anything to get work to be done at home, you are responding to an offer of merchandise for sale. From ideas to rabbits, you can probably get better merchandise at a lower cost.

"These tested, proven mail-order money makers can put you in the rich, fabulous mail-order business overnight — on a shoestring."

"Now you can build a profitable mail-order business on your own the proven way. Use professional mail-order ads. Your own catalogs. Pocket cash profits daily. Don't invest a cent in inventory. Large firms supply advertisements, catalogs and do all shipping for you. Amazing new plan for beginners requires little capital and previous experience. The ideal home business."

These ads are likely to be misleading. The promoter's sole purpose is to sell you something — cheap catalogs listing products with stale or dubious sales appeal and near-worthless oral and printed advice. Beginners who respond to misleading advertising featuring get-rich-quick ideas are not likely to find even a workable get-rich-slow method. What's more, the unscrupulous promoter does not expect them to. *Before you invest, investigate.*

There is no easy solution to the problem of questionable mail-order promotions, but there are some practical safeguards against them. People seeking "employment" and "business opportunities" on a part-time basis should:

- ☐ Study the business they are considering and learn all about its pitfalls as well as its opportunities.
- ☐ Evaluate the risks of establishing any business successfully without prior experience in the field.
- ☐ Investigate the reliability of anyone offering any sales proposition with the local Better Business Bureau.
- ☐ Check the performance claims made for the products involved. Make sure they are supported by competent evidence.
- ☐ Demand proof-of-earnings claims and verify whatever information is secured by direct contact with those whose earnings are reported.
- ☐ Read and understand the terms of any contract or agreement before signing it. Go over it with your lawyer.

When you become a sales agent, you act as an independent business person. Your reputation is at stake. It can be protected only if you are prepared to stand behind the product you sell and the claims made for it.

If You Are Dissatisfied

CONSUMERS HAVE THE RIGHT to expect that they will receive full value for every dollar they spend. But rights and responsibilities are as inseparable as the two sides of a coin. It follows that to secure fundamental consumer rights consumers should accept these responsibilities:

- ☐ Shop with care. Read labels. Evaluate consumer information. Choose dealers and retailers as carefully as you choose products and services.
- ☐ Follow manufacturers' use and care instructions.
- ☐ Speak up. Complain when products fail to perform or service is inadequate. Ask questions when use and care instructions are hard to understand, when advertising leaves questions in your mind, when you need a clear understanding of such essentials as warranty provisions, terms and conditions of a sales contract.

Think of consumer complaints and inquiries as a form of public service. The results of your effective communication with the business community go beyond the obvious personal benefits of resolving an individual complaint or getting an answer to your question. To responsible manufacturers and retailers, consumer complaints are used to signal problem areas in production and/or communication. To consumer service organizations such as the Better Business Bureau, complaint correspondence is an effective indicator of problem areas, providing the Better Business Bureau network with solid evidence of, for example, the need for industry-wide adoption of advertising and selling standards.

WHEN TO COMPLAIN

There are many reasons behind consumer complaints. For example:

- ☐ A food product — fresh, canned or frozen — is defective. It doesn't matter whether the item cost 39 cents or $7.99 — return it. The grocer will probably replace the merchandise or refund your money and make an effort to correct the problem at the

source. If the food is processed, write to the processor.
- ☐ A major appliance requires too many service calls. Why?
- ☐ Gadget X, a small appliance, has never performed properly. The dealer refuses to help.
- ☐ A new knit suit is a size smaller after its first cleaning. Is the cleaner or the fabric to blame?

Because most products meet consumer expectations most of the time, you probably won't need to file complaints very often. Because most retailers and service organizations are honest and interested in keeping their customers, most complaints will probably be resolved at the retail level.

However, if the retailer or service organization cannot or will not assist in arriving at a satisfactory resolution of your complaint, your next step is to contact the manufacturer of the problem product.

HOW TO COMPLAIN
Your clear, concise letter should contain the following information:

- ☐ **What you bought:** Supply information that will enable the company to identify the product — size, color, model number, serial number, etc.
- ☐ **Where you bought it:** Include the complete address of the retailer.
- ☐ **When:** The date of purchase is important.
- ☐ **How you paid for it:** Specify cash, check, credit card or money order. Include copies (*never send originals*) of receipts, canceled checks, sales contract, etc.
- ☐ **Describe the problem:** Be objective; allow the facts to speak for themselves.
- ☐ **What do you want?** State whether you expect a refund, a partial refund, repair or replacement of the product, delivery of merchandise or effective service.

Keep a copy of your letter. You should have a response within three weeks. Even if the problem is not solved in that period of time, you should at least have an acknowledgment from the firm indicating that the matter is being investigated.

If your initial communication fails to elicit action or response, you may want to get help from a third party, your Better Business Bureau. (For addresses of Better Business Bureaus, see pp. 375—379.)

At the state level, consumer protection is often a function of the Office of the Attorney General. Some states have established statewide toll-free telephone lines to receive complaints and requests for information from consumers.

You may also find that help is available from local television stations and newspapers who have assigned special reporters to assist with and report on a wide range of consumer problems.

You can save yourself time and effort if, before requesting assistance from any agency or organization, you make sure that your problem lies within their scope of activities.

The range of services of local consumer protection agencies will vary with the powers and responsibilities included in the enabling legislation, and with the funds budgeted for staff and services. This is true at the state level as well; many states have the "Little FTC Act" — legislation establishing the authority of a state agency to act against unfair and deceptive advertising and trade practices, but the enforcement of this law will also vary according to the administering agency's resources.

A valuable addition to the home filing system might well be a special section devoted to consumer assistance, containing brochures collected from local agencies and organizations describing services available.

Better Business Bureaus respond to inquiries and complaints. They urge consumers to check the reputations of local firms *before* making a purchase or entering into a contract. They do not recommend specific firms, but they do respond to inquiries with information including the number of years the firm has been in business, whether customers have had problems, the nature of the problems and whether and how the firm resolved them. They provide facts from extensive file records; you must draw your own conclusions.

Better Business Bureaus also attempt to resolve consumer complaints through **mediation** — the intervention of an interested, concerned third party. Your complaint must be presented in writing, preferably with *copies* of relevant correspondence (including your original complaint letter). The Bureau will then seek a fair adjustment of the complaint by the business.

The Better Business Bureau system also checks advertising claims, receives complaints concerning advertising, and works with industries to develop standards in advertising and selling (see ADVERTISING).

Better Business Bureaus do not:

- ☐ Handle complaints about the prices of goods and services, *unless the price has been misrepresented;*
- ☐ Appraise or evaluate products. Helping to judge whether one appliance, for instance, is better than another for your purposes is outside the Better Business Bureau's scope of activities. For this kind of information, check consumer research and rating publications available at the local library;
- ☐ Give legal advice or recommendations.

ARBITRATION OF CONSUMER COMPLAINTS

Most Better Business Bureaus have established arbitration programs, adding another step in their handling-of-complaints process beyond the more informal let's-talk-it-over approach of mediation.

Disputed consumer complaints can involve any amount of money and complex arguments on both sides. Some reach a point at which communication is impossible. An alternative to court action at this point is arbitration, in which an impartial third party — the arbitrator — is chosen from a pool of community volunteers to arrive at a resolution of the problem.

Better Business Bureaus use volunteer arbitrators trained in methods and procedures by a representative of the Council of Better Business Bureaus' national program. Volunteers often represent a cross section of the community — with attorneys, homemakers, labor mediators, businessmen and an assortment of other individuals and professionals available to serve.

At a private, informal hearing, each party has the opportunity to present an argument, present supporting documentation and call witnesses. Although parties may be represented by lawyers, they rarely are.

If an inspection of damaged or contested property seems called for, the arbitrator can inspect the property (together with an expert, if necessary), choose to hold the hearing wherever such inspection can take place — in the complainant's front yard, for example. (This is important; in a court case, the judge cannot take time for on-site inspections of property.) If the testimony of expert witnesses or a decision by an independent testing laboratory is required, these services can also be arranged.

The arbitrator's decision (called an *award*) is made quickly and delivered to both parties. The award is final. In virtually all states, an agreement to arbitrate is binding upon both parties and is enforceable by the courts.

WHERE TO GET HELP

In response to consumer complaints about products, service and warranties, complaint-handling mechanisms have been established by three major industries. These are called **Consumer Action Panels** (CAPs) and their functions include:

- receiving and investigating consumer complaints;
- studying industry practices;
- advising manufacturers in their respective fields of ways to improve services to consumers;
- developing and providing consumer information materials.

Their names and addresses are:

AUTOCAP
(Established by new car dealers in over forty metropolitan areas. Check with the National Automobile Dealers Association, 8400 Westpark Drive, McLean, VA 22101 for local addresses.)

Furniture Industry Consumer Action Panel (FICAP)
Box 951
High Point, North Carolina 27261

Major Appliance Consumer Action Panel (MACAP)
20 North Wacker Drive
Chicago, Illinois 60606

SMALL CLAIMS COURT

You may encounter an impossible situation in which you have sustained a loss as a result of some transaction with a recalcitrant businessman who refused to repair or replace defective merchandise, will not answer your letter, ignores correspondence from voluntary consumer protection organizations and says, in effect "Sue me."

In most states small claims courts are established where individuals can sue corporations (or other individuals) without having to hire a lawyer. State laws vary on methods, procedures and on the amount of money for which you can sue. Because of this variation in local law, the best way to find out where and how your state's small claims courts operate is to go to the court house and request information from the clerk of the court. Or call the local Legal Aid Society for information.

In most states the procedure will be something like this: The complainant (you) files the suit in the office of the clerk of the court, usually for a small fee. Be prepared to supply complete, accurate information as to the legal name of the defendant (the person or firm you intend to sue) and a complete address. If you are suing businessman X, remember that the legal name of the firm may be different from the name over the door of the shop. It is your responsibility to get the name right. If you are in doubt, double-check for the legal name in the business records filed in the office of the county clerk.

You must also state your name, your address, the reason for the suit and the amount of money you wish to collect.

The clerk will schedule the trial date and issue a summons (official notification that the suit has been filed and the date of the trial). Expect to pay a fee for the summons and for having it sent by registered mail. If you wish to call witnesses (and if you doubt that they will appear voluntarily) have the clerk issue subpoenas to them.

Both complainant and defendant present their own cases. Lawyers' services are usually unnecessary or not permitted in small claims court. This means you have no legal fees to pay. It also means you must prepare and document your case with care. Correspondence, receipts, canceled checks and other relevant records will all be important to your presentation. You should also spend some time thinking about the testimony of your witnesses. How do you expect them to help you? What points can they clarify for the judge?

Expect court action to be a longer, slower process than arbitration. Court calendars are often crowded. You may wait months for your case to be heard. Nevertheless, you may find the delay, the inconvenience and the time-consuming procedure worthwhile. You will have learned how to use due process of law to recoup your losses and to support a principle. And even if you lose, you learn.

FEDERAL REGULATORY AGENCIES

Federal regulatory agencies play an undeniably important role in the marketplace. Equally important, however, are the operations and activities of consumer groups, industry, state governments and the executive and legislative branches of the federal government.

Organized consumer groups have made their voices heard in the marketplace, creating public demand for and response to consumer-oriented legislation. For example, in response to public demand, the Consumer Product Safety Commission was established in 1972, and the Magnuson—Moss Consumer Product Warranties/Federal Trade Commission Improvements Act came into effect in July 1975 (see WARRANTIES). These are only two examples of the results of the increasingly effective voice of the consumer sector in the complex marketplace.

Federal agencies do not handle individual consumer complaints, though most agencies have established offices of consumer affairs responsible for communicating consumer concerns, consideration of consumer issues and direct response to consumers. Such offices exist in many agencies from the Department of Agriculture to the Department of State.

The following agencies have direct responsibilities in the marketplace.

1. **Office of Consumer Affairs,** 1009 Premier Building, Washington, D.C. 20201: Established to advise and represent the President on consumer interests. Federal activities in the area of consumer protection are coordinated here. In addition, the Office of Consumer Affairs carries on an extensive public information program, conducts investigations, holds conferences and conducts surveys on consumer issues.

2. **Consumer Product Safety Commission (CPSC),** 1111 18th Street, N.W., Washington, D.C. 20207: The commission has the power to:

    ☐ set safety standards for all common household and recreational products;
    ☐ seize and ban hazardous products from the marketplace;
    ☐ ban from the market any product that presents an unreasonable risk of injury;
    ☐ order manufacturers, distributors or retailers to notify purchasers about hazardous products and to repair, replace or refund the cost of such products.

CPSC's enabling legislation defines a consumer product as "any article or component part thereof, produced and distributed for sale to a consumer for use in or around a permanent or temporary household or residence, a school, in recreation... or for the personal use, consumption, or enjoyment of a consumer in or around a permanent or temporary household or residence."

In other words, almost everything you use in your home — except for products regulated by other agencies — is covered by this product safety legislation. Exceptions to CPSC's coverage are: tobacco and tobacco products; motor vehicles and related equipment; economic poisons (pesticides, fungicides, etc.); firearms; aircraft and related equipment; boats and related equipment; and food, drugs and cosmetics.

3. **Federal Trade Commission (FTC),** Washington, D.C. 20580: whose primary responsibility was set forth in enabling legislation as to the maintenance of a free and open marketplace, with jurisdiction over restraint of trade and unfair business practices and false and deceptive advertising. Its responsibilities now include administration of the Fair Packaging and Labeling Act, the Truth-in-Lending and Fair Credit Reporting Acts and warranty regulations (see WARRANTIES).
4. **Food and Drug Administration (FDA),** 5600 Fishers Lane, Rockville, Maryland 20857: responsible for overseeing the marketing of food, drugs, cosmetics and medical devices.
5. **U.S. Postal Inspection Service,** Washington, D.C. 20260: the oldest, and possibly least-known, law enforcement agency in the United States. The Chief Inspector's Office processes more than one hundred thousand complaints of fraudulent use of the mails each year, and conducts more than ten thousand full field investigations annually.

The fact that these and other federal agencies have well-defined consumer responsibilities does not mean that all products in the complex marketplace are inspected, approved or known to federal regulatory agencies. There is no practical system that allows total oversight of the marketplace. Therefore, the consumer's best protection system is knowledge of the system and its operations, and intelligent functioning within the marketplace.

When problems occur, redress mechanisms exist to correct them. *However, the greatest complaint-handling systems available will inevitably be less useful to the individual consumer than his or her own ability to avoid the necessity for making complaints.*

DIRECTORY OF BETTER BUSINESS BUREAUS

Council of Better Business Bureaus

HEADQUARTERS
1515 Wilson Boulevard
Arlington, VA 22209

IN NEW YORK CITY
845 Third Avenue
New York, NY 10022

The United States

ALABAMA
The BBB, Inc.
2026 Second Avenue, N.,
Suite 2303
BIRMINGHAM, AL 35203
Branch office: Montgomery
205-323-6127

BBB of North Alabama, Inc.
Central Bank Building
West Side Square
Suite 410
HUNTSVILLE, AL 35801
205-533-1640

BBB of South Alabama—
NW Florida, Inc.
307 Van Antwerp Building
MOBILE, AL 36602
205-433-5494

BBB of Montgomery
60 Commerce Street
Suite 810
MONTGOMERY, AL 36104
205-262-2390
(Branch office of BBB/
Birmingham)

ARIZONA
BBB of Maricopa County, Inc.
4428 North 12th Street
PHOENIX, AZ 85014
602-264-1721

BBB of Tucson, Inc.
100 East Alameda Street
Suite 403
TUCSON, AZ 85701
602-622-7651

ARKANSAS
BBB of Arkansas, Inc.
1216 South University
LITTLE ROCK, AR 72204
501-664-7274

CALIFORNIA
BBB of South Central
California, Inc.
705 Eighteenth Street
BAKERSFIELD, CA 93301
805-322-2074

BBB of Inland Cities
1265 North La Cadena,
P.O. Box 970
COLTON, CA 92324
Branch Office: Palm Desert
714-825-7280

BBB of Central California, Inc.
413 T W Patterson Building
FRESNO, CA 93721
209-268-6424

BBB of Los Angeles/Orange
Counties, Inc.
639 South New Hampshire Ave.
3rd Floor
LOS ANGELES, CA 90005
Branch Office: Tustin
213-383-0992

BBB of Metropolitan Oakland, Inc.
360 22nd Street
El Dorado Building
OAKLAND, CA 94612
415-839-5900

BBB of Palm Desert
74-273 1/2 Highway 111
PALM DESERT, CA 92260
(Branch office of BBB/Colton)
714-346-2014

BBB of Sacramento, Inc.
1401 21st Street, Suite 305
SACRAMENTO, CA 95814
916-443-6843

BBB of San Diego, Ltd.
4310 Orange Avenue
SAN DIEGO, CA 92105
714-283-3927

BBB of San Francisco
2740 Van Ness Avenue
Suite 210
SAN FRANCISCO, CA 94109
415-775-3300

BBB of Santa Clara Valley, Ltd.
P.O. Box 8110
SAN JOSE, CA 95155
408-298-5880

BBB of San Mateo County, Inc.
P.O. Box 294
20 North San Mateo Drive
SAN MATEO, CA 94401
415-347-1251, 52, 53

BBB of the Tri-Counties
P.O. Box 746
SANTA BARBARA,
CA 93102
805-963-8657

BBB of Mid Counties, Inc.
1111 North Center Street
STOCKTON, CA 95202
209-948-4880

BBB of Orange County
17662 Irvine Blvd., Suite 15
TUSTIN, CA 92680
(Branch office of BBB/Los
Angeles)
714-544-5842

COLORADO
Colorado Springs BBB
524 South Cascade
COLORADO SPRINGS, CO 80903
303-636-1155
(Branch office of BBB/
Denver)

Rocky Mountain BBB, Inc.
841 Delaware Street
DENVER, CO 80204
Branch office: Colorado Springs
303-629-1036

CONNECTICUT
BBB of Western Connecticut, Inc.
Fairfield Woods Plaza
P.O. Box 1410
2345 Black Rock Tpk.
FAIRFIELD, CT 06430
203-368-6538

BBB of Greater Hartford, Inc.
250 Constitution Plaza
HARTFORD, CT 06103
203-247-8700

BBB of SE Connecticut, Inc.
35 Elm Street
P.O. Box 2015
NEW HAVEN, CT 06510
203-787-5788

DELAWARE
Kent Sussex BBB, Inc.
20 South Walnut Street
P.O. Box 300
MILFORD, DE 19963
(Branch office of BBB/
Wilmington)
302-856-6969

BBB of Delaware, Inc.
1901-B West Eleventh Street
P.O. Box 4085
WILMINGTON, DE 19807
Branch office: Milford
302-652-3833

DISTRICT OF COLUMBIA
BBB of Metropolitan
Washington
1334 G. Street, N.W.
Prudential Building, Sixth Floor
WASHINGTON, DC 20005
Branch offices:
Bethesda, MD, Falls Church, VA
202-393-8000

FLORIDA
BBB of South Florida, Inc.
8600 N.E. 2nd Avenue
MIAMI, FL 33138
305-757-3446

375

GETTING MORE FOR YOUR MONEY

BBB of Palm Beach County, Inc.
3015 Exchange Court
WEST PALM BEACH,
FL 33409
305-686-2200

GEORGIA
BBB of Metropolitan Atlanta, Inc.
212 Healey Building
57 Forsyth Street, N.W.
ATLANTA, GA 30303
404-688-4910

BBB of Augusta, Inc.
First Bank Building
Suite 303
209 7th Street
P.O. Box 2085
AUGUSTA, GA 30903
404-722-1574

BBB of West Georgia—East
  Alabama, Inc.
1320 Broadway, Suite 250
P.O. Box 2587
COLUMBUS, GA 31902
404-324-0712

BBB of the Coastal Empire, Inc.
6822 Abercorn St.
P.O. Box 13956
SAVANNAH, GA 31406
912-354-7521

HAWAII
BBB of Hawaii, Inc.
677 Ala Moana Boulevard
Suite 602
HONOLULU, HI 96813
Branch Office: Maui
808-531-8131, 32, 33

The Maui BBB of Hawaii
P.O. Box 11414
LAHAINA, MAUI, HI 96761
(Branch office of BBB/
  Honolulu)
808-877-4000

IDAHO
BBB of Treasure Valley, Inc.
Idaho Building, Suite 324
BOISE, ID 83702
208-342-4649

ILLINOIS
BBB of Metropolitan Chicago, Inc.
35 East Wacker Drive
CHICAGO, IL 60601
312-346-3868

BBB of Central Illinois, Inc.
109 S.W. Jefferson Street
Suite 305
PEORIA, IL 61602
309-673-5194

INDIANA
BBB of Elkhart County, Inc.
118 South Second Street
P.O. Box 405
ELKHART, IN 46515
219-293-5731

BBB of Evansville
Old Courthouse Center, Room 310
EVANSVILLE, IN 47708
(Branch office of BBB/
  Indianapolis)
812-422-6879

BBB of Northeastern Indiana, Inc.
1203 Webster Street
FORT WAYNE, IN 46802
Branch Office: Marion
219-423-4433

BBB of Northwest Indiana, Inc.
2500 West Ridge Road
Calumet Township
GARY, IN 46408
219-980-1511

Central Indiana BBB, Inc.
15 E. Market Street
INDIANAPOLIS, IN 46204
317-637-0197
Branch Offices: Ball State
BBB, Muncie, IN (Serving
University Area only);
Evansville, Terre Haute

BBB of Northeastern Indiana, Inc.
204 Iroquois Building
MARION, IN 46952
(Branch office of BBB/Fort
  Wayne)
317-668-8954

Ball State University BBB
Whitinger Building
Room 160
MUNCIE, IN 47306
(Branch office of BBB/
  Indianapolis)
317-285-6375

BBB of South Bend
  Mishawaka Area, Inc.
230 West Jefferson Boulevard
SOUTH BEND, IN 46601
219-234-0183

BBB of Central Indiana, Inc.
105 South Third Street
TERRE HAUTE, IN 47801
(Branch office of BBB/
  Indianapolis)
812-637-0197

IOWA
BBB of Central and Eastern Iowa
234 Insurance Exchange Building
DES MOINES, IA 50309
Branch office: Davenport
515-243-8137

BBB/Quad Cities
619 Kahl Building
DAVENPORT, IA 52801
(Branch office of BBB/
  Des Moines)
319-322-0782

Siouxland BBB, Inc.
Benson Building, Suite 645
7th & Douglas Streets
SIOUX CITY, IA 51101
712-252-4501

KANSAS
BBB of Northeast Kansas, Inc.
501 Jefferson, Suite 24
TOPEKA, KS 66607
913-232-0454

BBB, Inc.
300 Kaufman Building
WICHITA, KS 67202
316-263-3146

KENTUCKY
BBB of Central Kentucky, Inc.
1523 North Limestone
LEXINGTON, KY 40505
606-252-4492

The Better Business Bureau, Inc.
844 S. Fourth Street
LOUISVILLE, KY 40203
502-583-6546

LOUISIANA
BBB of Baton Rouge Area, Inc.
2055 Wooddale Blvd.
BATON ROUGE, LA 70806
504-926-3010

BBB of Houma
300 Bond Street
P.O. Box 9129
(Branch office of BBB/New Orleans)
HOUMA, LA 70361
504-868-3456

BBB of Acadiana, Inc.
804 Jefferson Street
P.O. Box 3651
LAFAYETTE, LA 70502
318-234-8341

BBB of Southwest Louisiana, Inc.
1413 Ryan Street
Suite C, P.O. Box 1681
LAKE CHARLES, LA 70602
318-433-1633

BBB of Northeast Louisiana, Inc.
141 ONB Building, Suite 503
141 De Siard Street
MONROE, LA 71201
318-387-4600

BBB of Greater New Orleans
  Area, Inc.
301 Camp Street, Suite 403
NEW ORLEANS, LA 70130
Branch Office: Houma
504-581-6222

The Better Business Bureau, Inc.
320 Milam Street
SHREVEPORT, LA 71101
318-221-8352

MARYLAND
BBB of Baltimore, Inc.
401 North Howard Street
BALTIMORE, MD 21201
301-685-6986

DIRECTORY OF BETTER BUSINESS BUREAUS

BBB of Montgomery County
6917 Arlington Road
BETHESDA, MD 20014
(Branch office of BBB/
  Washington, DC)
301-656-7000

MASSACHUSETTS
BBB of Eastern Massachusetts, Inc.
8 Winter Street
BOSTON, MA 02108
Branch offices: Hyannis,
  Lawrence, New Bedford, Concord, NH
617-482-9151

Cape Code & Island BBB
The Federal Building, Suite 1
78 North Street
HYANNIS, MA 02601
(Branch office of BBB/Boston)
617-771-3022

BBB of Merrimack Valley
316 Essex Street
LAWRENCE, MA 01840
(Branch office of BBB/Boston)
617-687-7666

BBB of Southeastern Mass., Inc.
908 Purchase St., Room 305
NEW BEDFORD, MA 02745
(Branch office of BBB/Boston)
617-999-6060

BBB of Western
  Massachusetts, Inc.
293 Bridge Street, Suite 324
SPRINGFIELD, MA 01103
413-734-3114

BBB of Central New England, Inc.
32 Franklin Street
P.O. Box 379
WORCESTER, MA 01601
617-755-2548

MICHIGAN
BBB of Eastern Michigan
150 Michigan Avenue
DETROIT, MI 48226
313-962-7566

BBB of Western Michigan, Inc.
1 Peoples Building
GRAND RAPIDS, MI 49503
616-774-8236

MINNESOTA
BBB of Minnesota
1745 University Avenue
ST. PAUL, MN 55104
612-646-4637

MISSISSIPPI
BBB of Mississippi, Inc.
510 George St., Suite 217
P.O. Box 2090
JACKSON, MS 39205
601-948-4732

MISSOURI
BBB of Greater Kansas City, Inc.
906 Grand Avenue
KANSAS CITY, MO 64106
816-421-7800

BBB of Eastern Missouri &
  Southern Illinois
Mansion House Center
440 North Fourth Street
ST. LOUIS, MO 63102
314-241-3100

BBB of Southwest Missouri, Inc.
P.O. Box 4331
GS 319 Holland Bldg.
Park Central
SPRINGFIELD, MO 65806
417-862-9231

NEBRASKA
Cornhusker BBB of Lincoln, NE, Inc.
719 North 48th Street
LINCOLN, NE 68504
402-467-5261

BBB of Omaha, Inc.
417 Farnam Building
1613 Farnam Street
OMAHA, NE 68102
402-346-3033

NEVADA
BBB of Southern Nevada, Inc.
1829 E. Charleston Boulevard
Suite 103
LAS VEGAS, NV 89104
702-382-7141

BBB of Northern Nevada, Inc.
372-A Casazza Dr.
P.O. Box 2932
RENO, NV 89505
702-322-0657

NEW HAMPSHIRE
BBB of the Granite State
One Pillsbury St.
CONCORD, NH 03301
(Branch office of BBB/Boston)
603-224-1991

NEW JERSEY
BBB of South Jersey, Inc.
836 Haddon Avenue
P.O. Box 303
COLLINGSWOOD,
  NJ 08108
Branch Office: Toms River
609-854-8467

BBB of Central New Jersey, Inc.
Route 130 & South River Road
CRANBURY, NJ 08512
609-586-1464 Mercer County
201-536-6306 Monmouth Co.
 -297-5000 Middlesex,
  Somerset & Hunterdon
  Counties

BBB of Greater Newark, Inc.
34 Park Place
NEWARK, NJ 07102
(Branch office of BBB/Metro
  New York)
201-643-3025

BBB of Bergen, Passaic &
  Rockland Counties
2 Forest Avenue
PARAMUS, NJ 07652
(Branch office of BBB/Metro
  New York)
201-845-4044

Ocean County BBB
1721 Route 37 East
TOMS RIVER, NJ 08753
(Branch office of BBB/
  Collingswood)
201-270-5577

NEW MEXICO
BBB of New Mexico, Inc.
2921 Carlisle NE, Suite 102
ALBUQUERQUE, NM 87110
Branch offices: Santa Fe &
  Farmington
505-884-0500

BBB/Four Corners
2120 East 20th
FARMINGTON, NM 87401
(Branch office of BBB/
  Albuquerque)
505-325-1136

BBB of Santa Fe
227 East Palace Avenue
Suite C
SANTA FE, NM 87501
(Branch office of BBB/
  Albuquerque)
505-988-3648

NEW YORK
BBB of Western New York, Inc.
775 Main Street
BUFFALO, NY 14203
716-856-7180

BBB of Harlem
257 Park Avenue So.
New York, NY 10010
(Branch office of BBB/Metro
  New York)
212-533-7500

BBB of Metropolitan New
  York, Inc.
257 Park Avenue South
NEW YORK, NY 10010
Branch Offices: Harlem, Long
  Island, White Plains, Newark
  (NJ) and Paramus (NJ)
212-533-6200

BBB of Rochester, Inc.
1122 Sibley Tower
ROCHESTER, NY 14604
716-546-6776

BBB of Syracuse and Central
  New York, Inc.
120 East Washington Street
SYRACUSE, NY 13202
315-479-6635

BBB of the Mohawk Valley, Inc.
209 Elizabeth Street
UTICA, NY 13501
315-724-3129

377

GETTING MORE FOR YOUR MONEY

Long Island BBB
435 Old Country Road
WESTBURY, NY 11590
(Branch office of BBB/Metro
  New York)
516-334-7662

BBB of Westchester, Putnam
  and Duchess Counties
(Serving Orange & Ulster
  Counties)
158 Westchester Avenue
WHITE PLAINS, NY 10601
(Branch office of BBB/Metro
  New York)
914-428-1230, 31

NORTH CAROLINA
The BBB of Asheville/
  Western North Carolina, Inc.
29 1/2 Page Avenue
ASHEVILLE, NC 28801
704-253-2392

The BBB of the Southern
  Piedmont, Inc.
Commerce Center, Suite 1300
CHARLOTTE, NC 28202
704-332-7152

BBB of Central North Carolina, Inc.
3608 West Friendly Avenue
GREENSBORO, NC 27410
919-852-4240, 41, 42

Triangle Cities BBB
100 Park Drive Bldg., Suite 203
P.O. Box 12033
RESEARCH TRIANGLE
  PARK, NC 27709
919-549-8221

The BBB, Inc.
The First Union National
  Bank Building
WINSTON-SALEM, NC 27101
919-725-8348

OHIO
BBB of Akron, Inc.
209 South Main Street
Suite 201
P.O. Box F596
AKRON, OH 44308
216-253-4590

BBB of Stark County, Inc.
500 Cleveland Avenue, North
CANTON, OH 44702
216-454-9401

Cincinnati BBB, Inc.
26 East Sixth Street
CINCINNATI, OH 45202
513-421-3015

The BBB, Inc.
1720 Keith Building
CLEVELAND, OH 44115
216-241-7678

BBB of Central Ohio, Inc.
527 South High Street
COLUMBUS, OH 43215
614-221-6336

BBB of Dayton/Miami Valley, Inc.
15 East Fourth Street
Suite 209
DAYTON, OH 45402
513-222-5825

BBB Serving NW Ohio &
  SE Michigan, Inc.
405 N. Huron St.
TOLEDO, OH 45604
419-241-6276

BBB of Mahoning Valley, Inc.
903 Mahoning Bank Building
P.O. Box 1495 (44501)
YOUNGSTOWN, OH 44503
216-744-3111

OKLAHOMA
BBB of Central Oklahoma, Inc.
606 North Dewey
OKLAHOMA CITY,
  OK 73102
405-239-6081

BBB of Tulsa, Inc.
4833 South Sheridan
Suite 412
TULSA, OK 74145
918-664-1266

OREGON
Portland BBB, Inc.
623 Corbett Building
PORTLAND, OR 97204
503-226-3981

PENNSYLVANIA
BBB of Eastern Pennsylvania
528 North New Street
Dodson Building
BETHLEHEM, PA 18018
(Branch office of BBB/
  Philadelphia)
215-866-8780

Capital Division of BBB/
  Eastern Pennsylvania
53 North Duke Street
LANCASTER, PA 17602
(Branch office of BBB/
  Philadelphia)
717-291-1151

BBB of Eastern Pennsylvania
1218 Chestnut Street
PHILADELPHIA, PA 19107
Branch Offices: Bethlehem &
  Lancaster
215-574-3600

BBB of Western Pennsylvania, Inc.
610 Smithfield Street
PITTSBURGH, PA 15222
412-456-2700

BBB of Northeastern
  Pennsylvania, Inc.
Brooks Building
SCRANTON, PA 18503
717-342-9129

PUERTO RICO
BBB of Puerto Rico, Inc.
P.O. Box BBB
Fernandez Juncos Station
SAN JUAN, Puerto Rico 00910
809-724-7474

RHODE ISLAND
BBB of Rhode Island, Inc.
248 Weybosset Street
PROVIDENCE, RI 02903
401-272-9800

TENNESSEE
BBB of Greater Chattanooga, Inc.
716 James Building
735 Broad Street
CHATTANOOGA,
  TN 37402
615-266-6144

BBB of Greater Knoxville/
  E. Tenn., Inc.
P.O. Box 3608
KNOXVILLE, TN 37917
615-522-1300

Memphis Area BBB, Inc.
1835 Union Building
Suite 202
MEMPHIS, TN 38104
901-272-9641

BBB of Nashville/Middle
  Tennessee, Inc.
506 Nashville City Bank
  Building
NASHVILLE, TN 37201
615-254-5872

TEXAS
BBB of Abilene, Inc.
P.O. Box 3275
465 Cypress Duffy Bldg.
Suite 16
ABILENE, TX 79604
915-677-8071

BBB of the Golden Spread
1008 W. Kent Street
AMARILLO, TX 79101
806-374-3735

The Better Business Bureau, Inc.
American Bank Tower
Suite 720
AUSTIN, TX 78701
512-476-6943

BBB of Southeast Texas, Inc.
P.O. Box 2988
BEAUMONT, TX 77704
713-835-5348

BBB of Brazos Valley, Inc.
202 Varisco Building
BRYAN, TX 77801
713-823-8148

BBB of Corpus Christi, Inc.
109 N. Chaparral, Suite 101
CORPUS CHRISTI, TX 78401
512-888-5555

DIRECTORY OF BETTER BUSINESS BUREAUS

BBB of Metro Dallas, Inc.
1511 Bryan Street
DALLAS, TX 75201
214-747-8891

BBB of El Paso, Inc.
2501 North Mesa Street
Suite 301
EL PASO, TX 79902
915-533-2431

BBB of Fort Worth & Tarrant
County
709 Sinclair Building
106 West 5th Street
FORT WORTH, TX 76102
817-332-7585

BBB of Metro Houston, Inc.
P.O. Box 7499
HOUSTON, TX 77008
713-868-9500

BBB of the South Plains, Inc.
1015 15th Street, P.O. Box 1178
LUBBOCK, TX 79408
806-763-0459

BBB of the Permian Basin, Inc.
Air Terminal Building
P.O. Box 6006
MIDLAND, TX 79701
915-563-1880

BBB of San Angelo, Inc.
224 West Beauregard, Suite 310
SAN ANGELO, TX 76903
915-653-2318

BBB of San Antonio, Inc.
406 West Market Street
Suite 301
SAN ANTONIO, TX 78205
512-225-5833

BBB of Waco, Inc.
608 New Road
P.O. Box 7203
WACO, TX 76710
817-772-7530

BBB of Greater Wichita Falls, Inc.
First Wichita National Bank Bldg.
Suite 600
WICHITA FALLS, TX 76301
817-723-5526

UTAH
BBB of Utah Valley
40 North 100 East
PROVO, UT 84601
801-377-2611

BBB of Greater Salt Lake, Inc.
1588 South Main
SALT LAKE CITY, UT 84115
801-487-4656

VIRGINIA
The Northern Virginia BBB
105 East Annandale Rd.
Suite 210
FALLS CHURCH, VA 22046
(Branch office of BBB/
  Washington, DC
703-533-1900

BBB of Southeastern Virginia, Inc.
First & Merchants Bank
  Building, #620
300 Main Street, E.
P.O. Box 3548
NORFOLK, VA 23514
804-627-5651

BBB of Richmond VA, Inc.
4020 West Broad Street
RICHMOND, VA 23230
804-355-7902

BBB of Western Virginia
646 A Crystal Tower
145 West Campbell Avenue, SW
ROANOKE, VA 24011
703-342-3455

WASHINGTON
BBB of Greater Seattle, Inc.
2332 Sixth Avenue
SEATTLE, WA 98121
206-622-8067, 68

BBB of Spokane, Inc.
N. 214 Wall Street, Suite 630
SPOKANE, WA 99201
509-747-1155

Tacoma BBB, Inc.
P.O. Box 1274
TACOMA, WA 98401
206-383-5561

BBB of Central Washington, Inc.
P.O. Box 1584
424 Washington Mutual
  Building
YAKIMA, WA 98907
509-248-1326

WISCONSIN
BBB of Greater Milwaukee
740 North Plankinton Avenue
MILWAUKEE, WI 53203
414-273-4300

International

**NATIONAL HEADQUARTERS
FOR CANADIAN BUREAUS**
BBB of Canada
2 Bloor Street East, Suite 3034
TORONTO, Ontario M4W 3J5
416-925-3142

ALBERTA
BBB of Calgary, Inc.
630 8th Avenue, S.W.
Suite 404
CALGARY, Alberta T2P 1G6
403-269-3905

BBB of Edmonton & Northern
  Alberta
600 Guardian Building
10240 124th Street
EDMONTON,
  Alberta T5N 3W6
Branch Offices: Red Deer &
  Grande Prairie
403-482-2341

BRITISH COLUMBIA
BBB of the Mainland of British
  Columbia
788 Beatty Street
Suite 404
VANCOUVER, B.C. V6B 2M1
604-682-2711

BBB of Vancouver Island
P.O. Box M-37
635 Humboldt Street
VICTORIA, BC V8W 1A7
604-386-6348

MANITOBA
BBB of Metropolitan Winnipeg, Inc.
365 Hargrave Street, Room 204
WINNIPEG,
  Manitoba R3B 2K3
204-943-1486

BBB of New Brunswick
331 Elmwood Dr., Suite 3
P.O. Box 1002
MONCTON, NEW BRUNSWICK
E1C 8P2
506-854-3330

NEWFOUNDLAND
BBB of Newfoundland &
  Labrador, Ltd.
2 Adelaide Street, P.O. Box 516
ST. JOHN'S,
  Newfoundland A1C 5K4
709-722-2222

NOVA SCOTIA
BBB of Nova Scotia
P.O. Box 2124
1722 Granville Street
HALIFAX,
  Nova Scotia B3J 3B7
902-422-6581

ONTARIO
BBB of Hamilton & District
170 Jackson Street, East
HAMILTON,
  Ontario L8N 1L4
416-526-1119

BBB of Waterloo Region
58 Scott Street
KITCHENER,
  Ontario N2H 2R1
519-579-3080

BBB of Ottawa & Hull, Inc.
71 Bank Street, Suite 503
OTTAWA, Ontario K1P 5N2
613-237-4856

BBB of Metropolitan Toronto, Inc.
321 Bloor Street, East
Suite 901
TORONTO,
  Ontario M4W 3K6
416-961-0088

BBB of Windsor & District
500 Riverside Drive, West
WINDSOR, Ontario N9A 5K4
519-258-7222

GETTING MORE FOR YOUR MONEY

QUEBEC
BBB of Montreal, Inc.
2055 Peel Street, Suite 460
MONTREAL, PQ H3A 1V4
514-286-9281

Bureau d'ethique Commerciale
  de Quebec, Inc.
475 rue Richelieu
QUEBEC CITY, PQ G1R 1K2
418-523-2555

SASKATCHEWAN
BBB of Regina
2049 Lorne Street
Suite 3
REGINA, SASKATCHEWAN S4P 2M4
306-352-7601

ISRAEL
BBB of Beer-Sheva and the
  Negev District
Seven Hamuchtar Street
P.O. Box 578
BEER-SHEVA, Israel
Tel: 34222

BBB of Tel Aviv
Allenby Street
No. 53A
TEL AVIV, Israel
(03) 28-25-28

VENEZUELA
Etica Comercial de Venezuela, A.C.
Avenida El Cafetal
Edificio "CIEMI," Piso 1, #85
CARACAS, Venezuela
Tel: 323117

Index

accidents, *see* safety
advertising, 12—21; of automobiles, 48—50; of plants, 185; of home improvement, 204; and sales, 299—304
aged, care of, 279—281
air conditioners, 22—28; energy consumption of, 142—146; maintenance of, 203
aluminum siding, 205—206
American National Standards Institute (ANSI), 267
American Society of Travel Agents, 350
amplifiers, 39, 45—46
animals, 29—30
annuities, 237—238
antiques, 31—32
apartments, 33—35; *see also* condominiums, cooperatives
appliances, small, 36—38
asphalt shingles, 316
Association of Home Appliance Manufacturers (AHAM), 22—25
audio equipment, 39—46
automobiles, 47—67; depreciation, 47; new cars, 50—51; used cars, 52—54; maintenance, 54—56; repairs, 54—58; rental, 58—61; leasing, 61—63, 66—67; insurance, 63—65; energy consumption of, 146

"bait and switch" ploy, 164—165, 181, 335; *see also* advertising
banks and savings institutions, 68—71; and mortgages, 216
basements, waterproofing, 72—73
beds, *see* mattresses
Better Business Bureau (references throughout); history, 6—7; methods of working, 8—11; arbitration of complaints, 370—371
bicycles, 74—76
birds, *see* animals
Blue Cross and Blue Shield, 227
boxsprings, *see* mattresses
brand names, 37
brown-outs, 28
budget, preparation of, 111; for food shopping, 159; for medical care, 194
builders, 218—220
Bureau of Consumer Protection, 121

cable television, 338
calculators, 77—78
cameras, 288—295

INDEX

camps, 79—80; for adults, 80
carpets, 81—85; padding (cushions) for, 83
cars, *see* automobiles
cartridges, *see* audio equipment
cassettes, *see* audio equipment
cats, *see* animals
"chalking" of paint, 285—286
charitable giving, 86—88, 261
Chartered Life Underwriters, 235
charter travel arrangements, 349—350
checking accounts, 70
children: advertising and, 19—20; camps for, 79—80; clothing for, 89—90; and drugs, 125; and safety, 324—325; *see also* toys
civil service examinations, 327
clothing, 89—99; and fashion, 89; maintenance costs, 90—91 (*see also* dry cleaning); quality and fit, 91—92; fibers used in, 93—99
complaints, how to make, 368—374; about advertising, 20—21; about automobiles, 57; about cosmetics, 107; about door-to-door sales, 121; about magazine subscriptions, 257
completion certificates, 209
condominiums, 100—102; *see also* apartments
Consumer Action Panels, 371—372
Consumer Credit Protection Act, 120
Consumer Product Safety Commission (CPSC), 320—321, 347, 373 (address), 374
contracts, 103—104; in door-to-door selling, 118—119; with employment agencies, 136; for magazine subscriptions, 256—257
convection (turbo) ovens, 309
cooking, economy in, 144—145
Cooling Load Estimate Form, 24—25
"cooling-off" period, 103, 118—121, 354; on magazine subscriptions, 256
cooling systems, *see* air conditioning
cooperatives, 100—101; *see also* apartments
cosmetics, 105—107
credit (and finance), 108—114; for audio equipment, 46; for automobiles, 48; in contracts, 104; cost of, 109—111; for hearing aids, 201; for mobile homes, 265; for TVs, 339

credit unions, *see* banks and savings institutions

darkroom equipment, 294—295
day-care centers, 115—116
debt repayment, 112—113
deception, *see* fraud
dental care, 196—197; insurance for, 228
diamonds, 241—243
digital watches, 361
Direct Mail Marketing Association, 261
direct-mail solicitations, 88, 260—261
Direct Selling Association (DSA), 118
dishwashers, 117; energy consumption of, 144
doctors, *see* health and medicine
dogs, *see* animals
Dolby systems, 44
door-to-door (direct) selling, 118—122, 166, 168; by charity groups, 87; of encyclopedias, 141; of magazine subscriptions, 255; of vacuum cleaners, 354; *see also* "cooling-off" period
drills, electric, 296
driveways, 207—208
drugs: nonprescription, 123—127; prescription, 128—130; cost of, 128—129
dry cleaning, 131—134; *see also* clothing

electricity, hazards of, 323
electric power tools, 296—297
emeralds, 243
employment, 135—139; fraud in, 168; *see also* work-at-home schemes
Encyclopedia Buying Guide, 141
encyclopedias, 140
endowment life insurance, 236—237
energy, consumption of, 142—146; of air conditioners, 23; of small appliances, 37; in mobile homes, 267; of cooking ranges, 307
Energy Efficiency Ratings (EER), 144; of air conditioners, 22—23; of small appliances, 37; for refrigerators and freezers, 311
Equal Credit Opportunity Act, 113
Environmental Protection Agency, 189
escrow accounts, 349
exchange of goods, 314—315
executive career counseling, 137—138
executive search firms, 138—139

381

fabrics: types of, 93—99; stretch and laminated, 99; dry cleaning of, 131—134
Factory Mutual Laboratories, 149
Fair Credit Billing Act, 113
Fair Credit Reporting Act, 113
Federal Housing Administration (FHA), 210—212, 216
Federal Trade Commission (FTC), 374 (address)
fee schedules (of lawyers), 252—254
fibers: used in clothing (chart), 93—99; in upholstery, 180—181
film, 290—291
finance, see credit
fire: protection systems, 147—149; flame-resistant fabrics, 93; insulation and, 225; hazards of, 322—324
fire extinguishers, 148—149
first aid, 193—194
fish, see animals
Flammable Fabrics Act, 93
flatware, silver, 246
floor covering, 84—85; see also carpets
Food and Drug Administration (FDA), 321, 374
Food, Drug and Cosmetic Act, 106
food shopping, 150—160; see also nutrition
franchises, 161—163
fraud and deception, 164—169; in home maintenance, 205—207; in storm doors and windows, 335; see also "bait and switch" ploy
"free" gifts, 303—304
freezers, 310, 312—313
fuel costs, see energy consumption
funerals, 170—172
furnaces, 173—175; energy consumption of, 142—143; maintenance of, 203
furniture, 176—181
Furniture Industry Consumer Action Panel, 372
furs, 182—184

gardening and lawn care, 185—187
gasoline and gasoline-saving devices, 188—189
gems, see jewelry
gold, 244—245
guarantee, see warranty

hair dryers, 190
health and medicine, 192—197; see also insurance, health
hearing aids, 198—201
heating equipment: energy consumption of, 142; safety of, 322; see also furnaces
hi-fi, see audio equipment
home buying, 212—222; see also insurance, home
home maintenance and improvement, 202—211
Home Owners Warranty Corporation (HOW), 220—221
housing, 212—222; see also apartments, condominiums, cooperatives

installment buying, see credit
insulation, 223—225; and energy consumption, 143; see also storm doors and windows
insurance: automobile, 61, 63—65; of bicycles, 76; of savings accounts, 68—69; health, 194, 226—231; home, 232—234; life, 235—239; of mobile homes, 265; of motorcycles, 269—270; on moving house, 273
interest on loans, types of, 109—111
Interstate Commerce Commission (ICC), 272—273
Interstate Land Sales Full Disclosure Act, 250
inventory, for insurance purposes, 234
investment, see banks and savings institutions; insurance, life; land purchase
itinerant sellers, 166—167

jewelry, 240—247

labels: on clothing, 90—91, 131; on drugs, 123—124; on small appliances, 144; on fire extinguishers, 149; on food, 152—154; on furniture, 177—179; on furs, 182
land purchase, 248—251; fraud and, 165
laundry, energy consumption of, 145
lawn care, 185—187
lawyers, see legal services
leases: on apartments, 34—35; on automobiles, 61—63, 66—67; of mobile home sites, 266
legal clinics, 254

382

INDEX

legal services, 252—254
life insurance, *see* insurance, life
lighting, energy consumption of, 145
linoleum, *see* carpets and floor covering
loan companies, *see* credit
lumber, 206

magazine subscriptions, 255—257
mail-order: shopping, 258—261; life insurance, 238; work-at-home, 366—367
maintenance: of automobiles, 54—56; of clothing, 90, 131—134; of furs, 183; *see also* home maintenance
Major Appliance Consumer Action Panel, 372
management-consultant firms, 138
Magnuson-Moss Warranties Act, 355
mattresses and foundations, 262—263
Medicaid, 280
Medicare, 227, 280
medicine, *see* drugs; health
menu planning, 151, 154—155
microwave ovens, 308—309
mobile homes, 264—267
mopeds, 270
motorcycles, 268—270
mortgages, 215—218
movie cameras, 293—294
moving household goods, 271—275
multilevel marketing (pyramid selling), 167—168
musical instruments, 276—278
mutual savings banks, *see* banks

National Advertising Review Board (NARB), 20—21
National Association of Home Builders (NAHB), 220—221
National Association of Life Underwriters, 235
National Automobile Dealers Association, 371
National Credit Union Administration (NCUA), 69
National Fire Protection Association (NFPA), 267
National Hearing Aid Society, 200
National Highway Traffic Safety Administration, 269
National Home Improvement Council, 204

National Home Study Council, 326
National Institute for Automotive Service Excellence (NIASE), 54
National Retail Merchants Association, 301
natural foods, 159—160
nursing homes, 279—281
nutrition, 282—284; *see also* food shopping

Office of Consumer Affairs, 373 (address)
Office of Interstate Land Sales Registration (OILSR), 250—251
organically grown foods, 159—160

packaging, cost of, 151
painting and paints, 285—287
palladium, 246—247
pearls, 244
pets, *see* animals
Philanthropic Advisory Service (PAS), 87—88
photograph developing, 303—304
photographic equipment, 288—295
platinum, 246—247
Poison Prevention Packaging Act, 125
power tools, 296—297
prescriptions, *see* drugs, prescription
prices and sales, 298—304; of clothing, 92—93; of food, 151—152; of furs, 184
projectors: slide, 291—292; movie, 293—294
Property Reports, 250

quadriphonic equipment, 44

"R" value, 223
radial tires, 343—344
radios, 305—306; *see also* audio equipment
ranges, 307—309
rebuilt appliances, 38
reconditioned appliances, 38
records, *see* audio equipment
refrigerators, 310—312
refunds, 314—315
rental: of apartments, 33—35, 232; of automobiles, 58—63; of musical instruments, 277

383

repairs, automobile, 54—58, see also maintenance
"restored" antiques, 31—32
retirement income insurance, 235, 238
return (refund) policies, 314—315
roofs and roofing, 316—319
rubies, 243—244

safety, 320—325; of camps, 79; of clothing, 93; of cosmetics, 106—107; of drugs, 125—127, 193; when gardening, 187; of hair dryers, 191; when putting in insulation, 224—225; of motorcycles, 269; of power tools, 297
sales, see prices and sales
sander, orbital, 296
sapphires, 244
savings accounts, 70—71
savings institutions, see banks; insurance, life
saws, electric, 296
schools: home study, 326—328; vocational, 329—331
second-hand: appliances, 38; automobiles, 52—54
semiprecious stones, 244
service: automobile, see maintenance; TV, 340
sewing machines, 332—333
Sherman Anti-Trust Act, 252
silver, 245—246
slide projectors, 291—293
Small Business Reporter, 161
Small Claims Court, 372—373
smoke detectors, 147—148
speakers, stereo, 46; see also audio equipment
special offers: on food, 151; see also prices and sales
sports equipment, safety of, 325
Standard First Aid and Personal Safety, 194
stereo equipment, see audio equipment
sterling silver, 245—246
storage (of household goods), 273
storm windows and doors, 143, 334—335; see also insulation
stoves, cooking, see ranges
surety bonds, 349
surgery, 196
swimming pools, energy consumption of, 146

tapes, see audio equipment
taxes: and charitable giving, 87; and home ownership, 212
telephone: appeals 88; toll-free lines, 369
televisions, 336—341
tiles, see floor coverings
tires, 342—345
toll-free telephone numbers, 369
toys, 346—347; advertising of, 19; safety of, 324—325
Trade Practice Rules for the Jewelry Industry, 241
travel and travel agents, 348—350
Truth about Automobile Leasing, The, 63, 66—67
Truth-in-Lending Act, 120
turntables, see audio equipment
typewriters, 351—352

Underwriters Laboratory safety seal, 149, 191
unordered merchandise, 88, 261
upholstery, see furniture
U.S. Postal Inspection Service, 374

vacuum cleaners, 353—354
vapor barriers, 225
Veterans' Administration, 201, 217
video cassette recorders (VCR), 338
video home system (VHS), 338
vinyl floor covering, see floor covering
vocational schools, 329—331
VU meters, 44

warranties, 355—360; on audio equipment, 46; on automobiles, 55—56; in contracts, 103; on home improvements, 210; and mail-order shopping, 259; on mobile homes, 267; on musical instruments, 277—278; on photographic equipment, 295
watches, 361—362
water-conditioning equipment, 363—364
waterproofing, basement, 72—73
water temperature, energy consumption and, 143
work-at-home schemes, 365—367

zoning, 219, 249, 251